Curtiss-Wright

Greatness and Decline

TWAYNE'S EVOLUTION OF MODERN BUSINESS SERIES

Kenneth Lipartito, Editor

The American Aerospace Industry
Roger E. Bilstein

Curtiss-Wright
Louis R. Eltscher and Edward M. Young

The American Amusement Park Industry
Judith A. Adams

A History of Black Business in America
Juliet Walker

A History of Women and Business
Angel Kwolek-Folland

E. H. Harriman
Lloyd J. Mercer

Wal-Mart
Sandra S. Vance and Roy V. Scott

CURTISS-WRIGHT

Greatness and Decline

Louis R. Eltscher and Edward M. Young

Twayne Publishers
An Imprint of Simon & Schuster Macmillan
New York

Prentice Hall International
London Mexico City New Delhi Singapore Sydney Toronto

338.762913
E51c

Curtiss-Wright: Greatness and Decline
Louis R. Eltscher and Edward M. Young

Copyright 1998 by Twayne Publishers
All rights reserved. No part of this book may be reproduced or transmitted in any form
or by any means, electronic or mechanical, including photocopying, recording, or by
any information storage and retrieval system, without permission in writing from the
Publishers.

Twayne Publishers
An Imprint of Simon & Schuster Macmillan
1633 Broadway
New York, NY 10019-6785

Library of Congress Cataloging-in-Publication Data

Eltscher, Louis R.
    Curtiss-Wright : greatness and decline / Louis R. Eltscher and
Edward M. Young.
        p. cm. — (Twayne's evolution of modern business series)
    Includes bibliographical references and index.
    ISBN 0-8057-9829-3 (alk. paper)
    1. Curtiss-Wright Corporation—History. 2. Aircraft industry—
United States—History. I. Young, Edward M. II. Title.
III. Series.
HD9711.U63C873 1998
338.7'62913'0973—dc21   98-8599
                                                                       CIP
JK

This paper meets the requirements of ANSI/NISO Z3948-1992 (Permanence of Paper).

10 9 8 7 6 5 4 3 2 1

Printed and bound in the United States of America.

*To all the employees
of the Curtiss-Wright Corporation
and its predecessor companies.*

Contents

List of Illustrations   ix
Foreword   xi
Acknowledgments   xiii

1.   Introduction   1

2.   Origins to the End of World War I, 1909–1918   7

3.   Decline and Expansion, 1919–1929   26

4.   Decline and Resurgence, 1930–1937   53

5.   Rearmament, 1938–1941   82

6.   War Production, 1942–1945   95

7.   Demobilization, 1945–1948   122

8.   A New Identity, 1949–1990   141

Appendix A: Curtiss-Wright Corporate Genealogy and Organizational Charts   167
Appendix B: Wright Aeronautical and Curtiss-Wright Total Sales and Net Income   176
Notes and References   179
Bibliographic Essay   200
Index   203

Illustrations

Photographs

Glenn Hammond Curtiss   8

Curtiss JN-4 Jenny   15

Clement Mellville Keys   18

Curtiss H-16 flying boat   23

Curtiss P-1   34

Wilbur and Orville Wright   44

Richard F. Hoyt   46

Guy W. Vaughan and Charles R. Lawrance with Wright Whirlwind engine   48

Thomas Morgan   59

Curtiss Export Hawk II   68

Curtiss P-36   80

Curtiss C-46 transport and P-40 fighter   98

Curtiss SB2C Helldiver   103

Roy T. Hurley   146

Curtiss X-19   154

T. Roland Berner   158

Figures

1. Aircraft production: 1925–1929   37

2. Aircraft production: 1930–1935   54

3. Curtiss-Wright total assets: 1929–1934   62

4. Curtiss-Wright aircraft sales: 1932–1936   69

5. Aircraft engine production: 1930–1935   70

6. Net income: Curtiss Aeroplane versus Wright Aeronautical, 1931–1935   74

7. Curtiss-Wright: increase in personnel, 1936–1942   92

8. Aircraft production: 1936–1941   92

9. Curtiss-Wright production: 1939–1944   124

Foreword

Curtiss-Wright. The name recalls three of the great pioneers of aviation. One of the largest aviation companies in the world by World War II, Curtiss-Wright combined the barnstorming tradition of Glenn Curtiss with the inventors of powered flight, the bishop's boys, Orville and Wilbur Wright.

When Curtiss-Wright was formed in 1929, the aviation industry was still young and full of promise. It had just left the hands of individual inventors, men such as the Wright brothers and the former motorcycle builder Glenn Curtiss. In World War I, nations had seen that airplanes were destined to be one of the most important weapons of modern warfare. American airplane and engine manufacturers had supplied a major portion of this new military market. But then they suffered in the severe contraction of demand following the war. This boom-and-bust pattern would characterize the aviation industry throughout its history.

By the mid-twenties, airplane manufacturing was again soaring, and both the Curtiss and Wright companies were growing and profiting. Technological changes that began with the hothouse wartime years, coupled with government actions to promote a stable industry, made airplane stocks one of the hottest items on Wall Street in the great twenties bull market. It was in this environment that financiers Clement Keys and Richard Hoyt brought together the airframe-making talents of the Curtiss company with the superior radial engine designs of the Wright firm. Curtiss-Wright was born, unfortunately just in time for the Great Depression.

A series of reorganizations during the thirties got the aviation industry ready for a world rearming itself for World War II. Having survived the depression, Curtiss-Wright began to expand its operations in response to increased military demand, both foreign and domestic. But wartime orders shaped the fate of Curtiss-Wright in unexpected, unpredictable ways. The company had more productive capacity than any other airplane maker on the eve of World War II, and that advantage, ironically, helped to seal Curtiss-Wright's fate and number its days as a plane maker.

Curtiss-Wright was one of the most prominent airframe, engine, and propeller manufacturers in World War II. It ended the war number two on the list of American military contractors. It turned out the mainstay of the American fighter fleet, the P-40, along with the R-1820 engine, which powered many American and allied aircraft. Like all manufacturers, Curtiss-Wright had to struggle to keep up with vital wartime needs while staying on top of changing technology and dealing with material and labor shortages. In America in particular, war meant both incredibly rapid technological change and ever higher levels of production to supply the allied "Arsenal of Democracy."

It might seem that making money under such circumstances was easy, but wartime production was fraught with perils. Curtiss-Wright factories were ordered to turn out, at the fastest possible rates, current models when other firms were working on new designs. When the British developed jet engines, American military planners refused to allow engine manufacturers such as Curtiss-Wright to devote any company resources to this radical technological breakthrough. Work on the new engines went to other firms such as General Electric. As a result, Curtiss-Wright ended the war somewhat behind the technological curve, facing new competitors who were already starting to transform the postwar aviation industry.

This was the situation in which the company found itself after World War II. It was cash rich and had an overabundance of manufacturing facilities but was facing a rapidly changing market without the proper resources to compete. Curtiss-Wright made what turned out to be its most fateful postwar decision: to pay out profits to stockholders rather than reinvest in its great pool of engineering skill and talent to join the modern aviation industry.

Such conflicts between immediate stockholder benefit and longer-term corporate strategy are commonplace in our own day. At the end of the forties, Curtiss-Wright was one of the first firms to confront this issue. A bitter, drawn-out proxy fight indicated that it had no easier a time than do firms of today. Moved less by conscious decision than by a flow of events that no one in the company could quite master, Curtiss-Wright eventually left the airframe and airplane engine business. In the sardonic words of one employee, "Curtiss-Wright did five billion dollars worth of business in World War II and never recovered."

Curtiss-Wright survives to this day as a much smaller diversified investment concern and manufacturing subcontractor. It has managed to survive even after losing its historic legacy in the aviation industry. But we shall never know what the company might have been had it stayed the course and invested its resources into developing the products it knew best: airframes, engines, and propellers.

As told by Lou Eltscher and Ted Young, the story of Curtiss-Wright is a rich narrative of the complex, unpredictable nature of business evolution. It offers much to ponder: the unintended impact of war on industry; the difficulties managers confront in periods of unstable and rapidly changing technological design and fluctuating markets; the crucial historical importance of management decisions, whose full import can be grasped only in retrospect; the ever present trade-off between the value of a company's stock and its long-term investment strategy. The history of Curtiss-Wright is more than the story of a once famous company. It is the very human story of managers confronting abstract market and technological forces and making decisions on which turn the fate of a company and its people. We are proud to have this story as part of the Twayne Evolution of Modern Business Series.

Acknowledgments

This study represents the first attempt to write a general history of the Curtiss-Wright Corporation. However, it is just a beginning. We are fully aware of this volume's shortcomings, and we realize that much work remains to be done before a truly definitive history of the company can be written. Nevertheless, sufficient information has been secured from many sources, including the memories of people still living, to make that beginning. We hope the work will continue.

We are indebted to many people who have assisted us with this project. Special thanks go to the staff of the National Air and Space Museum for help provided in a variety of ways. Although the risks of inadvertent omissions inevitably accompany the naming of specific individuals, several members of the museum staff who have gone the extra mile must be recognized. They are Phil Edwards, Dan Hagedorn, Von Hardesty, Russ Lee, Dom Pisano, and Bob van der Linden. Others who have given their kind assistance are Harold Andrews, Gerry Beauchamp, Henry Borst, Lt. Col. Mike Devine of the USAF, George F. P. Kernahan, Richard Morley, Walter Warrick, and Howard Wolko. Several of these people read the manuscript in its entirety or portions thereof. They corrected factual errors, challenged questionable assumptions, and pointed out confusing or imprecise language. Their helpful comments and insights are deeply appreciated. Of course, responsibility for the final product is solely ours.

Thanks must also be given to Guy W. Vaughan Jr. and Burdette S. Wright Jr. for their perspectives on the Curtiss-Wright Corporation and for information on the respective roles played by their fathers; and to Mr. Robert A. Bosi, vice president, Finance, the late Arnold Kossar, vice president, Engineering, both of the Curtiss-Wright Corporation, and the late Joseph M. Mergen, director of engineering for Curtiss Wright's Propeller Division, all of whom were invaluable resource persons.

Many additional former employees, too numerous to name, must also be acknowledged for their help in providing information and insights from private papers and personal experiences. Their contributions to this project have been of inestimable value.

A considerable debt is owed to Ken Lipartito, the editor, who not only provided excellent constructive criticism but also gave many words of encouragement during the entire endeavor.

The greatest debt, however, is owed to our wives, who were immensely supportive throughout. They also lent their editing skills on several occasions and endured the whole process with long-suffering and quiet patience.

Chapter 1

Introduction

Companies, like empires, rise and fall. In every industry, famous names that once were synonymous with achievement, innovation, and leadership are now known only to a few. Once dominant firms now labor at the periphery or have faded away altogether. Ample evidence of this process can be found in the American aerospace industry, which has experienced much consolidation throughout the past four decades. Many famous companies with great and historic names have either disappeared or merged into a single entity. The post–Cold War era has been particularly wrenching. Erstwhile rivals are now partners in new combinations, such as Lockheed Martin and Northrop Grumman. Many other names have simply disappeared. For 30 years, one combined name—Curtiss-Wright—stood at the center of the American aviation industry, competing with the likes of Boeing, Douglas, and Lockheed. Yet few today have ever heard of the Curtiss-Wright Corporation, although it once challenged these and other firms for leadership of the industry. Today the company plays only a small, specialized role in aviation, providing a variety of services and products largely centered on metalworking technologies for government and the aerospace industry. The goal of this study is to tell the story of Curtiss-Wright's rise to greatness and its subsequent decline and to illustrate the factors that contributed both to the company's success and to its failure to sustain competitive advantage.

The history of the Curtiss-Wright Corporation parallels the formative years of the American aviation industry. Curtiss-Wright grew with the industry and experienced the challenges of technological change and the struggle to establish a viable market that characterized the aviation industry's period of infancy and early growth. The corporation's predecessors emerged from the greatest names in American aviation: Glenn Hammond Curtiss and Wilbur and Orville Wright. Over time, the company that Glenn Curtiss founded became renowned as a designer and manufacturer of airplanes, and the company that was the legacy of the Wright brothers turned to the manufacture of airplane engines and achieved equal, if not greater, success. Ironically, though Curtiss and the Wrights were bitter rivals in their lifetime, the companies they founded went on to merge into a powerful combination.

Before World War I, aviation in America could hardly be called an industry. The fragile wood-and-fabric airplanes that Curtiss and the Wrights built had little practical application. They were most often used to give exhibitions of flight at fairs across the country. Few people could afford this novelty. The American military had little use for the airplane and remained well behind the European powers even after the outbreak of the Great War in 1914 began to demonstrate the airplane's military potential. Before America's entry into that war, fewer than a dozen firms could be considered to be active in aviation, and of these only the Curtiss Aeroplane Company had any experience in building more than a few dozen airplanes in the course of a year.

World War I changed the direction of American aviation. Soon after the outbreak of hostilities, several European nations turned to the United States for badly needed supplies, including airplanes. As the largest airplane manufacturer in America, the Curtiss Aeroplane Company was soon the beneficiary of several comparatively large orders for seaplanes, which Glenn Curtiss had pioneered. The need to expand production capacity led to a reorganization of the company into the Curtiss Aeroplane and Motor Corporation. When the United States entered the conflict in April 1917, the Curtiss company was building a small but steady stream of seaplanes and training planes for England plus a smaller number for the United States Army and Navy. As the American military struggled to overcome years of neglect and prepared to make a significant contribution to the Allied war effort, Curtiss received a flood of orders. Politicians called for American industry to produce enough airplanes to darken the skies of Europe. The Wright-Martin Company, which was the successor to the original Wright Company, had begun building aircraft engines under license from the French government. Wright-Martin, too, soon found itself swamped with orders for thousands of engines. Curtiss's relations with the government provided valuable but often frustrating experience with what would be the company's major customer throughout its history. Although production for the United States Navy went relatively smoothly, the inability of the army to maintain a coherent production program led to innumerable delays and to the failure of American aviation to produce combat planes in anywhere near the promised numbers.

The end of the war left the Curtiss Airplane and Motor Corporation and Wright-Martin with significant advantages. Curtiss had produced more than 4,000 aircraft, more than any other manufacturer, and Wright-Martin had produced more engines than any other aviation engine company. Both companies had obtained invaluable experience in production and organization and had built up a core of capable engineers and design staff. Both had facilities that would create significant economy-of-scale advantages over their competitors for what many in the aviation industry believed would be the rapid development of commercial aviation in the United States. The commercial market failed to develop. The airplane, despite having made great technological strides under the pressure of wartime demands, had yet to demonstrate sufficient advances over existing modes of transport. Having fought the war to end all wars, the military had only a minimal demand for new aircraft. Even worse, the military instituted a system of competitive bidding that brought about a nearly ruinous state of competition within the aviation industry. All manufacturers were permitted to bid for production contracts for a particular design in open competition, with the lowest bidder winning regardless of whether it had developed the design or not. Innovative companies were thus unable to recover their costs of research and development. With no market for their products, neither Curtiss nor Wright-Martin could take advantage of their commanding position. A year and a half after the end of the war, having overinvested for the hoped-for boom, the Curtiss company stood on the verge of bankruptcy.

Clement Keys, an investment banker and Curtiss Aeroplane and Motor Corporation's vice president for finance during World War I, rescued the company from bankruptcy. Keys had faith in the ultimate future of aviation and felt that Curtiss's design and engineering excellence should not be allowed to disappear. Keys kept the company alive during the difficult first half of the twenties while supporting an intensive research and development effort built around the Curtiss D-12 engine, the finest liquid-cooled engine of the decade. Curtiss racing planes, powered by the D-12, brought several international speed records to the United States and helped reestablish American aviation technology, which had been so dependent on Europe during the war, to a prominent world position.

In 1926 the American government finally addressed the issue of the steady deterioration of military aviation and embarked upon five-year expansion programs for the army and navy. Curtiss was well placed to benefit from its technological lead and received large orders (for the time) for fighter and attack aircraft. The Wright-Martin Company, reorganized as the Wright Aeronautical Corporation, had abandoned airframe development altogether and was now a major airplane engine manufacturer. Under the influence of the navy, Wright began work on the development of the air-cooled radial engine, which over the next several years supplanted the liquid-cooled engines in both military and commercial service. The navy pressured Wright into taking over the small Lawrance Aero-Engine Corporation and provided capital for developing the radial engine designs of its president, Charles R. Lawrance. This merger began an era of air-cooled radial engine development and production that extended well beyond World War II and made Wright Aeronautical one of the two primary engine manufacturers in the United States.

Charles Lindbergh's flight to Paris in 1927 helped to stimulate a boom in aviation that had begun with the transfer of airmail services to private companies and with the expansion of military aviation. Flying became popular, boosting demand for small airplanes for private flying and air taxi services and for the formation of airlines to provide air transport services between major cities. The boom in aviation coincided with a general economic expansion and the stock market boom. Money poured into aviation stocks as investors sought to profit from the growth of this newest of industries. Clement M. Keys saw this as an opportunity to build a large aviation group, linking a variety of activities spread across the full spectrum of aviation. His goal was a vertically integrated aviation empire that would bring together manufacturing, airline operations, flying services, and airports under a single umbrella organization. Keys organized his new ventures around the Curtiss Aeroplane and Motor Company, and in 1929 he helped arrange a merger between his interests and those of the Wright Aeronautical Corporation, whose chairman, Richard F. Hoyt, had formed a similar aviation group around Wright Aeronautical.

The new Curtiss-Wright Corporation brought together more than a dozen separate companies under the parent holding company. Through other Keys and Hoyt interests, Curtiss-Wright was linked to a range of manufacturers and airlines. At its peak shortly after the merger, Curtiss-Wright had a market capitalization of $170 million, second in the industry only to the United Aircraft Corporation. The new corporation seemed well placed to obtain a dominant position in the growing aviation industry through its apparent financial strength and product range. This strength was to prove illusory.

The stock market crash and the ensuing depression brought an end to Keys's dream of creating an aviation empire. The market for private and commercial aircraft collapsed, and with it the demand for flight services and airport usage. Having invested heavily in expectation of a continued boom, the Curtiss-Wright Corporation and its subsidiaries found themselves vastly overextended. Keys withdrew from aviation, and Thomas Morgan became Curtiss-Wright's new president. Morgan instituted a policy of drastic retrenchment to reduce the corporation and its subsidiaries to a size commensurate with the level of actual business demand in the depressed aviation market. Morgan dismantled the group that Keys had built, leaving the corporation to concentrate on building aircraft and aircraft engines as its core activity.

The first half of the thirties brought home how dependent the aviation industry was on military orders. Only the military had a regular demand for aircraft due to high rates of utilization and wastage in military flying. Small private airplanes brought little profit, and the airlines had few large orders and tended to use their airplanes longer than the military. Government support was vital to the industry's survival, but government policies could distort normal investment strategies and affect the industry and individual companies in negative ways. The difficulty with military orders was that profits were limited. Even more damaging was that the army would not reimburse a manufacturer for development expenses. If a company failed to win an order, it had to absorb the losses, which could be crippling. In the first half of the decade, several companies were forced into bankruptcy because they failed to win new contracts.

Despite this, barriers to entry in the aircraft industry were not so high as to prevent new entrants. Curtiss-Wright found itself not only competing with existing companies but losing business to new entrants using new technologies. The corporation survived thanks to Wright Aeronautical's growing market share in the aircraft engine business as all-metal, multiengine aircraft made their appearance and demanded ever greater engine power. The steady earnings of the engine business cushioned the swings from profit to loss in the aircraft manufacturing subsidiaries, which benefited from Curtiss-Wright's success in penetrating foreign markets. With no military sales in the United States, Curtiss-Wright sold its military designs to smaller countries in Latin America and Asia.

The accession of Guy Vaughan, president of Wright Aeronautical, to the presidency of the Curtiss-Wright Corporation in 1935 was followed shortly by a revival of the industry's fortunes. As world rearmament accelerated, Curtiss-Wright was once again well positioned. In 1936 the company finally won a major order from the U.S. Army Air Corps for fighter planes, the largest single order granted since World War I. When several European and Asian nations looked to the United States for new equipment, they turned to Curtiss-Wright as the leading producer of fighter airplanes and aircraft engines. Foreign funds, particularly from the French government, helped Curtiss-Wright expand its production facilities to cope with the new orders flowing in. When America began its own rearmament in the late thirties, the government turned to Curtiss-Wright with large orders for airplanes and engines.

These orders proved to be a mixed blessing. While the corporation's sales and profits grew dramatically, the corporation's aircraft division was effectively trapped by the demand for quantity production of an obsolescent design. Demands for rapid quantity production of other types of aircraft stretched the corporation's managerial, engineering, and design capacities beyond their limits. Wright Aeronautical faced similar problems as it expanded production of its existing engines and worked feverishly to build an advanced engine for the planned B-29 long-range bomber. For the corporation as a whole, employment grew from 12,000 to 140,000 from 1939 to 1942 while production increased 1,500 percent during the same period. Coping with change of this magnitude would be a difficult challenge for any group of managers. For the Curtiss-Wright Corporation, it proved to be a severe strain.

Ironically, by the time the corporation reached the point of its greatest fame and financial reward, it was already in a process of decline. During World War II, the Curtiss-Wright Corporation produced more than 28,000 aircraft, and Wright Aeronautical built more than 130,000 airplane engines. At one point during the war, the corporation was the second-largest defense contractor. But the stress of managing the wartime production effort diluted management quality and diverted management's attention from planning for the postwar era. By the end of the war, Curtiss-Wright was effectively out of the business of designing and building aircraft. Wright Aeronautical continued as a builder of radial engines, but an attempt to enter the new field of jet engines fell afoul of internal corporate battles over the use of wartime earnings. During the fifties, Curtiss-Wright progressively withdrew from aviation and recast itself as a diversified, multi-industry and multinational investment conglomerate. By the late seventies, Curtiss-Wright had become a second-tier subcontractor to its former competitors.

The story of the Curtiss-Wright Corporation is a reminder that the world of business is dynamic, never static. Businesses are subject to constant changes in the economic environment, in technology, in industry, in government policy, and in many other areas. All these changes have an impact on the way a company conducts its business. Its response to change can, as in the case of Curtiss-Wright, dictate its success or failure. On the most fundamental level, change within an industry has a profound effect on a company's fortunes. Industries constantly evolve, moving from infancy to growth to maturity, and in some cases to decline. Throughout this process of evolution, the constellation of players within an industry will evolve as well. Dominant firms will emerge at different times. Some may achieve lasting dominance while others decline as new competitors emerge with the shift of technology or markets in new directions.

The goal of every company is to sustain long-term profitable growth. Michael Porter has written that the key to a company's success or failure is competition and a company's ability to respond to the competition it faces in its industry.[1] Industry structure will determine the nature of competition within an industry. From this, companies develop a competitive strategy. To survive and prosper, every company must seek to build a competitive advantage over its peers and must sustain this advantage as industries, markets, and products evolve. The story of the Curtiss-Wright Corporation is the story of one company's attempt to secure competitive advantage in its chosen industry and its ultimate failure to sustain that advantage.

In his book *Scale and Scope: The Dynamics of Industrial Capitalism,* Professor Alfred Chandler argues that the organizational capabilities of the firm are critical to achieving and sustaining competitive advantage. In Chandler's view, organizational capability is the core of the dynamic of industrial capitalism.[2] The ability to organize, coordinate, and integrate the total resources of the firm—physical plant, labor, management—was the source of the success of the modern industrial enterprise. Firms that could maintain their organizational capabilities could sustain long-term growth and adapt to changes in industry structure, markets, and products. In certain cases, firms could achieve "first-mover" advantages over their peers by being the first to achieve innovations in organization, process, technology, or other functional areas (or usually some combination of innovation). The first movers were the firms that could take advantage of economies of scale and scope and thus rise to dominant positions within their industry. Every first mover, however, faces new challengers. Sustaining first-mover, or competitive, advantage is not simple. Several times during its history, Curtiss-Wright had what could be termed first-mover advantages but could not capitalize on them.[3]

The ability of a firm to resist competitive challenges and sustain its own competitive advantage over time depends on the organizational skills of its senior and middle management. The successful firms not only had a high degree of organizational skill but also made continuous investments in three core areas: manufacturing, marketing, and management.[4] These correspond to the production of a product, its sale and distribution, and the management skills required to organize production and sale to achieve competitive advantage. Sustaining competitive advantage required constant attention to these three areas of organizational capability. As industries, markets, and products evolved, firms had to adjust their organizational structure and process to cope with the changes brought on by evolution and the rise of new challengers. The paradigm that Chandler has outlined in *Scale and Scope* has provided the framework for this history of the Curtiss-Wright Corporation.

Of the three core areas, Curtiss-Wright was most successful with its marketing activities. It developed a superb sales and marketing organization, beginning with the Curtiss Aeroplane and Motor Company, which successfully promoted the corporation's products worldwide. Wright Aeronautical also developed a worldwide market for its products. Curtiss and Wright maintained close, although not always harmonious, relations with the army and navy, its two main customers. The Curtiss marketing effort enabled the company to find markets for its airplanes once they were rejected or no longer considered suitable by the American army or navy. Wright Aeronautical benefited from its ability to anticipate its customer's need for engines of greater power.

Curtiss-Wright was weakest in its investment in management. The lack of effective management, and in several cases management turmoil, characterized much of the corporation's history. The use of a holding company structure with independent subsidiaries created an unwieldy organization that was difficult to manage. Although the corporation shifted to a divisional structure shortly before World War II, the pressures of wartime production amplified and deepened Curtiss-Wright's managerial problems. Many of its wartime difficulties can be attributed to a managerial base that was simply too small to accommodate the corporation's dispersed and greatly expanded production operations. The problems of rapidly expanding production were compounded by the difficulty of rushing complex aircraft and engine designs into service prematurely. Senior management proved reluctant to delegate and thus failed to develop a core cadre of skilled middle managers who could have overseen the wartime expansion more effectively. Curtiss-Wright came under severe criticism during World War II for its management deficiencies, which hindered the corporation's ability to meet production targets.

In the final analysis, a company's success depends on the resources it has available and the skill with which management can direct those resources to achieve its goals. Although Curtiss-Wright's managers were capable men, in the end the decisions they made in the course of managing their business could not equip the company to survive as a leader in its chosen industry. It is to these decisions, and the historical development that brought them about, that we now turn.

Chapter 2

Origins to the End of World War I, 1909–1918

The Beginning: From Engines to Airplanes

The Curtiss-Wright Corporation combines two of the most renowned names in American aviation history: Glenn Curtiss and the Wright brothers, Wilbur and Orville. Although Curtiss and the Wrights became bitter rivals, the companies they founded eventually merged, creating a great corporate enterprise in the American aviation industry. Glenn Hammond Curtiss was part of a unique group of individuals, the independent inventors, who in letting loose a torrent of invention at the turn of the century transformed America.[1] These men, among them Alexander Graham Bell, Thomas Edison, and Wilbur and Orville Wright, laid the foundations for entirely new industries with the products of their own inventive minds. Often from modest backgrounds and with limited formal education, these men flourished in an informal environment that supported a few chosen craftsmen who could pursue their ideas.[2]

Curtiss was born on 21 May 1878 in Hammondsport, a small town in the Finger Lakes region of New York State.[3] He received his only formal education at the local school, leaving at age 14 when his family moved to nearby Rochester.[4] Curtiss had an inventive mind, and from an early age, he demonstrated mechanical aptitude. He developed a fascination with speed. Attracted to bicycle racing, he became well known as a determined competitor and won many regional races.[5] Moving back to Hammondsport in 1897, Curtiss began working as an assistant at a local photographic studio. In 1900, at the age of 22, he opened a bicycle shop. He soon realized that by selling his own brand of bicycles, he could reap a greater profit then by selling national brands as an agent. He started building his bicycles at a nearby machine shop, selling them under the brand name Hercules. The bicycle shop proved to be a success, and Curtiss soon opened a second store in a nearby town.[6]

Curtiss remained fascinated with speed. In 1900, when the first motorcycles appeared in America, he determined to build one for himself. In 1901 he ordered a pair of engine cylinders from the E. R. Thomas Company in Buffalo, New York, adapting the rough engine to a frame of his own design and building his own carburetor and ignition system. He named his first effort the "Happy Hooligan." Soon thereafter, he built a second version, which proved to be more reliable than his first machine. Success convinced Curtiss that he could build

Glenn Hammond Curtiss.
Glenn H. Curtiss Museum, Hammondsport, N.Y.

motorcycles of his own and that he could design and build a better engine than any he could buy.[7]

In March 1902 he announced that he would concentrate on the manufacture and sale of motorcycles under the Hercules brand name. To promote his motorcycles, Curtiss entered races around New York State, winning a flood of orders for his motorcycles and particularly for his lightweight motorcycle engine. With demand for his new product exceeding the capacity of his small shop, Curtiss sought financial backing to expand. Several local businessmen contributed the needed capital. Curtiss named his operation the G. H. Curtiss Manufacturing Company.[8] The new company flourished. Curtiss proved to be a successful businessman, capturing a large share of an emerging market with a product that provided superior performance to what had been available. By 1907 his small factory in Hammondsport was producing 500 motorcycles a year.[9]

Curtiss became involved in aviation through his engines. In 1904 Thomas Scott Baldwin, who had extensive experience flying balloons at county fairs across America, designed a dirigible. Searching for an engine to power his design, he became aware of Curtiss's reputation for manufacturing light and powerful engines. Baldwin wrote to Curtiss asking him to build an engine for the new dirigible. With some reluctance, Curtiss agreed, and with a Curtiss engine, Baldwin's dirigible flew successfully at the 1904 Saint Louis Exhibition. In 1906 Baldwin moved his operations to Hammondsport. He managed to convince a skeptical Curtiss that there was a market for aeronautical engines and that Curtiss should pursue it.[10] Over the next few years, Curtiss built several engines for Baldwin and assisted him in experiments to develop more efficient propellers. Baldwin won a contract in early 1908 to provide the U.S. Army with a dirigible; Curtiss designed a special engine for it. This engine helped to convince the army to accept its first powered lighter-than-air vehicle.[11]

Curtiss became more actively involved in aviation through another aviation pioneer, Alexander Graham Bell. Renowned for his invention of the telephone, Bell was fascinated with the idea of flight. Since the 1890s, Bell had been experimenting with kites at his summer home in Nova Scotia. At the New York Automobile Show in January 1906, Bell came across the exhibit of the G. H. Curtiss Manufacturing Company. He ordered an engine from the Curtiss Company, and toward the end of the year, the two men met several times.[12]

In 1907 Bell decided to gather a group of young aviation enthusiasts to pursue the problem of manned flight and to see if the group could add to what the Wrights had already achieved.[13] He asked three acquaintances to join him: J. A. D. McCurdy, a Canadian and the son of Bell's secretary; Frederick W. "Casey" Baldwin, a recent engineering graduate; and Lt. Thomas Selfridge, seconded from the U.S. Army Signal Corps. Bell invited Curtiss to join as chief engineer. Although he considered himself more of a businessman than an experimenter, Curtiss agreed. The Aerial Experimental Association came into being on 1 October 1907. The association supported Bell's experiments with his unique tetrahedral-shaped kites and devoted its first efforts to working on Bell's designs. Soon, however, the younger members voted to concentrate on conventional airplane designs that held more promise. Moving to Hammondsport for the winter of 1907 to 1908, McCurdy, Baldwin, Selfridge, and Curtiss agreed that each would design an airplane that the others would help build and test. The association's first effort, a biplane that Lt. Thomas Selfridge designed, made a short flight from the frozen surface of Lake Keuka, near Hammondsport, in March 1908. This airplane, dubbed the *Red Wing* after the color of its fabric covering, was not a success. With an engine that Curtiss had designed and built in his shops, the airplane made only a short hop before crash landing. The next effort, the *White Wing,* was more successful. Designed by Casey Baldwin, the *White Wing* incorporated ailerons on its upper wings to give greater lateral control. On 17 May, Baldwin took the *White Wing* up for its first flight, covering 285 feet. When Curtiss took the controls for the first time four days later, he covered 1,017 feet in his first attempt. Clearly they were working in the right direction.[14]

Curtiss sponsored the next effort, which the group named the *June Bug.* The *June Bug* flew in late June and proved to be the most effective design to date; Curtiss was soon making flights of more than 1,000 yards. This achievement encouraged the members of the association to try for the Scientific American Trophy, which had been donated to the Aero Club of America to be awarded for achievements in aviation. The first trophy would be awarded for the first flight in a straight line over a distance of one kilometer. When the Wright brothers declined to compete for the trophy, the Aero Club sent representatives to Hammondsport to witness the Aerial Experimental Association's attempt. On 4 July 1908, Glenn Curtiss piloted the *June Bug* in a flight of more than one mile, easily winning the trophy and bringing immediate fame to himself and the association.[15]

Following the success of the *June Bug* in winning the Scientific American Trophy, and with work progressing on their next aircraft, named the *Silver Dart,* the members of the association began thinking about what direction they should take next. Success led them all to begin to consider the possible commercial applications of their effort. In early 1909, the members of the association gathered at Bell's home in Nova Scotia to discuss their prospects.[16] By now, Glenn Curtiss had made up his mind to commit himself to aviation. He had successfully designed and built an airplane, and with his entrepreneurial spirit, he now

began to consider what business opportunities might be available. Bell proposed the formation of a company with Curtiss as general manager and asked Curtiss for his assessment of
the possibilities. Curtiss argued that the main opportunities were for exhibition flights and
prize money offered for feats of airmanship. Apart from the military, he doubted that there
would be much demand for aircraft; therefore any company formed should pursue exhibition flights and military sales. At a meeting in February, Bell proposed that the members of
the association form a joint stock company with an initial capital of $100,000. The association
would transfer all its material and inventions to the new venture, and the shares would be
distributed among the members.[17]

Curtiss was considering a completely different offer, however. While the Aerial Experimental Association was deliberating its future, Curtiss received what he believed to be an
appealing offer from Augustus Herring. Herring was one of the first participants in the early
years of American aviation development, but his reputation far exceeded his actual accom-
plishment. Herring approached Curtiss with a proposal to form a company to manufacture
airplanes. Herring spoke of substantial financial backing for the venture from contacts he
had on Wall Street as well as a contract to supply an airplane to the U.S. Army. Most important, Herring told Curtiss that he held aeronautical patents that predated those of the
Wrights. This fact was critical. After the *June Bug* had won the Scientific American Trophy,
the Wrights had written to the Aerial Experimental Association to advise them that the
Wrights held a patent on adjustable flying surfaces. They warned the association that it had
no permission to use these features. Hence, any patent predating the Wrights' would be the
key to a successful defense. Bell, who had been involved in bitter patent battles over the
invention of the telephone, knew all too well what a blow a patent suit from the Wrights
would be to a new company, and the issue of possible litigation had not been far from the
deliberations within the association.[18]

To Curtiss, the opportunity of joining forces with Herring was far more attractive than
continuing his partnership with his colleagues in the Aerial Experimental Association. Curtiss was a practical businessman with a strong entrepreneurial instinct. Bell was an inventor,
and his orientation was toward experimentation, not business. Although Bell had a considerable reputation, he did not possess sufficient funds to invest in a new venture. Moreover, neither Baldwin nor McCurdy had the business experience, much less the contacts among the
financial community, that Herring claimed to have. Curtiss's motorcycle company had given
him firsthand experience in building a successful business based on a new technology. He
had a factory that was already producing the best airplane engines in America and skilled
craftsmen available who could build airplanes. A link with the seemingly renowned Herring
appeared to be the best possible approach to this new world.[19]

In his haste to take advantage of Herring's offer, Curtiss neglected to investigate or
demand proof of Herring's claims and simply took them on faith. Herring had also contacted
Cortland Field Bishop, a wealthy businessman who was then the president of the Aero Club
of America, who agreed to help organize the proposed company and provide a capital contribution. The formation of the Herring-Curtiss Company was announced at the offices of the
Aero Club of America on 3 March 1909. On 19 March, the Herring-Curtiss Company was formally registered in New York State with Glenn Curtiss as vice president and general manager
and Augustus Herring as secretary-treasurer; Cortland Bishop and Thomas Baldwin were
among the directors. As part of the process of forming the new company, Curtiss signed over
all the assets and property of the G. H. Curtiss Manufacturing Company. Although it would all
too soon end in failure, the Herring-Curtiss Company marked the beginning of what would
emerge as one of the greatest names in American aviation history.[20]

The Herring-Curtiss Company delivered its first airplane, named the *Golden Flyer,* to the Aeronautical Society of New York in June 1909. Based on the design of the *June Bug* and the *Silver Dart,* the *Golden Flyer* was the first civil aircraft sold in America. Up to that time, the Wrights had yet to sell one of their airplanes to any individual. On 17 July, Curtiss flew the *Golden Flyer* 25 miles around a circular course to win his second Scientific American Trophy.[21]

The sale of the *Golden Flyer* stirred the Wright brothers to action. The Wrights had specifically warned the Aerial Experimental Association that they would not allow anyone to gain commercial benefit from features that fell within their patent; now Curtiss had done exactly that. The genius of the Wright brothers had been their understanding that the key to flight was the ability to control the airplane. They had developed a method of control that they called "wing warping" and had patented their system in 1906. The Wrights had incorporated the broadest possible language in their patent application to include any movable surfaces on an airplane that imparted a measure of controlled flight. To the Wrights, the system of aileron control that Curtiss used in his airplanes was a clear infringement of their patent. On 19 August 1909, the Wrights filed suit in New York State to prevent the Herring-Curtiss Company and Glenn Curtiss from manufacturing, selling, and exhibiting airplanes. Wilbur Wright chose the date for maximum impact against his competitor. Curtiss was not in America but in France competing in the first great European air meet at Reims, where he won the prestigious Gordon Bennett Trophy and set several speed records. The news of the suit arrived as Curtiss was savoring victory.[22]

To his consternation, Curtiss learned in France that Herring's claims might be more apparent than real. Although Herring had promised to turn over to the Herring-Curtiss Company the patents and inventions he claimed to have, he had failed to do so. Even more damaging was his default on his contract to provide an airplane to the U.S. Army. The relationship between Herring and the other directors steadily deteriorated. In October the other directors of the company, determined to contest the Wright patent suit, passed a resolution ordering Herring to turn over his patents to the company; Herring procrastinated. At a final meeting in December, Herring simply slipped out of the meeting and ran away. The other directors faced the awful realization that Herring had nothing to contribute but empty words. In January 1910, the remaining directors obtained an injunction against Herring, preventing him from voting his shares. The month brought even more shattering news. On 3 January 1910, the federal circuit court in Buffalo issued an injunction preventing the Herring-Curtiss Company from selling and exhibiting aircraft.[23]

The injunction could not have come at a worse time. Curtiss's success at the Reims meet stimulated an enormous demand for exhibition flights in the United States. People across the country were clamoring for a chance to see the new wonder. Cities were eager to pay to have an airplane flight as the central attraction of their fairs and exhibitions and offered large prizes. By posting a $10,000 bond and filing an appeal, Curtiss could continue flying, though at considerable risk; should he lose his appeal of the Wright suit, the Wrights could claim any money he had earned before the final court judgment.[24]

Curtiss flew at the International Air Meet in Los Angeles in January, and in several other cities over the following months. The exhibition business was lucrative, but Curtiss could not exploit all the opportunities available, particularly with the financial risk of the Wright suit and his difficulties with Herring. Curtiss was determined to strike out on his own but needed a means of severing his connections with Herring. Ironically, the Wright suit provided the solution. The January injunction against the Herring-Curtiss Company brought the company's business to a grinding halt. With the injunction hanging over the company, customers were reluctant to purchase its airplanes. With no income, the company soon had trouble paying its creditors and filed for bankruptcy on 10 April 1910. Curtiss's unfortunate association with Augustus Herring ended on 2 December when the U.S. district court in Buffalo issued a decree of bankruptcy. The Herring-Curtiss Company ceased to exist, and Curtiss was finally rid of Herring.[25]

The following June, Curtiss won his appeal against the Wrights, and the injunction against him was overturned. Curtiss could now build airplanes and fly them, pending final judgment. To capture as much business as possible, Curtiss set up a separate company in September 1910—the Curtiss Exhibition Company—with a manager and several pilots. Although its profits were at risk owing to the Wright suit, Curtiss had to generate a source of earnings to keep his plant in operation, since the Herring-Curtiss Company was in bankruptcy.[26]

Profits from exhibition flying kept Curtiss going until the bankruptcy of the Herring-Curtiss Company was resolved. Once free of Herring, Curtiss moved quickly to set up his own manufacturing company. On 3 December 1910, Curtiss formed the Curtiss Aeroplane Company to manufacture airplanes. Two weeks later, on 19 December, he created a second organization, the Curtiss Motor Company, which incorporated the existing motorcycle business as well as the manufacture and sale of airplane engines. In both new companies, Curtiss maintained majority control. The following February, Curtiss bought back his original factory from the bankruptcy trustee. Freed from the injunction and with a company that he controlled, Curtiss was ready to build a business.[27]

Building a Business

To succeed as he had done in the motorcycle business, Curtiss needed a superior product and a market for it. He proceeded to develop both. He still believed that there were only two likely sources of profit for aviation: exhibition flights and sales to the government. The Curtiss Exhibition Company was doing well, with its pilots winning fame and prize money. Curtiss now turned to developing business with the government. In an astute bit of marketing, he wrote to the secretary of the Navy and the secretary of war in November 1910 offering to provide free flying lessons to selected army and navy officers.[28] After setting up his new companies, Curtiss moved to San Diego, where he established a flying school to take advantage of the fine winter weather in southern California. Accepting Curtiss's offer, the navy sent one officer to the San Diego school for instruction, and the army sent three.[29]

Close links between the Army Signal Corps and the Wright brothers led Curtiss to believe that he would have little success selling airplanes to the army. Thus he concentrated on the navy instead.[30] Perhaps equally important, Curtiss was intrigued with the problem of an airplane's landing on, and taking off from, water. In 1908 he had begun experimenting with the idea of what he called a "hydro-aeroplane," an airplane equipped with pontoons. On 28 March 1910, the Frenchman Henri Fabre made the first seaplane flight in history when a floatplane of his design successfully took off from a harbor near Marseilles. His frail airplane failed to convince the navies of the world that a practical seaplane could be developed, however. Yet if Curtiss could perfect an airplane that could land on, and take off from, water, he would have a product of great interest not only to the U.S. Navy but to other navies as well. He would have a patent that might be as important as that of the Wrights.[31]

Coincidentally, the navy had assigned a senior officer, Capt. Washington Irving Chambers, to investigate and advise on aviation. When Chambers met Curtiss in October 1910, they discussed his experiments with the hydro-aeroplane at length. Curtiss was convinced that if he could build a successful hydro-aeroplane, the navy would purchase it.[32] In the following month, the navy arranged for a trial flight from the deck of a navy ship. On 14 November, Eugene Ely, one of Curtiss's best exhibition pilots, flew the Curtiss *Hudson Flyer* off a specially prepared wooden deck built on the cruiser *Birmingham* and landed successfully onshore. On 18 January 1911, Ely performed the reverse feat at San Francisco, landing on a wooden deck on the armored cruiser *Pennsylvania*. Despite this successful demonstration, the navy felt that specialized decks were impractical. The immediate prize was still an airplane that could take off from, and land on, water. The secretary of the Navy wrote Glenn Curtiss to say that only when an airplane could land alongside a battleship and be hoisted aboard would he believe that the airplane had practical naval value.[33]

After arriving in San Diego at the end of 1910, Curtiss renewed his experiments with his hydro-aeroplane. He was not a trained engineer; nor was he given to theory. He was instead a practical inventor who simply went out and tried his ideas, tinkering with them until they worked or proved to be impractical. He used the same approach in developing the seaplane. After many experiments and numerous changes to the shape of the twin pontoons, Curtiss finally came up with a design that enabled the airplane to break free of the water with relative ease. On 26 January 1911, he made the first successful flight of the world's first practical seaplane. In the following month, he flew out to the *Pennsylvania,* landed alongside, and was hoisted aboard, thus answering the secretary of the Navy's challenge. Soon Curtiss was making flights off the water with a passenger. The navy recognized that it now had an airplane it could use. In May, with a new congressional appropriation for aviation, the navy placed an order with the Curtiss Aeroplane Company for two Model E airplanes, one equipped as a seaplane and one as a land plane. These aircraft, designated the A-1 and the A-2, were the U.S. Navy's first airplanes.[34]

By the middle of 1911, Curtiss was producing two types of aircraft, the Model D and Model E. Both were pusher biplanes, with the engine mounted behind the pilot. The Model D had a single seat, while the slightly larger Model E was a two-seater. That year Curtiss sold several aircraft to the government and to individual fliers. Ironically, given Curtiss's attempts to interest the navy in his airplanes, his first sale to the U.S. government was a Model D, which went to the U.S. Army Signal Corps in March. Later in the year, the army ordered three Model E pushers. The navy also bought a third pusher from Curtiss in 1912. Curtiss's success with his seaplane created interest among several foreign navies. During 1911 and 1912, he sold Model E seaplanes to the navies of Russia, Germany, and Japan. These early sales reflected a strong interest in foreign markets that would characterize the Curtiss Company throughout its history. Exhibition flights were still in great demand in the United States, and Curtiss sold several of his airplanes to noted exhibition fliers.[35]

When Curtiss returned to his winter flying school in San Diego in the fall of 1911, he began developing a true flying boat in which the hull would be part of the main structure of the airplane. Although his first design was unable to get off the water, the idea showed promise. He continued his experiments on his return to Hammondsport. His flying-boat No. 2 featured a true full-length hull structure, setting the pattern for all subsequent flying boats. This boat, unable to break the suction created as it moved across the surface of the lake, also failed to take off from the water. During trial runs, Curtiss followed alongside in a motorboat, watching the interaction of the hull with the water. He came up with the idea of breaking the smooth line of the hull by putting a wedge, or step, at the center of gravity. This enabled the front part of the hull to break free of the water, and with the reduction in drag, the flying boat was able to reach takeoff speed. Curtiss's inventive mind had found the solution. In July 1912, the world's first successful flying boat made its maiden flight.[36]

Curtiss's flying boat attracted the immediate attention of both U.S. military services and foreign navies. Even wealthy individuals showed interest. After continued experimentation, Curtiss developed a standard model, which the company designated the Model F. In 1912 the U.S. Army bought a Model F flying boat and ordered two more in 1913. The U.S. Navy purchased the first of five Model F flying boats in 1912, acquiring more over the next two years as naval aviation slowly expanded. The Model F was the first American military aircraft to be used in action when a navy version flew a reconnaissance mission over the Mexican town of Vera Cruz in 1914. Among foreign powers, the Austro-Hungarian empire bought several Model F flying boats for use in the Adriatic Sea, and the Imperial Russian Navy acquired 24 Model F flying boats before 1914. The standard Model F was a two-seater, but Curtiss built several multiseat versions for wealthy Americans, as well as several other specialized models.[37]

The sale of the standard Model D and E pusher airplanes and the Model F flying boats provided a small but steady flow of business to the Curtiss Aeroplane Company. In addition to manufacturing airplanes, the company also ran two flying schools, at Hammondsport and San Diego, providing instruction to military and civilian pilots from several nations. It managed to prosper from aircraft sales, exhibition flying, and flying training, although it was still under the threat of the Wright patent suit.

At this time, building airplanes was more a skilled craft than a production process. Made from wood and fabric and held together with wire and metal fittings, each airplane was handcrafted. None of the work was beyond the skills of a good woodworker. The pace of production was slow. Demand for aircraft was not great, and the actual production rate may not have been more than one or two airplanes a month in the early years. The Curtiss factory employed fewer than 300 men, including those who worked on the Curtiss Motor Company engines. Employees at the Hammondsport factory worked in a casual atmosphere, with "G.H.," as longtime employees called Glenn Curtiss, overseeing construction. Curtiss combined the roles of inventor, designer, engineer, test pilot, shop foreman, and manager. On first visiting the Curtiss factory, U.S. Navy Lt. John Towers asked Curtiss if he could see the detailed plans for the two navy planes on order from the Curtiss Company. Curtiss led Towers to a wall of the factory where Curtiss had simply sketched out his designs in pencil. The workmen would come over to the wall to check on their progress, then go back to work.[38]

In January 1914 the United States Circuit Court of Appeals issued a ruling in favor of the Wrights in their case against Curtiss. The court supported a broad interpretation of the original Wright patent and ruled that Curtiss had infringed on it. Curtiss struck back, hiring the patent lawyer who had helped Henry Ford win a patent fight in the automotive industry. A careful reading of the patent showed a loophole. The crux of the Wright's invention was the simultaneous movement of the control surfaces. In this regard, the Curtiss system of ailerons was similar to the Wright's wing warping. When the pilot moved the left aileron up, for example, the right aileron moved down accordingly. Curtiss revised his system, disconnecting the ailerons so that the movements were not simultaneous. This system was not covered in the Wright patent. Although the defense was not foolproof, Curtiss in effect forced the Wrights to bring an entirely new suit to the courts, with the prospect of further delays under appeal. By finding the loophole, Curtiss bought more time.[39]

Curtiss did not let the Wright patent suit distract him from continued developmental work. In 1912 the army expressed interest in a tractor design, in which the engine was placed in front of the pilot, rather than behind. Curtiss built the Model G tractor and sold two to the army in 1913, his first move away from the pusher. In fact, the pusher design was reaching the end of its capabilities. Airplane designers in Europe were abandoning the pusher in favor of the tractor airplane. The pushers had an unhealthy reputation for serious accidents. When a pusher crashed, there was risk of the engine breaking loose and crushing the pilot. The tractor airplane was safer. In 1914, following a series of fatal accidents, the U.S. Army Signal Corps instructed its pilots to stop flying pusher aircraft. At the same time, the army approached the Curtiss Aeroplane Company for an improved tractor airplane.[40]

Curtiss JN-4 Jenny.
Brian Flanagan Collection, courtesy of Stanley Teachman.

The Model G was a first attempt at a tractor design, but it was not a success. Curtiss realized that he lacked experience in designing tractor airplanes. On a European trip in the summer of 1913, he hired B. Douglas Thomas, a British engineer who had worked on tractor designs for the Avro and Sopwith airplane companies. After joining the Curtiss company, Thomas set to work designing the Model J, a tandem two-seat tractor biplane. The Model J proved to be a more successful design than the Model G, although the army could buy only two on its limited budget. At the same time, Curtiss began developing a parallel tractor design, the Model N. The Model N also showed promise, and the army bought the single prototype produced. In the Model J and the Model N, the Curtiss company had the seeds of one of the most successful aircraft it would ever build, the JN trainer.[41]

Even as the demand for more capable aircraft grew, Curtiss did not neglect the development of more powerful engines. By 1913 the Curtiss Motor Company was producing two standard water-cooled engines, a four-cylinder engine that produced 40 horsepower, and an eight-cylinder engine, the Model O, that came in either 60-horsepower or 75-horsepower versions. During 1914 Curtiss worked with his chief assistant for engine construction, Henry Kleckler, to improve the power of the Model O. They developed two engines, the Model OX, which generated 90 horsepower, and the Model OXX, which gave 100 horsepower. These engines powered the larger versions of the Model F flying boat and the new Model J and N tractor biplanes. The greater power available with these engines encouraged Curtiss to take on his most ambitious project.[42]

Curtiss had been working on an idea that would have seemed impossible only a few years before: an airplane that could fly across the Atlantic Ocean. He had first talked of the idea after successfully developing the flying boat in 1912. In the following year, Lord Northcliffe, publisher of the English *Daily Mail* newspaper, announced a prize of £10,000 ($50,000) for the first successful flight across the Atlantic. In August 1913 Rodman Wanamaker, an American retail magnate, asked Curtiss to design and build two flying boats to attempt the Atlantic crossing. The new flying boat, which Wanamaker named *America,* promised to be bigger than anything the Curtiss Company had yet built. Nearly twice the size of the Model F flying boat, Curtiss's new design featured an enclosed cockpit for the two pilots. Powered by two

90-horsepower OX engines, the *America* flew for the first time in June 1914. After successful test flights, the Atlantic crossing was scheduled for early August. On 4 August, Great Britain declared war on Germany, and all of Europe was now entangled in the Great War. The Atlantic flight had to be postponed until the war was over. All the effort devoted to the *America* appeared to have been in vain, but the outbreak of war would bring about an unexpected change in the fortunes of the Curtiss Company.[43]

The Curtiss Aeroplane Company was the largest airplane manufacturer in America in the summer of 1914, even though it employed fewer than 500 people. Although Glenn Curtiss was still not free from the Wright patent suit, he had managed to establish a successful business manufacturing airplanes and airplane engines. He had built up a small but capable engineering team that had produced two successful tractor designs and the impressive *America* flying boat. In business, timing can be a critical factor in a company's success or failure. Over the history of the Curtiss-Wright Corporation, product timing would be both a benefit and a detriment to the company's fortunes. In World War I, it proved to be a benefit. The war would transform not only the course of aviation but the fortunes of the Curtiss Aeroplane Company.

From Shop to Factory: Airplanes for the European War

With the beginning of hostilities in August 1914, the major European powers quickly mobilized their air arms and brought them to the front. While United States military aviation had stagnated, European armies and navies were quick to appreciate the airplane's potential contribution in time of war. In response, they had established army and naval air units. Although the early military airplanes had limited capability, they had demonstrated their usefulness in reconnaissance and sea patrol in prewar maneuvers. When they went to war, the military air units already had an idea of how best they could be employed. By the end of the year, the airplane had demonstrated beyond doubt its value in reconnaissance. With the emergence of static trench warfare, the airplane became the only means of ascertaining the enemy's strength and intentions. Under the demands of war, new roles soon emerged. Airplanes began to drop primitive bombs on enemy troops and supplies. Some pilots went aloft with rifles to prevent enemy reconnaissance machines from performing their task, thereby giving birth to the fighter plane.[44]

The course of the war and the airplane's success created an urgent demand for ever increasing numbers of airplanes, engines, and pilots. Few generals had expected the war to last more than a few weeks, but stagnation soon set in. Within months, German advances in the west and east had been halted. The attrition in men and aircraft over the front and in accidents during the first months of the war was greater than expected. The military had an immediate need for aircraft of all types, for combat as well as training. The European aviation industry was simply unable to cope with these demands in a short space of time.[45]

Even while moving as rapidly as possible to mobilize their own industries, both Britain and Russia had no alternative but to seek out aircraft from other sources. They turned to America and to the Curtiss Aeroplane Company. Some of the smaller European powers approached Curtiss as well. The Curtiss Company was a recognized leader in the design and construction of flying boats, which the naval air arms of Europe needed immediately. Moreover, Curtiss had in its Model J and Model N series the prototype of a serviceable training plane that could be put to use training the scores of pilots needed at the front.

The first of a flood of wartime orders came from the British Royal Naval Air Service (RNAS). Soon after the outbreak of war, the British Admiralty purchased the *America* flying boat and its sister ship for the RNAS. The aircraft were delivered to England in November

1914. After trials at the RNAS air station at Felixstowe, the RNAS placed an order with Curtiss for 62 production versions, designated H-4, for delivery during 1915. Late in the year, the RNAS placed an order for 8 Model JN-3 training planes, which combined the best features of the Model J and the Model N. At the same time, the Imperial Russian Navy ordered more Model F flying boats for its Naval Air Service. The Spanish navy also placed orders for the Model F.[46]

Glenn Curtiss quickly realized that the factory at Hammondsport had neither the space nor the labor force for large-scale production. Early in 1915, the Curtiss Aeroplane Company moved its headquarters and airplane production to a factory in Buffalo, a city that had a large supply of skilled labor. The Curtiss Motor Company remained in Hammondsport to continue manufacturing engines. Soon even the new facilities in Buffalo proved inadequate as the orders continued to come in from Europe. In March, with advances from the British against future orders, the company had an entirely new plant built in just 30 days. This factory, known as the Churchill Street plant, was devoted to airplane production. Shortly thereafter, another factory was taken over to expand engine production. At the same time, a subsidiary company was established in Toronto, Canada. It was the Curtiss Aeroplane and Motor Company, Ltd., under J. A. D. McCurdy, Glenn Curtiss's former associate in the Aerial Experimental Association. The Canadian company soon began producing airplanes under British contracts.[47]

Throughout 1915 British orders continued to come in. In March the RNAS ordered an additional 91 JN-3 training planes. Later the RNAS ordered 84 Model R-2 airplanes, a larger development of the Model N powered by a new Curtiss engine, the 160-horsepower V-X. In May the RNAS placed an order for 102 twin-engine bombers designed specially for the RNAS. Named the *Canada,* only 12 were built, and the original contract was later canceled. An even more ambitious project initiated in 1915 for the RNAS was the Model T, the largest seaplane in the world at the time of its construction and the first four-engine airplane built in the United States. The RNAS placed an order for 20 Model T seaplanes, intending to use them for long-range patrols over the North Sea. The *Wall Street Journal* reported that for the fiscal year ending 31 October, the Curtiss Company had produced more than $6 million worth of airplanes and engines under British contracts and held additional contracts worth $15 million.[48]

The magnitude of his success and the prospect of even more business to come made Glenn Curtiss realize that the scope of the Curtiss Company's activities was beginning to exceed his managerial ability. Curtiss had no experience running a large enterprise. He needed to reorganize the company and bring in more professional managers, namely, businessmen who were more familiar with the needs and problems of a large manufacturing company. In addition, continued expansion demanded more capital, and Curtiss had little experience in raising funds. Coincidental with the change in Curtiss's thinking, investors and investment banks on Wall Street were now keenly interested in the growing aviation industry. The prospects of lucrative wartime contracts held the potential for large profits, which made investing in the most successful companies an attractive proposition.[49]

In early January 1916, a syndicate led by the investment banking firm of William Morris Imbrie and Company purchased the controlling stock in the Curtiss Aeroplane Company and the Curtiss Motor Company from Glenn Curtiss. On 12 January 1916, the Curtiss Aeroplane and Motor Corporation was incorporated to take over the business of the two companies. The Curtiss Exhibition Company and the Curtiss Aeroplane and Motor Company, Ltd., of Canada, were brought into the new organization as well. Capital of the new company was established at $9 million, consisting of $6 million in 7 percent preferred stock, $3 million in 6 percent notes maturing over the following 18 months, and 150,000 shares of common stock. Overnight Glenn Curtiss became a millionaire. He reportedly received $5 million in cash, $3.5 million in preferred stock, and 75,000 shares of common stock in the new company. A month later, the Curtiss Aeroplane and Motor Corporation bought control of the Burgess Company, a small manufacturer of seaplanes founded in 1910 by W. Starling Burgess. With this acquisition, Curtiss gained a factory in Marblehead, Massachusetts, and 200 skilled workers. Over the course of the year, he brought in several prominent businessmen and bankers from Buffalo and New York City to sit on the board of directors. One of these men was Clement M. Keys, an investment banker who would figure prominently in the company's future.[50]

Keys was an intriguing figure. The son of a minister, he grew up in a small town near Toronto and attended the University of Toronto. He taught classics at a small Canadian college for several years and in 1901 left for New York City to seek his fortune. He worked as a journalist, first at the *Wall Street Journal* and then at the monthly journal *World's Work,* where he soon became the financial editor. He left in 1911 to set up his own investment bank, underwriting securities and advising wealthy clients on investments. Glenn Curtiss sought Keys's investment advice soon after selling his company and then asked Keys to join the Curtiss Aeroplane and Motor Corporation as vice president for finance.[51]

It was not simply the company's size and structure that were changing. The task of designing and building airplanes and engines was becoming more complex and required a more disciplined approach. In a profound shift from the days when Curtiss and a few employees would cut and hammer until they got it right, the company established a research and test department to complement the work of the engineering department. It used the latest scientific methods for testing new designs. As the technology advanced, the need for an extensive research and development effort and for highly capable design engineers became ever more important. This would become one of the defining characteristics of the aviation industry. Flush with wartime contracts, few gave much thought to the expense of the design effort.[52]

Nineteen sixteen proved to be another good year for the Curtiss Company. The RNAS ordered 84 improved flying boats designated the H-12. That summer the British ordered 105

Clement Mellville Keys.

Davies, *Airlines of the U.S. since 1914,* 50.

JN-4 trainers, a modified version of the earlier JN-3. In November Curtiss built a refined version of the JN-4 as the JN-4A, which incorporated changes in design the British had requested. In total, the British Admiralty placed orders for 250 JN-4 and JN-4A airplanes for use by the RNAS and the Royal Flying Corps.[53]

During the year, the Curtiss company received its first sizable orders from the United States Army and Navy. Despite the rapid growth in military aviation in Europe, military aviation in the United States remained stagnant. Senior army and navy commanders begrudged any expenditures on aviation and paid little attention to the role of aviation in the European war. In July 1914, Congress established the Aviation Section of the Army Signal Corps, but with meager appropriations, the Aviation Section acquired few aircraft. During 1914 the army purchased 11 airplanes for the Aviation Section, and in the following year only 18, including 8 Curtiss JN-2s. Naval aviation was in similar shape, with the naval aviators at Pensacola still flying pusher floatplanes and Curtiss Model F flying boats.[54]

In 1916 attitudes within Congress and the military began to change. Congress, aware of the greater risk of American involvement in the war, passed the National Defense Act in June 1916, which authorized the expansion of the Aviation Section. In August Congress passed the first large appropriation bill for army aviation, allocating $13,281,666 for the Aviation Section. With more money available, the army placed orders with several manufacturers; Curtiss received contracts for 21 Model JN-4 aircraft and 53 Model R-4s. That same month, naval aviation was allocated $3.5 million under the naval appropriations bill. In November the navy ordered 30 Model N-9 airplanes (basically a JN-4 equipped with floats) from Curtiss. The navy also ordered what could be considered its first real warplane, a single example of the Curtiss H-12. This was followed by an order for 19 more H-12s for delivery in 1917.[55]

To Darken the Skies with Aircraft: America Goes to War

When America declared war on Germany on 6 April 1917, the air arms of the army and navy were woefully ill prepared for the conflict they were about to enter. The army had 56 trained pilots and approximately 300 airplanes, not one of which was suitable for combat. Naval aviation was in similar shape. The navy had 48 officers and 54 airplanes, but with the exception of the single Curtiss H-12, they were all training planes. From this motley collection of aircraft and inexperienced pilots, the United States had to build an air arm capable of fighting against the most advanced airplanes German industry could produce.[56]

Neither the American army and navy nor the American aviation industry were prepared for war. Of the 16 firms that had received orders for military aircraft before America entered World War I, only 6 had built more than 10 airplanes.[57] Now this small industry, which employed in total only a few thousand workers, was being called on to undertake an immediate and massive expansion.

To many American observers, the airplane seemed to offer a solution to nearly three years of stagnant slaughter in the trenches. After the American declaration of war, calls went out for enough airplanes to darken the skies over Germany. The French premier called for 4,500 airplanes from America. Underlying this belief in the efficacy of the air weapon was an unbounded faith in American productive capacity and the American system of mass production. With no knowledge of the actual difficulties involved, supporters of a massive air force believed that American industry could simply and rapidly churn out thousands of airplanes just as it had produced automobiles and countless other products. All that was needed was the will and sufficient funds.[58]

Not surprisingly, given the widespread acceptance of this vision, the men who came to dominate American aviation policy in the first year of the war came from the automotive industry. They were firmly committed to the idea that American production technology was superior to that of Europe and that the mass production techniques of the automotive industry could be effortlessly adopted to produce thousands of airplanes, along with the engines to power them. Promoting this idea through speeches and the press, they helped persuade Congress to authorize a massive spending program for aviation. In May the Aircraft Production Board was created to advise the military and the aviation industry on the aviation program. A month later, the Joint Army and Navy Technical Board proposed a program to build 12,000 combat planes, 5,000 training planes, and 24,000 engines by July 1918. To finance this program, on 24 July, Congress approved an appropriation of $640 million for army aviation, the largest single appropriation ever passed; over the summer, additional funds were approved to expand naval aviation. The navy came up with its own plan for building 1,700 patrol and training airplanes.[59]

Under pressure from the government, which had no desire to pay the royalties demanded under the Wright patent suit on the huge number of airplanes it planned to build, the airplane manufacturers agreed to a solution to the patent problem. A Manufacturers Aircraft Association was set up to hold all patents in a cross-licensing agreement. The Curtiss Aeroplane and Motor Corporation and the Wright-Martin Company, which held the Wright patents, would receive reduced royalties on every aircraft built up to a specified amount. This agreement gave all manufacturers access to all patents, clearing the way for wartime production.[60]

To speed production and meet the aggressive targets that had been set, the military and the Aircraft Production Board decided to copy the best and most advanced designs then in production in Europe rather than have American firms design new aircraft. These automotive men naively believed that the process of converting these designs to American mass production methods would be simple. In parallel, the army decided to design and build a standard airplane engine that would also be suitable for mass production. This engine would be available in several different horsepower ratings and would be used in the European aircraft models chosen for production in America instead of the European-made engines for which the aircraft were designed.[61]

Even before the army and the Aircraft Production Board had decided on the aircraft to be produced, Curtiss began to receive orders from both the army and the navy. The military establishment had an immediate need for training airplanes to cope with the demand for more pilots. Following the American declaration of war, the navy placed contracts with Curtiss for 150 training airplanes.[62] Then, in June, the army ordered 600 JN-4D trainers. These orders dwarfed the company's previous production for the British. Although the company had been building the JN-4 for more than a year, the process of expanding production was not well managed. The company was simply not prepared for such a rapid increase in production and lacked the management staff to oversee the expansion. Many of the production processes were in the heads of the engineers and were not written down. A shortage of working capital led to further delays. An army audit done in the summer of 1917 revealed frequent disruptions from unplanned changes in design, a waste of materials, and a lack of inventory control.[63]

Curtiss and the other directors clearly perceived that with the demands on the company about to shift by a significant order of magnitude, they needed managers with more experience. The company's strengths lay in aircraft design and development, not in the mass production of standard types of airplanes. Curtiss turned to his friend John North Willys, president of the Willys-Overland Company, one of the leading automobile manufacturers of the day. Willys was a man with an established reputation as an expert on production. Curtiss proposed that the two companies combine. In June Willys agreed. The Willys-Overland Company took a controlling interest in the Curtiss Aeroplane and Motor Corporation through a purchase of preferred and common stock. Glenn Curtiss became chairman of the Curtiss Aeroplane and Motor Corporation, and John Willys was appointed president. Willys immediately brought in new management. He recruited William A. Morgan, a Buffalo industrialist, as vice president and general manager, and James E. Kepperly, a Willys-Overland vice president. Willys also injected $2 million in new cash and followed this with an issue of 63,000 shares of new common stock to raise additional capital.[64] Curtiss now had a partner whose central focus was production. Willys-Overland had the experience needed to coordinate the supply of a vast number of parts, materials, and subassemblies from a host of subcontractors.[65]

In late July, Willys and his new directors met with the Aircraft Production Board to discuss the army's future requirements for aircraft and engines and the likely demands that would be placed on the Curtiss Company. The board asked the directors to come up with a plan for producing 3,000 fighter planes and 1,000 heavy bombers, the specific types to be determined later. It also urged the company to transfer production of the JN-4 to other manufacturers and concentrate instead on fighter and bomber production. But Curtiss insisted on continuing production of the JN-4 at his own plants. He had no interest in having plant and workers idle while new aircraft were introduced into the production line. Curtiss estimated that the company could produce 2,000 JN-4D aircraft, 3,000 fighters, and 1,000 bombers by July 1918.[66] Based on these discussions, Willys authorized the construction of a new plant in Buffalo to provide capacity for the expected orders of 6,000 airplanes. This new facility became known as the Elmwood Avenue plant.

Over the next six months, the Curtiss Company struggled to cope with the constant and often conflicting demands from the army. The attempt brought the company to the edge of bankruptcy. On 15 September the U.S. Army Signal Corps's Equipment Division placed orders with Curtiss for 3,000 French Spad XIII fighters, 500 Italian Caproni bombers, and an additional 1,400 JN-4D trainers. Since the government could not advance funds to cover the cost, the company used its own funds and borrowed additional money from banks to purchase the new facilites, machine tools, and materials. The army had assured the company that the cost would be covered in the contract for the planes.[67]

Problems arose almost immediately. The army gave Curtiss conflicting instructions on the type of engines it wanted for its Spads. Having told Curtiss to redesign the Spad for one type of engine, the army then told the company to use another. The same degree of confusion occurred over the Spad's machine guns. The army instructed Curtiss to redesign the Spad to accommodate an American-made machine gun, and Curtiss did. In October, however, the army changed its mind and ordered Curtiss to go back to using the Spad's standard British machine gun instead.[68] Each design change caused delays as blueprints had to be redrawn, calculations redone, and production processes reconfigured. While still involved in gearing up for production of the Spad, the army placed an order with Curtiss for 1,000 Bristol fighters.[69]

Then, on 7 November, the company was shocked to learn that the army had canceled the entire Spad order, fearing that new German aircraft would make the plane obsolete by the time it reached the front in 1918. The fast pace of technological innovation prompted the decision to leave the design of single-engined fighters to England and France. The army also canceled its contract for the 500 Caproni bombers. General manager William Morgan, soon to leave the company owing to a nervous breakdown from the accumulated stress, promptly told the army that the cancellation would be disastrous. The company owed the banks a $1 million payment in April. Additional money had been spent purchasing raw materials and hiring a large labor force for the planned production of the Spad fighter. Without these contracts, the company faced bankruptcy.[70]

As a stopgap, Curtiss received an order for 700 additional JN-4Ds on 29 December. The army told Curtiss to concentrate on the Bristol. On 10 January 1918, the original order for 1,000 Bristol fighters was increased to 2,000 fighters at a cost of $12 million plus an additional $2,476,185 in spare parts. To enable Curtiss to complete its wartime contracts, the government loaned the company $12 million, which allowed Curtiss to repay its outstanding bank debt and retire its bond issue.[71]

The attempt to manufacture the Bristol fighter proved to be an even greater exercise in frustration and demonstrated the fallacy of assuming that mass production techniques could easily and quickly be applied to the production of aircraft. The army insisted on redesigning the Bristol fighter to take the new American-designed Liberty engine then entering mass production, a more powerful but far heavier engine than the Bristol's Rolls-Royce Falcon. Instead of designing an airplane around a specific engine, as the Curtiss engineers wanted to do, the army insisted on forcing the Liberty into an airplane for which it was not designed, with predictable results. The company undertook the laborous process of redesign and built a sample aircraft by hand. After months of delays, the first example was completed, and test flights began in early March 1918. The Curtiss-built Bristol fighter proved far too heavy due to the weight of the Liberty engine. The first example crashed on a test flight, and the second crashed a short time later, killing the crew. After a third crash, the airplane was deemed unsafe, and on 20 July the army canceled the entire contract.[72]

The failure of American industry to produce a flood of aircraft for the European front caused an outcry among the public and produced a political scandal. The automotive men who dominated the Aircraft Production Board had failed to appreciate that building an airplane demanded a much higher degree of skill, finer tolerances, and thousands more parts than building an automobile.[73] Airplanes of the day were simply not suited for mass production in the quantities originally intended. An official investigation failed to reveal any evidence of fraud or collusion, but suspicion of industry malfeasance would linger for years to come. What the investigations did confirm was a chaotic situation of constant changes in designs, plans, and contracts.

In its own defense, the Curtiss Company issued a statement in *Aerial Age Weekly,* a leading aviation journal, documenting the conflicting orders and cancellations it had received since the start of the war. On the credit side of the ledger, Curtiss had delivered more than 4,000 JN trainers and 5,000 engines; six other firms built nearly 2,000 additional JN trainers under license.[74] But even in the more successful production of a trainer of its own design, the company encountered quality problems; mass production of wood-and-fabric aircraft was not a simple process.

Although Curtiss's experience with the army had been one of almost constant frustration, the company's work for the U.S. Navy was one of the American aviation industry's few success stories during World War I. Curtiss built approximately 1,800 flying boats and seaplanes for the navy. When the Senate investigators asked William Morgan, the Curtiss production manager, why the company's production for the navy differed from that for the army, he replied simply, "The navy seemed to know what they wanted and never changed."[75]

The U.S. Navy entered the war needing flying boats for convoy and antisubmarine patrol. Like the army, the navy wanted hundreds of training planes to accommodate the demand for hundreds of new pilots. Soon after America entered the war, the navy placed orders with Curtiss for 704 seaplane and flying boat trainers.[76] Curtiss flying boats were the backbone of the navy's patrol squadrons. The navy ordered 124 large flying boats from Curtiss, but the flying boat built in the greatest quantity was the Curtiss HS-1L, which was adopted as the navy's standard coastal patrol plane. Curtiss built 675 examples, and other manufacturers

Curtiss H-16 flying boat.

Bowers, *Curtiss Aircraft, 1907–1947,* 94.

built 417 under license. In the spring of 1918, the navy began shipping Curtiss flying boats to England and France, where they flew patrol missions searching for German U-boats. U.S. Army fliers in Europe relied almost completely on European aircraft for combat until nearly the end of the war, while the U.S. Navy flew nearly 800,000 nautical miles on patrol in Curtiss-built flying boats.[77]

In the last year of the war, the Curtiss Aeroplane and Motor Corporation built a remarkable aircraft for the navy that was the start of the company's long association with fighter planes. As part of his agreement with John Willys, Glenn Curtiss set up the Curtiss Engineering Corporation, a special research and development facility located at Garden City, Long Island. Curtiss gathered around him some of the most talented engineers in the company.[78] When the Aircraft Production Board allowed American aviation manufacturers to develop their own designs, the navy asked Curtiss to design a two-seat fighter plane and placed an order for two examples in March 1918.

Charles Kirkham, one of the leading designers at the Curtiss Engineering Corporation, designed a streamlined triplane around a new and powerful 12-cylinder engine that he had been developing for several years. In the K-12, Kirkham incorporated several innovations that improved on the best engine the European allies produced at that time. Kirkham paid particular attention to reducing the width of his engine so that the frontal area of any airplane designed around it could be kept to a minimum, thereby reducing drag. While not without faults, the K-12 represented a considerable advance over existing engines, providing as much power, but with smaller size and lighter weight.[79]

Kirkham's aircraft design became the Curtiss Model 18-T. With the 400-horsepower K-12 engine, the Model 18-T achieved a record speed of 163 miles per hour on 19 August 1918. The following year, the 18-T set a world altitude record of 34,610 feet. The navy purchased two examples of the Model 18-T, which could be flown as a land plane or a seaplane; after borrowing one example for tests, the army ordered two Model 18-B land planes. The end of the war removed any chance that Curtiss would receive a production contract for the Model 18 from either the army or the navy. However, the Model 18 was an important demonstration that the Curtiss Company had caught up with European designers. In the Model 18, the company held two of the seeds of its future success; a design for a streamlined, high-speed fighter plane, and a powerful, compact engine of advanced design. It would take several years and much hard work for this combination to come to full fruition. Unknown to the company's engineers and its management, this combination would be the source of the company's very survival and resurgence in the years to come.[80]

The Achievement

The armistice of 11 November 1918 brought an end to four years of warfare. Within a few days, the army and navy, with no warning to the aviation industry, canceled contracts amounting to $100 million. From April 1917 to the end of the war, the American aviation industry had built 13,894 airplanes and 41,953 airplane engines.[81] Although more than 4,000 of those airplanes were bombers of British design, a significant number of which entered frontline service, America's inability to built combat airplanes in the promised tens of thousands left a lasting impression of failure. In its final report on the aviation production program, the government investigation judged that much of the $640 million authorized for army aviation had simply been wasted. The goals of the Aircraft Production Board had been flawed, and the lack of understanding of the complexities of aircraft design and construction on the part of the automotive industry men who ran the production program had severely hampered the aviation industry. The constant changes in orders and direction had only compounded the problem.

The American aviation industry did produce two technological successes: the Liberty engine and the Curtiss flying boats. These aircraft were superior to any of the indigenous multiengined flying boat designs in Europe. Glenn Curtiss's pioneering efforts had given the American aviation industry a clear lead in this one area. The Curtiss H series of flying boats gave admirable service in the British and American navies; these aircraft formed the backbone of the long-range sea patrol effort of both countries during World War I.

The war transformed the Curtiss Company beyond all recognition. Curtiss produced more aircraft than any other American airplane manufacturer in World War I. At its peak, the company employed more that 18,000 workers in nine plants. It owned the largest factory in American devoted to the manufacture of aircraft, and in the Curtiss Engineering Corporation, the company had one of the finest groups of aeronautical engineers in the country. The pressure of war had compressed and accelerated the pace of technological development. The company had gained enormous experience during the war as it was catapulted into a leading position within the American aviation industry.

The gains were not made without cost. Neither the company's management nor its manufacturing processes were prepared for the demands of government once America entered the war. So much had to be learned at once: the development of production designs and production plans, the coordination of suppliers and subcontractors, the management of thousands of unskilled workers in an industry that demanded a high degree of skilled assembly. New management made assumptions and mistakes that nearly bankrupted the company, but much of the expansion that John North Willys engineered was due to his faith in the mistaken assumptions of the Aircraft Production Board. There was undeniable waste and inefficiency as the company's management struggled with the huge volume of orders from the U.S. Army Air Service, the U.S. Navy, and the British government. Yet the company learned valuable lessons and in the end effectively organized the production of complex aircraft.

The Curtiss Aeroplane and Motor Corporation emerged from the war with significant advantages. It now had an experienced management familiar with aircraft production. It had honed its manufacturing skills and had absorbed many of the new technologies and processes that came from Europe. America's aviation industry had essentially caught up with Europe's, although this fact would not become readily apparent for several more years. The Curtiss Company was at the forefront of this development. In management and in manufacturing, the company's skills were perhaps the best in the industry. What its management could not have known was how difficult the search to find a market for its products in the early years of the following decade would be.

Chapter 3

Decline and Expansion, 1919–1929

The Curtiss Aeroplane and Motor Corporation was the largest aviation manufacturer in America at the end of World War I. The company's designs were equal, and in certain cases superior, to European designs. With a top-quality design staff, capable management, and the most modern production facilities in the industry, Curtiss seemed poised to capture a leading position in the new era of commercial aviation that many people in the industry believed was about to begin. This vision proved decidedly premature. Within two years, the Curtiss Aeroplane and Motor Corporation would be teetering on the brink of bankruptcy.

To the Brink

The American aviation industry experienced a severe contraction following the end of World War I. After the armistice, the U.S. War Department canceled hundreds of millions of dollars of outstanding contracts for aircraft and engines.[1] The Curtiss Aeroplane and Motor Corporation received notices canceling between $50 million and $75 million in government contracts. Yet neither John Willys nor Glenn Curtiss gave any thought to withdrawing from the aviation industry now that the war was over. Both believed that the company should pursue the further development of aviation and produce a broad range of both commercial and military aircraft and aircraft engines. The airplane had established itself as a weapon of war. Managers of the leading airplane companies were convinced that a demand for military aircraft would continue. The challenge lay in the field of commercial aviation.

The aviation industry has three markets for its products: military, commercial (airlines and private flyers), and exports of both military and commercial aircraft. Large airliners and specialized high-performance military aircraft generate much higher profit margins than small single-engine aircraft that are produced for the private flyer. Traditionally, the military market has been the most important for the aviation industry. Only the military has a regular demand for high-performance aircraft. In 1919 a commercial market for aircraft did not exist, but Willys and Curtiss were confident in the future of commercial aviation. The airplane had made such tremendous strides during the war and offered such potential for commercial use that it was hard to believe that commercial aviation would not develop. What was needed were practical, purpose-built aircraft designed for purely commercial activities. Entering this new field was not without challenge and risk, but many in the aviation industry besides John Willys and Glenn Curtiss believed in this vision.[2]

Willys and Curtiss set about reorganizing the company to meet the commercial demand they were sure was forthcoming. Glenn Curtiss devoted his efforts to creating new commercial aircraft designs, while Willys developed an effective marketing network with dealers and distributors that could both stimulate demand and respond to it. One of Willys's first steps was to create a sales department with Curtiss dealerships in the major cities around the United States. In a move that would become characteristic of the company's approach to marketing its aircraft, the sales department aggressively sought out foreign markets. The company set up dealerships in Europe and East Asia. A separate sales mission went to Latin America.[3] Willys also established a separate sales promotion effort to educate the public and the business community on the benefits of the airplane. Throughout 1919 the company organized demonstration flights of its new aircraft to popularize the idea of commercial aviation and attempted numerous record flights to gain additional publicity.[4]

During 1919 the Curtiss company produced several commercial airplanes, beginning with a simple conversion of the Navy MF flying boat. Dubbed the Seagull, it had accommodations for three passengers. The first true commercial design was the Oriole, a light commercial aircraft and personal sports plane.[5] The most ambitious Curtiss effort was the Eagle, a three-engined airliner that could accommodate six to eight passengers in relative comfort plus a crew of two. The Eagle had a range of 350 to 475 miles, suitable for the type of intercity air travel the Curtiss Company thought would develop.[6] To promote widespread interest in aviation, the company purchased 2,716 surplus trainers and 4,608 surplus OX-5 engines from U.S. Air Service stocks, and a number of surplus MF flying boats from the navy.[7] Curtiss acquired these airplanes to provide an inexpensive alternative to the Oriole, hoping that by stimulating general flying activity, they could generate more sales.

The hoped-for boom in commercial aviation failed to materialize. The best efforts of Curtiss and other like-minded companies could do nothing to stimulate demand when it simply did not exist. The American people had come to accept the airplane as a valued weapon of war, but they were not yet willing to put their trust in the airplane as a means of transport. The wood-and-fabric aircraft of 1919 were neither reliable nor equal in comfort or speed to existing modes of transport. With no public interest in air transportation, there was little chance of achieving the volume of traffic that would generate the sustained returns necessary to attract capital to commercial aviation. Without airline companies, there was no demand for new aircraft for the manufacturers. The few air taxi services and pleasure flights that did start up could just as easily make do with a surplus JN-4 as a brand-new and far more expensive Oriole. Moreover, the infrastructure needed to support commercial aviation simply did not exist. There were few landing fields, no laid-out routes, no law or regulation of air commerce. In short, none of the elements that were needed to sustain aviation as a business were present.

The American military market failed to offset the lack of demand for commercial aircraft. Both the army and the navy rapidly demobilized after the end of the war and returned to an earlier pattern of austerity, offering few opportunities for the sale of new aircraft. Having just won "the war to end all wars," Congress had little inclination to support more than the bare minimum of military expenditure. Appropriations for military aviation contracted sharply.[8] The hundreds of surplus aircraft and engines remaining from the war were more than sufficient for military needs. In the climate of strict economy that soon prevailed, the army and navy had little alternative but to use up their surplus stocks of matériel before they could order new aircraft in quantity. Over the next several years, America's military establishment would order comparatively few new aircraft, and with a few exceptions, most new orders were in small lots. Rarely could a manufacturer recover costs, let alone make a profit.

Even more damaging to the fortunes of the remaining manufacturers was the system of competitive bidding Congress imposed on the industry. In the eyes of many congressmen, the aviation industry emerged from the war with the taint of scandal. The apparent wastage of hundreds of millions of dollars on aviation could only have come about through fraud, favoritism, and collusion. Congress was determined that this would never happen again. Through its powers over appropriations and contracting, it insisted on a bidding and contracting system that created, in the words of one historian, "a destructive, competitive regulatory environment for aircraft manufacturers."[9] To avoid favoritism or possibility of collusion, Congress required the most open form of competition possible. The contracting system did not recognize a manufacturer's proprietary right to a design. The military could solicit bids from the industry, but the winning design then became the property of the military, not the manufacturer. Any production contract was thrown open to competitive bidding, with the lowest bidder winning the contract.

The impact of this system of competitive bidding was even more damaging given the excess capacity that remained in the industry. With 15 firms chasing the few contracts available, competition became truly ruinous. A slow Darwinian process of natural selection took place in the years after the war. Firm after firm was either forced out through lack of business or simply withdrew from the industry.[10] In a system in which there was no recognition of proprietary rights to a design and in which competitors were willing to bid for contracts below cost, the advantages that would normally apply to a market leader such as Curtiss did not exist. Like every other manufacturer, Curtiss had to scramble for whatever business it could get. Given the excellence of its engineering staff, Curtiss did have some competitive advantage over rival firms in bidding for experimental contracts, but in competition for the marginally more lucrative production contracts, the company had no guarantee of success. Sometimes it came up with a winning bid, and sometimes not.

The Curtiss Company's third field of effort, the foreign market, brought some results but no substantial orders. The Curtiss sales mission to Latin America arrived to find that official military missions from England, France, and Italy had already made significant inroads into the markets for military and civil aircraft with sales of their own surplus airplanes. Despite being late on the scene, the Curtiss representatives sold a number of flying boats to the Argentine, Brazilian, and Peruvian navies and established flying schools using Curtiss aircraft in Argentina and Brazil.[11] This foothold, however, could only generate sales of small numbers of aircraft in the face of powerful European competition. In East Asia, Curtiss sold a few flying boats, but conditions in Asia were even less conducive to creating demand for many airplanes.[12]

By early 1920, the Curtiss company was facing a critical problem. The minimal level of sales achieved could not support the level of assets committed to the business. One plant in Buffalo was sold, and leases on three other facilities were canceled. The engine plant in Hammondsport was shut down and sold, ending Curtiss's long association with the town. Production was then consolidated in the remaining Buffalo Churchill Street plant and one in Garden City. These drastic measures reduced the value of the company's plant and property from $6,589,370 in June 1919 to $502,111 by June 1920. Parts and raw materials proved more difficult to deal with. The company had more than $5 million in materials and supplies on its books and had little prospect of converting these assets into sales of aircraft.[13]

Prospects for sales deteriorated further that spring. The British government's Aircraft Disposal Company, set up to dispose of Britain's surplus aircraft, made a concerted effort to sell large numbers of its aircraft in the United States. Though the American aviation industry blocked this threat through litigation, the British action did have the unintended effect of forcing the U.S. government to unload its own stocks of surplus aircraft on the market. The army and navy posted prices below what Curtiss was offering for the reconditioned JN-4s it had bought from the government. Curtiss had no alternative but to cut its own prices, further reducing the prospects for sales of its new Oriole. This action also reduced the profits the company could make on sales of its own stocks of surplus aircraft and engines. Clearly, the company was headed for a substantial loss.[14]

To compound these problems, the American economy in 1920 began sliding into what turned out to be a severe recession. The automotive industry was not immune to these forces. As the situation worsened, John Willys had to devote more of his time and energy to his car company. The recession forced Willys to reconsider his commitment to aviation. To say the least, the prospects of the Curtiss Company were not promising. It was selling small numbers of Orioles, but the commercial market was flooded with surplus aircraft. There was little likelihood of any expansion in commercial aviation. The military sales situation was equally grim. With no proprietary design rights, a manufacturer could not hope to recoup the high costs of design and development. Willys decided that the only alternative was to withdraw from aviation.

One Friday in August 1920, representatives of the Willys-Overland Company called on Clement Keys, who had continued his role as vice president for finance, at the Manhattan offices of his small investment bank, C. M. Keys and Company. The Willys representatives informed Keys that on the following Tuesday, approximately $650,000 of bank debts for the Curtiss Aeroplane and Motor Corporation were coming due. The Willys-Overland Company did not intend to pay them. Failure to pay these debts would force Curtiss into receivership, but the Willys-Overland Company saw no alternative. Curtiss was in serious financial trouble. The company's sales prospects were poor, it was headed for a substantial loss, and it was technically bankrupt; the company's assets could not cover its liabilities. The Willys-Overland Company's first duty was to protect its automotive interests. Keys told the Willys representatives that it would be a pity to let Curtiss go into receivership and asked if he could give the matter some thought over the weekend to see if there was anything he could do.[15]

Keys thought long and hard. That the Curtiss Aeroplane and Motor Corporation was in serious trouble there could be little doubt. Yet Keys had faith that aviation would ultimately succeed and prosper. He believed that the failure of the Curtiss Company would be a disaster for the future of American aviation. As vice president for finance, he had come to know the company's strengths and its potential. In his view, no other company in America had a group of engineers that were as capable of competing with those in Europe. He was convinced that the Curtiss Company had the capacity to equal or surpass the Europeans. But now, if bankruptcy forced the Curtiss engineering staff to disband, it would take years for any other company to rebuild such a team. America would remain a second-rate power in aviation, a follower of the Europeans. Keys could not let that happen.[16]

On the following Monday, Keys went before the combined boards of the Curtiss Aeroplane and Motor Corporation and the Willys-Overland Company and offered to buy their holdings of common stock for cash equal to the amount of debts coming due on the following day. The two boards agreed. Glenn Curtiss chose not to participate financially in the new ownership but agreed to take an unsalaried position as chairman of the Engineering Committee. On Tuesday, Keys, as the new president of the company, went out and raised $650,000 using his own credit and paid off the banks. The fate and fortunes of the Curtiss Aeroplane and Motor Corporation were now his responsibility.[17]

The Road to Recovery

Soon after taking control, Keys journeyed to Washington to meet with representatives of the army and navy. They discussed the possibilities of generating a level of business sufficient to sustain the research and development that he knew was the key to his company's future.

Keys told Newton Baker, the secretary of war, that he would maintain the Curtiss Aeroplane and Motor Corporation as a going concern and devote every dollar the company earned to research. He had rescued the company to preserve its engineering division. He promised Baker to use the company's engineering skills not only to develop new airplanes and engines but also to bring American aviation to a level that would equal or exceed Europe's best.[18]

For the first few months, the financial situation remained precarious. At times, Keys had to pay the firm's debts from his own funds. More than once, he contemplated simply liquidating the company. Keys realized that Curtiss had to undergo a further contraction to survive in the contemporary climate. Production would be tailored to actual, rather than expected, orders, and the scale of the company's effort would conform to the actual business outlook. To improve the company's financial condition, Keys continued the program of writing off assets that no longer had value and canceled contracts for materials that could not be converted into salable aircraft. Receivables, patents, and inventories were all written down to more realistic values. The cost of getting rid of the dead wood was steep; after full depreciation, the company suffered a loss of $1,756,583 for the year.[19]

Keys's new strategy combined his faith in the future of aviation with the current realities of the industry. Most important was the reality that the aviation industry had only one customer, the military. Keys had no alternative but to seek what business he could from the army and navy. The development effort would continue, but in the absence of any commercial market, it would be directed toward military aviation. Keys believed that improvements in engines, the design of aircraft, and construction methods gained from military work could be readily translated into improvements for commercial aircraft when the demand for such aircraft finally emerged. The trick was to survive until a supportive governmental policy could create the infrastructure necessary for commercial aviation. Keys decided to shrink the Curtiss Company to a size that the business from military contracts could sustain while concentrating on developing innovative products that would enable the company to capture a large share of the military and civil markets once demand improved. He was confident that with his excellent engineering staff and facilities, he could win sufficient business from the army and navy to sustain his firm.[20]

Keys could not afford to rely solely on the American military. He was determined to seek out markets for aviation products wherever he could find them, especially among the military air services of other nations. He continued to develop sales of Curtiss products in foreign markets, an orientation few other American aviation companies pursued with such persistence. Foreign markets and foreign military air services would remain a focus for the Curtiss Company's sales efforts in the decades before World War II. In 1921 Keys organized the Curtiss Aeroplane Export Corporation as the foreign sales arm of the Curtiss Company. Although initially the export company had few business prospects, the marketing effort and the network of contacts built up were not abandoned.[21]

Competition for military orders remained fierce under the prevailing bidding system. As long as it was kept in place, no rational company would invest in development, since there was no hope of earning a return on the funds invested. Ultimately, the system would drive capital out of the industry, a point that became clear as more and more firms were forced out or withdrew from aviation. Curtiss won a number of experimental contracts from the army and navy but won few of the production contracts by which the company might have recovered its costs. In the fall of 1920, the company failed in its bid for the largest single army order of the decade, 200 Thomas-Morse MB-3 pursuits. The relatively new Boeing Airplane Company won with a bid that was $534,000 lower than Curtiss's.[22] During 1921 Curtiss won a contract to produce 34 examples of the TS-1, the navy's first carrier-borne fighter, designed by the Bureau of Aeronautics. Curtiss also won an order for 50 NBS-1 bombers, underbidding the Glenn L. Martin Company for production of its own design. These contracts helped carry Curtiss through difficult times, but they provided little in the way of return and could not always cover the costs incurred on some of the company's experimental contracts.[23]

The experience of Curtiss in designing and building the CS-1 torpedo bomber for the navy is an example of the problems that bedeviled the aviation industry during the first half of the decade. In 1922 the navy approached Curtiss with a design for a new and more versatile torpedo plane. The Curtiss engineering staff realized that the weight of the aircraft had to be reduced to achieve the required performance. They proposed an airplane partly built with lighter metal tubing instead of wood. Metal tubing was then coming into general use, although Curtiss itself had only experimented with the technology. The proposed navy plane was a significant advance over anything Curtiss had built before. It involved an entirely new construction process, and it would cost one and a half times more than a wooden airplane. The navy agreed to the proposed price, and in June 1922 it gave Curtiss a contract to produce six aircraft under the designation CS-1.[24]

Construction of the CS-1 proved to be more difficult than expected. Metal tube construction cost three to five times more than wood. Delays arising from testing the design, and difficulties in perfecting metal construction added additional costs. By the time the first airplane flew in November 1923, Curtiss had spent an additional $180,000 of its own money to ensure that the CS-1 met the navy's specifications. Tests demonstrating the advances in range and endurance the navy wanted proved that the CS-1 more than met the navy's expectations. Nonetheless, the navy refused to reimburse Curtiss for its additional development expenses.[25]

When the navy approached Curtiss in 1924 to bid on a production order for 35 of the torpedo bombers, Curtiss submitted a bid that would help it recoup some of its development costs. The navy, realizing it could obtain lower bids from manufacturers who did not have the burden of development costs, opened the contract to competitive bidding, much to the distress of Curtiss. Ironically, the Glenn L. Martin Company won the contract with a bid of $20,000 per airplane, $12,000 lower than Curtiss's bid.[26] Curtiss then built an improved version, the CS-2. Once again it had the frustration of seeing the Martin Company outbid it for a second production order for 40 aircraft.[27] As Keys later complained in congressional testimony, having solved all the design, engineering, and production problems, Curtiss was forced by the competitive bidding system to turn all the solutions over to its competitors. Firms that maintained no design staffs or that spent no money on research and development would always be in a position to underbid design firms for the production contracts.

The D-12 Engine

While competing for the few available military aircraft contracts, the Curtiss Company had been devoting considerable effort to developing what would prove to be its most significant contribution to American aviation during the twenties: the D-12 engine, one of the finest aircraft engines ever designed. Its origins are found in the Curtiss K-12 engine that Charles B. Kirkham designed during World War I. The K-12 was a radical advance over its contemporaries, but it needed considerable development to make it thoroughly reliable. In the aftermath of the war, John Willys was unwilling to devote the resources needed for this development, prompting Kirkham to leave the company. Clement Keys argued for continued development of the K-12, however, convinced that its considerable promise should not go to waste. With his urging, and despite financial pressures to cut research and development expenditures, the Curtiss Company continued its work on the design, coming up with a revised version, the C-12.[28] This engine powered the first of a new generation of superb racing planes built by Curtiss for the army and navy in the early twenties.

In the decades between the two world wars, speed records became tests of national prowess and prestige. Military air services had a constant demand for aircraft of ever higher performance.[29] The air force that had a faster and more powerful fighter held a clear advantage in time of war. Air racing provided a demanding test of an engine and airframe. An aircraft capable of withstanding the stress of high-speed racing demonstrated the characteristics needed in fighter aircraft. As a result, the speed races of the twenties received the active support and participation of the military air arms of several countries. These races were the laboratories where new types of engines and aircraft underwent grueling tests and where advances in the state of the aviation art were introduced.[30]

Keys, recognizing that high-speed racing planes were in effect prototypes of fighter planes, realized that by building a successful racer, they had a potential fighter design to offer the military. In 1921 a Curtiss racing plane built for the navy captured first prize in the Pulitzer Trophy Race, the premier American high-speed air racing event. Later in the year, this racer set an American speed record with a speed of 197 miles per hour.[31]

In the following year, both the army and the navy ordered racing planes from Curtiss for the 1922 Pulitzer Race, the CR-2 for the navy and the R-6 for the army. What was new about these airplanes was the engine that powered them. Keys did not yet have a product that would interest the military, but he was determined that Curtiss should keep trying. Curtiss's young chief motor engineer, Arthur Nutt, undertook a complete redesign of the C-12 engine, which became the D-12. Curtiss now had a real winner. The D-12 was the finest in-line liquid-cooled engine of its day; it set the pattern for subsequent development of the liquid-cooled engine. In the streamlined Curtiss racers, the D-12 was unbeatable.[32]

In the 1922 Pulitzer Race, the Curtiss racers placed first, second, and third, with the army R-6s taking the honors and setting a new course record of 205 miles per hour. The D-12 became the first engine to power an airplane to speeds faster than 200 miles per hour. The Curtiss racers' real moment of glory, however, came in the following year at the Schneider Trophy seaplane race in England. On 28 September 1923, the navy's Curtiss CR-3 astonished the European aviation industry by winning the Schneider race with a new course record of 177 miles per hour. A few weeks later, Curtiss racers swept the 1923 Pulitzer Race, and in November they set a new world's speed record of 266 miles per hour. In the D-12, Curtiss had an engine superior to all others.[33]

The army and navy Curtiss racers went on to win more victories in the Pulitzer and Schneider races, but none was as important as the 1923 triumph. Curtiss Aeroplane and Motor achieved what Keys had promised. The United States had recaptured world records, and Curtiss demonstrated convincingly that America was on par with Europe in aviation technology. The company had developed and perfected the D-12 entirely at its own expense; neither the army nor the navy contributed any funds. A small but highly skilled team of engineers and mechanics had built small numbers of these engines for the Curtiss racers. To keep this little team together and to recoup its heavy investment, the company now had to find orders for the D-12.

Even while supporting the development of the D-12, Keys managed to improve the company's financial position. He reduced losses and in some years achieved a modest profit. Yet Curtiss was still unable to pay any dividends. Keys pulled capital out of the business and reduced assets and debt, but he still felt the company was overcapitalized. To remedy the situation, he came up with a novel reorganization idea. He divided company assets into two distinct categories. The Curtiss Aeroplane and Motor Corporation continued to hold large inventories of surplus aircraft and engines, as well as aircraft patents on which it still received royalties. Keys proposed that these assets be separated and set up in a new company that would use the proceeds from asset sales and the royalties on patents to provide a stream of dividends to the preferred stockholders. The manufacturing assets would then be reorganized in a new company that would be more in line with the expected business volume. With a reduced level of capital supporting only the assets it needed in the manufacturing process, the manufacturing company would be in a position to support its obligations and would have a better chance of providing some dividend, however small.[34]

The reorganization plan went into effect on 12 May 1923. Two new companies emerged. The Curtiss Aeroplane and Motor Company, Inc., took over the manufacturing assets of the old corporation. Its $5.6 million of assets were funded through a new issue of preferred and common stock. The new Curtiss Assets Corporation was incorporated on the same date to take over and liquidate the designated assets of the corporation, amounting to $2.5 million.[35]

The reduction in assets at the manufacturing company helped the newly reorganized Curtiss Aeroplane and Motor Company to achieve its first operating profit in three years. Yet the outlook for the industry remained so uncertain that Keys and the other directors decided that the company had no alternative but to cut back on engineering development and shrink the assets and capital invested in the firm. There seemed to be little prospect of recovering the more than $1.2 million the company had invested in developing the D-12 engine and the Curtiss racers. Still smarting from the navy's refusal to recognize the additional sums spent developing the CS-1 torpedo bomber, Keys wrote in the 1924 annual report that the company would no longer undertake experimental work regardless of the cost to the company. The company's fortunes were about to take a turn for the better, however.[36]

Return to Profitability

In early 1923 Curtiss approached the U.S. Army Air Service with a proposal for a new fighter plane that the company had designed and built at its own expense. Incorporating the lessons learned from the Curtiss racers, and powered with the new D-12 engine, the new fighter offered a significant advance over the standard Thomas-Morse pursuit then in service. The Air Service purchased the prototype and ordered two additional examples as the XPW-8. Following further testing, the Air Service ordered 25 PW-8 aircraft in September 1923. Contradicting its own rules, the Air Service did not submit the PW-8 contract to competitive bidding. On its own initiative, it directed the contract to Curtiss. At the same time, the Air Service placed a contract with Boeing for a competing fighter, the PW-9, also powered by the D-12 engine.[37]

During 1924 the Air Service continued testing the Curtiss and Boeing prototypes. The Curtiss fighter proved faster, but the Boeing fighter was more maneuverable. In the fall, the Air Service awarded a contract to Boeing for 30 PW-9 aircraft. Curtiss received small consolation from the fact that the PW-9 used its D-12 engine. The Air Service asked Curtiss to redesign the XPW-8 to incorporate a new wing and radiator. In March 1925, the Air Service placed an order for 15 of the new fighters and in September gave Curtiss an order for a further 25 examples of an improved version. The new Curtiss fighter became the P-1. The navy was also acquiring new fighters, and that same month, it ordered 9 naval versions of the P-1, designated F6C-1.[38]

Curtiss named its new fighter the Hawk. The Hawk fighter evolved into a family of airplanes that retained the basic biplane configuration of the initial P-1 but incorporated progressive changes in power plant and design to improve performance. The Hawk family would be a mainstay of the Curtiss Company for 13 years. The last versions of the Hawk

Curtiss P-1.
Bowers, *Curtiss Aircraft, 1907–1947,* 245.

were still in production as the first all-metal monoplanes entered service in the mid-thirties. Between 1925 and 1938, Curtiss built more than 700 Hawk fighters for the U.S. Army, the U.S. Navy, and for export to countries around the world.[39]

During 1924 the Air Service organized a design competition to select a new observation aircraft to replace the venerable DH-4. Curtiss designed a two-seat observation aircraft using the same advanced construction as its new P-1 fighter. Although the examining board thought highly of the Curtiss entry, the young Douglas Aircraft Company won the contest with its O-2 design; the Curtiss O-1 placed second. In 1925 the Air Service arranged a second contest for observation aircraft using a new engine built by the Packard Company. The Curtiss O-1 won handily, and the company received an order for 10 O-1 aircraft equipped with the more reliable Curtiss D-12 engine. Curtiss named its new aircraft the Falcon. Like the Hawk fighter, the Falcon developed into a series of observation and attack aircraft that Curtiss sold successfully to the army, the navy, and foreign air forces. The Falcons, together with the Hawks, would be premier products of the Curtiss Company into the early thirties.[40]

These government contracts and some foreign orders for the D-12, coupled with strict inventory control and continued debt reduction, enabled the company to post profits in 1924 and 1925. For the first time, the preferred shareholders received a dividend. In the 1925 annual report to shareholders, Clement Keys sounded a note of cautious optimism. Contractual relations with the army and navy had improved because the military had realized the destructive impact of competitive bidding on the aviation industry. Half of the new orders on the company's books had come from new military orders, but Keys noted a renewed growth in commercial orders as well. Most important for the future of the company, the year had seen what Keys characterized as a "widespread public awakening" to the need for a comprehensive policy for military and commercial aviation. The commitment to commercial aviation's development and to a healthier aviation industry for which Keys and other leading aviation figures had been calling was about to take place.[41]

By 1925, the years of parsimonious budgets, together with a lack of replacements, had reduced the number of army and navy aircraft, further weakening the military capabilities of both services. In June of that year, the Air Service had on hand 1,436 aircraft, of which 1,040 were classed as obsolete.[42] Since World War I the aviation industry had been subjected to more than 20 congressional investigations, but none had resulted in any improvement in the industry's condition. In October 1924 a new congressional committee was formed under the leadership of representative Florian Lampert to investigate the condition of the aviation industry and the military air services. The Lampert Committee acted as a stimulus to several congressional initiatives on aviation. During 1925 the committee conducted the most thorough and open investigation to date. Following the crash of a navy dirigible later in the year, Brig. Gen. William Mitchell, an outspoken advocate of air power, launched a blistering attack on the senior officers of the army and navy for their neglect of aviation. The intemperate attack resulted in Mitchell's court martial that fall, but the public outcry over Mitchell's claims forced President Coolidge to appoint his own presidential commission under Dwight Morrow, a noted banker, to investigate how to develop aviation for national defense.[43]

In testimony before the Lampert Committee and the Morrow Board, Clement Keys and other aviation industry leaders argued for an end to the destructive competitive bidding system and a recognition of the proprietary rights of design. The aviation industry urged the government to adopt a regular procurement program so that the manufacturers could afford to retain the skilled workers and engineering staff so vital to the design and production of improved aircraft. The Lampert Committee and the Morrow Board agreed that a healthy aviation industry was important to national defense. The nation needed a comprehensive and consistent government policy toward military aviation. The strength of the industry would depend for some time to come on military orders. Both the Lampert Committee and the Morrow Board recommended that the government adopt a comprehensive procurement program. This would provide continuity in orders over a period of several years. Additionally, they proposed a modification of the system of competitive bidding that would recognize proprietary rights of design.[44] Plans for a new government body to regulate air commerce and to meet the need for clearly defined airways across the United States with adequate navigational and weather facilities came out of these investigations as well.[45]

These recommendations formed the basis for congressional action to address the problems confronting the military air services and commercial aviation. In early 1926 Congress began work on a legislative program that would be a landmark in the history of American aviation. What finally emerged ended much of the uncertainty that had plagued the aviation industry since the end of World War I and set the stage for the industry's recovery. The building of an aviation infrastructure was about to begin.

The Air Commerce Act of 1926, which became law on 20 May, provided the "legislative cornerstone" for the development of commercial aviation.[46] The act established the right of the federal government to regulate interstate air commerce. Combined with the earlier Kelly Act of 1925, which transferred the operation of air mail services from the Post Office Department to private operators, the Air Commerce Act provided the framework for commercial aviation and established the regulatory and legal certainty that was necessary to attract capital and investment to the newly formed airlines.[47]

That summer, Congress passed the Army and Navy Five Year Aircraft Program Acts. The Army Act changed the name of the U.S. Army Air Service to the U.S. Army Air Corps and authorized a five-year expansion program. The newly established Air Corps received permission to maintain a force of 1,800 serviceable airplanes and replace all existing obsolete aircraft, although Congress limited yearly purchases to no more than 400 aircraft. The Navy Five Year Aircraft program Act approved an increase of the navy's authorized aircraft strength to 1,000 serviceable aircraft. Here at last was the consistent purchasing plan the industry had longed for. The one significant failing of the two five-year procurement acts was that they represented not appropriations but merely authorizations. The actual funds to purchase new aircraft had to come from Congress, which did not always approve the amounts requested. In addition, Congress failed to take into account normal rates of attrition, so that over time the Air Corps would be hard pressed to meet its target of 1,800 serviceable aircraft.[48]

To the great concern of the industry, the Air Corps Act failed to correct the industry's greatest complaint, the competitive bidding system and the lack of proprietary design rights. The act attempted a compromise between those congressmen sympathetic to the industry's position and those who still harbored a suspicion of collusion and fear of excessive profits. The Air Corps Act gave the military more leeway in placing orders for new airplanes, but the fundamental requirement for competitive bidding remained in place. Ever mindful of the chaotic conditions that had been so damaging to the industry, the War Department employed what was later termed an "artful evasion" of the act in order to award production contracts to the firms who had developed a design. Although not entirely within the spirit of the new law, the approach was perfectly legal, and the War and Navy Departments employed it during the five-year term of the expansion programs.[49]

In the Curtiss Aeroplane and Motor Company annual report for 1926, Clement Keys commented that in ensuring a relatively stable flow of business over the coming five years, the new legislation turned the manufacture of airplanes into "a business instead of an adventure."[50] Charles Lindbergh's flight to Paris on 19 May 1927 captured the imagination of the American people and helped stimulate an enormous interest in aviation. The flight of a single-engined airplane from New York to Paris without incident helped to convince many skeptics that flying was not simply for daredevils and that air travel might well be practical. When the stock market began a record boom, demand for aviation securities exploded. Tens of millions of dollars became available for investment, and the industry, starved for capital since the end of World War I, gobbled it up.[51]

From 1925 to 1929, aircraft production in the United States soared, owing to the Air Corps and navy expansion programs and the explosion of popular interest in flying. The Curtiss Aeroplane and Motor Company was well placed to benefit from the expansion in military aviation, and it did so. During this period, total assets of the company grew four-fold while profits grew from $156,780 to $623,859.[52] Curtiss held several of what could be termed "first-mover" advantages. In a technologically intensive industry, the company had one of the best research and engineering groups in the country, a management that understood the process of development and production of advanced airplanes, and extensive contacts and experience in dealing with the military, the company's primary customer. Most important, Curtiss had products already in service with the military, and in the D-12, it had the finest liquid-cooled engine in the world.

These advantages by no means guaranteed success, however. The military field was not without challenges from other existing competitors and new entrants. As technology advanced, the relentless pressure to keep up with the latest developments proved to be a significant barrier to entry into the more advanced segments of the aviation industry, but it did not prevent competition. Competitors could incorporate the latest technology in their designs and thereby produce aircraft that exceeded the performance of existing aircraft by a wide margin. Curtiss built excellent airplanes, but so did other firms. Nevertheless, Curtiss continued to compete successfully in the military market, and the military remained its largest customer. During the late twenties and into the early thirties, three-quarters of the company's sales were to the army and navy.[53]

Although Curtiss did not win every military contract it sought, the company benefited from the breadth of its activities. Selling several types of aircraft to the army and the navy enabled Curtiss to build up a steady volume of business as the five-year expansion programs got into full swing. Larger production runs meant economies of scale and support for the

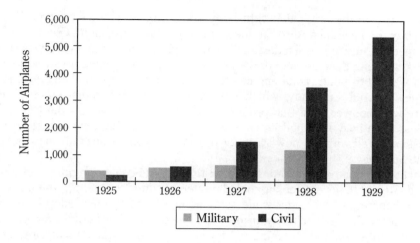

Fig. 1.   Aircraft production: 1925–1929

company's pool of engineering talent. During the period, Curtiss had its greatest success building fighters and observation and attack aircraft. The company competed fiercely with Boeing to supply fighters and with the Douglas Aircraft Company and the Chance Vought Corporation to supply observation aircraft to both services. Curtiss was successful in selling its Hawk fighter and Falcon observation and attack aircraft in what was for the period a substantial quantity.

With the Hawk and the Falcon, Curtiss demonstrated an ability to take a basic design and develop from it several specialized types of aircraft that could perform a number of different roles and thus appeal to a wider range of customers. Curtiss had more success than Boeing in selling fighters during the initial years of the Air Corps expansion program. In the first phase, the Air Corps purchased 83 P-1 fighters and an additional 75 models as advanced trainers. Smaller numbers of the Hawk fighter went to the navy. By the end of the Air Corps expansion program, Curtiss had sold them more than 300 Falcon aircraft. The company had less success in the bomber field, however. The Curtiss entry in a 1927 competition for a new bomber proved to have the best performance of any of the competing designs, but it failed to win a large production contract. The Curtiss B-2 lost to the Keystone LB-6 because the LB-6 was cheaper and less expensive to operate.[54]

Curtiss, the leading exponent of the liquid-cooled engine, remained committed to the progress of this technology. In 1928 the company unveiled the Conqueror, a more refined and more powerful engine than the D-12. The Conqueror produced 600 horsepower and increased the maximum speed of the P-1 by 20 miles per hour over the same airplane powered by the older D-12 engine. These promising results with the new engine encouraged the Air Corps to order 18 new Conqueror-powered fighters as the P-6 and P-6A.[55]

Even as Curtiss worked to improve the liquid-cooled engine, however, the navy and the Air Corps were moving toward the lighter and more reliable air-cooled radial engine. The liquid-cooled engine allowed a more streamlined design, but it paid a significant weight penalty with its bulky cooling system. The system's complexity made the liquid-cooled engines of the day less reliable. The navy's Bureau of Aeronautics was committed to developing the aircraft carrier and needed airplanes that could be flown over the sea for extended periods. In the early twenties, the navy pushed the development of the radial engine, first with the Wright Aeronautical Corporation, the other leading manufacturer of aircraft engines and the lineal descendant of the original Wright Brothers company. The navy forced Wright Aeronautical to buy the Lawrance Aero Engine Company, whose president, Charles R. Lawrance, had developed a promising radial design. When Wright Aeronautical proved less than enthusiastic about pushing development of the new engine, the navy encouraged a group of engineers who wanted to build radial engines to set up a new company. This became the Pratt and Whitney Aircraft Company, which introduced a powerful radial engine, the famous Wasp. Here was a power plant that produced the same horsepower as the Curtiss D-12 but weighed less. The navy now had its engine and began ordering new fighters from Boeing and Curtiss powered with the new Wasp for the navy's two new aircraft carriers, the *Lexington* and the *Saratoga*.[56]

The Curtiss Company remained dedicated to its liquid-cooled engines and made only a halfhearted attempt to develop an air-cooled model. In contrast, Boeing, which had been less successful competing with Curtiss while using liquid-cooled engines, adopted the air-cooled radial wholeheartedly. As Curtiss worked on its next series of fighters for the Air Corps, Boeing produced a new radial engine fighter as a private venture. Incorporating the Pratt and Whitney Wasp, the Boeing Model 83 fighter obtained a much higher performance than previous aircraft. First flown in the summer of 1928, the new Boeing design won a navy production order for 27 aircraft. Boeing's F4B-1 fighter came just at the right time to capture the lion's share of the fighter business for the next five years. In November, Air Corps pilots tested the navy's new fighter and were so impressed that the Air Corps placed an immediate order for nine of these aircraft as the P-12. Altogether Boeing sold 555 F4B/P-12 aircraft between 1929 and 1932. After 1929 the Boeing company supplanted Curtiss as the preeminent supplier of fighter aircraft to the American military, a position Boeing would hold until the technology of military aircraft went through a further evolution in the mid-thirties.[57]

Although many at Curtiss looked on commercial aviation as a great opportunity, the company's initial efforts in the field met with limited success. Curtiss built several specialized mail planes in small numbers, as well as the Curtiss Condor transport, an 18-passenger airliner based on the B-2 bomber design. None of these aircraft achieved much success, however. The most successful Curtiss commercial design was the Robin, a single-engine cabin monoplane that could carry a pilot and two passengers. Designed for the private flyer and air taxi operator, the Robin was built in greater numbers than any other single Curtiss aircraft during the twenties and thirties.[58]

After 1925 the company's production and sales rose steadily, with sales reaching $5.9 million at the end of 1928.[59] Over the same period, operating profit before interest and taxes grew from $288,277 to $1,017,083.[60] Keys worked hard to improve the financial condition of the Curtiss Company. By the end of 1928, he had repaid all of its outstanding mortgages and retired the preferred shares. The company was now funded purely through common stock. Keys believed that equity was a more appropriate form of financing for a new industry in the process of rapid change. Aviation was a field in which knowledgeable businessmen, prepared to take a business risk, should be the primary investors; aviation was not a field for "widows and orphans."[61]

Expansion in Scale and Scope: Building the Curtiss Group

Keys saw many more avenues for growth emerging as aviation expanded. As a businessman and banker, he understood that making aviation a profitable business meant careful organization, planning, and, above all, attention to detail. He coined the phrase "10 percent of aviation is in the air and 90 percent on the ground." The romance of aviation, he felt, turned attention away from the mundane but crucial application of sound business principles. The struggle for survival was over. Now he could begin work building a business in a more certain climate.[62]

Keys divided the aviation industry into four categories: the manufacture of airplanes and engines, freight transport, passenger transport, and airplanes for personal uses.[63] Each area had its own particular characteristics and its own unique requirements and methods of operation. The degree of specialization would likely increase as the activities in these other areas expanded in scope. Manufacture of airplanes and engines was itself divided into specialized categories. Military and commercial aircraft were beginning to diverge, reflecting the different demands and requirements of military and commercial operations. Keys wanted to create separate specialized business units that would be responsible for covering different segments of the aviation industry. He envisioned a vertically integrated manufacturing group with a research and design center that would be the focus of all design activities. The designs created there would be sent to separate manufacturing entities to manufacture airplanes for military, commercial, and private use. An engine firm would manufacture engines of different capacities for each class of airplane. Keys then wanted to create distribution networks, one for the domestic market and one for exports around the world. This structure would give his group the benefits of economies of scale in production and distribution.[64]

Keys also intended to broaden the range of products and services his group could offer, thereby creating economies of scope.[65] In the air transport field, he planned a similar vertical integration to manufacturing. There would be airlines and air transport companies to transport people and goods; airport service companies to run the airports the airlines needed; and a network of flying service companies to train future pilots, provide air charter services, and help foster interest in aviation and air travel. The activities of the entire group would be integrated to enhance the economies of scale and scope. The airlines and flying service companies would provide a captive demand for the output of the manufacturing units, and the flying service companies would act as the domestic distribution arm for the manufacturing companies.[66]

Keys had already expanded the scope of his own activities in aviation. In 1925 he and a group of businessmen formed National Air Transport, one of the first business groups to enter the field of commercial air transport. In 1928 he helped organize Transcontinental Air Transport to operate a passenger service from New York to Los Angeles. In the field of aircraft manufacturing, Keys's first step was to develop the capacity to build smaller commercial aircraft. These were designed at the Garden City engineering facility. The Curtiss Buffalo plant concentrated on military and large aircraft.

In January 1928 the Curtiss Company established a partnership with Maj. William Robertson, owner of Robertson Aircraft Corporation, a small Saint Louis firm that flew the mail route to Chicago and operated a flying service. The new company, the Curtiss-Robertson Airplane Manufacturing Company, opened a factory in Saint Louis and began building the Curtiss Robin, which had been designed at Garden City. Toward the end of the year, Curtiss acquired a 50 percent share of the Reid Aircraft Company of Montreal, Canada, to form the Curtiss-Reid Aircraft Company, Ltd., to build a small light airplane called the Reid Rambler. To fund these and other acquisitions, the Curtiss company took advantage of the booming stock market. In the early part of 1928, the company issued 72,686 shares of common stock at $50 a share, raising an additional $3.6 million in capital. In August it issued an additional 58,149 shares at $100 a share, raising another $5.8 million in capital. Toward the end of 1928, Curtiss stock hit a high of $192 a share, a nearly four-fold increase in less than a year. At its lowest point in 1924, the company's common stock had traded at $4.50 a share.[67]

Throughout 1928 Keys embarked on new ventures and broadened the activities of what was becoming the Curtiss group of companies. In January he had reorganized and recapitalized the Curtiss Aeroplane Export Corporation to strengthen the overseas distribution network. Keys restructured the Curtiss Flying Service, which traced its origins back to the old Curtiss Exhibition Company, and which operated a series of flying schools and air taxi services around the country. A new company was incorporated in Delaware and issued 750,000 new shares of common stock, raising $6.75 million for its expansion. Riding the seemingly inexhaustible wave of interest in aviation stocks, Keys set up several financial companies to acquire aviation stocks and to provide financing for the purchase of aircraft.[68]

The culmination of Keys's activities during the year was the formation of North American Aviation, Inc. North American evolved into a holding company and management vehicle through which Keys could invest funds and coordinate the activities of his rapidly diversifying group without calling on the financial or management resources of the existing Curtiss companies. North American's directors were a group of influential businessmen and bankers. Through them Keys raised $25 million in investment funds, acquiring the Sperry Gyroscope Company, a maker of aircraft instruments, Pitcairn Aviation Inc., which held the airmail route from New York to Miami, and a host of other aviation stocks.[69]

Keys continued his expansion drive into the new year. In January 1929 the Curtiss-Caproni Corporation was incorporated to manufacture in the United States the large airplane and seaplane designs of the Italian aviation engineer Gianni Caproni. A stock issue raised $2.5 million for the new company. The next creation was the Curtiss Airports Corporation, which was incorporated in May to own and operate a group of airports located near several large and medium-size cities across the country. For this new venture, Keys raised $25 million in the stock market.[70]

By the spring of 1929, Keys had assembled a group of more than 20 subsidiary and affiliated companies. There were six companies in the manufacturing sector, three in sales and service, four in transportation, and seven in finance.[71] The Curtiss group, as it came to be called, was in fact a rather loosely organized structure of separate operations. There was no overall holding company directing and controlling the operation of subsidiary units. The Curtiss Aeroplane and Motor Company did not hold controlling shares in all the members of the group. The companies were linked through cross-holdings. Keys apparently believed that having several small companies operating independently but under a common general policy was a better form for managing the diverse set of businesses than grouping them in a single company.[72] Continuity and the coordination of policy came through the most senior level of management. Keys and a few of the top managers of the Curtiss Aeroplane and Motor Company were on the boards of directors of all the companies in the group. Keys began to delegate responsibility for certain aspects of the group's operations to important individuals who had relevant expertise, but the lack of an administrative structure to support these senior managers in their day-to-day management of the business placed a heavy burden on them as well as on Keys himself. In diversifying into other activities, Keys chose not to undertake a major restructuring of the administrative function as other companies in other industries had done. This failure would become a serious handicap in time of stress.[73]

Clement Keys was not the only businessman or banker attracted to the new opportunities in aviation. By the end of 1928, the aviation boom was in full swing. The U.S. Army Air Corps and the U.S. Navy were into the second year of their expansion programs, and a record 1,219 military aircraft were built during the year. The growth in civil aircraft production was dramatic, recording a five-fold increase over 1926 as the number of air transport companies and air services grew and private flying blossomed. Moreover, the war surplus aircraft and engines that had depressed demand for so long were no longer flyable, adding further stimulus to demand. Between the end of 1925 (the last full year of airmail operations under the U.S. Post Office Department) and the end of 1928, the total mileage of air routes in the country grew five-fold. By the end of that year, 32 airline companies were operating with a fleet of 294 single-engine and multiengine aircraft. The growth in the demand for military and civil aircraft stimulated the entry of new companies into the manufacturing sector in all segments of the market. At the end of 1928, 53 companies were producing airplanes or airplane engines. But few men were as comprehensively involved in so many aspects of aviation or had as broad a vision as Clement Keys.[74]

The financial community generally recognized that aviation had become a business. In a report on the aviation industry issued in September 1928, the New York brokerage firm of Pynchon and Company stated that with the recent developments, "aviation passes from a dangerous speculation into the realm of everyday business."[75] But the report sounded a note of warning, saying that "the tremendous possibilities of future development tend to inspire one to financial risks which would not be considered in other fields."[76] In the great speculative bull market of 1928 to 1929, few people listened, particularly when large, well-known institutions such as the National City Bank of New York, Lehman Brothers, and Hayden, Stone were underwriting sizable investments in the industry. Investment money came pouring into the industry. Before 1928 there had been few issues of aviation stocks into the market; between March 1928 and December 1929, the stock market absorbed $300 million in new issues.[77] Keys alone raised nearly $70 million for the Curtiss group of companies and North American Aviation.

The flood of capital helped accelerate the passage of the aviation industry through the normal stages of industrial development. In the early phase, one or more individuals or companies would typically introduce a new product, technology, or process that would create a new market. The industry would then expand as demand increased and as new competitors entered the market. Then would follow a period of overexpansion, with too many competitors in the market, leading to a contraction and a consolidation of the industry through acquisition or merger into a small group of stronger players. From 1898 to 1902, many of the industrial sectors in America had gone through this process of consolidation through merger as firms sought both economies of scale and stronger competitive positions within their respective markets. One of the key issues in the ability of firms to merge and expand through integration or acquisition was their ability to raise capital.[78] The stock market boom of the late twenties and the widespread availability of credit mirrored the conditions around the turn of the century and allowed the consolidation of the aviation industry and the formation of several large groups.[79]

By the middle of 1929, four groups had emerged as the leading players in the aviation industry. They were:

1. The United Aircraft and Transport Corporation
2. The Aviation Corporation
3. The Curtiss Aeroplane and Motor Company/Clement Keys group
4. The Wright Aeronautical Corporation/Richard Hoyt group

Organized in February 1929, the United Aircraft and Transportation Corporation combined the interests of the Boeing Aircraft and Transportation Company with Pratt and Whitney. Boeing Aircraft and Transportation had been formed in the previous December from a combination of Boeing Aircraft, Boeing Air Transport, and Pacific Air Transport. The Pratt and Whitney Company was then building engines for Boeing's military and commercial airplanes. The new holding company comprised the Boeing Aircraft Company, Boeing Air Transport and Pacific Air Transport, the Pratt and Whitney Aircraft Company, and the

Chance Vought Corporation, another large Pratt and Whitney customer and builder of observation planes for the U.S. Navy. William Boeing became chairman, and Frederick Rentschler, president of Pratt and Whitney, became president of the new group. From the start, Boeing and Rentschler intended the individual companies to operate independently, but with a single management at the holding company level establishing policy. This combination of aircraft manufacturers, airline companies, and one of the premier engine manufacturers created a powerful competitor in the industry.[80]

The Wright Aeronautical/Hoyt group was similar in structure to the Curtiss group. Several diverse companies were built around a major manufacturer, the Wright Aeronautical Corporation, and were linked through cross-shareholdings and the presence of Richard Hoyt, chairman of Wright and a senior partner in the investment banking firm of Hayden, Stone and Company, on the board of directors. By this time, Wright Aeronautical was, with Pratt and Whitney, the principal manufacturer of air-cooled radial engines in America. The companies in the Hoyt group built a range of military and commercial aircraft and were involved in airport operation and finance. The Keystone Aircraft Corporation produced bombers for the Air Corps, and the Travel Air Company built small four- and six-seat passenger planes. In two areas, airlines and financial activities, the interests of the Wright/Hoyt group overlapped with those of the Curtiss/Keys group. Richard Hoyt was a director of Transcontinental Air Transport, where Keys served as president; Hoyt and Keys were directors of the National Aviation Corporation, an investment firm dealing in aviation securities, while Hoyt was also chairman of the Aviation Credit Corporation, in which the Curtiss group held an interest and several seats on the board. Like Keys, Hoyt had organized the companies in his group into a loose affiliation rather than the holding company structure of United Aircraft and Transport.[81]

United Aircraft and the Curtiss group of companies (including the companies North American Aviation controlled) appeared to be the leading players in the industry. At the time, it was by no means clear that other rivals would not emerge to present a serious challenge. An article written in April 1929 on the mergers in the aviation industry concluded its analysis by saying that "it was not beyond the realm of possibility that one or another of the present independent companies ... may become the nucleus of still another grouping excelling in importance those herein listed."[82] The Aviation Corporation (AVCO) appeared to have this potential. Organized in March 1929 with a capital of $35 million AVCO had substantial backing from the Wall Street firms of Lehman Brothers and W. A. Harriman. AVCO quickly invested in a number of airline companies and aviation manufacturers. Promising small and medium-size companies such as the Douglas Aircraft Company and Western Air Express remained independent. With the stock market still booming, further combinations seemed possible. With the constellation of industry leaders still in the formative stage, competition for market share and competitive position could only continue.

What was clear enough was that United Aircraft would be a formidable competitor for the Curtiss group. The most obvious disparity between United Aircraft and Curtiss was that Curtiss was still committed to the liquid-cooled engine and had no capacity to produce an acceptable air-cooled radial, while in Pratt and Whitney, United Aircraft had the manufacturer of one of the finest radial engines ever built. By 1929 the movement of large segments of aviation in America toward the radial engine was evident. The navy had already committed itself to the radial. In the commercial air transport field, the three large airliners then in service—the Boeing Model 80, the Ford 5-AT Trimotor, and the Fokker F-10—were all equipped with the Pratt and Whitney Wasp. Even the U.S. Army Air Corps had begun to change, ordering the new Boeing fighter with Wasp engines and the Keystone LB-6 bomber with the Wright Cyclone radial engine. Engine technology was driving aviation into a new direction, and neither the Curtiss Aeroplane and Motor Company nor any of its related companies had the capacity to follow along.

Two other issues were becoming apparent to observers of, and participants in, the aviation industry. The technologies of airplane design, construction, and motive power were in a process of change. The emergence of the air-cooled radial engine was the most obvious change, but other innovations were slowly appearing in government and corporate laboratories. Practical application of some had already begun. The government's National Advisory Committee for Aeronautics (NACA) had devoted considerable work on aerodynamics and aircraft streamlining. Aircraft structures were improving as well. There was greater use of metal in place of wood and fabric, and more attention was being given to reducing drag. Although a combination of all the new features capable of maximizing their benefits was not yet technically possible, these advances pointed toward the potential that lay ahead. The successful manufacturers would be those who could undertake the intensive research and development effort that was necessary.[83]

Technological competition among the leading aviation manufacturers could only intensify. Firms with inadequate research and development capacity could only fall behind in the competitive battle. Frederick Rentschler of United Aircraft addressed this theme directly in June 1929 when he remarked that in the future, the most important competitive factor in the aviation industry would be engineering ability.[84] Success would come not simply from having a large number of engineers but from the ability to realize economies of scale in the research effort. Economies of scale could come only through attention to the development of a supportive administrative structure in which the resources of a firm could be effectively coordinated.[85] The holding company structure that the United Aircraft and Transportation Corporation had adopted was a far better structure for building a coordinated engineering effort than the loose affiliation that both Keys and Hoyt had used to develop their respective groups. To compete with United Aircraft, they would have to change. In the spring of 1929, Clement Keys and Richard Hoyt began to discuss a plan that was full of historic irony: the merger of the Curtiss Aeroplane and Motor Company with the Wright Aeronautical Corporation. The names of the bitter rivals, Curtiss and the Wrights, were shortly to become united in one company.

Growth of the Wright Aeronautical Corporation

The Wright Aeronautical Corporation had an illustrious heritage, tracing its ancestry back to Wilbur and Orville Wright. In one of the many ironies that came out of this merger, Curtiss, the engine builder, achieved fame and financial success building airplanes, whereas the company bearing the name of the inventors of the airplane became best known as a manufacturer of airplane engines. The Wright brothers had received many lucrative offers, but they did not find backers with whom they felt comfortable until the fall of 1909, when a group of prominent New York businessmen and bankers offered support for an American company to manufacture and sell Wright aircraft. On 22 November 1909, the Wright Company was incorporated in the state of New York with a capital of $1 million and Wilbur Wright as president.[86]

Over the next two and a half years, the two brothers spent considerable time pursuing their patent suit against Curtiss and others. The Wright Company concentrated on building small numbers of aircraft, developing new models, and running a training school for both military and civilian flyers. When Wilbur Wright died in 1912, Orville took over as president. Orville never had his older brother's drive, however. Nor did he feel comfortable running a business. He remained wedded to the designs he and his brother had developed, and the Wright Company fell behind its competitors in America and Europe. When the U.S. Army

The Wright brothers. *Left,* Wilbur: *right,* Orville.
Courtesy of Special Collections and Archives, Wright State University.

banned further instruction in its Wright machines and began shifting to tractor designs from Curtiss and Glenn Martin, the Wright Company had no competing tractor design available.[87]

Orville Wright recognized that he had not managed the company well and that he was not the person to reverse its fortunes. He bought back the shares of the original investors and then sold the company in October 1915 to a new syndicate of investors from the New York financial community. They included representatives of the investment banking firm of Hayden, Stone and Company, who would play a key role in the company's future.[88] The new company's first attempts to restore its position in the manufacture of aircraft were not a success. The Wright pusher models could not compete with the newer Martin and Curtiss trainers. Fortunately, new management, attracted to the potential that the war in Europe offered to American manufacturers, had already been exploring other alternatives in the aviation field.

These investors decided to begin building aircraft engines. The prospect of a long war meant a steady demand for engines. There was no reason why an American manufacturer could not become a significant supplier to Europe. With this goal in mind, the syndicate purchased an interest in the Simplex Automobile Company, which had built a plant in New Brunswick, New Jersey, for the production of automobiles and high-quality engines. In November 1915, the directors sent the chairman of the Simplex Automobile Company and his chief engineer to France to study the current airplane engines. The two men selected the new 150-horsepower Hispano-Suiza engine as the most promising design. In January 1916 the French government granted the Wright Company a license to manufacture the Hispano-Suiza in the United States, on the condition that the output of their plant should be for

France. The Wright Company received a contract to build 450 Hispano-Suizas—popularly known as "Hissos"—for delivery later in the year. The Wright Company raised $2 million to build and equip a new plant at the New Brunswick site to manufacture the new engines.[89]

In the interim, the directors of the Wright Company sought another means of becoming involved in the manufacture of aircraft. In the summer of 1916, they approached Glenn Martin, president and driving force behind the small Glenn L. Martin Company in Los Angeles. Their proposal was a merger with the Wright Company into a new, larger enterprise. Martin, who was then producing training planes on a small scale for the army and the navy, had recently received a contract from the Netherlands for 20 trainers for the Dutch East Indies. He agreed to the proposal, and in August the formation of a new company, the Wright-Martin Aircraft Corporation, was announced. Martin became vice president responsible for aircraft production and development but remained at the Los Angeles factory.[90]

When America entered the war in April 1917, the Wright-Martin Aircraft Corporation was the only company in America apart from Curtiss that was working on a usable airplane engine. Soon after war was declared, Wright-Martin received a contract to produce 500 150-horsepower Hispano-Suiza engines to be used in the Curtiss JN-4 advanced trainer. By October Wright-Martin had received a contract for 4,000 additional Hispano-Suiza engines of larger horsepower.[91] Wright-Martin concentrated on engine production. The Aircraft Production Board decided that Glenn Martin's Los Angeles plant was too small for volume production and asked Wright-Martin to manufacture airplanes instead of Martin. Wright-Martin submitted a proposal to the Aircraft Production Board, but the company could not get the board to agree to more favorable terms on its contracts and did not pursue the opportunity further. Frustrated by the parent company's lack of commitment to aircraft manufacturing, Glenn Martin resigned and returned to the east coast to start up a new firm under his own name.[92]

At this juncture, two men entered the firm who would play pivotal roles in the company's future: Richard Hoyt and Guy Vaughan. Hoyt was an investment banker. He had joined the investment banking firm of Hayden, Stone and Company after graduating from Harvard University in 1910. He soon developed a strong interest in aviation and became a sportsman-aviator. When America entered the war, he spent several months working as a civilian assistant in the aircraft and motor development program at McCook Field in Dayton, Ohio. Hayden, Stone had helped organize and underwrite the Wright-Martin Aircraft Corporation and was the largest shareholder of the company's preferred stock. With Wright-Martin about to expand significantly as it took on government contracts, Hoyt joined the company as secretary and assistant to the president. As Keys had done with the Curtiss Aeroplane and Motor Corporation, Hoyt helped arrange financing to expand Wright-Martin's wartime production.[93]

Manufacturing aircraft engines was a new endeavor, but the rapid development of the automotive industry in the United States had created a pool of engineering talent on which companies such as Wright-Martin could draw. The company's organizers had purchased the Simplex Company to get the engineering skills they needed. As wartime orders for more engines began to come in, the company hired additional engineering talent. One of these men was Guy Vaughan, who brought with him nearly 20 years of experience working in the auto industry.

Guy Warner Vaughan was born in Bay Shore, Long Island, in 1884 and grew up in New Rochelle, New York. Like so many young men of his era, he became fascinated with the automobile, and after graduating from high school in 1898, he went to work for the Desberon Motor Company of New Rochelle. While there, he did something typical for ambitious young men of that day who lacked the financial means to attend college: he enrolled in the International Correspondence Schools, signing up for an engineering course. He subsequently

Richard F. Hoyt.
New Jersey Aviation Hall of Fame.

joined the Standard Automobile Company and rose to the position of vice president and chief engineer.

Vaughan's interest in automobiles led to automobile racing, and at the age of 18, he began a career as a race car driver that lasted for some five years. In 1909 he designed and produced his own auto, the Vaughan Runabout. Some 80 examples were manufactured. In addition, he was a consulting engineer for various companies, including the Olds Motor Works of Lansing, Michigan. He also helped to develop the Knight automobile engine. Vaughan's association with the aviation industry began when he joined Wright-Martin in 1917 as quality manager. He later became factory manager of company plants in New Brunswick and Long Island, supervising all engine production.[94]

Thanks largely to Vaughan's efforts, Wright-Martin's production was accelerating rapidly by the spring of 1918. Within a year, the company had increased its rate of production from 10 to 12 engines per month to 500 engines per month. In April 1918, the army ordered Wright-Martin to begin work on a contract for the 300-horsepower Hispano-Suiza engine. The French and British governments decided that the new 300-horsepower engine, which was essentially an enlarged version of the standard Hispano-Suiza, would be used in several advanced aircraft planned for introduction in 1919.

When the engine factories in Europe were found to have insufficient capacity to expand production, Wright-Martin was given a contract for an additional 2,000 engines. The company's New Brunswick plant could not handle the production of two different types of engine, however. Hence the army made a government-owned plant in Long Island City available exclusively for manufacturing the 300-horsepower Hispano-Suiza. The Long Island City plant was rapidly preparing for a production rate of 1,000 engines per month when the war ended in November.[95]

Between April 1917 and November 1919, when the last of the wartime contracts had been completed, Wright-Martin delivered 5,816 Hispano-Suiza engines.[96] With the end of the war, all but one of the automotive companies that had shifted production to aircraft engines went back to producing automobile engines, leaving only three companies in the aircraft engine field: the Curtiss Aeroplane and Motor Corporation, the Packard Motor Car Company (which had built the famous Liberty engine), and Wright-Martin. The Wright-Martin directors were determined to remain in the aviation industry but decided to concentrate solely on manufacturing aircraft engines and not to become involved in designing or manufacturing airplanes. Commitment to this strategy, which essentially recognized the reality of the company's strengths, warranted a reorganization. The Wright-Martin Aircraft Corporation was dissolved, and a new company, the Wright Aeronautical Corporation, was incorporated in October 1919. George Houston continued as president, but he recruited a new group of senior engineers and managers to help him run the company, as a number of the wartime staff, including Vaughan, had left. Frederick Rentschler, an engineer and wartime army captain who had been directly involved in production of the Hispano-Suiza at Wright-Martin, was recruited as vice president and general manager. After Houston retired in 1921, Rentschler became president of the company, and Richard Hoyt became chairman of the board of directors representing the Hayden, Stone interests. Houston and Rentschler arranged to sell the New Brunswick plant and most of the company's assets to the International Motor Truck Corporation. In the following year, the Simplex Automobile Company was sold. Rentschler found new facilities for an aircraft engine plant at Paterson, New Jersey.[97]

Wright Aeronautical started business in a favorable position. It continued to hold the manufacturing licenses for the Hispano-Suiza engines, and in 1919 it was manufacturing three versions: the Model I of 150 horsepower, the Model E of 180 horsepower, and the Model H of 300 horsepower. After the war, the Hispano-Suiza name was dropped, and the engines became known simply as Wright engines. Unlike Curtiss, Wright Aeronautical did not overexpand but chose instead to concentrate on improving its existing designs. The company received a steady flow of business from the military, even as the army and navy both cut back their orders. Most of the American fighter planes developed in the first few years after the war used the Wright-built 300-horsepower Hispano-Suiza engine.[98]

Over the next four years, Wright Aeronautical earned steady profits from sales to the military. The engine business proved to have more stable earnings and cash flow than aircraft manufacturing. Although Moody's Investors Service still considered Wright Aeronautical's common stock a speculative investment, it gave the Wright Company a higher rating than the Curtiss Aeroplane and Motor Corporation.[99] The company's core business remained the Wright version of the Hispano-Suiza. The company then developed a large liquid-cooled engine developing even greater horsepower as a replacement for the Liberty engine. Wright sold this engine in quantity to the U.S. Navy for the Curtiss and Martin torpedo planes and for long-range patrol planes. Wright Aeronautical had established itself as a major supplier of aircraft engines and had built up a solid business. The direction of its business, however, was about to undergo a radical shift.[100]

Liquid-cooled engines gave Wright Aeronautical a firm foundation in the aviation industry; the air-cooled radial engine would bring the company a fortune. Wright began working on radial engines with reluctance and only as a result of pressure from the U.S. Navy. In seeking an alternative to the liquid-cooled engine, engineers and airplane designers hoped to achieve more power for less weight and greater simplicity in operation and maintenance. The liquid coolant, radiator, and related tubing that these engines required imposed a heavy weight penalty. Moreover, they needed constant maintenance. In the United States, both Curtiss and Wright had worked on a radial engine design for the U.S. Army Air Service in the early twenties, but neither company had much success, and both remained committed to the liquid-cooled engines they were then developing.

Left, Guy W. Vaughan; *right,* Charles R. Lawrance with Wright Whirlwind engine.

Courtesy of Louis Eltscher.

Charles R. Lawrance, a young engineer who had trained in Europe, was at the forefront of radial engine development in the United States. Lawrance had begun designing and building radial engines in 1916. In 1919, with help from the U.S. Navy, he built a small three-cylinder engine that showed promise. The navy was taking a strong interest in the radial engine as it began to plan the development of carrier aviation, which needed more reliable engines for its aircraft. With the navy's encouragement, Lawrance continued his developmental work. In May 1921, he delivered an experimental nine-cylinder engine to the navy that produced 200 horsepower, as much as the liquid-cooled Wright Model E. This engine, the J-1, led to a navy order for 50 engines. It became the first American-built radial engine to successfully complete a 50-hour endurance test. Lawrance was on the right track.[101]

The Lawrance Aero Engine Company was too small to undertake quantity production. The navy needed an experienced manufacturer and approached both Curtiss and Wright Aeronautical, but neither was enthusiastic. Wright saw no reason why it should manufacture an engine that would compete directly with its own Model E. The navy, however, was determined to have its new radial design and exerted pressure on Wright Aeronautical by the simple expedient of telling the company that unless it agreed to build the J-1, the navy would buy no more Model E engines. In May 1923 Wright Aeronautical acquired the capital stock of the Lawrance Aero Engine Company and arranged for the merger of the two companies. Charles Lawrance became a vice president at Wright Aeronautical and continued to work on developing the J-1 engine.[102]

Among its capable engineering staff, Wright Aeronautical had two men of exceptional talent, George Mead and Andrew Willgoos. Working with Mead and Willgoos, Lawrance modified and improved his J-1 engine. The first version to be accepted by the navy was the J-4, which the navy used to power the Vought UO-1 observation plane and the navy-designed TS-1 built by Curtiss. The engine still needed more work to increase power and reliability. To this end, Wright Aeronautical recruited a brilliant English engineer, Samuel Heron, who had been working for the U.S. Army Air Service at their McCook Field, Ohio, development laboratories. Heron was the world's leading expert in the design of air-cooled cylinders for radial engines. During 1925 he redesigned the cylinders for the basic Lawrance engine to produce the J-5, known as the Whirlwind. Developing 220 horsepower, it demonstrated remarkable reliability and achieved enduring fame as the engine that powered Charles Lindbergh's Ryan monoplane, the *Spirit of St. Louis,* from New York to Paris. Lindbergh's flight, and several other long-distance flights that took place shortly thereafter, proved beyond doubt the value of the air-cooled radial engine.[103]

Timing has a great deal to do with the success of any business, and in this regard, Wright Aeronautical was fortunate. The successful introduction of the J-5 Whirlwind came at a time when American aviation was beginning its recovery and the war surplus material that had depressed sales of new equipment was finally wearing out. The Whirlwind found a ready market as the power plant for several small single-engine passenger planes and in combination as the engine for the new airliners then just entering production, such as the Ford 4-AT Trimotor and the Fokker F.VIIa. In addition, Wright Aeronautical won two big contracts from the navy and the Air Service for Whirlwinds. The company's sales increased steadily, and profits doubled. Engine production doubled as well, and the company built up a healthy backlog of orders.

Timing is also a factor in the emergence of challengers to an established firm. With the Whirlwind, Wright Aeronautical had what appeared to be a commanding lead in a new technology. But aviation was developing across a broad range of activities that created and demanded special capabilities. As newer and more specialized aircraft emerged to serve particular segments of the aviation market, a demand for a broader range of engine power was created. The Whirlwind was a superb engine, but it lacked power. The liquid-cooled engines then available had much higher horsepower ratings, more than 400 horsepower for the Curtiss D-12 and more than 500 horsepower for the Wright T-2 and T-3. Convinced that the radial engine offered significant benefits, aircraft designers now wanted more power. Given this demand, the emergence of a challenger to capture a share of the growing market was inevitable. A challenger did emerge, not from among Wright Aeronautical's competitors, but from within Wright itself.

Frederick Rentschler resigned as president of Wright Aeronautical in September 1924, over a disagreement with Richard Hoyt and the other directors on the amount of profits the company would devote to research and development. As an engineer, Rentschler understood the need to invest in developmental work to sustain a company's position in the market and to ensure future sources of profit. Rentschler came to feel that the directors were not wholly committed to the radial engine at a time when the radial badly needed further development. In frustration, he left the company.[104] After some months, Rentschler decided to reenter the aviation engine business. He approached the navy, which agreed to give him some experimental funds if he could come up with a new engine. The navy hoped to foster competition for Wright Aeronautical. Recruiting George Mead, Andrew Willgoos, and several other capable engineers from Wright, Renstschler persuaded the Pratt and Whitney Company, a machine tool manufacturer in Hartford, Connecticut, and a subsidiary of the Niles-Bement-Pond Company, to invest in his new venture. Taking his main investor's name, Rentschler incorporated the Pratt and Whitney Aircraft Company in July 1925. Six months later, the new company produced its first engine, the 425-horsepower Wasp, which was an instant success. The navy immediately placed an order for 200 Wasp engines.[105]

Although Wright Aeronautical had the frustration of seeing the navy's new fighters and observation aircraft flying with the Pratt and Whitney Wasp, the Whirlwind was still generating a substantial amount of business for the company as the aviation boom gathered steam. Nevertheless, the resignation of Mead and Willgoos was a severe blow. With Rentschler's departure, Charles Lawrance became president of Wright Aeronautical, and Guy Vaughan, who had returned to the company as factory manager in 1924, was made vice president and general manager in 1925. During 1927 the company sold 624 engines and had total sales of $3,990,546, the highest levels achieved since the end of the war. Even more promising, the company ended the year with $4,466,519 in back orders, more than double the figure from the previous year. In the first three months of 1928, the company received an additional $3,327,274 in orders. For the first time, Wright Aeronautical sold more engines to commercial operators than to the military, reflecting the popularity of the Whirlwind for commercial operations. So great was the demand for the Whirlwind that the company had to expand its Paterson plant facilities.[106]

As the navy had hoped, the entry of Pratt and Whitney into the market spurred Wright Aeronautical's effort in the radial engine field. Under the leadership of Charles Lawrance and Guy Vaughan, and with Samuel Heron's engineering genius, Wright Aeronautical worked hard to develop a competitive response. Wright first boosted the performance of the Whirlwind through a complete redesign of the engine that became the J-6 and brought the power up to 300 horsepower. The company then began developing a family of Whirlwind engines that offered 165, 220, and 300 horsepower, all with interchangeable parts. Conceding the middle power range to the Pratt and Whitney Wasp, Wright decided to concentrate on building a more powerful engine that could produce more than 400 horsepower. For some time, Wright engineers had been working on a large engine with nearly double the capacity of the Whirlwind. This engine, the P-2, was expected to produce around 450 horsepower, but with the introduction of the Wasp, this would not be enough. After more development, Wright introduced a new large nine-cylinder radial engine for the U.S. Navy in 1927. Named the Cyclone, Wright's new engine produced 525 horsepower. Pratt and Whitney had also developed an engine in this class, the Hornet, but the Cyclone proved to be a tough competitor, winning orders from the U.S. Navy, the U.S. Army Air Corps, and commercial operators.[107]

For Wright Aeronautical, 1928 proved to be an exceptional year. Both the army and the navy were in the midst of their five-year expansion programs, and commercial aircraft sales were accelerating. During the year, the company built 1,644 engines, more than double the prior year's figure. The Whirlwind still made up the bulk of the production, but the new Cyclone had begun to sell well, with the navy ordering a large number for new patrol and torpedo planes. The company's sales during the year more than doubled to $8,781,516, while profits from operations went up three-fold to $2,381,408. In the first three months of 1929, the company received $7,658,398 in new orders. To support this level of production, Wright Aeronautical undertook a major expansion of its facilities. Capitalizing on the booming stock market, the company raised nearly $5 million through the issue of 50,000 new shares. Approximately $4 million went for purchasing an additional 21 acres of land at the Paterson, New Jersey, facility and for building and equipping new factory space to expand production capacity to 500 engines per month.[108]

The senior managers and directors of Wright Aeronautical could look back on the year with no small sense of satisfaction at what they had achieved. Quite apart from achieving record sales and profits, the company's real success was in following American aviation's transition from the liquid-cooled engine to the air-cooled radial. Neither of Wright's old competitors, the Curtiss Aeroplane and Motor Company and the Packard Motor Car Company, had developed a successful radial engine. With the U.S. Navy having firmly committed itself to the radial, and the new commercial airlines moving in the same direction, Wright Aeronautical could look forward to a growing market. Already, in a short time, the dominance that Wright and Pratt and Whitney had established in the radial engine field had created significant barriers to entry; any new competitor would have to make a prohibitively expensive investment to compete. The battle in the American market would be between Wright and Pratt and Whitney. Having Boeing and Vought as captive customers under the United Aircraft umbrella seemed to give Pratt and Whitney a competitive advantage.

The Curtiss and Wright Merger

The idea of merging the Curtiss and Wright groups had been discussed for some time, both inside and outside the two companies; Frederick Rentschler had predicted to the navy that if Wright Aeronautical proved too successful a competitor with its radial engines, Curtiss would seek a merger.[109] Discussions between Hoyt and Keys became more serious during the spring of 1929 as each viewed the competitive evolution of the aviation industry. By June they had reached a decision to merge their respective groups and create a new holding company structure with Hoyt as chairman and Keys as president of the parent company. On 27 June 1929, the directors of the Curtiss Aeroplane and Motor Company, Wright Aeronautical, and the Keystone Aircraft Corporation announced that a new company, the Curtiss-Wright Corporation, would soon be formed.[110]

The formation of the Curtiss-Wright Corporation created the largest aviation holding company in the country. The combined group had assets of more than $75 million. In a statement to the press, Keys listed the advantages the new corporation would have. First among these were the economies of scale that would be possible by coordinating the operations of the different group companies. Research and development work could be concentrated in one or two centers and thereby greatly expanded. The new corporation would also offer a full line of aircraft and engines for both the military and commercial markets. Supporting the manufacturing side was a strong distribution network and an organization of dealers based at many of the most important airports in the country. The new corporation began on a solid financial base with no funded debt.[111]

The senior management of the new corporation included representatives from the main companies in the group. Charles Lawrance, president of Wright Aeronautical, and Walter Beech, president of Travel Air, became vice presidents; J. A. B. Smith, secretary and treasurer of the Curtiss Aeroplane and Motor Company, became executive vice president and secretary; F. H. Russell from Curtiss and J. F. Prince from Wright were appointed treasurers. In a gesture to the history of the company, Glenn Curtiss was appointed a member of the technical committee, although he had not been active in the company or in aviation for more than six years. On 9 August, the Curtiss-Wright Corporation was incorporated in Delaware, and six days later, the corporation gained control of its 12 subsidiary companies through an exchange of shares.[112]

For Keys, the merger of Curtiss with Wright Aeronautical was the pinnacle of his achievement and the culmination of his vision. In an article that appeared in the *New York Herald Tribune* a few weeks before the merger, the journalist Howard Mingos had labeled Keys "the Harriman of aviation," a reference to Edward Harriman, builder of one of the greatest railway empires in American history.[113] But for Keys, the Curtiss-Wright merger was merely a stepping-stone to a larger vision. He knew that although aviation had taken off as a business, much remained to be done. The airlines and air routes that he foresaw crisscrossing America had hardly begun. The operations of Transcontinental Air Transport and National Air

Transport were a mere fraction of what was needed. The aircraft that flew daily along these early routes were far from the speedy, efficient, and reliable airliners that passengers wanted. He was building the infrastructure needed to supply the airplanes, engines, pilots, and trained staff that the industry would need, and he was bringing that infrastructure under the control of one management. His vision was not limited to America; he foresaw the same developments occurring around the globe, and he was already pursuing similar ventures in China and Latin America.[114]

For the Curtiss Aeroplane and Motor Company, the merger culminated a decade of profound change. Entering the postwar era full of confidence in the future of aviation, the company had paid a heavy price for its premature faith and had narrowly avoided bankruptcy. Curtiss had subsequently struggled to survive while building the tools that could turn a vision into a reality, namely, better and more capable aircraft with powerful and more reliable engines. The company had made significant contributions to American aviation through its racing planes and the D-12 engine; its Hawk fighters were among the finest fighter planes in the world, and its other military aircraft were building solid reputations for performance. Although the company's failure to develop a successful radial engine put it at a competitive disadvantage, its new partnership with Wright Aeronautical held considerable promise for the combination of Curtiss-designed aircraft with Wright engines. The financial rewards of success had been tangible. In the summer of 1929, the company was in solid financial condition with sales and earnings at record levels.

For all the companies in the Curtiss-Wright Corporation, the future looked bright indeed. Aircraft and engine sales were well ahead of the records posted in 1928, and a new postwar record seemed likely. There was much to be done to realize the full potential of the new corporation. On 9 September 1929, the *New York Times* reported that 80 officials of the component companies of the Curtiss-Wright Corporation were meeting that day to discuss the coordination of their activities, including the formation of a unified plan for engineering development.[115] Fifty days later came the great stock market crash, followed by the Great Depression, and with it the collapse of the empire Keys had struggled so hard to build. Within a few short but harrowing years, Keys would leave the industry a broken man while the Curtiss-Wright Corporation would teeter on the brink of bankruptcy once again.

Chapter 4

Decline and Resurgence, 1930–1937

The End of the Aviation Boom

During 1929 the aviation industry produced 6,034 military and commercial airplanes. Few participants would then have believed that within 2 years, production would fall to barely one-sixth of this figure, or that it would take 10 years for the industry to exceed the production level attained in 1929. It would take the urgent need for rearmament, not the growth of commercial and private flying, to repair the damage the Great Depression inflicted on the aviation industry.

The depression brought about the collapse of the aviation boom. The value of production sank from the 1929 high of $44.5 million to a mere $12.7 million in 1932.[1] In the general collapse of the stock market that began with the October 1929 crash, aviation stocks were hard hit, falling to a fraction of their 1929 values as the depression deepened. The demand for commercial aircraft shrank dramatically. The demand for small aircraft for private flying, on which so many in the industry had placed great hopes, simply evaporated. Military sales sustained some manufacturers during the early years of the depression, but when the army and navy five-year programs ended in 1931, military sales dropped as well. Congressional parsimony and fiscal restraint depressed military sales until the middle of the decade. The period between the end of the five-year programs and the renewed military orders that began in the second half of the decade demonstrated again how critically dependent the American aviation industry was on military orders. With little commercial demand and few military contracts, the aviation industry experienced a sharp contraction in capacity and total assets employed.

As the financial condition of the industry worsened, several firms were forced into bankruptcy. Even some of the larger and more powerful groups had a difficult time surviving the early years of the depression. The structure of the industry changed as well. Following the airmail industry hearings in 1934, the government mandated the separation of airline and manufacturing companies, thus ending the dream of vertically integrated monopolies that would dominate the industry. The firms that had established leading positions in the industry, such as Boeing, Curtiss-Wright, Douglas, and Vought, competed fiercely among themselves, but they were not able to dominate the industry and prevent the entry of new com-

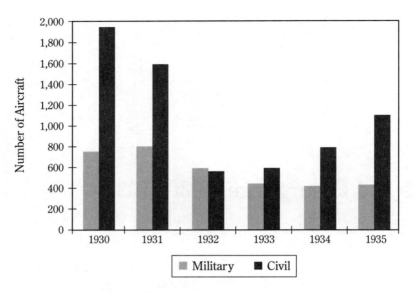

Fig. 2.   Aircraft production: 1930–1935

petitors.[2] Surprisingly, given the financial condition of the aviation industry for much of the decade, new entrants continued to emerge. Firms such as Grumman, Bell, North American, and Seversky succeeded in winning new business at the expense of the longer-established firms.

What gave these new entrants their opportunity was the revolution in aviation technology that took place during the late twenties and early thirties. This revolution resulted not from a single development but from the synergistic application of a series of design features, principally in aerodynamics (the design of the airplane) and propulsion.[3] During the twenties, research clearly demonstrated that the most effective way of improving an airplane's performance was through streamlining and creating a design that offered the least amount of drag, or resistance to the air, as possible. The struts, bracing wires, and fixed landing gear of the standard biplane created significant drag. Engineers found that by eliminating the struts and bracing wires, the speed of the airplane could be increased. Using metal instead of fabric and wood for construction enabled the structural support and bracing to be done internally. Shifting to a monoplane form decreased the drag even further, and with a strong metal wing, the landing gear could be made retractable, offering even more improvement. Refinements in the placement of engines and the development of streamlined cowlings for radial engines gave additional benefits. Many of these innovations had been developed during the twenties, but it was not until they could be combined into a single airframe that the full benefits of the individual improvements could be realized. Using the same Pratt and Whitney engine as the Boeing P-12 biplane fighter, the streamlined Lockheed Orion monoplane airliner proved to be 30 miles per hour faster.[4]

In aircraft construction, the six-year period from 1929 to 1936 saw the shift to all-metal construction as the standard for aircraft of all types. More powerful and efficient engines together with variable pitch propellers (i.e., varying the angle at which the propeller strikes the airflow), when combined with better aerodynamic design, brought about steady increases in speed, range, and productivity. However, the shift from wood to all-metal construction required a change in production processes, and this increased costs. All-metal air-craft were more expensive and more difficult to build than their fabric and metal-tube prede-cessors. Development costs increased as well. Complexity in design required more design specialists and a heavier investment in research and development. This increase in costs occurred against a backdrop of financial pressure as companies struggled to survive during the lean years of the depression. Leading firms in the aviation industry thus faced a three-fold challenge of coping with costly technological change, fewer potential contracts, and more competition.

For Curtiss-Wright, these were difficult years indeed. Clement Keys had entered into the merger with Wright Aeronautical to form the cornerstone of an aviation empire. Under the financial stress of the depression, his empire could not be sustained. The Curtiss-Wright merger was the pinnacle of his success; within a few years, his group of companies would be dismantled and he himself ruined. During the course of this drastic retrenchment, the Curtiss-Wright Corporation would sustain staggering losses. Financial recovery came slowly and only after the middle of the decade, once the retrenchment had been completed and new orders had begun to trickle in.

Curtiss-Wright seemed to lose its competitive edge in the first half of the decade, espe-cially in aircraft design. The mantle of leadership in innovation fell to other firms. Only after 1935, under the leadership of Guy Vaughan, did the company recapture its reputation and position within the industry. The end of the period would see a resurgent Curtiss-Wright on the verge of a vast wartime expansion. What helped Curtiss-Wright survive these lean years were the export markets for American aircraft and, more important, Wright Aeronautical's leading position as an engine manufacturer. Export and engine sales sustained Curtiss-Wright, giving management time to restructure the company and organize a recovery when world rearmament began a few years later.

The Decline of Curtiss-Wright

In the minds of many Americans, the collapse of the stock market on 29 October 1929 marked the end of the great economic boom of the twenties. The boom had in fact ended some months before. Beginning in the spring and early summer, the American economy began to slide into recession. Production in leading industries—automobiles, steel, housing construction—started a gradual decline that would accelerate in the following year with the country sinking into a full-blown depression. The stock market crash was symbolic of the end of what business leaders and politicians had hailed as a new era of permanent prosperity. Few could have guessed the extent of the disaster that was about to engulf them.[5]

Aviation stocks did not escape the crisis. As beneficiaries of the speculative boom, avia-tion stocks had soared in value during 1928 and 1929 in expectation of the vast profits to be made in this new industry. The gains from two years of a bull market were wiped out in a matter of days. The average share price of aviation stocks declined from $60 per share to around $15 per share following the crash.[6] United Aircraft and Transport fell from its all-time high of $160 per share to $30 per share, while Curtiss-Wright's common stock fell from $31 to $9.[7] The inflated dreams of the industry's most vocal promoters evaporated.

The actual performance of the aviation industry during 1929 mirrored the gradual decline in the rest of the American economy. Although American aircraft manufacturers produced more aircraft than ever before, aircraft sales declined sharply during the second half of the year. During 1928 private flying and aerial taxi services grew rapidly; manufacturers could not keep pace with the demand for aircraft. In the expectation that demand could only grow during 1929, many manufacturers expanded their rate of production and their production facilities. In fact, they assumed a rate of growth that was beyond reasonable expectations. Sales began to decline during the second half of the year, leaving many manufacturers with large unsold inventories.[8]

Toward the end of the year, most manufacturers cut back on production but viewed these cutbacks and consolidation of facilities as a reasonable and conservative reaction to the excess of supply over demand. Most leaders in the industry believed that once this readjustment was completed, sales would surge again and would likely exceed the record set in 1929. Writing in the February 1930 issue of the industry magazine *Aviation,* both Clement Keys and Frederick Rentschler, president of United Aircraft and Transport, predicted substantial sales during 1930, particularly in commercial aviation. Keys looked to the growth of private aircraft ownership by individuals and business corporations as the key to success in 1930.[9]

For its first six months of operations, the Curtiss-Wright Corporation had consolidated sales of $26,047,904 and incurred a consolidated net loss of $668,532.[10] During the year, all the companies within the group undertook significant expansion. Production at the manufacturing facilities was impressive. The Curtiss Aeroplane and Motor Company built 233 airplanes and 914 engines at its Buffalo plant, primarily for the army and navy, and Wright Aeronautical produced 2,148 engines, the highest level of sales it had ever achieved. The Curtiss-Robertson Airplane Manufacturing Company in Saint Louis produced several hundred Curtiss Robin airplanes. The decline in sales caught the manufacturing subsidiaries off guard; by the end of the year, Curtiss-Wright had 585 unsold airplanes in inventory. As the manufacturers sold a large portion of their production to Curtiss-Wright distributors, who then held the aircraft in inventory until they could be sold, the distributors carried the burden.[11]

Although results in the final months of the year were worrisome, Keys and the other directors of Curtiss-Wright had grounds for cautious optimism. The directors had thought it prudent to charge the large development and consolidation expenses Curtiss-Wright incurred during the year directly to income to strengthen the corporation's financial position. Plans to further consolidate airplane and engine manufacturing, as well as the engineering and development departments, were well in hand with the promise of further savings from greater economies of scale. Collectively, the manufacturing subsidiaries had more than $10 million in back orders. In his first annual report to Curtiss-Wright shareholders, Keys wrote that he and the other directors were confident that they had taken all necessary steps to meet the current situation, which Keys attributed more to the need for the industry to pass through a necessary period of readjustment than to the state of the economy. Curtiss-Wright's size and important position within the industry, coupled with the projected savings in manufacturing costs from further consolidation, would ensure that the corporation would continue to prosper.[12]

In an article written in January 1930, Keys admitted his disappointment with the aviation industry's results for 1929. Neither the manufacturing business nor passenger transportation had lived up to the expectations of industry leaders. Nevertheless, in his view, the industry began 1930 in a stronger position. The consolidations in the industry and the expansion in the quantity and quality of manufacturing facilities augured well for future growth. Clearly the immediate task was to reduce the inventories of aircraft that had built up at the end of the year, but Keys did not think that this period of inventory adjustment would take long. The real challenge was to build up passenger transportation. His conclusion was that, "unless all signs fail . . . it would not be surprising to me if aviation as a whole did a great deal better in 1930 than in 1929".[13]

The condition of the American economy was the most important "sign" for the aviation industry. In the months following the stock market crash, the signals for the future direction of the economy were disturbing. The decline in industrial production continued, and more worrying, it spread to more industries. Not only production but factory payrolls and employment also showed declines.[14] Despite these signals that something was seriously wrong with the economy, most public statements from business leaders in early 1930 reflected an unshaken optimism and a belief that the decline was only temporary, but as the months wore on, the American economy sank inexorably into depression. The index of industrial production, which had peaked in June 1929, had fallen 30 points by July 1930.[15] The fall in production reflected a sharp decline in overall demand in the economy. As production fell, so did capital investment and employment, further deepening the crisis. The economy did not hit bottom until 1933; it then took five years to recover.[16]

The aviation industry had a difficult year. Military sales provided some cushion, as the army and navy had not yet reached the end of their five-year programs, but commercial sales fell sharply. Most manufacturers spent the first half of the year trying to unload their inventories of unsold airplanes built up during 1929. They slashed prices to clear out the older 1929 models and make room for sales from current production. The market for small private airplanes, on which so many manufacturers had placed their hopes, proved to be negligible. Sales to the airlines and air service operators could not fill the gap. The airlines had doubled the number of airplanes in service during 1929; 1930 saw a net gain of only 66 airplanes. Moreover, the number of air service operators fell during the year. Although the industry sold 2,324 commercial airplanes in 1930, this was not enough to clear out all the inventory left from 1929 and the inventory built up during 1930.[17]

For the Curtiss-Wright Corporation, 1930 proved to be a disaster. The company posted a net loss for the year of $9,012,919, nearly as much as its two principal subsidiaries, Curtiss Aeroplane and Motor Company and Wright Aeronautical, had earned in the previous 10 years. The year did not begin well and got steadily worse. By midyear the corporation was clearly hemorrhaging. In September, Richard Hoyt announced the half-year results; Curtiss-Wright had suffered a loss of $5,351,661.[18]

Continued military sales under the five-year programs cushioned the Curtiss Aeroplane and Motor Company from the sharp fall in commercial sales. Similarly, the Keystone Aircraft Corporation continued to produce bombers for the army, receiving contracts during the year for an additional 64 bombers.[19] However, production of single-engine cabin monoplanes, which formed the bulk of Curtiss-Wright's commercial airplane production, was hard hit. By cutting prices, Curtiss-Wright whittled down its own inventory from 585 aircraft at the beginning of the year to 151 by year's end. The decline in demand hurt the introduction of new models as well. In 1929 Curtiss-Wright had introduced the Kingbird, a small eight-passenger airliner. When production began in 1930, however, the market for this type of aircraft had evaporated. Curtiss-Wright sold a mere 12 Kingbirds, all of which went to Eastern Air Transport, which was controlled by Clement Keys. In all, Curtiss Aeroplane and Motor managed to post a net profit of $555,003 for the year.[20]

Wright Aeronautical, however, incurred a substantial loss. In expectation of the boom in aviation, Wright had nearly doubled manufacturing capacity at its Paterson engine plant. During 1930, despite strong sales to the military, Wright Aeronautical's total sales fell by nearly 50 percent, leaving the company with a large inventory of engines and parts and sizable depreciation charges on its new plant facilities. To compound its problems, Wright Aeronautical suffered a prolonged strike in the last months of the year in response to management's attempt to cut costs and improve productivity.[21] For the full year the company posted a loss of $2,198,424.[22]

While the manufacturing subsidiaries struggled to cope with the decline in demand, problems at the Curtiss-Wright Airports Corporation and the Curtiss-Wright Flying Service represented the most serious drain on the company's resources. Clement Keys's vision had been a vertically integrated group that would participate in all phases of aviation, from manufacturing airplanes, to training pilots, to running airports. With the money that had flooded into the aviation industry during 1929, the Curtiss-Wright Airports Corporation had invested heavily in airports around the country. By the end of 1930, the corporation had total assets of $26 million. Similarly, Keys had reorganized the old Curtiss Flying Service, Glenn Curtiss's original exhibition company, into the Curtiss-Wright Flying Service. With money raised from the sale of stock, Keys made substantial investments in airplanes, equipment, and personnel to provide flying training and air taxi services. At the end of 1929, the Flying Service had total assets of $10 million, with 350 airplanes in operation at 37 airports across the country. Keys was convinced that private flying by both individuals and business corporations would be a big part of the aviation boom.[23]

Despite an increase in both commercial and private flying, the investment in airports far exceeded the revenues that could be generated through tariffs on airport usage and ancillary services. Curtiss-Wright Airports Corporation could not even meet its operating costs. Even worse, the need to write off certain investments helped boost the net loss for the year to $2,247,030. The situation at Curtiss-Wright Flying Service was equally grim. Here, too, the investment in facilities and equipment far exceeded demand under the depressed market conditions. Even though the Flying Service carried nearly three times as many passengers as it had in 1929, the company suffered an operating loss of $2,104,356. Reducing the number of aircraft the company owned, as well as writing off investments in other equipment, brought the total loss to $3,597,772.[24]

Compounding the financial problems was the incredible difficulty of completing the merger between the Curtiss and Wright companies. Imposing an efficient system of administration and management on a loosely linked network of companies would have been a challenge even in the best of times. In the midst of an aviation market in steep decline, coordinating activities within the Curtiss-Wright group became not only imperative but also a far more formidable task to complete. The entire corporation suffered from a shortage of skilled managers, a recurring problem that would bedevil the company in years to come. Many of the managers within the Curtiss-Wright companies were young engineers who had unbounded enthusiasm and faith in the future of aviation but little practical business experience or managerial acumen. Curtiss-Wright's situation was precarious and required drastic action to avoid a disaster.

Glenn Curtiss did not live to learn of the magnitude of the problems confronting the company he had founded 20 years before. On 23 July 1930, he died of a pulmonary embolism two weeks after an apendectomy. He was 52 years old. In May, Curtiss had taken his last flight in an airplane when he flew a Curtiss Condor airliner down the Hudson River on the 20th anniversary of his famous Hudson River flight. The Condor was a far cry from the *Hudson Flyer.* Aviation had progressed beyond his own skills as an inventor, but without the pioneering efforts of the Wright brothers and Glenn Curtiss, American aviation would undoubtedly not have achieved its current state of advancement. Curtiss was buried in Hammondsport, close to the meadow where he had made his first flight.[25] Orville Wright was the last of the triumvirate and survived until 1948.

By mid-1930, the magnitude of the problems facing Curtiss-Wright was readily apparent. Keys and Hoyt instituted an aggressive program to liquidate excess facilities and operations and to consolidate the activities of the manufacturing units. All engine manufacturing was concentrated in the Wright Aeronautical plant at Paterson, New Jersey. Production of the Curtiss liquid-cooled engines moved from the Buffalo factory to Paterson, although the strike at the Wright plant that fall delayed the transfer and added substantially to the cost of the move. The design and construction of military aircraft shifted completely to Buffalo. The engineering facility at Garden City, Long Island, was closed at the end of the year. The Travel Air Corporation in Wichita, Kansas, which had been in the Hoyt-Wright group, and the Curtiss-Robertson Airplane Manufacturing Company in Saint Louis, Missouri, were reorganized into the Curtiss-Wright Airplane Company to concentrate on the manufacture of commercial airplanes. In addition to reducing the number of aircraft at the Curtiss-Wright Flying Service, several unprofitable operations were shut down, and greater emphasis was put on the sale of aircraft and services. At the end of the year, the directors of Curtiss-Wright set up a further contingency reserve of $6 million against the possibility of having to make further write-downs on assets of the corporation. The year 1930 ended on a note of cautious optimism. While the losses were a tremendous disappointment, both Hoyt and Keys believed that the consolidation and reorganization undertaken in the second half of the year had put the corporation in a position to take advantage of the renewed level of activity they expected for 1931.[26]

By the spring, two things had become clear. Recovery was not in sight, and the measures Keys and Hoyt had introduced were insufficient to deal with a worsening economy. The cost of operations and the carrying costs of the corporation's extensive investments simply exceeded the revenues that could be expected from the business. For the first half of the year, the corporation reported a loss of $1.4 million.[27] More drastic measures were needed, but neither Hoyt nor Keys could devote the time required to deal with the many problems confronting the corporation and manage a recovery plan. Both men had extensive commitments above and beyond their positions at Curtiss-Wright, and in the midst of an economic crisis, the calls on their time and energy were incessant. Beset with problems across the broad range of his aviation holdings, and facing mounting personal financial losses, Keys could simply not take on the full-time management of a recovery. Instead Keys and Hoyt arranged a change in management to bring in more support. On 25 June, Hoyt and Keys

Thomas Morgan.
New Jersey Aviation Hall of Fame.

announced that Thomas A. Morgan had been elected president of the Curtiss-Wright Corporation.[28] Morgan, an engineer, had been president of the Sperry Gyroscope Company when it was acquired by North American Aviation. At Keys's request, Morgan had successfully reorganized the Berliner-Joyce Aircraft Company, another North American Aviation holding. Hoyt remained chairman, and Keys became chairman of the executive committee. At the same time, Keys relinquished his position as president of Curtiss Aeroplane and Motor Company to J. A. B. Smith, who had been secretary and treasurer of the company.[29]

Morgan quickly determined that the prospects for the aviation industry looked grim. The commercial market was effectively nonexistent, with no sign of recovery to be seen anywhere. The only real market left was the military, but both the U.S. Army Air Corps and the U.S. Navy were coming to the end of their five-year expansion programs, and there was little prospect of increases in appropriations once the programs had ended.[30] In light of the depressed market conditions, Morgan realized that without a comprehensive plan and immediate action, Curtiss-Wright might not be able to survive. At that time, the Curtiss-Wright Corporation was losing money at the rate of nearly $4 million per year. Many of the subsidiaries were carrying excessive inventories, and the Curtiss-Wright Airports Corporation and the Curtiss-Wright Flying Service constituted a heavy drain on the group's resources.[31]

Morgan realized that the factor essential to Curtiss-Wright's survival was to stem the operating losses as quickly as possible. Curtiss-Wright had to scale back its operations to a level that current market conditions could sustain. Keys and Hoyt had not gone far enough; the operating units had to retrench even further. As painful as it would be, they had to eliminate excess inventories and reduce assets to more realistic levels. To implement the plan, Morgan gathered a small team of senior managers from among the group of companies: Guy Vaughan, who had become president of Wright Aeronautical in April 1930, J. A. B. Smith and Burdette Wright from the Curtiss Aeroplane and Motor Company, T. P. Wright, chief engineer and manager of the Curtiss Kenmore plant in Buffalo, J. S. Allard from the Curtiss-Wright Export Corporation, Ralph Damon from the Curtiss-Wright Airplane Company, and Charles W. Loos from the Curtiss-Wright Flying Service. Morgan and his team began the task of restoring Curtiss-Wright to profitability.[32]

The consolidation of manufacturing units was completed by the end of 1931. In Buffalo, the Curtiss Aeroplane and Motor Company concentrated all production in its Kenmore plant and closed all other facilities. The Wichita, Kansas, factory was closed, and production of commercial aircraft was concentrated in the Curtiss-Wright Airplane Company's plant at Robertson, Missouri, near Saint Louis. After the failure of the bitter strike at Wright Aeronautical, all engine production was shifted to the Paterson plant. Significantly, Wright managed to generate a profit for the year. Ralph Damon cut the operating losses at the Keystone Aircraft Corporation. Throughout the group, salaries and wages were slashed, the number of employees were reduced, and economies were instituted wherever possible. The Curtiss-Wright Flying Service sharply curtailed its activities, and Morgan appointed J. S. Allard as the new president of the company to oversee a further retrenchment. Through these and other measures, the operating loss for the group as a whole was trimmed from $6.7 million in 1930 to $1.9 million for 1931. Although additional deductions took the total loss for the year to $4.2 million, Morgan and his team were clearly making progress.[33]

The most drastic measure implemented by Morgan was an aggressive write-off of assets. At the end of the year, the directors approved a reduction in the par value of the corporation's stock to $1.00 a share, creating a surplus to absorb accumulated operating losses plus a reduction in property values of close to $20 million. Following the write-off, net plant and property assets shrank from $48 million at the end of 1930 to $21 million at the end of 1931. Most of the write-downs took place at the Curtiss-Wright Airports Corporation, which cut total assets by nearly half, recognizing that the corporation's property assets were grossly overvalued. For the Curtiss-Wright Corporation as a whole, total assets declined from $67 million at the end of 1930 to $41 million at the end of 1931.[34]

At this juncture came the surprising news that C. M. Keys was severing his connections with the Curtiss-Wright Corporation and withdrawing from the aviation industry. On 7 January 1932, Keys announced that he was resigning from all his offices, ostensibly for reasons of health. At the time, Keys was chairman or director of 16 companies in the aviation industry that were involved in manufacturing and transportation. His contributions to the development of the aviation and airline industries were substantial, not the least of which was the rescue of the Curtiss Aeroplane and Motor Corporation from certain bankruptcy after World War I. He had provided organizational and financial leadership when few businessmen showed much interest in aviation, and he was a tireless spokesman for the industry in a field of many doubters. He had achieved his own vision of creating an aviation empire to mirror that of the railroad leaders he so admired.[35]

Perhaps his very success led, in an excess of hubris, to the actions that prompted his resignation and withdrawal from the endeavor that had consumed him for more than a decade. When Keys organized North American Aviation at the end of 1928, he raised $25 million through the sale of shares in North American to invest in the stocks of aviation companies. Keys arranged for all of these transactions to flow through his own investment banking firm, C. M. Keys and Company. He further arranged for North American's excess cash to be deposited with C. M. Keys and Company in the form of a call loan. On 30 June 1929, this excess cash on deposit amounted to $8.8 million.[36]

Keys, without informing the other directors of North American, used this money for his own personal speculation in aviation stocks, earning a substantial profit for his own account. Following the stock market crash, he was apparently unable to pay back the call loans in full. This came to light in the fall of 1931 when the directors decided to write down the company's investments to reflect the fall in market values. An audit revealed that Keys owed North American $766,000 and could only provide collateral worth less than $100,000. A short sentence in the North American Aviation annual report for 1931 announced that as of 6 January 1932, Keys had resigned his position as chairman of the company. Although the true story is not known, Keys was apparently given the opportunity to withdraw with his reputation, if not his wealth, intact. The fact of his dereliction in his fiduciary responsibilities never appeared in print. Why Keys should have engaged in what was clearly an inappropriate and reprehensible activity is difficult to comprehend. On the next day, he announced his resignation, his career in ruins, his fortune all but gone. Thus, quietly and with little notice, the Keys era at Curtiss-Wright ended.[37]

As market conditions worsened during 1932, Curtiss-Wright had little alternative but to follow the trend of the market, seeking business where possible and ruthlessly cutting back where there was none. Thomas Morgan and his team continued their drastic pruning of Curtiss-Wright's operations, struggling to shrink the corporation to a level that the depressed market could sustain. Early in the year, the Curtiss-Wright Airplane Company stopped production at its Saint Louis plant and cut back operations to a bare minimum when it became apparent that there were simply no commercial sales to be had. In the spring, the Keystone Aircraft Corporation closed down; after completing its existing navy and Air Corps contracts, Keystone could not find new business. The Keystone name disappeared from the industry. Ralph Damon was promoted to president of the Curtiss-Wright Airplane Company and returned to Saint Louis.[38]

J. A. B. Smith, president of the Curtiss Aeroplane and Motor Company, worked with T. P. Wright, general manager of the Curtiss Buffalo plant, to improve the efficiency of production and reduce costs wherever possible. Under their leadership, the company renewed its development of new products, this effort having been neglected in the struggle to shrink the company's operations and cut losses. Under Guy Vaughan's management, Wright Aeronautical improved its own production and cut operating costs through a substantial reduction in excess inventories and plant; total assets shrank by 50 percent. Improved operating performance enabled Wright to devote more attention to development as well.[39]

Morgan pushed relentlessly to cut costs and excess investment throughout the corporation. During the year, the excess inventory of commercial airplanes was whittled down from 277 in January to 46 by the end of December. Despite intensive efforts to turn the problems at the Curtiss-Wright Flying Service around, the company could simply not attract sufficient business to sustain an economic level of operation. Early in the year, Morgan recommended that the company be liquidated. The board agreed, and throughout the rest of the year, Curtiss-Wright Flying Service closed down its network of operations, leaving only a few at airports owned by Curtiss-Wright. The operations of the Curtiss-Wright Airports Corporation went through a further drastic reorganization, with total company assets of $27 million shrinking to $15 million, and net losses being reduced from $2.3 million to $749,000. Total assets of the entire Curtiss-Wright Corporation again shrank dramatically, from $41 million at the end of 1931 to $29 million at the end of 1932. In a little more than two years, the apparently powerful combine that Clement Keys and Richard Hoyt had created became a shadow of the aviation empire the two men had envisioned.[40]

By the fall of 1932, Thomas Morgan felt sufficiently confident to report to Hoyt and the executive committee of the Curtiss-Wright board that the situation had stabilized and that Curtiss-Wright was out of immediate danger. Production facilities had been rationalized, and production reduced to a level the market could support. The diversification across the full spectrum of aviation activities that had been so central to Keys's vision had proved to be unsupportable in the midst of a depression. Morgan had cut back all activities that could not sustain a profit and had returned the company to its original purpose: the design and production of military aircraft and engines.

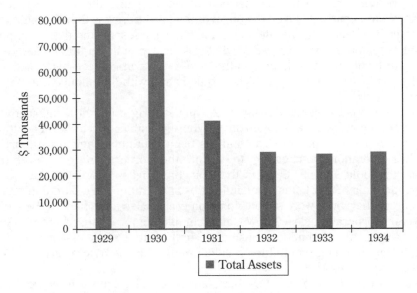

Fig. 3.   Curtiss-Wright total assets: 1929–1934

He had directed the surviving units, principally the Curtiss Aeroplane and Motor Company and Wright Aeronautical, to resume their developmental work and come up with new products that would achieve sales in what he presumed would be a difficult market for some years to come. He was not then aware of just how difficult the market would be.

The Struggle for Survival

The Curtiss Aeroplane and Motor Company and Wright Aeronautical, the two main divisions of the Curtiss-Wright Corporation, had always depended more on military sales than on the commercial market. With the commercial aircraft market in a severe depression, sales to the military became all the more important. Both Curtiss Aeroplane and Wright Aeronautical had been significant beneficiaries under the Air Corps and navy five-year expansion programs. In the difficult years following the completion of those programs, the companies' fortunes would be markedly different. The Curtiss Aeroplane and Motor Company's attempts to win business from the Air Corps during these years would meet with repeated frustration, whereas Wright Aeronautical would flourish. The technological revolution was demanding ever-increasing power from the airplane engine.

In 1930, in the middle of the expansion program, Curtiss Aeroplane held a solid position in the competition for military aircraft sales. The company sold a broad range of aircraft to both the Air Corps and the navy. Completion of the five-year programs and the deepening depression changed the competitive dynamics within the industry. Appropriations for new military aircraft were cut back as the Hoover and Roosevelt administrations sought to economize on government expenditures wherever possible.[41] Overall appropriations for the U.S. Army Air Corps and U.S. Naval aviation suffered sharp cuts and remained essentially flat from 1932 to 1935. Fewer contracts for new aircraft created intense competition for the few contracts available. What made the competition worse was rapid technological change. An airplane that might be thought superb one day could be made obsolete in a few months as the pace of change accelerated. Moreover, changing technology allowed new entrants into the military aircraft field, despite the daunting prospects. In the first half of the decade, Curtiss Aeroplane faced multiple challenges from both old and new competitors as it too struggled to cope with the change in technology.

Commercial competition, not the military, drove much of the innovation. To compete with the railroads, the airlines had to offer their customers a significant savings in time; this required faster airplanes. To improve their own profitability, the airlines needed airplanes that were more efficient, that could carry a greater weight of mail or passengers with the same amount of engine power and fuel. The airline industry thus stimulated the demand for higher performance and greater efficiency. However, as the gap in performance between the new commercial airplanes and existing military aircraft began to grow, it was clearly only a matter of time before the design revolution would shift to military aircraft. An air force consisting of elderly biplanes would be in no position to engage a force of more modern, more powerful, all-metal monoplanes. The military biplane had reached the end of its development. During the first half of the thirties, the Air Corps shifted to monoplane designs for its combat aircraft. Some of the aircraft the Air Corps accepted represented a transitional stage as aircraft designers struggled to master and incorporate innovations in their designs. With no potential conflict on the horizon in the first part of the decade, the Air Corps was perfectly willing to accept aircraft that offered only incremental increases in performance.[42] The life span of these transitional aircraft was short; within a few years of their introduction, they became obsolete. The all-metal monoplane with all the features associated with modern aircraft would emerge after the middle of the decade and would undergo progressive refinements in response to urgent demands for increased performance as the world edged again toward war.

The difficulty for Curtiss and other manufacturers was that the "state of the art" during this transitional period was often a moving target. An aircraft manufacturer has to predict what performance criteria will meet the needs of the military and then determine what design features are not only practical and economically feasible but also possible within the technology available. The combination of factors that contributed to the state of the art was changing rapidly. During the early thirties, a difference of a few months in the start of a design could have a profound impact on the final result, which in turn could mean the difference between success and failure in winning a contract.[43]

Air Corps attack aviation was the first sphere of American military aviation to accept the monoplane and give Curtiss its first and only success with the Air Corps until 1936.[44] In early 1930, Curtiss approached the Air Corps with a new all-metal monoplane attack design to replace the older Curtiss Falcon attack plane. While incorporating several new features, the Curtiss design retained a fixed landing gear and the use of external bracing common to the older biplanes. Nevertheless, the new design proved to be nearly 40 miles per hour faster than the Falcon and could carry twice the bomb load. The prototype flew in June 1931 and beat out a similar design from Fokker, winning an order for 13 service test models under the designation Y1A-8. After tests, the Air Corps placed an order for 46 aircraft in February 1933.[45] Curtiss Aeroplane delivered the 46 aircraft, designated the A-12 Shrike, during 1934, but the design failed to win any follow-on orders. A newer design from a new competitor had appeared, offering significant improvements over the A-12 just entering service. The Northrop Corporation, a subsidiary of Douglas Aircraft, had modified a commercial all-metal monoplane design into an attack aircraft. The early versions first flew in July 1933, two years after the first flight of the Curtiss attack prototype. Two years of design progress made a significant difference. The Northrop airplane was a newer, more streamlined design that gave a 30-mile-per-hour increase in speed, longer range, and a larger bomb load than the A-12 Shrike. In December 1934, Northrop won a contract for 100 A-17 attack planes, effectively shutting Curtiss out of the market.[46]

In 1931 the Air Corps began a search for an all-metal monoplane bomber design that would be a significant improvement over its standard Keystone bombers. Keystone entered the competition, but its design failed to arouse any interest, and the company ceased production. The Boeing Company developed an impressive aircraft in its XB-9, but the winner proved to be the Martin Company, which introduced the revolutionary XB-907. Martin won a contract for 48 aircraft, designated the B-10, in January 1933. The B-10 was as fast as any Air Corps fighter aircraft then in service and was the first true modern bomber. In June 1934, the Martin Company won a further contract for an additional 103 bombers.[47]

Even before the Air Corps completed the bomber competition, the need for a new fighter with the speed to catch the new generation of bombers then under development was obvious. Boeing began work on a new monoplane fighter in September 1931. Designated the XP-936, the prototype flew in March 1932. The prototype and two additional aircraft were delivered to the Air Corps for testing as the XP-26 fighter. The P-26 was an all-metal monoplane, with a fixed landing gear, open cockpit, and wire bracing reminiscent of its biplane predecessors. With the encouragement of the Air Corps, Curtiss Aeroplane designed a new monoplane fighter at the same time. The Curtiss design, the XP-934, was similar in appearance to the Boeing XP-936. Borrowing from experience with its new attack plane design, Curtiss built an all-metal monoplane with fixed landing gear, but with the innovation of an enclosed cockpit. Powered with a Curtiss Conqueror engine, the XP-934 proved to be slower and far heavier than the Boeing fighter. Boeing won the production contract to supply 111 P-26A fighters to the Air Corps.[48]

From the end of 1931 to the end of 1935, the Curtiss Aeroplane and Motor Company won only a single large production contract from the Air Corps. This lack of success was intensely frustrating for Morgan, who claimed in testimony before a House military affairs subcommittee in April 1934 that he believed the Air Corps was deliberately excluding the Curtiss Aeroplane and Motor Company from competition for new airplanes. Curtiss, Morgan maintained, was being "pushed out" for reasons he could not fathom.[49] At the same hearings, however, Morgan admitted that when he had become president of Curtiss-Wright, he had felt that the Curtiss Aeroplane and Motor Company was suffering from a lack of progress in engineering.[50] Curtiss Aeroplane was "not going ahead fast enough".[51]

The Curtiss Aeroplane and Motor Company's experience competing for Air Corps business during the first half of the decade reflects the difficulties of developing competitive products in a period of rapid technological change. In some cases, the Curtiss products were perfectly adequate, but superior designs emerged within a relatively short time. In other cases, such as the fighter contest, the Curtiss design was simply not as good as the winning design. No deliberate policy of exclusion could hide the fact that the Boeing P-26 and the Northrop A-17 were simply superior airplanes.

Curtiss Aeroplane had better luck with sales to the U.S. Navy. In the early thirties, the navy ordered small production runs of several types of fighters. The navy was more reluctant than the Air Corps to shift to monoplanes, fearing that higher monoplane landing speeds would make them unsuitable for carrier landings. Thus the navy remained with the biplane for a few years longer, which gave Curtiss an opportunity to sell developments of its existing Hawk fighter to the navy. Curtiss had been refining and developing the basic Hawk fighter for nearly a decade, using different types of engines and alterations to the fuselage to achieve improvements in performance. Curtiss had built several experimental models for the Air Corps using the Wright Cyclone radial engine in addition to the liquid-cooled Curtiss Conqueror. As a private venture with an eye to potential foreign markets, Curtiss Aeroplane had adapted the basic P-6E airframe for the Wright Cyclone engine and built a private demonstrator. Curtiss offered the demonstrator to the navy, which bought the prototype in April 1932 as the XF11C-2 and ordered a second prototype with a slightly less powerful Wright engine as the XF11C-1.[52]

The XF11C-2 proved to be a good fighter plane and a capable dive-bomber. In October the navy placed a production order with Curtiss for 28 F11C-2s; these were delivered during 1933. Curtiss took the fifth production F11C-2 and developed a retractable landing gear for the fighter, which the navy ordered under the new designation of BF2C-1 (Bomber-Fighter) to emphasize the fighter's dual role as a dive-bomber. The navy ordered 27 of the new BF2C-1 fighters in February 1934 for delivery later in the year.[53]

Through small incremental improvements, Curtiss Aeroplane had stretched the life of its Hawk fighter for a decade, but even with improvements, the Hawk was an old design. The real plum to be had was the contract to develop a replacement for the navy's standard fighter, the Boeing F4B. This went to a new competitor, the Grumman Aircraft Engineering Corporation, whose fighter designs, while still biplanes, were more advanced than the Curtiss Hawk. Whereas Curtiss adhered to fabric and metal tubing for its fighters, the Grumman XF2F had a streamlined all-metal fuselage and a more robust structure. When the navy received additional funds under an allotment from the National Industrial Recovery Act, Grumman won a contract in early 1934 for 54 of its F2F fighters. A year later, Grumman won another order for 54 of the revised F3F fighters. With the Grumman fighters in place, Curtiss had little hope of winning any further orders.[54]

Where Curtiss Aeroplane did achieve a success, and its largest contract in five years, was in a competition for an observation floatplane to serve from the navy's battleships and cruisers. The navy's specification called for a biplane design. Built to an older standard using fabric and metal tubing, the Curtiss entry beat rivals from Douglas Aircraft and the Chance Vought Division of United Aircraft and won a production order in March 1935 for 135 SOC-1 aircraft. Curtiss received two further contracts from the navy, building 258 airplanes in all.[55]

Curtiss-Wright's commercial aircraft sales remained in the doldrums. The market for small private airplanes disappeared. Sales of the original Condor airliner had been disappointing, so Curtiss Aeroplane and Motor Company set about developing an improved design that could be put on the market quickly using existing technology and design skills. When Ralph Damon, who had returned to Saint Louis as president of the Curtiss-Wright Airplane Company, heard about the new airliner, he proposed that the design effort shift to Saint Louis and production begun as soon as possible to enable the Saint Louis plant to continue operating.[56]

The new airliner, named the T-32 Condor II, featured retractable landing gear, better streamlining, and greater passenger comfort, but it was a traditional biplane design using fabric and metal tubing in its construction. The prototype first flew in January 1933 and soon won orders from Eastern Air Transport and American Airways (the predecessor of American Airlines). The Curtiss-Wright Airplane Company developed a special "sleeper" version of the Condor for American Airways, which was looking for an airplane that would offer greater comfort on long flights across the continent. American Airways ultimately bought 9 T-32 Condors and 10 of the more advanced AT-32 version. In total, the Curtiss-Wright Airplane Company sold 45 Condors to domestic and foreign airlines and to several military users.[57]

The Condor II was nothing more than a stopgap to generate quick sales and cash flow without a heavy investment. It provided a badly needed source of revenue to the Curtiss-Wright Airplane Company and prevented the Saint Louis factory from shutting down completely. But the Condor II was an anachronism from the day of its first flight and a dead end as a design. A month after the Condor II made its first flight, Boeing flew its Model 247, the first of the truly modern airliners. Seven months later, the Douglas Aircraft Company flew its DC-1, which when developed as the DC-2 became the first airliner to generate a profit simply from carrying passengers. The DC-2/DC-3 family dominated the airline market for the rest of the thirties.[58]

By 1935 the Curtiss Aeroplane and Motor company had obtained only two contracts of significant size from the military, while the Curtiss-Wright Airplane Company had the single but limited success of the Condor II. It is ironic that in this period of technological transition, the Curtiss-Wright Corporation's successes should be with airplanes that in design and construction could be said to belong to the previous era. Curtiss spent considerable time and effort designing what could be called transitional aircraft that were an attempt to bridge the biplane and monoplane eras. One could argue that the Hawk fighters were as much a stopgap as the Condor II and that they represented an attempt by a financially strapped company to win sales by squeezing a bit more performance out of an existing design at minimal expense. Given the financial problems that beset Curtiss-Wright in the early thirties, the company may in fact have had little alternative. The innovations belonged to other companies: Boeing, Douglas, Martin, and Northrop.

Only if a manufacturer had a steady flow of contracts could it maintain the research and development effort and up-to-date plant facilities and skilled staff. Before World War II, the manufacture of aircraft never achieved a level that could be called mass production, but larger contracts usually meant longer production runs and enabled a certain degree of economies of scale to be achieved.[59] Manufacturers often faced periods of feast or famine, struggling to survive between contracts. Not all firms were successful. The ideal position was to have a series of contracts from multiple sources. In part, this could be achieved by competing for contracts from the U.S. Army Air Corps and the U.S. Navy, and for multiple contracts from each service. By early 1935, the Curtiss Aeroplane and Motor Company had achieved a fair position with the navy. Although sales of the Hawk fighters had ended, Curtiss had won the SOC contract, and the navy was interested in a promising Curtiss design for a dive-bomber. What Curtiss lacked were contracts from the air corps. The alternative, which Curtiss-Wright had been pursuing with exceptional vigor, was selling airplanes abroad.

The Export Market

For certain airplane companies such as Curtiss-Wright, the export markets were to prove an invaluable cushion against the decline of sales in the United States. Exports provided an attractive alternative to aircraft sales to the American military or the commercial market. With no government limitations on profits, sales abroad were substantially more profitable than sales to the U.S. Army Air Corps or the U.S. Navy. During much of the early thirties, sales in foreign markets contributed to badly needed production volume and revenues. Moreover, foreign markets provided outlets for airplanes that failed to attract sales in the domestic market. Neither the American military nor their European counterparts were willing to allow their best aircraft to be sold abroad, and they placed restrictions on the ability of their manufacturers to sell their most advanced models to foreign air forces. Smaller countries in Latin America and Asia did not have the capability of building an indigenous aviation industry that could compete with the state of the art in Europe or America, nor could their air forces afford the most modern equipment. What these air forces needed were relatively reliable and inexpensive airplanes whose performance did not necessarily have to match that of the more advanced nations. An airplane design no longer considered suitable for a modern air force might find a home in the air arm of a smaller power.[60] Curtiss-Wright achieved substantial success in selling older but still serviceable designs to air forces in Latin America and Asia.

Curtiss-Wright had a tradition of selling airplanes in foreign markets dating back to the days of Glenn Curtiss, who had sold examples of his early pushers and seaplanes in Europe and Latin America before World War I. Clement Keys was a strong supporter of export sales and pushed the development of export markets in Europe, Latin America, and Asia. In 1923 he helped organize the Curtiss Aeroplane Export Corporation with C. W. Webster as president. Webster concentrated on Latin America, where the many small air forces offered possible sales opportunities. Competition with European manufacturers was fierce, but Curtiss won orders from the Chilean air force for the P-1 Hawk fighter and the Falcon observation plane and sold small numbers of the P-6 Hawk to the air force of the Netherlands East Indies and to Cuba. Small numbers of the Curtiss Fledgling trainer went to Brazil and Argentina.[61]

The decline in both the military and commercial markets domestically made the need for greater sales abroad imperative. Having built up a network of sales representatives in Latin America and Asia, as well as extensive contacts among the army and navy air arms in the region, Curtiss-Wright was well placed to pursue foreign sales through the renamed Curtiss-Wright Export Corporation, now led by J. S. Allard as president. In the early thirties, the prospects for selling military aircraft abroad looked promising. Several of the smaller air arms in Latin America and Asia sought to replace their twenties vintage fighters and observation aircraft. A more important stimulus to demand was armed conflict. In Latin America,

Peru had clashed with Colombia over what was called the Leticia affair, and Bolivia and Paraguay would go to battle in the Chaco War. In China the so-called Shanghai incident of 1932 demonstrated the inability of the Chinese to counter the Japanese air forces involved in the conflict and emphasized China's need to build a more modern air force.

In the Hawk fighter and the Falcon observation plane, Curtiss had airplanes that were ideally suited for smaller air forces. Both the Hawk and the Falcon were well built and capable of operating from the rugged airfields and weather conditions that characterized much of Latin America and Asia. Curtiss adopted the Wright Cyclone radial engine for both the Hawk and the Falcon, bringing not only greater reliability but also an increase in all-around performance. In early 1932, the Curtiss Aeroplane and Motor Company built a new version of the Hawk fighter, the Hawk II, designed for the export markets. At the same time, the Curtiss-Wright Airplane Company had developed a militarized version of its CW-14 light sportsplane design. Dubbed the Osprey, the CW-14B could be equipped with one fixed machine gun for the pilot and one flexible machine gun for an observer in the rear cockpit. Racks under the wings could carry several light bombs. The Osprey was a versatile aircraft that could serve as a trainer, observation or communications aircraft, and even a light attack plane. With the Hawk, Falcon, and Osprey, Curtiss-Wright could cover most of a small air force's needs.[62]

Curtiss-Wright's aggressive foreign sales effort soon began to achieve results. During 1932 the Curtiss Aeroplane and Motor Company sold 29 Hawk fighters to Bolivia, Colombia, and Turkey. The following year proved to be even better. With the Leticia border conflict between Colombia and Peru and the Chaco conflict between Bolivia and Paraguay erupting, Curtiss Aeroplane found a ready market in Latin America. During 1933 the company sold 13 Hawk fighters and 34 Falcon observation planes to Colombia, Peru, and Bolivia, and China purchased 50 Hawk fighters. In 1933 an estimated 40 percent of Curtiss Aeroplane's revenues came from foreign sales, giving the company its first profit in three years. All the Cur-

Curtiss Export Hawk II.
Bowers, *Curtiss Aircraft, 1907–1947,* 282.

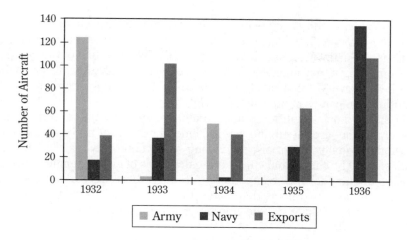

Fig. 4.   Curtiss-Wright aircraft sales: 1932–1936

tiss Aeroplane aircraft were equipped with Wright Cyclone engines, which contributed to Wright Aeronautical's profits. During the same year, the Curtiss-Wright Airplane Company sold approximately 30 CW-14s to Latin America. In all, during 1933 the Curtiss-Wright Export Corporation generated sales of $3.3 million, approximately one-third of the Curtiss-Wright Corporation's total revenues for the year.[63]

Sales of the Hawk II continued in 1934, with Colombia and Siam purchasing a dozen each. When the more advanced version of the Hawk fighter with retractable landing gear became available for export as the Hawk III, Siam bought 24 to reequip its growing air force, and in 1936 China ordered 72, the largest export order Curtiss Aeroplane had ever received. China also ordered 20 examples of the export version of the Air Corps A-12 Shrike attack plane. The Chinese orders came to more than $1.5 million, nearly 10 percent of the total sales of the entire Curtiss-Wright Corporation for 1936.[64]

The importance of export sales to the survival of the Curtiss Aeroplane and Motor Company and the contribution that foreign markets made to the Curtiss-Wright Corporation as a whole cannot be overestimated. Between 1932 and 1936, Curtiss Aeroplane sold approximately 288 airplanes abroad, roughly 40 percent of the total number of airplanes the company sold during the period. The Curtiss-Wright Airplane Company sold 78 trainers and 11 military versions of the Condor II. Many of the larger aircraft were equipped with Wright Cyclone engines. Wright Aeronautical also had substantial sales of engines abroad that were used in the aircraft of other manufacturers. Curtiss sold more Hawk fighters abroad than it did to either the U.S. Army Air Corps or the U.S. Navy. This enabled Curtiss Aeroplane to offset the decline in sales to the American military. Sales of the Hawk fighter provided a certain degree of economies of scale. Development costs of the Hawk II and III were modest, and both models were produced in large numbers that enabled Curtiss Aeroplane to enjoy greater profits per unit. The group's sales abroad were a resounding success.

The Key to Survival: Wright Aeronautical

A good case can be made for the argument that export sales saved the Curtiss Aeroplane and Motor Company; what saved Curtiss-Wright was the Wright Aeronautical Corporation.

Wright Aeronautical was without question the cornerstone of the Curtiss-Wright Corporation. Through the difficult first half of the thirties, when Thomas Morgan and his team struggled to restore Curtiss-Wright to financial health, more than half of the company's revenues came from Wright Aeronautical. Wright's consistent and growing profitability provided a bulwark that gave Morgan relief from the competitive and financial storms that were battering the other companies in the Curtiss-Wright group.

The aircraft engine business differed in several fundamental ways from the manufacture and sale of aircraft. The aircraft engine was a tremendous feat of precision engineering. It required the highest-quality materials, machining to exceptionally precise standards, and detailed engineering. The capital and engineering demands of engine manufacturing created effective barriers to entry for new competitors. Although there were a number of manufacturers of smaller engines, two firms dominated the market for the larger, more powerful engines required by the military and the commercial airlines: Pratt and Whitney and Wright Aeronautical.

Airplanes were usually designed for a specific engine that gave a specific power; while the aircraft manufacturer might offer his customer a choice of engines, aircraft engines were rarely interchangeable on the same model of airplane. A customer could order an airplane with a Pratt and Whitney engine or a Wright engine but could not in the normal course change the engine model after it was installed. Once the aircraft designer chose an engine type, that particular engine manufacturer was granted an effective monopoly for that airplane. For example, the Boeing Company built more than 550 P-12/F4B fighters for the U.S. Army Air Corps and the U.S. Navy, all of which were powered by the Pratt and Whitney Wasp engine. Being selected as the engine manufacturer on a winning design meant receiving a guaranteed revenue stream for as long as that airplane was in operation. As a result, there was fierce competition between Pratt and Whitney and Wright to have their respective engines chosen.

The aircraft engine business benefited from greater stability in both design and demand. Engine designs did not change as rapidly or as dramatically as airplane designs. The tremendous increase in engine performance during the thirties came more from incremental

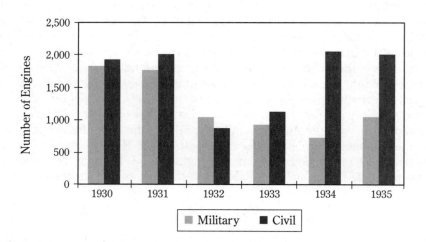

Fig. 5.   Aircraft engine production: 1930–1935

improvements and refinements of existing designs rather than a constant stream of new models. The Wright Cyclone engine had first appeared as an experimental model in the mid-twenties; the same basic engine, with double the power output, was still in demand 15 years later. The demand for aircraft engines was more stable than demand for the aircraft they powered. The wear and tear on an aircraft engine was greater than on an airplane. It was not unusual for an airliner or a military airplane to work through several sets of engines over the course of its service life. To ensure that the airplane was always available for service, the commercial or military operator had to keep spare engines on hand and substantial amounts of spare parts. Spare parts sales were estimated to be at least one-quarter of an engine manufacturer's revenues.[65]

Regular demand, limited competition, relatively lower development expenses, and annuity-like revenue streams made the aircraft engine business the most profitable sector of the aviation industry. Although profits on any particular engine contract could vary considerably, the Air Corps estimated that both Pratt and Whitney and Wright Aeronautical had obtained an average profit on Air Corps contracts of 17 percent over a period of 10 years; profits on commercial sales were higher.[66] Although a direct comparison is difficult to make because of different accounting treatments, Curtiss Aeroplane and Motor Company's return on sales between 1930 and 1936 ranged from a high of 12.3 percent to nothing when the company suffered a loss.

What Guy Vaughan inherited when he became president of Wright Aeronautical in April 1930 was a far cry from a strong, profitable business. During 1929 Wright Aeronautical had expanded production facilities at its Paterson, New Jersey, plant to more than double its yearly production capacity. When the collapse of the aviation boom left the manufacturers with extensive inventories of unsold aircraft, demand for aircraft engines evaporated. Wright Aeronautical's sales were cut in half, and the company suffered a severe loss. Vaughan instituted sharp cuts in wages along with changes in production methods to cut costs, having few other methods of quickly restoring Wright to profitability. His approach produced an angry strike by workers at the Paterson plant that lasted until April 1931.[67] At the same time, Vaughan had to oversee the transfer of all engine production within Curtiss-Wright to the Paterson plant, which meant moving the engineering staff and production tooling from the Curtiss Aeroplane plant in Buffalo to Paterson. The move turned out to be a costly and drawn-out process, but it had the benefit of adding a pool of highly qualified engineers led by Arthur Nutt, who had developed the Curtiss D-12 engine.

In spite of the financial pressure on Wright Aeronautical, Vaughan continued to develop the company's principal products, the Whirlwind series of small air-cooled radial engines, the more powerful Cyclone radial engine, and the liquid-cooled Curtiss Conqueror series, which had replaced the Curtiss D-12 as the best available liquid-cooled engine. While the Conqueror would give several more years of good service and satisfactory sales, it was clear by 1930 that the radial engine would dominate the commercial and military aircraft scene in America. Vaughan knew that Wright Aeronautical's future lay with the radial engine, and the future of the radial engine meant developing greater power.

In the early thirties, the American airlines were a greater influence on Pratt and Whitney and Wright Aeronautical than the military.[68] The airlines wanted greater power to carry more passengers and mail at lower cost. In the late twenties and early thirties, passenger volume increased dramatically, rising from 52,934 passengers in 1928 to 504,575 in 1932.[69] Airlines that had depended solely on government airmail contracts for their survival now found themselves beginning to earn a substantial amount from carrying passengers. The McNary-Watres Act of 1930, which amended the Kelly Air Mail Act of 1925, gave further impetus to the growth in passenger revenues as the main source of airline earnings. The act changed the formula for calculating airmail payments from a pound-per-mile basis to a formula based on the amount of space available in the airplane to carry mail. This provided a strong incentive for the airlines to buy larger aircraft that were suited to carrying more passengers as well.[70]

But to make the air transportation business profitable, the airlines required more efficient aircraft. Writing in early 1932, Guy Vaughan stated that the airline business could not be self-supporting until the cost of operations had been reduced to a point where the cost of air travel to the average passenger was competitive with other forms of transportion.[71] This meant improving the percentage of payload (of mail and passengers) that could be carried by an airplane of a given weight. The engine manufacturers had to improve mechanical reliability and decrease engine weight per horsepower. Vaughan commented that "there is far more reduction in overall operating costs to be gained through finding means to increase the reliable power output of a given airplane engine without materially increasing the weight than is to be gained through mere reductions in the cost of manufacture of a given engine."[72]

Greater efficiency meant more profits, and engine performance was a critical component of aircraft efficiency. The improvements in aircraft design and construction that characterized the technological revolution in aviation would have been far less effective in creating the economical airplane without the concurrent improvement in engine performance and reliability.[73] A reduction in drag meant lower fuel consumption, while higher speeds from the combination of improved aerodynamics and more powerful engines meant greater aircraft utilization. An airplane that could make three trips a day instead of two could generate that much more revenue.[74] The availability of more powerful engines enabled aircraft designers to incorporate the features of design and construction that made airplanes more efficient. Greater power also meant a larger payload, which meant more earnings. More reliable engines meant less time between engine overhauls and less money spent on spare parts and replacements. Guy Vaughan clearly understood what the airlines needed; he directed his energy to ensuring that Wright Aeronautical could provide it.

Designing a completely new engine would take time and money. The immediate solution was to step up the power of Wright's most powerful radial, the Cyclone. Vaughan set Philip Taylor, Wright Aeronautical's chief engineer, to the task. The first version of the Cyclone had a cylinder capacity of 1,750 cubic inches. To get more power, the size of the cylinders was enlarged and total capacity increased to 1,820 cubic inches. This enabled the Cyclone to generate an additional 50 horsepower taking the engine power to 575 horsepower, equal to the Pratt and Whitney Hornet. The E model Cyclone incorporated a new design for the cylinder head that improved the flow of cooling air around the cylinder. This incremental improvement reduced the cylinder head temperature, thereby reducing the stress placed on the cylinders and pistons within. Wright Aeronautical announced its new R-1820 Cyclone E model toward the end of 1930 and was rewarded with a contract from the U.S. Navy for 343 engines for the navy's patrol planes.[75]

Philip Taylor and his team at the Paterson plant did not let up in their relentless pursuit for more power from the Cyclone engine. Getting more power out of an engine meant creating more heat in the combustion process. To prevent cylinder damage, engineers had to find some means of dissipating the heat through the cylinder and out into the atmosphere. By concentrating on the design of the cylinder, and particularly on improving the method of cooling, the Wright engineers sought to squeeze more power out of the Cyclone without changing its size.[76]

Wright introduced the R-1820 Cyclone F in the summer of 1932. With a new cylinder head design and several other improvements, Wright engineers had boosted the power of the R-1820 from 575 horsepower to 700 horsepower, a significant improvement. With the higher-octane fuels that began coming into use over the next two years, the power output went up to 715 horsepower. In early 1935 Wright introduced the R-1820 Cyclone F-50 series, with the most powerful engine in this series producing 820 horsepower. By the end of the year, Wright had advanced to the R-1820 Cyclone G, which was rated at 950 horsepower. In five years Wright engineers had managed to nearly double the power of the Cyclone, a remarkable feat of engineering.

Aircraft designers were quick to take advantage of the greater power that the R-1820 Cyclone offered. Several all-metal single-engine monoplane designs emerged in the early thirties as high-speed passenger and mail planes. They were powered by the R-1820. Wright's biggest success was with the revolutionary DC-1/DC-2/DC-3 family. The availability of 700-horsepower engines such as the R-1820 and its rival, the Pratt and Whitney R-1830 Twin Wasp, enabled Donald Douglas and his team of engineers to design the DC-1 as a twin-engine airplane rather than the more complicated trimotor.[77] The Douglas Aircraft Company tested the DC-1 with both the Cyclone and the Twin Wasp, but most operators of the larger production version of the Douglas transport, the DC-2, chose the R-1820 over the Twin Wasp. When the larger DC-3 came into service, the majority of airline operators specified the R-1820, giving Wright a commanding lead in the commercial market over Pratt and Whitney.

As the military services demanded more power for their airplanes, sales of the Cyclone to the army and navy and to the export markets increased as well. The navy had chosen the Cyclone for several of its large patrol planes and for the Hawk fighters it ordered from Curtiss. The Air Corps selected the Cyclone for the first versions of the Martin B-10 bomber and for the main production version, the B-10A. The Cyclone also sold well abroad. Several foreign airlines chose the Cyclone for their DC-2s and later the DC-3, and the Martin Company selected the Cyclone for its Model 139W, the export version of the B-10 bomber, which it sold in considerable quantities. Northrop sold 49 Cyclone-powered 2E attack bombers to China, and all the Hawk and Falcon aircraft that the Curtiss Aeroplane and Motor Company sold abroad came with Wright Cyclone engines.[78]

Not all of Wright Aeronautical's engines were as successful as the Cyclone. Wright's first attempt to develop a two-row radial engine in competition with Pratt and Whitney failed. When the navy asked Pratt and Whitney to develop an engine with the same power as the larger Cyclones and Hornets but a smaller diameter to reduce drag, Pratt and Whitney designed the 14-cylinder R-1535 Twin Wasp Junior, with two rows of seven cylinders back-to-back. At the same time, Pratt and Whitney used the two-row design for the R-1830 Twin Wasp, its answer to the more powerful versions of the Cyclone. Wright then developed the R-1510 Whirlwind, a two-row engine with smaller cylinders and a smaller diameter than the Cyclone. Wright built a few examples of a slightly larger version as the R-1670, but neither engine was a success. Wright's early two-row engines were used in several prototype aircraft but never received a production contract. Although the Twin Wasp Junior did win some military contracts, neither of these Pratt and Whitney and Wright attempts to build small two-row radial engines found much favor with either the military or the airlines, who could get the same, if not more, power from the simpler and less-complicated single-row Cyclone or the larger Twin Wasp.[79]

Wright Aeronautical's financial contribution to the Curtiss-Wright Corporation during the first half of the thirties was critical to the corporation's survival. Between 1931 and 1935, Wright Aeronautical had total net profits of $2,201,525, compared to a cumulative loss at Cur-

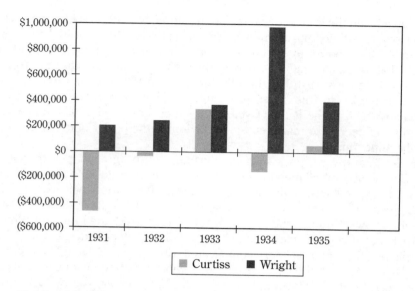

Fig. 6.   Net income: Curtiss Aeroplane versus Wright Aeronautical: 1931–1935

tiss Aeroplane and Motor Company of $374,210.[80] Wright's profits illustrate the differences between the engine and the airframe business. The stability of Wright's profitability is especially important. With one exception, once Wright Aeronautical had recovered from its overexpansion, its profits increased year by year. The contrast between the aircraft and the engine business could not have been lost on Guy Vaughan and doubtless influenced his thinking as he later contemplated Curtiss-Wright's place in post–World War II America.

The key to Wright's success was the R-1820 Cyclone. The ability of the Wright engineers to boost the power of the Cyclone enabled airplane designers to design bigger, faster, and more efficient airplanes whose success created the demand for more Cyclone engines. Wright Aeronautical's promise to Douglas Aircraft to get 1,000 horsepower out of the Cyclone engine is said to have made the Douglas DC-3 possible.[81] The Cyclone changed Wright's competitive position with Pratt and Whitney. By 1930, Pratt and Whitney had captured nearly 60 percent of the engine market with its superb Wasp and Hornet engines.[82] Wright's sales and market share rebounded during the thirties thanks to the Cyclone. For the first half of the decade, Wright's market share was equal to that of Pratt and Whitney, with each company taking around 40 percent of the market.[83] While competition remained fierce, Wright more than held its own.

What Wright Aeronautical gave the Curtiss-Wright Corporation above all was time; time to recover financially, time to dismantle the structure that Keys had built, and time to shrink the entire organization to match a scale that the market could support. By the beginning of 1935, this process was more or less complete. The subsidiary companies had rid themselves of excess inventory and plant facilities. Unprofitable operations at the Curtiss Flying Service and the Curtiss Airports Corporation had been curtailed, and the excessive investment in airport facilities were drastically reduced. More importantly, the companies in the group were devoting more effort to developing new products. Writing in the 1934 annual report, Thomas Morgan felt confident that the corporation's financial and market position would continue to improve. Curtiss-Wright had survived; now it needed to grow and regain the momentum it had lost.

Return to Growth

Richard Hoyt, chairman of the Curtiss-Wright Corporation, died suddenly on 7 March 1935.[84] On 20 March the board of directors of Curtiss-Wright elected Thomas Morgan as the new chairman; Guy Vaughan succeeded Morgan as president of the corporation. Morgan had brought Curtiss-Wright through the most difficult years of the depression and had managed the corporation's financial recovery. Vaughan's task was to restore the corporation's growth and profits.

Vaughan became president of Curtiss-Wright as the American aviation industry and the American economy had begun a slow recovery from the nadir of the depression. There were clear signs that after several years of drift and cutbacks, the army and the navy were about to embark on a modest expansion of their air arms. The dismal performance of the U.S. Army Air Corps during the airmail crisis of February to March 1934, when President Roosevelt canceled all government airmail contracts with the airlines and turned operation of the airmail over to an unprepared Air Corps, raised a storm of protest and criticism about the poor state of the Air Corps. A special investigative board under former secretary of war Newton Baker conducted a thorough review of the Air Corps, and the board's final report, issued in June 1934, recommended that the Air Corps be authorized a peacetime strength of 2,320 aircraft and additional pilots. Implementing these recommendations took time, but the Baker board signaled the beginnings of a new approach to the Air Corps. Although Air Corps appropriations were actually cut for fiscal year 1935 (June 1934 to June 1935), Congress approved an increase of $10.4 million in appropriations for fiscal year 1936 and specified that $13.7 million was to be spent on new combat aircraft.[85]

Cuts in appropriations for naval aviation had been equally harsh, and the U.S. Navy also remained below the aircraft strength planned under its five-year program. In March 1934, however, President Roosevelt signed into law the Vinson-Trammel Naval Bill, which authorized the navy to acquire additional ships, including two new aircraft carriers. The Vinson-Trammel Act also authorized the navy to acquire sufficient aircraft to equip its new carriers when they were completed. For fiscal year 1935, the navy received an increase in appropriations for naval aviation of $12.8 million and an additional $5.9 million for fiscal year 1936.[86]

These increases in appropriations for military aviation took place against a backdrop of disturbing trends abroad. The world order that had emerged out of the wreckage of World War I was crumbling. Japan's seizure of Manchuria in 1931 and its subsequent departure from the League of Nations in 1933 demonstrated that the league was powerless to prevent aggression. The league's attempt to arrange a disarmament treaty among the major powers also failed. An increasingly strident and resurgent Germany under Adolf Hitler, now chancellor, demanded not disarmament but equality with England and France. In October 1933, Germany withdrew simultaneously from the Disarmament Conference in Geneva and the league. Germany's increase in armaments during 1934 prompted England to announce its own rearmament program on 1 March 1935. Nine days later, Hermann Göring announced the existence of the Luftwaffe. France then decided to accelerate her own rearmament program. By the end of 1935, all the major powers of Europe as well as Japan had begun to rebuild their air forces. The world seemed once again to be heading for war.[87]

World rearmament meant more business for Curtiss-Wright. The threat of war has always spurred the development of military hardware. Every nation seeks to have weapons superior in quality and quantity to those of its enemies.[88] The prospect of war leads to a race to acquire the most advanced and most powerful weapons available. The emergence of the militant dictatorships in Europe and Japan sparked the accelerated development of military aviation as both the dictatorships and the democracies sought to gain a military advantage. If the major powers were building bigger and better air forces, smaller air forces around the world, who were buying Curtiss Hawks and Falcons in large numbers, would need to acquire more modern aircraft for their own protection so as not to fall too far behind.

By the mid-thirties, the all-metal monoplane was firmly established as the principal aircraft type. As always, the air forces of the world wanted bigger, better, and faster airplanes. The capabilities of one type of airplane often determined what was required in another type. Many air forces during the thirties believed that the bomber was the primary instrument of air power and that it would play the key role in future warfare. Pioneering theorists of air power developed the concept of strategic bombing, which would destroy not just military forces but a country's ability to make war. To achieve this, bombers needed to carry a greater bomb load for a greater distance and at greater speeds. To defend against the modern bomber, fighter airplanes needed to be faster, better armed, and able to climb more rapidly. Performance of other types of aircraft such as attack and observation planes had to improve as well.

Demands for increased performance put intense pressure on the manufacturers to develop new and improved military aircraft. The design and development of all-metal airframes was far more demanding than for building conventional tube-and-fabric airplanes. The pressure for better performance was relentless because as always, "superior performance . . . wins contracts".[89] Curtiss-Wright had the potential for more military and export business, but only if the products the company had to offer could meet the higher standards now required. The Hawk fighters and Falcon observation planes were selling well but were clearly at the end of their development life. If the military air forces of the world were moving to standardize on the all-metal monoplane, as the commercial airlines had already done, then Curtiss-Wright had no choice but to move in the same direction. Both the Curtiss-Aeroplane and Motor Company and the Curtiss-Wright Airplane Company had to break away from the transitional airplanes they had been building and develop more technologically advanced designs for military and commercial aircraft.

Underlying the demand for more capable aircraft was the demand for more powerful engines. Neither military nor commercial aircraft could fly faster and longer and carry greater loads without more powerful engines. The R-1820 was approaching the magic figure of 1,000 horsepower, but it could not be pushed much beyond that. Airplane designers were already thinking about larger multiengine airplanes that would require greater power than even four R-1820s could provide. In 1934 the Boeing Company had won a contract to design an experimental long-range bomber that dwarfed contemporary airplanes. During 1935 Boeing introduced its four-engine Model 299, forerunner of the great B-17 bomber, and the Martin Company produced the first of its Martin M-130 four-engine flying boats for Pan American Airways. Both Boeing and Martin were starting work on large multiengine flying boat designs that demanded more powerful engines. To a greater extent than the Curtiss Aeroplane and Motor Company, Wright Aeronautical had been at the forefront of its industry, but Wright could not afford to relax its own development effort in its competition with Pratt and Whitney. Along with Curtiss Aeroplane, Wright had to look to the next generation of engines.

As Curtiss-Wright edged toward financial recovery, the Curtiss Aeroplane and Motor Company began work on several new projects. Some work had begun even before Guy Vaughan was appointed president of the corporation. In June 1934, Ralph Damon, then president of the Curtiss-Wright Airplane Company, was appointed vice president and general manager of the Curtiss Aeroplane and Motor Company and moved to Buffalo. Damon helped oversee and manage two design initiatives for a new attack airplane and a new fighter.

One would be an innovative design but would fail to win a major order; the other would prove to be one of Curtiss Aeroplane's biggest successes.

The first of these two projects was an all-metal twin-engine attack plane that was a successor to Curtiss's own A-12 Shrike. Powered by two Wright R-1820 Cyclone engines, the Model 76 was a streamlined design with retractable landing gear that was 40 miles per hour faster than the contemporary Northrop A-17. First flown in July 1935, the Model 76 attracted the interest of the Air Corps, which purchased the prototype in November. In July 1936 the Air Corps ordered 13 service test examples as the Y1A-18, Curtiss Aeroplane's first sizable Air Corps contract since 1933. In squadron service, the A-18 proved the benefits of having two engines for greater speed, safety, and bomb load. Yet the A-18 failed to win a production order; it cost three times as much as the Northrop A-17. The Air Corps chose quantity over quality. Having chosen 100 A-17As earlier that year, it decided not to order the A-18 in quantity.[90]

The design of a new fighter plane proved to be a long, drawn-out, but ultimately far more successful saga. In the early fall of 1934, the Air Corps had sent out a circular to the aviation industry announcing a competition for a new single-seat fighter to be held in May 1935. The Air Corps wanted a significant advance over its then standard fighter, the Boeing P-26. The specifications called for a monoplane design with all-metal construction and a speed of 300 miles per hour, 70 miles an hour faster than the P-26. This represented a challenge for any aircraft designer, but one that Curtiss was keen to take on. Having lost the earlier fighter contract to Boeing and the attack aircraft contract to Northrop, Curtiss saw the fighter competition as the best opportunity to win a big Air Corps contract. To improve the company's chances, Ralph Damon hired Donovan Berlin, the former chief engineer at Northrop, who had left the firm. At Northrop, Berlin had participated in the design of the all-metal single-engine monoplanes that Northrop made famous in the early thirties. Moving to Buffalo, Berlin immediately began work on the new fighter project, which was designated Design 75.[91]

Curtiss flew the prototype of its new fighter, now called the Model 75, in May 1935. In just two years, fighter design had undergone a complete transformation. The airplanes that participated in the 1935 fighter contest had more in common with the fast commercial airliners already in service than with earlier fighter planes. Donovan Berlin designed an all-metal low-wing monoplane with a radial engine enclosed within a streamlined metal cowl. Structural support and bracing were completely internal. The new fighter featured an enclosed cockpit and retractable landing gear. The Model 75 was not a revolutionary design, but it was clearly a break with the past.

Curtiss immediately ran into problems with the experimental Wright engine it chose to power the new fighter. Fortunately, none of the other competing firms was ready either, so the Air Corps postponed the contest until August. Several competitors entered with new designs, but the real challenge came from a new firm, the Seversky Aircraft Company. Alexander P. de Seversky, a Russian émigré, had set up his company in 1931 and had recruited another Russian émigré, Alexander Kartveli, a brilliant aircraft designer. Seversky used its first design, a highly streamlined single-engine floatplane, as the basis for a single-seat fighter but had asked the Air Corps for additional time to prepare a prototype.[92]

In the interval between May and August, Curtiss Aeroplane tried several Wright engines in the Model 75, but problems with engine reliability plagued the new fighter; the Wright engines failed to provide sufficient power. For the August competition, Curtiss Aeroplane switched to a rival Pratt and Whitney engine, but even with this engine, the Model 75 was underpowered. The Air Corps favored the Seversky entry, the SEV-1XP, but when Curtiss protested about the extra time given to Seversky to modify their design, the Air Corps agreed to postpone the contest until April 1936. This gave Curtiss time to install a new engine, a more powerful Wright Cyclone, but even with the Cyclone, the Model 75 could not reach the speed Curtiss had promised to deliver. Although neither the Model 75 nor the Seversky SEV-1XP could attain the promised 300 miles per hour, Seversky proved to be the winner. In June the Air Corps awarded a production contract to Seversky for 77 P-35 aircraft, the first of the new generation of fighters.[93]

While losing the contract to Seversky was a blow, the fighter competition was not a complete failure for Curtiss. The Air Corps recognized that the Model 75, despite its engine problems, was an excellent design that was in many ways superior to the Seversky and held promise for further development. In July the Air Corps awarded Curtiss a contract for three service test aircraft, designated Y1P-36. The Air Corps directed Curtiss to use the Pratt and Whitney R-1830 Twin Wasp engine, which offered more power than the version of the Wright Cyclone Curtiss had used.[94] With world rearmament accelerating, the Air Corps would soon need more fighter aircraft. Curtiss still had a chance for an Air Corps contract.

In other areas, Vaughan's first full year as president of Curtiss-Wright proved to be a success. The navy had received authorization to acquire more aircraft to equip its newest carriers, the *Enterprise* and the *Yorktown,* and wanted a new scout-bomber type to replace older models. For several years, Curtiss had been working on a design for the navy that appeared in several different guises as a two-seat fighter and as a scout plane. Curtiss reworked the design and submitted a prototype to the navy as the XSBC-2. A slightly refined version was submitted to the navy as the XSBC-3. The navy approved the design and awarded Curtiss a contract for 83 SBC-3s in August 1936. Two months later, the navy awarded Curtiss a follow-on contract for 40 additional SOC observation planes.[95]

For Wright Aeronautical, the year proved to be a financial and technical success. The Cyclone engine sold exceptionally well; within the first six months of the year, Wright had sold more than 1,000 Cyclones.[96] In January the Air Corps awarded a contract to the Douglas Aircraft Company for 82 twin-engine B-18 bombers, derived from the Douglas DC-2 airliner and powered with the same Wright R-1820 Cyclone engine. In June the Douglas contract was increased to 132 aircraft. The Douglas contract resulted in an order for more than 600 Cyclone engines from Wright Aeronautical. At about the same time, Boeing received a contract for 13 service test examples of its new Model 299 four-engine bomber, designated Y1B-17 by the Air Corps. The company chose to replace the Pratt and Whitney Hornet engines that were on the prototype with the more powerful Cyclone in the service test aircraft. This decision had far-reaching consequences for Wright Aeronautical because those 13 Y1B-17s were the first of thousands of Cyclone-powered B-17 bombers produced in World War II.[97]

The Cyclone was generating strong commercial sales as well. The G series Cyclones now generated 1,000 horsepower for takeoff, which was ideal for the new DC-3 airliners Douglas introduced in 1936. By the end of the year, Douglas had sold 55 DC-3s to United Air Lines, TWA, American Airlines, Eastern Air Lines, and the Dutch airline, KLM. In addition, Douglas had sold eight DST sleeper versions of the DC-3 to American. All but United chose the Wright Cyclone for their DC-3s. Working closely with TWA, who wanted an engine designed specifically for the demands of the airlines, Wright engineers developed the G-100 Cyclone toward the end of 1936. The G-100 boosted the takeoff power to 1,100 horsepower. Pleased with this result, TWA placed an order for 41 DC-3s from Douglas.[98]

The pressure for more performance was relentless. Wright Aeronautical's first attempts at building twin-row engines, with two rows of cylinders back-to-back, were both failures. There had been nothing wrong in principle with the idea of using two rows of cylinders. The problem had been in using cylinders of a smaller size to reduce the drag of the engine. The idea of using a larger number of smaller-size cylinders to generate the same or greater power than the R-1820 Cyclone simply didn't work. To make the next leap in power, Wright engineers went back to the larger cylinder size of the R-1820 Cyclone, accepting the fact that while a larger engine diameter meant additional drag, greater power was the more important factor. Wright designed a new engine with two rows of seven cylinders each, with a total capacity of 2,603 cubic inches. As the R-2600, the new engine made its first test run in September 1936. Aiming at 1,500 horsepower, Wright intended the R-2600 to take over from the R-1820 Cyclone in the new large multiengine transport aircraft then on the drawing boards at Boeing and Martin.[99]

In September Vaughan began reorganizing the entire group. Since the 1929 merger, Curtiss-Wright had continued to operate as a holding company with separate subsidiaries as the operating units. Integrating the disparate parts of the group had proved to be difficult and a constant drain on the small number of experienced managers. Moreover, separate subsidiaries inevitably created duplication of effort, particularly in staff functions. During the twenties and early thirties, a number of large industrial and manufacturing companies had shifted to a multidivisional structure to improve the administration and management of their diversified operations. Vaughan wanted the parent company, the Curtiss-Wright Corporation, to have more direct control over the operations of the subsidiary companies to facilitate coordination and to promote greater efficiency.[100] A change in tax laws relating to subsidiary companies gave him the opportunity.

With the concurrence of the other directors, Vaughan set up a divisional structure. All the subsidiary companies, with the exception of Wright Aeronautical, were reorganized as separate divisions or abolished. The Curtiss Aeroplane and Motor Company became the Curtiss Aeroplane Division. The Curtiss-Wright Airplane Company of Missouri and the dormant Curtiss-Wright Airplane Company of Delaware were merged into the Saint Louis Airplane Division. The Curtiss-Wright Export Corporation became the Export Sales Division, and the Curtiss-Wright Airports Corporation became the Airports Division. For a number of years, the Aeroplane Division in Buffalo had operated a propeller department, which had pioneered many innovations in propeller design. Under the new organization, a Curtiss Propeller Division was set up to take over propeller production. The introduction of the new constant-speed propeller for both commercial and military airplanes had created a level of demand that warranted a separate organizational structure.

Vaughan took the opportunity offered by his reorganization plan to dissolve the Curtiss-Caproni Corporation, which had never been more than a legal entity. The administrative and staff functions of the subsidiaries shifted to the parent company. Through the reorganization, Vaughan simplified the corporate structure, eliminated unnecessary units, and brought about more direct reporting lines to the office of the president.[101]

Having lost the production contract to Seversky, the renamed Curtiss Aeroplane Division set to work on the three Y1P-36 aircraft the Air Corps had ordered. At the same time, and with a keen eye on the lucrative export markets, Curtiss engineers began working on an export version of the Model 75 that the company could market as a replacement for the older Hawk III fighters. Realizing that smaller air forces would require a less-complicated aircraft that would be easier to maintain, Curtiss developed the Hawk 75, which featured a fixed landing gear instead of the retractable gear on the Model 75/Y1P-36 for the Air Corps. Curtiss also realized that it would be unlikely to get approval from the U.S. government to export an airplane with the same capability as a first-line fighter in the Air Corps. Reverting to the Wright Cyclone engine, the Hawk 75 had a top speed of about 280 miles per hour. While not

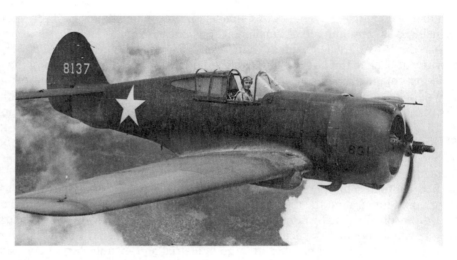

Curtiss P-36.
Courtesy of Louis Eltscher.

quite up to the fastest fighters coming into service, the Hawk 75 did offer a respectable increase in performance over the Hawk III. Using its own funds, Curtiss built a single Hawk 75 demonstrator, which had its first flight in May 1937. In August the Hawk 75 was shipped to China, where its performance, together with the outbreak of the Sino-Japanese War, led to an order for 30 Hawk 75 fighters. A second Hawk 75 demonstrator went to Argentina, which purchased 29 Hawk 75s. A third order came early in the following year from the Royal Siamese Air Force, which purchased 12. Curtiss's extensive marketing network and marketing effort, combined with its understanding of the requirements of the export markets, enabled the company to offset its initial lack of success with the Air Corps, proving once again the importance of developing multiple markets to ensure continued sales.[102]

Perseverance with the Air Corps brought success. During 1936 Congress approved an increase in the authorized strength of the Air Corps to 2,320 aircraft and increased the appropriations. The Air Corps decided to hold a second competition for fighter aircraft in May 1937. Curtiss had delivered the Y1P-36s to the Air Corps in March and April. Flight tests soon revealed that the combination of the Model 75 design with the Pratt and Whitney R-1830 engine was a winner. The Y1P-36 had a higher speed, faster rate of climb, and a higher ceiling than the P-35. Although the aircraft did not yet attain the goal of 300 miles per hour, a more powerful Pratt and Whitney engine soon to be in production would make this speed easily achievable. In tests at Wright Field, the Y1P-36 proved its clear superiority over the Seversky entry. On 7 July 1937, the Air Corps awarded Curtiss a contract worth $4.1 million for 210 P-36 fighters, the largest fighter contract since World War I.[103]

Curtiss-Wright Resurgent

At the end of 1937, the Curtiss-Wright Corporation posted sales of $24 million and a net income of $1.9 million, the highest sales and earnings figures the corporation had ever achieved. Curtiss-Wright was a far smaller and leaner company than at the time of its birth, but financially it was far stronger. Excess investment in activities unrelated to the core business had been ruthlessly cut, and Keys's grand vision was abandoned. Curtiss-Wright would not participate in all phases of aviation but would concentrate on building aircraft, engines, and propellers. Wright Aeronautical remained the cornerstone of the corporation's financial strength, contributing more than half the revenues and most of the profits. The Curtiss Aeroplane Division now had large contracts with both the U.S. Army Air Corps and the U.S. Navy, as well as a new range of products for the export market. The Saint Louis Airplane Division had begun selling a new all-metal military trainer and had begun designing a large transport that held promise, the Model 20.

Gratifying as this success must have been, Guy Vaughan sensed that it was only a beginning. The European nations were rearming at a frantic pace and on a huge scale, each rushing to achieve supremacy over its enemies. The air forces of the major powers were already getting 100 percent of the output of their aviation industries and were demanding more. Smaller nations would be forced to turn to other sources for their own rearmament. But even some of the major powers were having problems coping with the urgent demands for more planes and more engines. An ill-conceived program of nationalization had devastated the French aviation industry; French manufacturers could not supply all that the French air force needed. Vaughan saw this as an opportunity. With the level of unfilled orders growing, and in anticipation of future orders coming in, he authorized an expenditure of $1.8 million on the expansion of production facilities. For the first time since 1932, Curtiss-Wright would grow. Few then could have anticipated how fast and how far the great company would expand.

Chapter 5

Rearmament, 1938–1941

The Race for Air Supremacy

International political instability was escalating at an alarming pace by the late thirties as the European powers began their inexorable descent into the abyss of war. As late as 1935, preserving peace had seemed possible. The events of the next three years carried a clear message, however. The revisionist world powers, Germany, Italy, and Japan, preferred military force as the method for achieving political change. Moreover, the diplomatic maneuverings that eventually brought these states together in the Axis alliance only underscored the West's vulnerability, and the pathetic attempt by the Western nations to resolve the Czech crisis peacefully with the Munich agreement in the fall of 1938 only made conflict more likely.

These events emphasized the need for a rapid modernization and expansion of the British and French military establishments, especially their air forces. Smaller countries, which were the likely victims of Axis aggression, faced a similar problem and were particularly vulnerable. However, the demands being placed on the aviation industries of all these nations were greater than any of them could sustain over the short run. A comparison of the production figures for the years 1937 and 1938 gives some idea of the challenge facing the West. In those two years, France and the United Kingdom together manufactured 7,105 airplanes, whereas Germany and Italy produced 12,691.[1] These statistics must be used with caution, however, because such factors as type and quality of aircraft, and the long-term ability of the industry in each country to convert to war production after mobilization, all must be considered in assessing the overall capability of the respective air forces. The danger was nevertheless evident. If only in numbers, the Western air forces were well behind their adversaries in 1938, and time was running out as darkening war clouds loomed ever closer.

Hence the race for military supremacy was fully under way by 1938, and the Western democracies pursued rearmament with growing desperation. France, whose recently nationalized aviation industry was in complete disarray, was especially anxious. The French air force, Armee de l'Air, had suffered from years of neglect, and in an attempt to modernize it, the government had initiated a crash program to develop new aircraft designs. Unfortunately, political pressure by industry lobbyists only made matters worse. A surfeit of designs resulted, only a few of which were worthy of development. Consequently, the Armee de l'Air entered the conflict in 1939 with insufficient numbers of first-class airplanes.[2]

Great Britain's aviation industry was in better condition. A rearmament program in place since the early thirties had accelerated after 1935, and the Munich agreement, for all its political implications, gave the Royal Air Force (RAF) a year of grace to further expand and modernize its equipment and organization. Aircraft production in the United Kingdom rose to 7,940 units in 1939, up from 2,827 the previous year.[3] Moreover, much of this production was devoted to frontline aircraft. The RAF was not growing rapidly enough, however. One historian notes that its "capacity capable of meeting the maximum strategic demands was developed between 1936 and 1941."[4] Were a conflict to erupt in 1938 or 1939, air defenses would be inadequate. Help for equipping the RAF would have to come from the outside.

The Western military problem was compounded by misperceptions and propaganda. If the Germans underestimated the strength of the democracies, Great Britain and France consistently overestimated German strength.[5] The leaders of the Western powers allowed themselves to be deceived into believing that the German military machine, especially the Luftwaffe, was much more formidable than it really was. However, governments, like people, often respond to perceptions rather than the realities behind them. Moreover, the threat, if exaggerated, was real. With anxieties heightened by this psychological cat-and-mouse game, both Paris and London frantically looked westward across the Atlantic for help.

Fortunately for the democracies, the American aviation industry was able to respond. Thanks to the general recovery from the Great Depression and to rapid technological change, the industry was recovering its health. Commercial and especially military orders continued to grow. Foreign orders merely increased the pressures for further growth. The American aviation industry was about to experience a massive transformation.

At the beginning of the decade, aircraft and engine manufacturing companies more closely resembled the cottage industries of an earlier era than their contemporary counterparts in other manufacturing industries. Aviation industry products were essentially handmade items fabricated for a small domestic and foreign market. The catalyst of war brought significant changes, however, as the industry entered an era of high mass production and consumption unprecedented in its short history.

The Curtiss-Wright experience reflected these changes. One of the largest and most diverse companies within the industry, Curtiss-Wright also enjoyed certain first-mover advantages in marketing and manufacturing that put it ahead of the competition in the rearmament race. Thanks to its success with the Model 75 (H75) in the U.S. Army Air Corps fighter competition, the Curtiss Aeroplane Division was well placed to respond to the increased foreign and domestic demand. Moreover, a modification of the Model 75, the Model 81, brought improved performance that resulted in another U.S. government contract and additional foreign orders. The Model 81 became the P-40, one of the most significant fighters of World War II. Thanks to those sales, P-40 production lines were already in place by early 1940. Competitive designs were either in the prototype and testing stage or still on the drawing boards, allowing the Curtiss division to fill the void. Moreover, Wright Aeronautical's sales continued to grow rapidly.

Nevertheless, existing counterforces eventually helped to undermine Curtiss-Wright's favored position. The pressures of war would distort the normal process of aircraft design and development. As in World War I, the government was pursuing incompatible goals in its demand for ever greater quantities of the most up-to-date aircraft of increasingly higher performance. In response, manufacturers had to reconcile the mutually contradictory demands of quality and quantity. This delicate balancing act continued throughout World War II, and Curtiss-Wright failed to maintain it.

Foreign Sales

By the late thirties, foreign export sales accounted for 15 percent of the American aviation industry's total production. The chaotic state of the French aviation industry prompted that country to turn to the United States for help in equipping its Armee de l'Air. The French government ultimately sent three purchasing missions to the United States between January 1938 and September 1939. Great Britain had a purchasing mission in America as well.

All this activity resulted in a significant volume of business for American companies. In February 1939 the British increased their total aircraft order to 650. They committed more than $25 million to North American and Lockheed for aircraft and facilities. In the same month, the French government placed orders in excess of $60 million for 615 aircraft from Douglas, Curtiss, Martin, and North American. Pratt and Whitney and Wright Aeronautical also received sizable contracts for aircraft engines.[6] More was to come in the following months as the numbers steadily increased. By the end of 1939, Great Britain and France had contracted for some 2,500 aircraft from American manufacturers. These orders provided a tremendous stimulus to expansion.[7]

Curtiss-Wright was one of the first American companies to commit to heavy capital expansion. It began in 1937 with the first part of what eventually became a three-stage expansion program. This first phase commenced with the enlargement of the Kenmore plant in Buffalo. Built in 1929 for the manufacture of Curtiss engines, the plant was converted into an airframe-manufacturing facility for military aircraft soon after the Curtiss and Wright merger took place. The Kenmore facility was expanded several times between 1937 and 1940, with total floor space growing from 420,000 square feet to 665,502 square feet. Part of this expansion included enlarging the company's Propeller Division and the facilities of Wright Aeronautical as well.[8]

When the first French mission arrived in Washington, D.C., in January 1938, it had authority to negotiate the purchase of 1,000 aircraft of the types then in U.S. Army Air Corps service, plus engines, machine tools, and licenses. After examining the various aircraft models, the French representatives concluded that the only single-seat American fighter worthy of consideration was the latest Curtiss Model 75, the H75A. Negotiations with the Curtiss Aeroplane Division began in February for the purchase of 300 H75As. To their dismay, the French learned that only 100 could be produced and not before March 1939. Negotiations continued for the next several months and concluded with a contract that was signed on 13 May 1938. It contained an option for an additional 100 airframes. With French financing, production was expanded, and the first H75As arrived in France at the end of 1938. By the time war broke out in September 1939, some 200 H75As had been shipped. Subsequent deliveries were made in late 1939 and early 1940, with Great Britain receiving the remainder of the shipments after the fall of France on 22 June 1940.[9]

Although the H75A played only a marginal role in World War II, it was a very important airplane for Curtiss and the United States. Foreign and domestic sales of the Model 75 series kept the Curtiss production lines in Buffalo open; moreover, this airplane was parent to a more famous descendant, the immortal P-40.

The Model 75 was a versatile design. It had a sturdy airframe that could be uprated to meet the minimal combat requirements of modern air warfare, even though it was never able to match the performance of newer fighter aircraft soon to go into production. Curtiss engineers mated the Model 75 with a new engine, the Allison V-1710. The Allison Engineering Company, a division of General Motors, had been developing the V-1710, a liquid-cooled V-12 engine that caught the attention of the U.S. Army. The Model 75 could easily accommodate the V-1710, and the 10th production P-36 (the Air Corps' designation for the Model 75) was taken off the assembly line and mated to the Allison engine.

This airplane became the XP-40, which first flew on 14 October 1938. It won the U.S. Army fighter competition in January 1939 and a $12,872,898 order on 27 April for 524 production P-40s (Model 81). The first examples entered squadron service in July 1940, replacing the P-36 as the first-line fighter for the U.S. Army Air Corps.[10] The P-40 went on to become one of the most significant aircraft of World War II and arguably the most successful design ever produced by Curtiss-Wright.

The French, already pleased with their H75As, were anxious to get the new P-40. Passage in November, 1939 of the Fourth Neutrality Act allowed the purchase of war goods on a cash-and-carry basis. Consequently, France ordered 230 P-40s to be delivered between June and December 1940.[11] However, the French collapse on 22 June prevented those deliveries from taking place. They went to the British instead.

Curtiss-Wright had a distinct advantage in this early fighter competition. The Buffalo Kenmore factory, which had already been enlarged to accommodate the booming business in export sales of the Model 75, could easily be adapted to produce the P-40. Although the engine change required some rather complicated design adjustments, the airframe from the firewall back was essentially the same. Tooling could be readily modified for the new model, and production could be expanded very quickly.

Other manufacturers were much farther behind on the production curve with fighter aircraft. Although most of the American combat airplanes of World War II were at various stages of development by the time the XP-40 flew, full-scale mass production was several years away. Even the factories were not yet built. A comparison of the P-40 with the Lockheed P-38 is instructive. Designed as a high-altitude interceptor, the P-38 was closer to the P-40 in its development time than any of the other fighters of the new generation. The prototype P-38 had its maiden flight on 27 January 1939, the same month the XP-40 won the Air Corps fighter competition. Although superior to the Curtiss fighter in most respects, the P-38 had a long development period and would not be produced in quantity until well into the war. The newly created United States Army Air Forces (USAAF) did not begin receiving delivery of the first 30 examples until the early summer of 1941. The first P-40s had gone into service a full 12 months earlier. Lockheed's production facilities were not ready for full-scale P-38 production in 1940. The company was forced to purchase an abandoned distillery where some of the airframes were assembled.

By contrast, Curtiss-Wright could readily respond to fighter demand. Thanks to the foreign orders for the Model 75, the company had factories and assembly lines in place ready to turn out P-40s, which were in full-scale production by April 1940. In addition to the French order, the British took delivery of an additional 930 later-model P-40s in early 1941. The majority of these aircraft were sent to RAF squadrons serving in the western desert of North Africa and went into combat for the first time in the spring of 1941. The RAF flew greater numbers of P-40s in the North African campaign of 1941 to 1942 than any other type of fighter. Ultimately, 4,172 P-40s in various models flew in RAF livery.[12] As these figures suggest, Curtiss-Wright's manufacturing and marketing skills, especially in foreign sales, gave it a significant head start over the competition at the beginning of the war. Over the long run, however, that head start did the company little good because it failed to exploit this advantage.

The Challenge

Disintegrating political conditions in the late thirties highlighted one glaring fact. America's military force—especially its air arm—was completely inadequate for its combat needs. The commander of GHQ Air Force, Maj. Gen. Frank M. Andrews, described the U.S. Army Air Corps in early 1939 as a "fifth-rate air force."[13] On 1 September 1939, the day Germany invaded Poland, the Air Corps had only 2,400 combat aircraft of all types available for service, and many of them were obsolete. U.S. military intelligence estimated that the comparable figure for the Luftwaffe was 8,000. Data captured at the war's end showed the actual numbers to be even higher. Conditions were no better in the navy. First-line naval air units were still flying obsolete biplanes as late as 1939.

Nevertheless, the long drought for America's airplane builders was already coming to an end as government coffers began to open in response to deteriorating world conditions. By the fall of 1938, mobilization plans called for 12,000 combat aircraft in the first six months after mobilization day (M-day). This figure was well beyond the existing capability of the American aircraft industry. In 1938, for example, the entire industry produced just 3,623 civil and military airplanes for the total domestic market. Manufacturers were unable to give the Air Corps the detailed information it needed to meet its mobilization objectives.[14] The swiftly moving pace of international events made even the most optimistic estimates obsolete almost overnight.

In the meantime, the White House was lending its prestige to the push for an expanded Air Corps. On 12 January 1939, President Roosevelt requested $300 million for the manufacture of 3,000 warplanes. Congress responded on 3 April by authorizing the creation of an air force "not to exceed six thousand serviceable airplanes."[15] The U.S. Army Air Corps then initiated a plan of expansion calling for a maximum of 5,500 airplanes by 1 July 1941. Orders for aircraft began immediately and culminated on 10 August with contracts amounting to $86 million. It was "the largest single day of business in the history of the industry up to that time."[16]

Yet the full scope of military demand had hardly been reached. The Nazi conquests in 1939 and 1940 sent American military leaders into a mad scramble to revise obsolete defense programs. President Roosevelt went before Congress on 16 May 1940 and made a dramatic appeal for weapons, including 50,000 airplanes per year. This figure was roughly equal to the United States' entire aircraft production since the Wright brothers' first flight in 1903. Congress, shaken by the events in Europe, overcame many of its isolationist inhibitions and responded to the president's call by voting the largest peacetime military budget in history: $5 billion for direct defense purchases plus an additional $13 billion for future construction contracts. The stage was now set for the expansion of America's aircraft industry and the creation of the "Arsenal of Democracy." Aircraft production methods would have to be significantly revamped before this arsenal could become truly effective, however.

Since the beginning of the air age, aircraft manufacturing had been based on low-volume production with a small investment in tooling, all of which resulted in a high unit cost. The business of building airplanes had been a "job shop" process in which airframes were fabricated in a piecemeal manner. The products were essentially handmade and were manufactured in "batches" or "lots." Parts usually were not interchangeable and required much hand finishing, making the production process highly labor-intensive but demanding a relatively small capital investment. Although job shop methods were well suited to the low volume of production that prevailed up to that time, wartime demands made them wholly inadequate. High-volume mass production was now essential. The industry faced a herculean challenge.

A delicate balance between quantity and quality had to be maintained in aircraft production during wartime. The development of superior aircraft required design fluidity, whereas mass production demanded design stability. Quantity and quality in this context were mutually exclusive goals, as the experience of World War I had already demonstrated. Attempts to freeze production of a particular aircraft model at a time of rapid technological change could lead to disaster if a large quantity of obsolete and useless aircraft was turned out. The manner in which this trade-off was addressed could mean the difference between victory and defeat.[17]

Despite mounting pressures, industry was reluctant to change. It feared overexpansion. Memories of the post–World War I depression and the collapse of the Lindbergh boom in the early thirties haunted many aviation leaders. The volatility of international politics also created many uncertainties. A dramatic improvement in the prospects of peace could evaporate the market for military airplanes and engines overnight. Following a rapid buildup, the aviation business would be facing yet another disaster. Consequently, expansion came slowly at first, and when it did come, the stimulus was usually from foreign military orders. In effect, foreign governments financed much of the American aviation industry's prewar buildup. Otherwise, additions to plant capacity took place "only when necessary and frequently were paid for out of operating profits."[18]

Unfortunately, operating profits in the thirties were slim, contributing to a shortage of money capital. Although net profits rose steadily for the 18 top manufacturers from 1935 to 1938, the figures are somewhat deceptive. Corporate earnings of Curtiss-Wright and United Aircraft were part of that total figure. The profits of these two industry giants included sales of engines and propellers as well as airframes, thus distorting the picture somewhat. Furthermore, this was the era of the technological revolution that transformed aircraft design and structures. The costs of research and development that spawned this revolution were very high and were paid out of often meager profits. The low level of production that was typical for the period further narrowed the profit base and left little for capital expansion.

Expansion required infusions of money capital, but long-term borrowing for capital expansion was not generally a part of aviation's financial picture. The reason for this was simple: such a commitment would require fixed-interest charges, which would in turn substantially increase operating costs. The uncertain nature of the aviation market made this alternative an unappetizing prospect to airframe manufacturers. Consequently, the aviation industry acquired little funded debt before World War II. One of the few exceptions was Curtiss-Wright, which had acquired a "heavy burden" of funded debt brought on by the 1929 merger and the other activities of Clement Keys. However, thanks largely to the efforts of Thomas Morgan, the company was far stronger by 1939 than it had been just a few years earlier.

The third source of money capital was the stock market, but again there were serious disadvantages. For one thing, the sale of stock diluted managerial control of the company, and most industry leaders disliked this idea. At the time, the aviation business was still controlled by a relatively small number of pioneers who had a proprietary interest in their companies. Moreover, stockholders are interested in dividends, which require occasional profits. However, profits had been scarce in the industry for some time, making the stock market an unreliable source of capital.[19] The problem of managerial control versus stockholder interests would come back to haunt Curtiss-Wright shortly after World War II.

There were other investment deterrents as well. Several manufacturers such as Curtiss-Wright had become heavily overcapitalized as a consequence of the short-lived Lindbergh boom. This lowered their earnings potential and diminished their appeal to investors. Additional factors such as the rapid evolution of aircraft design and the low level of production reduced the percentage of profits and made investment in aviation manufacturing a less than appealing prospect. A 1937 publication suggested that owing to the unsettled nature of the aviation business, investors were "unwise to take a long-term viewpoint with regard to the purchase of aviation stocks."[20]

Guy Vaughan was especially sensitive to the many problems of financing and expansion, having ridden the aviation roller coaster since World War I. Even during the unprecedented prosperity that was to come with World War II, he never entirely escaped the fear of yet another collapse of the aviation market once the war was over. This fear was to have a significant impact on his planning for Curtiss-Wright in the postwar world. His company was one of the few to enlarge and improve its existing facilities before 1939, but the expansion took place largely because of secure foreign military orders. Vaughan's contract policy, from which he seldom deviated, called for "cash up front."[21]

Despite the many difficulties of financing capital expansion, the major companies, Curtiss-Wright included, did manage to raise a total of $30 million in new capital through stock offerings between 1933 and 1939.[22] Nevertheless, speculation, rather than investment, provided the inducement for these purchases. Volatility and instability, always a part of the aviation business, characterized the industry on the eve of World War II. Hence an adequate response by the industry to the impending war emergency required a direct investment in new plants and equipment by the U.S. government.

By 1940, the pressures for additional expansion were becoming irresistible. President Roosevelt's call for 50,000 airplanes per year changed everything. Job shop practices were increasingly discarded as new high-speed, labor-saving machinery, which had appeared several years earlier, proliferated. Assembly line techniques used in other industries—called "line production"—were applied to aircraft manufacturing. By 1944 most aircraft and engine production was organized into high-volume mass production.[23] Thanks to Mars and his insatiable demand for the tools of his trade, the mass market for airplanes had arrived at long last. Whether it would continue after the war's end remained the nagging question.

Although reorganizing production methods helped to meet the wartime boom, existing facilities could be enlarged only so much. New productive capacity was needed by 1940. Of several options available, the three most promising were new plant construction by the companies themselves, subcontracting, and licensing. The first option had the advantage of permitting direct company control. The drawback was the danger that company resources might become seriously overextended, especially if saddled with excess plant capacity once hostilities ceased. The second and third possibilities avoided the pitfalls of the first but generated their own set of problems. Aircraft and engine manufacturers feared that subcontracting and licensing would provide a basis for new competition once the war was over. Many of the firms outside the industry also lacked the requisite skills and facilities to perform the work. Manufacturers such as Curtiss-Wright thus opted for new plant construction as a better alternative. Only about 35 percent of the airframe weight produced during World War II came from subcontractors, and only 10 percent from licensees.

Although the industry had been either unwilling or unable to finance its own expansion in the late thirties without outside help, this state of affairs was beginning to change. By the end of 1940, the aircraft companies had spent $83 million of their own money on new plants and equipment. The British government contributed an additional $74 million. Nevertheless, the seemingly limitless demand for war goods exceeded the financial resources of both the industry and foreign governments. France had been defeated in June and was now out of the war. Great Britain was at the end of its financial tether. Its gold reserves were exhausted, and it could no longer meet the demands of the cash-and-carry provision under existing U.S. neutrality legislation. In January 1941, the United States Congress began debating the Lend-Lease bill, which would provide the means for Great Britain and the other allies to secure access to the American productive cornucopia. The time for the U.S. federal government to provide direct financial aid to the industry had arrived.[24]

The Response

Existing Curtiss-Wright facilities had been enlarged to their limits by 1940, and new construction was necessary to accommodate the increasing numbers of war-driven foreign and domestic orders. The second phase of the company's expansion began in November 1940 when it launched a dramatic construction program that ultimately increased its total plant capacity ten-fold. This phase was part of an industry-wide expansion effort in which the seven major airframe manufacturers—Curtiss-Wright, Douglas, Consolidated, Boeing, Martin, Lockheed, and North American—enlarged their combined floor space from some 8 million to more than 18 million square feet at an estimated cost of $83,082,000. Financing was provided by the Defense Plant Corporation, a subsidiary of the federal government's Reconstruction Finance Corporation, which built new facilities and then leased them to manufacturers.

The Curtiss-Wright expansion was the largest of the seven, some 3 million square feet. Three cities—Buffalo, Columbus, and Saint Louis—were chosen as the new factory sites, reflecting a government-inspired dispersal policy for aircraft manufacturing facilities. Many older factories were concentrated on the east and west coasts, supposedly making them vulnerable to enemy attack. Another obvious benefit of this policy was a wider distribution of government largesse to various communities throughout the hinterland. Considerable political pressure was exerted by congressional delegations and local authorities to bring these facilities to their respective communities. The Columbus, Ohio, Chamber of Commerce, for example, is said to have "lobbied hard to bring one of the new airplane factories to Columbus."[25]

Buffalo and Saint Louis were logical sites for Curtiss-Wright's expansion, since they were well inland and the company already had factories in those two cities. Labor shortages required a third city, and Columbus was the choice. Located almost on a direct line about halfway between the other two cities, Columbus was also not far from Lockland, Ohio, a northern suburb of Cincinnati, where a large engine plant was under construction for Wright Aeronautical. Engines manufactured at Lockland could be readily shipped the 100 or so miles to the new aircraft factory at Columbus and installed in the airframes going down the assembly line there.[26]

The first ground-breaking ceremonies took place in Buffalo on 9 November. The factory was built on a 124-acre site adjacent to the municipal airport along Genesee Street in the Buffalo suburb of Cheektowaga. It began operating within 193 days and was formally dedicated on 14 August 1941. Officially listed as "Plant #2," it was also variously known as the airport plant and the Genesee Street plant.[27] The original Curtiss-Robertson factory at Lambert Field, Saint Louis, was the site of the second ground-breaking ceremony on 19 November. The new plant was literally built around the old one, which was razed after the new factory was half built. Construction was planned so that all of the departments could be moved into the first half of the new building before the old one was dismantled.[28] The third ground breaking took place in Columbus on 28 November. The new factory was located on an 85-acre site at the southwest corner of the Port Columbus airport. Construction began on 20 January 1941, and on 16 June parts production commenced in the completed half of the building. Full production got under way just 319 days after construction had started. A transition team comprising management, engineering, and flight test personnel came from Buffalo to assist in bringing the Columbus plant to full operational status. It opened officially on 4 December 1941.[29] This factory became the manufacturing center for Curtiss naval aircraft in World War II.

By the time construction on these three factories was completed in 1941, total plant capacity for the company's airframe manufacturing facilities had increased from 1,140,508 square feet to 4,264,410 square feet. These facilities were equipped with the latest technological innovations to enhance the mass production of airplanes and were modern in every sense of the word.

The ground-breaking ceremonies held in each city were elaborate affairs and were attended by prominent civic and national officials. Civic interest ran high; not only did this expansion contribute significantly to the military preparedness program, but it also gave a tremendous boost to the local economies. The initial payroll for the two Buffalo factories alone was increased to 22,500 employees, giving this city of 630,000 a ratio of one Curtiss-Wright employee for every 28 Buffalonians. Employment in Columbus and Saint Louis totaled another 22,500 in the first year of operation. The workforce at Columbus, the smallest of the three plants, would increase to almost 25,000 by February 1944. In addition, the government spent more than $30 million in Columbus alone for plant expansion during World War II, much of it going into the local economy. In dollar terms, the total payroll for the combined plants in all three cities in this early period was an estimated $1.5 million per week. By war's end, Curtiss-Wright employed more than 180,000 workers in its many factories, making it a major element in the economic health of these communities.[30]

The construction of the three new aircraft manufacturing plants was accompanied by a reorganization of the corporation's aircraft manufacturing operations. In June 1940, the Saint Louis Airplane Division and the Curtiss Aeroplane Division were combined into one administrative unit known as the Airplane Division of the Curtiss-Wright Corporation. Burdette S. Wright, who had been head of the Buffalo subsidiary since 1935, was named vice president and general manager. The Columbus facility was subsequently added as the third branch of the division; a fourth branch, an assembly plant at Louisville, Kentucky, was built in 1942.[31] The company made these organizational changes in an attempt to improve managerial efficiency.

The three aircraft factories erected in 1941 were just a portion of Curtiss-Wright's second phase of expansion. Along with the rapid growth of airframe manufacturing after several years in the doldrums came a similar recovery in the aircraft engine business. Two developments provided the stimulus for engine production in the late thirties. The first was a significant increase in commercial transcontinental air travel and a modest growth of transoceanic flying. The new multiengine airliners that flew these routes required reliable power plants. Wright Aeronautical stood ready to provide them. The second factor was the deteriorating international political scene. Foreign demand for airframes was matched by a similar call for engines. As early as 1938, demand for engines necessitated a $1.35 million expansion of the Paterson factory, which resulted in a nine-fold increase in its size compared to a decade earlier. By 1939 the entire output of the two largest aircraft engine manufacturers, Pratt and Whitney and Wright Aeronautical, was some 400 units per month. With delivery of the H75s to the Armee de l'Air delayed by lack of engines, the French Air Ministry ordered the third French purchasing mission in the United States to finance a doubling of engine output from the two companies.

Both Curtiss-Wright and Pratt and Whitney feared that existing neutrality legislation could force an abrupt termination of foreign purchases and insisted that France and Great Britain underwrite the costs of this expansion. The British refused, but the French government agreed because of the desperate state of its air defenses. This financing represented an investment of $5 million to each company. Foreign investment capital was helping to finance the expansion of the American aviation industry at no cost to the American taxpayer.[32]

Growing commercial and military demand in the late thirties had obliged Wright Aeronautical to operate its existing facilities at peak capacity by early 1939. The outbreak of war on 1 September had caused a sudden demand for even more engines. The company needed more plant capacity. Consequently, it enlarged the original Paterson plant, built a new factory, and took over three former silk mills, all within the Paterson area, and refurbished them for engine manufacturing. Additionally, a magnesium foundry was built in nearby Fair Lawn, New Jersey.

Another expansion of Wright Aeronautical took place in 1941 with the construction of a new engine factory in the Cincinnati suburb of Lockland, Ohio, as part of the second-phase expansion program. The government authorized this plant after finding Wright Aeronautical adamant in its desire to retain control over final engine assembly. The company was willing to expand subcontracting but was reluctant to grant licenses for the manufacture of complete engines. Nevertheless, the burdens of wartime manufacturing eventually forced Wright Aeronautical to grant licenses.

The Lockland factory added 2,120,000 square feet to Wright Aeronautical's plant capacity. At the time of its completion, this building reputedly was America's largest single-story structure. Further expansion would come to Wright Aeronautical with the completion of the engine plant in Wood-Ridge, New Jersey, in 1942.[33]

The Curtiss Propeller Division, established in Buffalo in 1937, moved to Clifton, New Jersey, in August 1938. A year later, the Clifton plant was enlarged as part of the company's first-phase expansion program. The Propeller Division expanded again on 1 November 1939 when it acquired the propeller blade business of the Pittsburgh Screw and Bolt Corporation. Still further expansion began on 8 July 1940 with ground-breaking ceremonies for a factory in nearby Caldwell, New Jersey, formally dedicated on 19 April 1941. A fourth propeller plant in Indianapolis was opened in December 1940, and a fifth plant was built in Beaver, Pennsylvania, in 1941. These additions helped to establish the Curtiss Propeller Division of Curtiss-Wright as one of the dominant producers of aircraft propellers in World War II.[34]

Within the space of two years, the total plant capacity of the Curtiss-Wright Corporation had increased more than six-fold. On 1 September 1939, the date World War II began, the company had four factories for aircraft, engine, and propeller production, one each in Buffalo, Saint Louis, Paterson, and Clifton. Combined floor space was 1.7 million square feet, and employment numbered some 8,500 workers. By October 1941, 15 factories, comprising a total of 11 million square feet, were encompassed within the Curtiss-Wright empire, and 50,000 workers were on the payroll. Corporation spokesmen claimed that these facilities were greater than those of the entire American aircraft industry just two years earlier. This dramatic expansion reputedly made the Curtiss-Wright Corporation the largest manufacturer of aviation products in the nation and exemplified the changes that were transforming the entire aviation industry from a series of small cottagelike enterprises into industrial colossi.[35]

Like the rest of the industry, Curtiss-Wright understandably was now going for all the business it could get. Memories of the lean years less than a decade old were still vivid. Orders were hard to turn down, and by the end of 1941, they were coming thick and fast. The comparative yearly figures for the dollar value of the company's consolidated shipments gives an idea of the magnitude of the changes that were taking place. In 1938 Curtiss-Wright shipped close to $35 million worth of finished products. By 1940 that figure had jumped to $135 million, and by the end of 1941, it was almost $375 million. Airframe production for the industry gives a similar picture. In 1939 the total number of airframes produced by the American aviation industry was 5,856. In the next year, that figure more than doubled to over

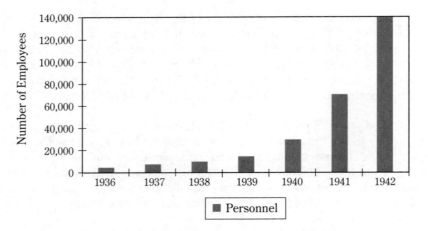

Fig. 7.   Curtiss-Wright: increase in personnel, 1936–1942

12,800, and in 1941 it jumped to more than 26,000. By the fall of 1941, the total backlog of orders on the books of aviation manufacturers was reported at $6 billion, of which $1 billion was on the books of Curtiss-Wright. It was just the beginning. In January 1942, President Roosevelt raised the production figure to 60,000 for that year and to 125,000 for 1943. Ultimately, the American aircraft industry produced almost 300,000 airplanes between July 1940 and August 1945.[36]

By the end of 1941, Curtiss-Wright was fully committed to the war effort. The Airplane Division was pursuing a host of projects. In fact, it seemed to be going in every direction at once to secure all the government contracts it could lay its hands on. P-40 production continued unabated as the design was steadily improved in response to combat experience. A variety of new designs, including trainers, scout and observation aircraft, a twin-engine transport, a dive-bomber, and several experimental fighters (among which was an unorthodox

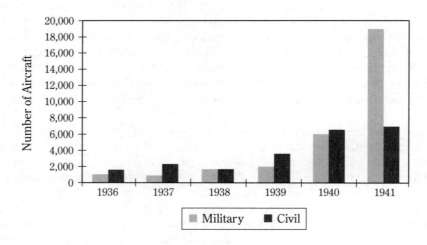

Fig. 8.   Aircraft production: 1936–1941

design with its wing and engine in the rear), were in various stages of development for the army and navy. None of the fighters was good enough to secure a production contract, however.

The two most successful of these designs were the twin-engine transport that became the C-46 and the dive-bomber that was given the navy designation SB2C. The C-46 was a military adaptation of the Model 20 commercial transport that had been under development at the Saint Louis plant since 1936. The SB2C story began in 1938 when the U.S. Navy's Bureau of Aeronautics invited American aircraft manufacturers to submit proposals in a design competition for a new dual-purpose scout and dive-bomber to replace the earlier generation of scout bombers then in service. The Curtiss design eventually won the competition, and a final contract to develop a prototype was signed on 15 May 1939. The new airplane became the SB2C (Scout Bomber, second type, Curtiss) and was given the name Helldiver.[37] Like many designs of that era, the urgency of war brought these two airplanes into production before they were ready. The resulting problems were to bring considerable distress and embarrassment to Curtiss-Wright, as well as to the government, before the two airplanes achieved operational success.

By the time America entered World War II, Wright Aeronautical was fully committed to developing and producing its three primary wartime engines: the Cyclone R-1820, which had been under continuous development since the mid-twenties; the R-2600, which first appeared in 1936; and the biggest and most powerful reciprocating engine ever built by Wright, the massive R-3350, which had been introduced in 1937.[38] The origins of the R-3350 can be traced to four experimental aircraft under development by the end of 1941. They were an army bomber and three navy flying boats. All were very large multiengine aircraft, and all required very powerful engines. The Wright R-3350, which had been undergoing tests since 1936, was a logical choice for these giants. At the time, it had the largest displacement of any engine then under development, and it had a good growth potential.

In the meantime, strategic bombing had become a central feature of Air Corps doctrine. Plans being developed in 1939 and 1940 called for a new "superbomber" with a range and payload exceeding that of the bombers then entering Air Corps service. Specifications for such an airplane were drawn up by the Air Corps and distributed to the industry in January 1940. Of the four "superbombers" initially proposed, only two, the Boeing B-29 and the Consolidated (Convair) B-32, reached production. The B-29 was clearly the superior design, and Boeing was awarded a major contract in September 1941 to manufacture 250 production units. Contracts for 1,499 additional airframes were signed in the months following Pearl Harbor.

The Wright R-3350 engine was chosen as the power plant for the new bomber. Consequently, Wright Aeronautical received a contract, signed on 15 April 1941, for more than 30,000 fully tested and operational R-3350 engines on a greatly accelerated production schedule. The engine was to be manufactured at the new Lockland, Ohio, plant.[39] Regrettably, this engine was destined to become one of Curtiss-Wright's most controversial products of World War II. Like the SB2C and the C-46, the R-3350 entered production prematurely and created massive headaches for Wright Aeronautical.

The Pitfalls of Wartime Production

The years following Pearl Harbor revealed that the rapid expansion of the American aviation industry was not a trouble-free endeavor. In the case of Curtiss-Wright, the war would create a manufacturing empire but in the process would also stretch the company's managerial, engineering, and production resources to the limit and beyond. One of the greatest challenges facing Curtiss-Wright and its competitors as they pushed production to unprecedented levels was the preservation of a technological edge in product performance. They had to reconcile high-volume production with a rapid rate of technological change. Some companies responded quite well; others were less successful. In the case of Curtiss-Wright, government demands for quantity would induce the Airplane Division to keep the P-40 in production until November 1944. Yet the need for ever better performance would prompt the division to devote scarce company resources to incremental design improvements on the P-40 while working constantly to produce a worthy successor. Although the P-40's performance would improve, the search for a successor would fail.

Was there a connection between continued P-40 production and the failure to produce a second-generation fighter? Certainly, the variety of new fighter designs that appeared at Curtiss would indicate that this was not necessarily the case. Nevertheless, the record of the Airplane Division during World War II clearly shows that something was wrong. Although the degree to which continued concentration on P-40 production hindered the development of a more successful fighter design may never be known, what is known is that the Airplane Division consistently failed to get its new designs "right."

The highly fluid state of aircraft design only compounded the industry's wartime problems. The half decade after 1938 was a time when combat experience could change military requirements almost literally overnight. This could work against manufacturers who would be the first to design an airplane to existing specifications only to see those specifications change abruptly. The end result would be wasted time and resources on an obsolete airplane. Curtiss-Wright had encountered the problem of rapid design obsolescence in the early thirties and would face it again on several occasions in World War II. A classic example was the O-52, a two-seat heavy observation airplane that first flew in 1941. Overtaken by the rapidly evolving demands of modern warfare, the O-52 was obsolete practically from its inception. The mission for which it was conceived no longer existed by the time it was available. There was nothing wrong with the airplane itself; it simply lacked a useful function. The O-52 has been accurately described as the last of a breed.[40] There are times when being a close second is preferable to being first.

The proliferation of design projects at the Airplane Division could only exacerbate Curtiss-Wright's problems. The company had only a finite number of personnel such as managers, engineers, and test pilots, and a finite amount of financial and material resources. Most important, it had only a finite amount of that most precious of all commodities, time. The great corporation had a full plate when America entered World War II. It was in fact too full. Curtiss-Wright very quickly became overextended with its many commitments. Too many projects, from airplanes to propellers to engines, were being pursued by corporate resources that were too limited. Ultimately, those commitments exceeded the great company's ability to fulfill them. The seeds of future trouble were being sewn during this period of rapid expansion, 1938 to 1941.

Chapter 6

War Production, 1942–1945

The Price of Success

World War II created the mass market for aviation products that took the industry out of the job shop era and into the age of high-volume production. The Curtiss-Wright Corporation was one of the first companies to move into the new age. Enjoying the first-mover advantages conferred by the P-36 and P-40 fighters and bolstered by sales of the Cyclone engines, Curtiss-Wright became one of the most successful producers of aviation products in World War II.

Unfortunately, success exacted its price. As long as the circumstances of war forced the Allied powers to concentrate on numbers instead of performance in their aircraft purchases, the Curtiss-Wright Airplane Division remained a prime aircraft manufacturer. By 1943, however, the equation was changing. The tide of battle was shifting against the Axis, and the "Arsenal of Democracy" was in high gear. America and its allies could now afford the luxury of demanding both quality and quantity. Curtiss-Wright could not meet the challenge. The newer Curtiss fighters were not competitive, and the Airplane Division began to slip badly.

The quality issue affected the company in yet another way. Like the rest of the American aviation industry, Curtiss-Wright was under considerable governmental pressure to pursue the development of its new products while maintaining a high level of current production, especially of the P-40 and the R-1820 and R-2600 engines. The company's most promising new projects, the SB2C dive-bomber, the C-46 cargo transport, and the R-3350 engine, represented the latest in technological refinement and showed great promise. But time was needed to fulfill that promise. Additional testing and development was necessary before they would be ready for mass production and combat operations. Yet the government's search for a qualitative edge in military hardware led to quantity orders for all three products before 7 December 1941 and before they had been properly developed. The problems that resulted from this action were not fully corrected until late in the war.

Overexpansion of a company already very large and diverse also took its toll. Both management and engineering talent were stretched thin and weakened by wartime demands. Company policy only deepened this problem. Unwilling to create competition for itself after the war and unsure of the quality of products manufactured by licensees, Curtiss-Wright chose to enlarge its own production facilities in response to the increasing number of war contracts. This course of action was a mistake. Neither the management nor the engineering staff could keep up with the crushing workload. A depleted talent pool industry-wide left Curtiss-Wright unable to correct the problem by hiring additional personnel. Thus a series of wartime reverses dissipated those first-mover advantages enjoyed in 1940, and the corporate giant never recovered its equilibrium. By 1943, there were clear signs that Curtiss-Wright was faltering.

The Airplane Division's Contribution to Victory: The P-40

The attack on Pearl Harbor came at a terrible time for America's defense industries because the initial rearmament program had not yet been completed. Although new war plants had been built, none of those authorized after June 1940 to manufacture combat aircraft had produced a single airplane by 7 December 1941. Full production would not be reached until 1943. Conversion of existing facilities was still unfinished as well. The prospect of a full-scale war on two fronts made existing plans dangerously deficient, and production goals were revised sharply upward.[1] Government officials at all levels appealed for increased production.

In the aftermath of the Japanese attack, the government authorized construction of additional aircraft plant capacity. Six new aircraft assembly plants were contracted with Bell, Curtiss-Wright, Douglas, the Fisher Body Division of General Motors, North American, and Republic, all within two weeks of Pearl Harbor. In all, "new [plant] construction authorized (for the most part in the first four months after Pearl Harbor) actually exceeded the facilities provided during the previous year."[2] The Curtiss-Wright airframe assembly plant at Louisville, Kentucky, and the massive engine plant at Wood-Ridge, New Jersey, were both built at this time. The Lockland, Ohio, engine plant was enlarged as well. This construction represented the third and final phase of Curtiss-Wright's World War II expansion program, the first two phases having been completed before Pearl Harbor.[3]

As these new facilities became operational, the American aviation industry moved quickly into high-volume production of the most advanced models of aircraft and engines. At the same time, production of existing models had to be continued to meet immediate combat needs. The quantity-quality pas de deux continued.

A fuller understanding of the difficulties facing the industry at the beginning of 1942 can be reached by considering the time constraints under which the manufacturers were working as they moved to enlarge their productive capability. For example, the time lag between ground breaking and full production for a new aircraft assembly plant might be as much as three and a half years. The average elapsed time was 31 months, of which 18 were necessary to bring the first production model through the line. It took an overall average of 21 months to expand the production of an existing aircraft assembly plant, and 28 months to change from one type of aircraft to another. The actual time lost was normally much less than 28 months because the new model was gradually brought on-line as the older one was phased out.[4]

In light of these figures, it is small wonder that the U.S. Army Air Forces (USAAF) turned to Curtiss-Wright for P-40s, which had seen extensive combat by early 1942. Comparative production figures indicate the importance of the Curtiss fighter to the Allied forces. In 1940, for example, 778 P-40s and 451 H75s rolled out of the doors of the Buffalo factory. The combined fighter production of all other U.S. manufacturers was only 152 airplanes. The following year, Curtiss built 2,246 P-40s, and Bell Aircraft produced 926 P-39s; the total production figure for all other U.S. fighters in 1941 was 609. As late as 1942, the other manufacturers were still well behind Curtiss-Wright. Although a new generation of U.S. fighters had made its appearance, these models were far down the production curve compared with the Curtiss fighter. Although the Lockheed P-38 was closest to the P-40 in development time, Lockheed could not match Curtiss-Wright's ability in quantity fighter production. In 1942, only 1,264 P-38s came off the assembly lines. The figure for P-40s was more than three and a half times as great, 4,453.[5]

Thus the P-40 was practically the only fighter America had in 1941 and 1942. It continued to provide the backbone of fighter strength for the USAAF until 1943. According to one estimate, a production change to a new model in 1941 would have meant a thousand fewer aircraft for the Allies at a time when the Axis powers, seemingly invincible, were advancing on several fronts and appeared to be close to victory. Although not a spectacular performer, the P-40 was adequate for the immediate needs. More important, it was available. A USAAF officer later summarized the problem very succinctly: "If we had not had the P-40, we would not have had any pursuit." Even as late as July 1943, the P-40 and the Bell P-39 constituted more than half the total fighter strength of the USAAF. Before September of the same year, over half of all USAAF fighters committed overseas were P-39s and P-40s.[6]

The air forces of many nations eventually flew various models of the venerable Curtiss fighter in World War II. A versatile airplane, the P-40 carried out a variety of combat duties and served in most of the major campaigns and in every combat theater. The most famous P-40s by far were those flown in China by the American Volunteer Group (AVG), better known as the Flying Tigers. Their exploits were spotlighted in the American press and in Hollywood films, and the Curtiss-Wright Corporation basked in the reflected glory. It was the high noon of the Airplane Division's achievements.

The total number of P-40s accepted by the USAAF is officially listed at 13,738, just behind the Republic P-47 (15,683) and the North American P-51 (14,686), making the P-40 the third most numerous fighter to emerge from American factories in World War II.[7] With improvements and design modifications, it soldiered on until the end of the war. Despite shortcomings, it was produced in greater numbers than any other airplane in company history. It represents Curtiss-Wright's finest hour in World War II. Never again would the corporation enjoy the public acclaim or the prominent position within the industry that it held in 1943.

Meanwhile, the Airplane Division was straining to produce a successor to the P-40 and to bring the C-46 and SB2C to quantity production. Work continued on several experimental fighters, but performance was disappointing, and the projects were eventually abandoned. To make matters worse, new and better fighter designs were beginning to move down the assembly lines of the competition. The C-46 and SB2C projects were proving to be particularly troublesome. A closer examination of these two programs gives some idea of the misfortunes that were beginning to affect the performance of the Airplane Division.

The C-46

By the time the prototype Model 20 civil transport made its maiden flight in March 1940, military needs were beginning to take precedence over civilian demands. The Air Corps had no heavy cargo transport in its inventory. The Douglas DC-3 was available, and adapted for military cargo operations as the C-47, it eventually became the air transport workhorse of World War II. Nevertheless, it lacked the load-carrying capability that Air Corps officials wanted in a cargo airplane. The Model 20 appeared to be the answer. Much bigger than the DC-3, the Model 20 ultimately carried a payload twice that of the Douglas transport. Consequently, the

Air Corps placed an order in September 1940 for 200 Model 20s to be modified as cargo transports. The design was given the military designation C-46. A follow-up order in May 1941 called for an additional 256 Commandos, as the C-46 was now known.[8]

The Air Corps, following a practice that was becoming all too prevalent, completely bypassed the normal procedure of acquiring several service test aircraft for extended trials before placing any quantity orders for the C-46.[9] As a result of this and other actions, both the manufacturer and the Air Corps were effectively prevented from gaining any practical experience in the day-to-day operations of the transport. Unfortunate consequences followed in the months to come. A design as new and as complex as the Commando inevitably had a significant number of "bugs" to be worked out. The duress of war put the airplane into production before it was ready, and the defects remained hidden until after the design had gone into service. Curtiss-Wright was unfairly criticized for producing a flawed airplane. The real culprit was the war emergency.

With construction delays threatening to prevent the completion of the Saint Louis plant on schedule, Curtiss-Wright transferred the major portion of C-46 production to the new Genesee Street plant at the Buffalo airport. The first C-46 rolled off the assembly line in May 1942 and was ready for USAAF acceptance by July.

As those Commandos exited the Buffalo factory, events transpiring in a faraway corner of the world would soon have a significant impact on the Curtiss-Wright Corporation. Japanese armies sweeping northward into Burma conquered the entire country by the middle of May. All Allied influence in Southeast Asia east of India was now eliminated. Access to the Burma Road, the only land route into western China, was cut off as well. This meant that all Allied military forces in western China, including the Flying Tigers, were trapped. A failure to resupply these forces could well lead to a collapse of the entire China front, a development that would be catastrophic for the Allies. Somehow, those Allied forces marooned in China's western provinces had to be supplied. An airlift from the Assam Valley of northeast India over the Himalaya Mountains—known as "the Hump"—into western China was the only way.

In the summer of 1942, this seemed an impossible task, given the performance capabilities of available aircraft and the conditions under which they would have to operate. Abom-

Curtiss C-46 transport and P-40 fighter.
Courtesy of Louis Eltscher.

inable weather, together with the world's highest mountain ranges, made this region the most forbidding and dangerous in the world for air operations. Moreover, existing cargo aircraft either had a limited load capability or were not available in sufficient numbers to maintain an effective airlift.

This was the breach into which the C-46 was thrust. Unfortunately, the C-46 was a new and very complex airplane that for all practical purposes was completely untested. Nevertheless, it seemed at the time to be the only solution to the problem. A call went out to Curtiss-Wright for more C-46s. In response, production at the Buffalo airport plant was accelerated.

The Commandos began their first flights from the Assam Valley into western China in May 1943. Operational problems surfaced almost immediately. Some were merely annoying. Others were lethal, as accidents began to occur with alarming frequency. By August, Washington was beginning to receive reports from the field that all was not well with the C-46. The feeling was summed up by Brig. Gen. Edwin S. Perrin, the deputy chief of the Air Staff, when he wrote, "The C-46 situation in China is terrible!"[10] The Airplane Division struggled for many months to correct the Commando's interminable deficiencies, most of which were eventually overcome through improved maintenance procedures and engineering changes. The cost in lives and matériel was high, however.

Eventually, the Curtiss Commando became the workhorse of the China airlift operation. It carried a greater tonnage over the Hump than any other airplane. Unfortunately, the many problems associated with early Commandos left the airplane with a bad reputation. The official USAAF history of World War II unfairly called the C-46 a killer.[11] Others unkindly labeled it the "Curtiss Calamity." Nevertheless, it eventually became a good, reliable transport aircraft and one of Curtiss-Wright's finest contributions to the Allied victory in World War II.

The SB2C

Despite the Commando's achievements, the negative publicity it generated was a blow to Curtiss-Wright's reputation as an airplane builder. The monumental problems that accompanied the third of the company's major World War II production aircraft, the SB2C Helldiver, only tarnished that reputation further.

The SB2C became an object lesson in the way in which things could go wrong when an American airframe manufacturer tried to bring a new airplane from the drawing board to mass production under the pressures of war. Not the least of the many problems the Airplane Division faced with the SB2C were the design specifications established by the U.S. Navy's Bureau of Aeronautics. This new airplane had all of the modern refinements that had become standard in aircraft design by the late thirties. It also had many internal systems that were brand-new and not fully tested. The SB2C has been described as "probably the most complex single-engined design of its time."[12] Inevitably, snags became commonplace. For example, engineers were forced to redesign the rear gun mount even while the airplane was still in the mock-up stage. Although this was not an uncommon problem in military aircraft so configured, it was a disturbing omen nonetheless.

More significant, another specification became the source of an unending series of problems for both the navy and Curtiss-Wright. The overall airframe dimensions had to be small enough to permit two aircraft to ride on a 41-by-48-foot aircraft carrier elevator with an all-around minimum clearance of 1 foot. The purpose was to launch aircraft quickly. But this demand became almost impossible to meet, given the other stipulations. It was the biggest design hurdle of the entire project. The end result was an overly compact and excessively heavy airframe that was "a lot of airplane in a small package."[13] Its aerodynamic configuration was a potential kiss of death. The SB2C tended to be unstable and tail heavy. Furthermore, like all new designs, it was expected to exceed the performance of comparable aircraft then in service, always a challenge. The additional burden of the size limitations created seemingly unattainable requirements.[14]

The SB2C seemed to be jinxed from the start. Two factors contributed to this state of affairs. First of all, Curtiss-Wright entered a new and unknown regime of aerodynamics with the SB2C. The Helldiver was on the cutting edge of aircraft engineering design and was pushing the state of the art to the limits. The airplane broke new ground in aeronautical technology because it was asked to carry a heavier load under more restrictive conditions than any other previous aircraft.[15]

The SB2C was required to sustain a 10,000-foot vertical dive and pull out with a maximum of 8 Gs (i.e., eight times the force of gravity). The navy wanted similar performance from other aircraft as well, such as the Chance Vought F4U Corsair. Vought persuaded the navy to drop the requirement after a Corsair experienced severe control problems during buildup practice dives. An SB2C disintegrated in the air under similar circumstances, killing the pilot.[16] Hence the performance specifications of the U.S. Navy contributed as much as any other factor to Curtiss-Wright's troubles with the Helldiver program.

The SB2C's checkered career can also be attributed to the World War II emergency, which was generating pressures to do things never before accomplished and to do them much faster than normal. The nation's aircraft manufacturers responded with varying degress of success as the rapid growth of America's military forces after 1938 compressed the usual process of aircraft development into the smallest possible time frame. The 1940 aircraft expansion program, for example, forced the navy to completely bypass its standard policy of thoroughly testing a prototype before ordering production aircraft, and the Bureau of Aeronautics placed an initial order on 29 November 1940 for 370 SB2Cs to be delivered beginning in December 1941, and reaching a rate of 85 aircraft per month by April 1942.[17] The prototype had not yet made its first flight, but the navy's decision to go into production was based on the promising results of preliminary wind tunnel tests and design studies. In addition, the navy's long and successful association with the Curtiss-Wright Corporation, together with the company's long-standing reputation for building reliable airplanes, undoubtedly contributed to the belief that the manufacturing giant could master the difficulties of producing this airplane on schedule. This assumption, however, proved to be unwarranted.

The first flight of the prototype XSB2C-1 took place in Buffalo on 18 December 1940 with Curtiss test pilot Lloyd Child at the controls. Problems developed immediately. Most significantly, the airplane displayed a pronounced instability, which was not surprising, given the restriction on fuselage length imposed by the navy. With their design freedom thus limited, Curtiss engineers encountered additional problems as they tried to improve the airplane's stability. They had to achieve a compromise between the size and weight of the tail sufficient to provide adequate strength. Yet they also had to ensure a stable airframe, an almost impossible task given the overall airframe size requirements.[18]

That was not all. Unfavorable wind tunnel tests the previous July had forced a redesign of the wing, which reduced the airplane's top speed. Nevertheless, the inevitable weight increases of the XSB2C-1 would have rendered it inoperable from aircraft carriers without the wing redesign. A vicious circle was beginning to develop as a correction in one area produced unfavorable consequences in another. For example, as the test program continued throughout 1941, the navy relented a bit by permitting the engine mount to be extended one foot, thereby lengthening the fuselage and improving stability. However, the benefits of this change were largely negated because a larger fin and rudder were now required to compensate for the increased fuselage length. The dog was chasing its own tail with ever-increasing ferocity.

Flight testing of the XSB2C-1 continued in Buffalo from December 1940 until 9 February 1941, when the prototype crashed as a result of engine failure during a landing. Flight testing with the rebuilt airframe did not resume until 6 May, whereupon a second landing accident several weeks later caused further delay. Fortunately, the damage this time was minimal, and the airplane was back in the air by the end of the month. By now, the testing program was seriously behind schedule.

Additional changes were made to the airframe as the accelerated flight test schedule proceeded. As pressure to get the project back on track increased, the number of test flights rose to an average of close to one a day throughout July and August. In a move to coordinate development testing and production, the XSB2C-1 was ferried to Port Columbus, Ohio, on 12 November 1941 for further dive tests. Although the Buffalo division had been the designated builder of the corporation's military airplanes since the 1929 merger, those facilities were operating at full capacity by 1940. Consequently, Helldiver manufacturing was switched to the new plant in Columbus.

On 21 December, the XSB2C-1 disintegrated in the air while attempting to recover from a vertical dive. The test pilot, Barton T. "Red" Hulse, bailed out safely, but the airplane was completely destroyed. Subsequent investigation revealed the cause to be a failure of the horizontal tailplane. Further strengthening of the tail assembly was required, which would add more weight to the tail and exacerbate the airframe's balance and stability problems. The crash also eliminated the program's only test airplane. A year had now passed since the original production contract had been signed. April, the target date for a production schedule of 85 airframes per month, was a scant four months away. Moreover, the Pearl Harbor attack had taken place two weeks earlier, and America was now in a full-scale war. The SB2C was needed more than ever.[19]

With the prospect of meeting the April 1942 production schedule all but nil, the navy assigned the first four production SB2Cs special priority. Curtiss-Wright was ordered to speed up the construction of these four airplanes by using the older job shop hand fabrication process, along with additional subcontracting. The first SB2C-1, serial number 00001, came off the assembly line in June 1942 and made its first flight on the 30th. It was never accepted by the navy but remained with Curtiss-Wright as a test aircraft.[20] Subsequent aircraft were assigned to various navy testing units for operational testing, training, and evaluation. Production of the SB2C-1 was thus initiated while tests were still under way and many of the critical design and engineering problems had not yet been solved. Accelerating wartime needs were distorting the normal process of aircraft development. The Battle of Midway, which had demonstrated the importance of the dive-bomber in naval air warfare, had taken place on 4 to 6 June, scarcely four weeks before the first flight of 00001. The navy, desperate for the new airplane, increased its initial order of 370 airframes to 3,865.

In the meantime, the army had placed an order in December 1940 for 100 examples of its own version of the SB2C, the A-25. Not to be outdone, the U.S. Marine Corps also expressed an interest in a specialized float-equipped seaplane version of the Helldiver. Finally, the British Royal Navy decided that it, too, needed dive-bombers and requested 450 SB2Cs from a production order for 1,000 U.S. Navy Helldivers to be built under license by the Canadian Car and Foundry Company of Fort William, Ontario.[21]

Unfortunately, standardization of the army's A-25 with the navy's SB2C was almost impossible to achieve, and two separate design teams were necessary to deal with the different sets of specifications. Since the Columbus facilities were already heavily burdened with the navy order, the Saint Louis plant was selected to build A-25s. This decision required further coordination in engineering and manufacturing, which put an additional strain on a company whose managerial and engineering facilities were already overloaded. Likewise, the contract with Canadian Car and Foundry, although representing an attempt to ease the strain on Curtiss-Wright, required the Columbus plant to supply the Canadian firm with its own set of production drawings. Similar difficulties arose when additional production was assigned to the Canadian branch of the Fairchild Aircraft Corporation, which built 300 SB2Cs for the U.S. Navy.

Another vicious spiral had been set into motion. Increased orders created additional stresses on the company's facilities, and every attempt to ease the burden only deepened the problem. The government's official engineering history of the SB2C states that the production program at Curtiss-Wright "suffered" as a consequence of the Canadian commitment.[22] Helldiver production continued at an increasing rate throughout the summer and fall of 1942. Nevertheless, deliveries were still running some nine months behind schedule at year's end.[23] The navy's policy of placing quantity orders for a brand-new airplane, the prototype of which was still undergoing flight testing, created king-size headaches for Curtiss-Wright. This practice, which was also followed by the army, resulted from the critical need to get quantity production under way as quickly as possible to ensure a reasonable delivery time to the armed forces. Some aircraft, such as the C-46, experienced problems that were a near duplicate of the SB2C's woes. The Martin Company faced similar delays with its controversial B-26 bomber and endured the same kind of adverse publicity as Curtiss-Wright. Other designs fared better. For example, the navy placed a quantity order for the Grumman TBF Avenger several months before the first flight of its prototype, and the airplane was successful almost from the start. However, the Avenger was designed to much more realistic specifications than the SB2C, and the Grumman company matched its commitments with its resources more adequately. Once more, the quality-quantity dilemma precipitated by the war emergency created severe problems for Curtiss-Wright.

As continued testing revealed additional design flaws in the Helldiver, changes had to be made in the fabrication process, which inevitably slowed the rate of production even more. It was scarcely any wonder that the first production SB2C-1s were less than sterling examples of high-quality American craftsmanship. Hydraulic leaks, cracked exhaust manifolds, brake failures, cracked bearings in the wing-fold joints, carburetor air-scoop fractures, malfunctioning electric propeller governors, leaking self-sealing fuel tanks and other deficiencies all were testimony to the problems of putting a new aircraft into quantity production.[24]

The difficulties at Columbus have been succinctly summarized as follows: "An inadequately trained workforce, handicapped by a shortage of experienced engineers and supervisors, was turning out a product that was then subject to careless inspection."[25] Under the circumstances, the end product could hardly have been other than seriously flawed. Various modifications and fixes were made to the design, and in December 1942, the first SB2C-1s entered squadron service.

The problems multiplied. Several operational accidents occurred that were attributed either to pilot error or to mechanical malfunction. Although the deficiencies that caused these accidents were serious, they were manageable and could be corrected by minor design changes and improved manufacturing processes.[26]

Not so easy to solve, however, was the persistent problem of the horizontal tailplane's structural integrity. A fatal accident occurred on 25 January 1943 that was a near duplicate of the December 1941 crash that had destroyed the XSB2C-1. This time, the first production Helldiver, number 00001, came apart in the air, killing Curtiss test pilot Byron A. Glover. The crash marked the nadir of the Helldiver's fortunes. An intensive program involving the Curtiss-Wright Research Laboratory in Buffalo, the National Advisory Committee for Aeronautics (NACA), and the U.S. Navy's Bureau of Aeronautics was launched to discover the cause of the tragedy. The culprit, little understood in 1943, was an aerodynamic phenomenon known as compressibility. In high-speed dives, the SB2C was approaching the realm of transonic flight (i.e., just below the speed of sound). The airframe simply could not accommodate the change of aerodynamic forces. Further strengthening of the tail and wing, along with restricting the velocity of high-speed dives, prevented a recurrence of the problem.[27]

As the SB2C-1 testing program dragged on into 1943, the company struggled to get production on schedule. The Columbus factory faced staggering challenges from the beginning, including the training of an unskilled workforce to produce the navy's most complicated carrier airplane. Only 2 percent of the first job applicants acknowledged any prior experience in aircraft production. A training program was quickly set up to teach the necessary skills to the new workers. Columbus was also being swamped with military orders. Not only was a navy scout and observation plane, the SO3C, moving down the assembly lines, but initial development work was also beginning on a new navy scout, the SC. Plant capacity had to be expanded to accommodate the increased workload. Although SB2C production was improving by early 1943, deliveries were still running some nine months behind the original schedule, partly because all of the completed airframes had to go through the modification line, some more than once.[28]

Delay followed postponement. The year 1943 wore on into summer and early fall, and still no SB2C-1s were ready for combat. Four years had passed since the original contract had been signed. In the meantime, production increased as carrier qualification trials proceeded. The tests continued to go badly, but Curtiss-Wright and the U.S. Navy persisted. Continued fixes and changes were made to the airplanes, both in modification lines and in production. By the end of October, the first combat-ready Helldivers were headed for the South Pacific.

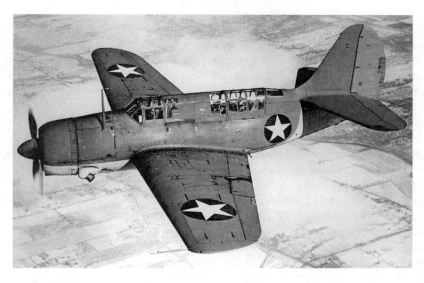

Curtiss SB2C Helldiver.
Courtesy of Harold Andrews.

They went into action for the first time in November 1943 and gave a good account of themselves. About a year and a half late, the Helldiver was part of the U.S. Navy's air arm. Considering the obstacles that had to be surmounted, this was not too shabby a time frame.

As improved models came out of the Columbus factory in late 1943 and 1944, SB2Cs gradually replaced the aging Douglas SBDs in naval air combat units. Helldivers went on to participate in most of the Pacific campaign's major air battles during the last year and a half of World War II. Tough and rugged, these Curtiss dive-bombers performed well and eventually won a measure of respect, if not always affection, from their crews, who often referred to the airplane as "the Beast," after one pilot allegedly was heard to remark after his first flight, "My God, what a Beast!" The Curtiss public relations department also used the appellation to promote the Helldiver as a ferocious animal. By the end of the war, the Beast had been effectively tamed to become, in the words of one pilot, "A useful military weapon of good striking power . . . but not an outstanding performer."[29] Given the circumstances surrounding its origins and development, that is tantamount to high praise. Later models of the Helldiver continued in frontline service with the U.S. Navy until 1949 and remained in the inventory of foreign air forces for another 10 years. This is not a bad service record for an airplane that had such an inauspicious beginning.

Yet the Helldiver, like the Commando, is mostly remembered as a seriously flawed airplane. The Helldiver's later combat and service record is often forgotten or ignored. In fact, the Airplane Division's accomplishments with this airplane were considerable given the serious constraints under which it had labored. A totally new factory had been built and equipped, a completely unskilled workforce had been trained, two test aircraft had been lost, and production had been initiated too hastily. Moreover, the engineering team had encountered and surmounted colossal design problems. The Airplane Division's experience with both the Helldiver and the Commando provided ample evidence that new and complex aircraft require time to make them fully operational. War rarely permits such time.

Wright Aeronautical and the R-3350

As the tribulations of the Airplane Division mounted, the Wright Aeronautical Corporation was experiencing its own full measure of troubles. They centered on its largest engine, the R-3350. The entire R-3350 wartime program cast a very long shadow and eventually attracted the unwelcome attention of the United States Senate. Once again, the urgency of war had pushed a complicated piece of machinery into service prematurely, and the manufacturer was ill-prepared to meet the challenge.

Of the four large experimental airplanes that had been powered by the R-3350, only two had actually flown before 1942, and none ever went into quantity production. The R-3350 engine development program for these earlier airframes had been minimal. Testing had been largely confined to low altitudes at low power ratings. Understandably, no engine troubles were encountered.

Another reason for the lack of attention given to the R-3350 before 1941 was Wright Aeronautical's preoccupation with its R-1820 and R-2600 engines, which were then being developed for an expanding market. The company did so with good reason. According to one source, the R-1820 powered almost three-quarters of the Douglas DC-2 and DC-3 airliners worldwide during the thirties. Additionally, foreign military orders, especially from Great Britain and France, along with the U.S. government's own rearmament program, had expanded the production of the R-1820 and R-2600 engines.[30]

When Wright Aeronautical signed the 15 April 1941 contract for 30,000 operational R-3350 engines, it put a severe strain on its facilities, which were already heavily committed to producing its other engines. Almost overnight, a low-priority program had been given one of the largest and highest priorities of the entire war production program; some said *the* highest. Yet only seven R-3350 engines had been shipped to the U.S. Army Air Corps and its successor organization, the USAAF, for test purposes between 1936 and 1 January 1942. An additional handful went to the U.S. Navy for the three experimental flying boats. Moreover, those seven army engines had produced only 2,000 brake horsepower for takeoff, whereas the B-29 required an additional 200 brake horsepower. Clearly, Wright Aeronautical had the makings of a sizable problem on its hands.

A further burden on the company was the need for additional factory space. Although the new facility in Lockland, Ohio, was built for R-3350 production, still more plant capacity was needed. In response, the factory in Wood-Ridge, New Jersey, was constructed in 1942 to manufacture R-3350s exclusively. It was scheduled to produce 850 engines per month beginning in May 1943. Wood-Ridge actually began shipping the new engines in July.[31]

By early 1942, the pressures on the R-3350 program were becoming severe. Allied grand strategy, developed before Pearl Harbor, gave the United States the dominant role in defeating the Japanese enemy. Moreover, the deteriorating military situation in East Asia gave special urgency to the development of all weapons with which to strike back at Japan as soon as possible. The centerpiece of this effort as envisioned by USAAF strategists was the B-29 with its long-range bombing potential. General H. H. Arnold, the USAAF commander, was especially anxious to maintain the B-29 schedule. The first 25 production-standard B-29s were to be ready for service by February 1943.[32] Time was of the essence. Unfortunately, that was one commodity in very short supply at Wright Aeronautical, as delays in the R-3350 program occurred almost immediately.

Another item in short supply was manpower, especially engineers. The problem was industry wide. Military leaders, industry executives, and college presidents met in July 1943 to consider the engineer shortage. With large numbers being siphoned off to the armed services, the industry was left seriously understaffed, and critical programs such as the B-29/R-3350 project suffered. An agreement was reached whereby industry could request the return of specific men, but this was a relatively long-term process and was of little help in resolving the immediate R-3350 crisis.

Critical raw material shortages developed in several areas. For example, supplies of a special casting sand from Madagascar were in danger of being cut off by German U-boat activity. Another threatened shortage was mica, a material used in all spark plug insulation. Mica came from the mountains of eastern India that were being threatened by advancing Japanese armies. These and other shortages created bottlenecks that were not easily overcome. Substitute materials were found, but they required many hours of developmental testing.[33]

The flight test phase of the R-3350 program also experienced time constraints. To speed things up, no flight testing of the R-3350 took place at Wright Aeronautical before the B-29 airframe went into its own flight testing. This was to have disastrous consequences. Not unexpectedly, the new engine produced many headaches. High oil consumption, cracked nose sections, and reduction gear failures were common occurrences. More ominously, the carburetion and ignition systems proved troublesome as well.

Flight testing continued until the end of the year, and in early January 1943, an intensive review of the entire R-3350 project was held at Wright Aeronautical headquarters in Paterson. Discussion centered on completing and equipping the new Wood-Ridge plant and expediting the production phase of the new engine. The review identified technical problems and noted the difficulties associated with this phase of the program. Said engineer Robert E. Johnson of Wright Aeronautical, "There were so many chances for error in the process, with so many new people and machines that special care was required at every step."[34] Nevertheless, the company was confident that a steady flow of combat-ready R-3350 engines would soon be coming off the assembly lines. And then disaster struck.

On 18 February 1943, the second XB-29 prototype crashed in Seattle, Washington, killing all on board. Early reports listed an in-flight engine fire as the probable cause. All aircraft powered by the R-3350 were temporarily grounded. A team from Wright Aeronautical went to Seattle to investigate the crash. Its report found no evidence of in-flight fires on any of the four engines. Instead, the culprit was an improperly functioning fuel filler system. Regardless, the engine manufacturer was criticized for sacrificing quality for quantity, and the USAAF was condemned for pushing Wright Aeronautical to that extreme. In fact, the normal five-year engine development cycle had been compressed by the war emergency to two years.[35]

A Special Wright Engine Committee, established by the USAAF after the XB-29 crash, was given responsibility for expediting R-3350 production. The committee's personnel included representatives of the USAAF and Wright Aeronautical. After compiling a comprehensive list of engine troubles, the committee had to determine how engine production would be affected by the changes required to correct the troubles. In some cases, minor problems were ignored. These could be rectified later at the modification centers set up at various points in the United States to remedy deficiencies in the manufacturing process or to bring airframes and engines up to combat standards. Other problems, such as a change to standardized ignition components desired by the USAAF, could be corrected, but all took time. Wright engineers constantly had to ask themselves the question: "How many early production engines do we lose if this change is required?"[36]

Many nagging problems, such as determining the proper type of piston ring and locating a vendor to supply it, caused maddening delays. A more serious problem was the tendency of the engines to overheat at high altitudes. The solution was to use forged, rather than cast, cylinder heads. However, the forging capacity in the United States at the time was insufficient to meet the B-29 engine production schedule. Consequently, early B-29s went into service with substandard engines. Another more significant and potentially dangerous problem was improper carburetion, which sometimes caused engine fires. This problem was eventually corrected by replacing conventional carburetion with a fuel injection system. However, further delays were caused by the supplier's inability to provide a steady supply of fuel injectors.[37] Eventually the bottleneck was overcome, and once the new equipment was installed, overall engine performance improved significantly. A report of a Wright Aeronautical service representative who made a field trip to the western Pacific in 1945 stated in July that fuel injection "will definitely overcome the backfiring problem and gives good indication of doing much to alleviate valve and cylinder troubles."[38] By then, of course, the war was all but over.

By 1943, many individuals, including some in public life, were joining a chorus of criticism directed at Wright Aeronautical and the R-3350. This engine was a highly visible piece of merchandise because it was associated with the B-29 and the strategic bombing campaign against Japan. People saw a weapons system not performing as expected, and they wanted to know why.

Like many wartime products, the R-3350 became operational before the innumerable design problems were solved and before the engine was ready for combat. Its development time was simply too short, and that Wright Aeronautical's wartime commitments exceeded its resources only made a bad situation even worse. Negative publicity was beginning to beset the company, typical of which was an episode that occurred on 29 June 1943 when the first flight of a production B-29 built at Boeing's Wichita plant took place. The Wright service teams had worked almost literally around the clock to bring the engines up to flight status. As news of the impending flight spread to the community, many townspeople came out to the field and took positions on a nearby hill to observe the event. The entire plant was shut down so that all the employees could watch. Robert E. Johnson, a senior engineer for Wright Aeronautical, was there too:

The plane was rolled out, the engines checked, and it took off. Immediately smoke poured out behind one engine, the flight was aborted, and it came around and landed safely some minutes later. . . . where do you hide? [The problem] turned out to be an oil leak from a small gasket on the engine nose section. The oil blew back over the exhaust system and created the smoke.[39]

Although minor, this episode typified the kind of negative publicity that the Curtiss-Wright Corporation was receiving by the middle war years, and it was attracting the attention of people in high places.

The Truman and Mead Committees

As Curtiss-Wright's production miseries mounted in 1943, still another blow to its prestige came from an unexpected source, the United States Senate. On 10 July, the Senate's Special Committee to Investigate the National Defense Program released to the public the latest in a series of reports on the state of America's defense industries. The committee had spent the previous months monitoring the nation's defense industries, and its chairman, Missouri senator Harry S. Truman, had sent investigators to many war plants to secure firsthand information on their operations. He and the other committee members also visited various facilities in person.

According to Truman, the committee was established at his initiative. Concerned about the possibility of waste and graft in the growing defense industries, he submitted a resolution to the Senate on 10 February 1941 calling for a special committee to investigate the conduct of the entire defense program. It was authorized and directed "to examine every phase of the entire war program."[40] He wanted "to obtain facts and suggest remedies where necessary." Rather than wait until the war was over, he preferred to study the defense program as it was operating so that corrective measures could be taken to improve it. As Truman put it, he wanted to play the role of the surgeon curing the patient, instead of a pathologist performing an autopsy after the patient had died.

In an effort to maintain a high level of objectivity, the committee was given a bipartisan membership of 7 senators, later enlarged to 10. Truman wanted to avoid sensationalism and publicity. In his words, the committee wanted neither a "whitewash [nor] a smear," but "only results." The committee held its first hearings on 15 April 1941 and continued its work throughout the war.[41] Truman remained chairman until August 1944, when he resigned to become President Roosevelt's vice-presidential running mate in the 1944 election. Fellow committee member Senator James Mead of New York became the new chairman.

Despite Truman's avowed goal of avoiding publicity, the 10 July report created a sensation nationwide. Reflecting the directness and plainspoken nature of its chairman, the Truman Committee, as it was popularly known, bluntly criticized both the government and the aviation industry in their operation of the aircraft production program. Of those companies denounced for having poor management policies and inferior products, Curtiss-Wright was named as one of the worst offenders. Noting the traditionally close ties between Curtiss-Wright and the military, the Truman Committee declared that "the Curtiss-Wright Corporation has enjoyed spectacular and unprecedented success in obtaining war contracts." The report went on to note that Curtiss-Wright was second only to General Motors as a manufacturer of war goods in the United States. Out of a total of almost $105 billion in total supply contracts granted by the government from 1 June 1940 through 1 March 1943, Curtiss-Wright had received more than $4.7 billion.[42] The report cited the "excessive ability and zeal of its [Curtiss-Wright's] salesmen and the extent and nature of the relations which it has built up with the War and Navy Departments through the years preceding the war." It suggested that Curtiss-Wright's skilled personnel, especially in its engineering departments, had become spread too thin as a result of the large number of contracts the company had received. The War and Navy Departments were also condemned for contributing to the problem by failing to seek additional sources of supply and relying instead on existing suppliers. The report noted that several contracts were awarded to Curtiss-Wright even when the company's own officers believed these contracts would "overload its own facilities."[43] These observations quite accurately and succinctly summarized the corporation's war-born troubles.

Two products of the Airplane Division, the P-40 and SB2C, were singled out for special criticism. The report blamed both Curtiss-Wright and the army for continued production of the obsolescent P-40 at a time when other, more advanced aircraft such as the P-47 and P-51 were under development. The army was condemned for failing to recognize the importance of the new designs and for not ordering them into production sooner. For its part, Curtiss-Wright was credited with making "a number of modifications" to improve the P-40's combat performance, but the report implied strongly that the company had pushed P-40 sales excessively.[44]

The Truman Committee failed to recognize, however, that P-47 and P-51 production facilities were not yet adequate in 1943 to maintain a constant flow of viable fighter aircraft to USAAF combat units. The only way to keep that flow coming was to keep the P-40 production lines open. In short, the committee failed to appreciate the delicate balance between quantity and quality that weapons procurement policy must preserve. The army, in fact, had tried to speed up the process in early 1942 by directing the Airplane Division to end P-40 production and begin manufacturing advanced versions of the P-47. In this way, the Curtiss assembly lines would be turning out aircraft of the latest design, even if it was not one of their own. It didn't work. The Buffalo plants produced only 354 P-47s, and delivery did not begin until December 1942. By this time, fighters were desperately needed on the North African and Russian fronts, and Curtiss resumed an accelerated production schedule for the P-40 while phasing out the P-47 lines. Retooling for the newer fighter was simply too time-consuming. Perhaps one lesson to be learned from the P-40 story is that wartime production has a tendency to take on a life of its own. The manufacture of a sophisticated weapon of war simply cannot be turned on and off like a faucet. Moreover, the committee also neglected to note that later P-40 production was used to supply training schools with fighter aircraft, thus releasing designs with higher performance for combat operations.[45]

The report noted that much of Curtiss-Wright's production was taking place in plants that had been constructed with government funds. It failed to consider that the Buffalo Kenmore plant, which had built P-40s before Pearl Harbor and was continuing to produce a steady stream of P-40 components, had been constructed close to 15 years earlier with company funds. That much of the earlier expansion of the P-40 assembly lines had been financed by foreign countries rather than the U.S. government was also not mentioned.

The Truman Committee was on firmer ground when it criticized the Airplane Division for failing to produce a more modern fighter for military service. Curtiss-Wright had received a large contract to develop the XP-60, but the airplane was a disappointment. Moreover, Curtiss-Wright had been given three of nine experimental contracts awarded by the army for single-engine fighter development and was one of four manufacturers to receive an army contract for a twin-engine fighter.[46] None of these contracts resulted in a production aircraft from Curtiss-Wright, clearly one of the company's greatest failures in World War II. The failed fighter program is discussed more fully later in this chapter.

Understandably, the Truman Committee was especially unhappy with the SB2C program, which had been floundering since its inception in 1939. The committee report noted that despite generous infusions of public monies amounting to more than $125 million, production was still "hopelessly behind schedule" and that to date "not a single SB2C" was ready for combat operations. Side effects of the delays were also noted, such as the ramifications for subcontractors and the negative psychological impact on plant workers and morale throughout the Columbus area.[47] Regrettably, the report failed to consider the many constraints under which both Curtiss-Wright and the navy were operating in their struggle to produce a viable dive-bomber.

Curtiss-Wright was also criticized for promoting the Helldiver as "the world's best dive bomber"; the report observed that the costs of such "eulogistic self-praise" amounted to $12,448.95. The committee also noted that the cost for advertising the company's other products in 1943 amounted to some $872,821, a significant portion of which would be borne by the federal government; Curtiss-Wright treated these costs "as an expense of doing business before computing profits on which the government would be entitled to receive excess-profits taxes at the highest rate." The report condemned this practice as "self-praise at the expense of the government."[48]

The Truman Committee reserved its most scathing criticism of Curtiss-Wright for the operations of the Lockland, Ohio, plant, which was producing the R-2600 and R-3350 engines. Years later, Truman himself remembered the affair during a conversation with author Merle Miller:

Down at Curtiss-Wright at the airplane plant in Ohio, they were putting defective motors in planes and the generals couldn't seem to find anything wrong. So we went down, myself and a couple other senators, and we condemned more than four or five hundred of those engines. And I sent a couple of generals who'd been approving, who'd okayed those engines to Leavenworth, and I believe they are still there. I certainly hope so. . . .

The whole time only about three or four people went to jail.[49]

Of course, neither Truman nor any other president of the United States could simply send "a couple of generals to Leavenworth" in the manner suggested in this passage.

In his memoirs, Truman explained the episode in greater detail. Noting his committee's discovery that the Lockland plant was turning out defective engines, he declared that they were causing the death of trainee pilots. This was an unlikely claim, since neither the R-2600 nor the R-3350 were installed in training aircraft, although some combat aircraft were used for training purposes. In any case, the committee condemned 400 engines. Truman then approached both Curtiss-Wright and the army without making any public announcement of his committee's findings, giving them several weeks to conduct an internal investigation of the inspection procedures at the Lockland plant. When both reported nothing wrong, Truman set up a subcommittee to inspect the plant and hold hearings. A succession of witnesses testified to improper inspection procedures that had allowed defective parts and engines to be turned over to the army.

The committee was very critical of the army inspectors, claiming that they showed an "undue regard for the well-being of the Wright Aeronautical Corporation." On too many occasions, "they seemed to be motivated by a desire to protect the company and its interests." For its part, the company was accused of "gross negligence" in failing to correct inspection procedures at Lockland, "despite the fact that it knew that the safety of pilots and crews of aircraft were dependent thereon." Specifically, Wright Aeronautical was charged with falsifying tests, destroying records, improperly recording test results, forging inspection receipts, failing to segregate substandard materials and destroy them, orally changing tolerances allowed on parts, skipping inspection operations, and, perhaps most significantly, allowing production to override the inspection force, thereby destroying morale of both company and army inspectors. Ironically, increased production was the very thing the army and navy were demanding. According to Truman, a subsequent army investigation confirmed the committee findings, and as Truman put it, the "dangerous and dishonest practice was thus brought to an end."[50]

As a consequence of the investigation, a lawsuit against Curtiss-Wright, its president, and officers, was filed in the U.S. district court in Trenton, New Jersey, charging the company with selling "defective, substandard and unsatisfactory" war materials to the U.S. government. A second suit was filed in Ohio at about the same time. These cases were never pursued, however.[51]

Response to the Truman Committee charges was not long in coming. In August, one month after the committee report was made public, Curtiss-Wright president Guy Vaughan issued a statement in which he vigorously defended his company's war record and accused the Truman Committee of misinterpreting "standard and recognized manufacturing and inspection procedures." He categorically denied selling products to the government "known to the company to have contained defective parts." He quoted from the army's investigative report, which defended Curtiss-Wright and declared that the charges of the Truman Committee were unsubstantiated. The most significant statement from the army board report may well have been the following: "Defects may appear during service which even the most rigid inspection and tests will fail to reveal."[52]

Others criticized the Truman Committee report by blaming Congress for the rather sorry state of the aviation industry before World War II. *Aviation* magazine, for example, editorialized as follows: "Congress, and Congress alone, is responsible for the low base upon which expansion of the aircraft industry was started."[53] Citing the niggardly appropriations that had effectively starved the industry in the twenties and early thirties, the editorial noted that many companies may well have expired had it not been for foreign orders that had kept them afloat. It was small wonder that the industry became severely overloaded when wartime demands suddenly descended on it. The perspective of history suggests that this assessment is essentially correct.

The whole sorry episode at the Lockland plant was as much an indictment of army inspection procedures as it was of Wright Aeronautical's manufacturing practices. Neither party came out of the affair untarnished. The incident demonstrates all too clearly what can, and probably will, happen when control of a company's operations becomes lax and the pressures for high-volume wartime production take precedence over every other consideration.

Why was Curtiss-Wright seemingly singled out for special criticism by the Truman Committee? Were conditions in the Curtiss-Wright factories that much worse than in the factories of other manufacturers? Probably not. However, the company's size alone warranted special attention. The committee's report of 10 July 1943 named Curtiss-Wright as the largest contractor in the U.S. aviation industry.[54] Hence the company was very visible. It also was very vulnerable; after all, the World War II record of the Curtiss-Wright Corporation was hardly unblemished.

Was greed the culprit? Certainly, history provides many examples of businessmen whose quest for profits has overwhelmed all other considerations. Indeed, the post–World War II history of the Curtiss-Wright Corporation itself provides ample evidence of this, as will be seen. Often the truth is more complex and mundane, however. People occasionally become overwhelmed by circumstances over which they have little or no control and are swept along by events. Nowhere is this more evident than in that most pervasive of all human activities, warfare. Total war takes on a terrible logic of its own and subordinates everything to the drive for complete victory. The need for equipment, although it may be substandard or even defective, becomes paramount, and the cost in human lives is discounted. Such was the case when substandard R-3350 engines with cast, rather than forged, cylinder heads were installed on operational B-29s.

The wartime decision-making process often brings together an inseparable mixture of elements, including personal interests and patriotism. It becomes impossible to determine which motive influenced which decision. Whether the decisions that led to the shipment of defective engines from Wright Aeronautical were prompted exclusively by avarice is difficult to say. However, venality alone seems to be an inadequate explanation for Curtiss-Wright's actions during World War II. More likely, the vast manufacturing empire had grown too quickly and had gotten too big, and its engineering and managerial resources simply had not kept pace. Consequently, they were not strong enough to direct and control the company's operations. Curtiss-Wright was not actually accused of any criminal wrongdoing by the Truman Committee, and no criminal indictments were handed down against the corporation and its officers as a result of the committee's investigations. Yet there were later accusations in Congress that the whole affair had been swept under the rug.

Perhaps the Truman Committee grasped the immensity of the problems facing Curtiss-Wright when it softened its criticisms by noting the "signal contributions" the company had already made to the war effort and by concluding with the following summary statement:

Its engines, airplanes and propellers, although not always of the best, have been of great value at the fighting fronts. Some of its products have been exceptionally good, and its performance taken as a whole has been creditable. The company and those employed by it should continue the work which they have started to correct the defects referred to in this report, so that the company may continue to merit the high reputation which it previously had obtained as a producer of fine airplanes and engines.[55]

The Truman Committee's July 1943 report was not the end of the matter. In January 1945, Senator William Langer of North Dakota brought charges of improper conduct by Curtiss-Wright to the floor of the U.S. Senate. Langer, an ardent populist and isolationist before the war, had all of the upper Midwest agrarian prejudices against big business and the "internationalist" Wall Street banking interests. He began his offensive by placing into the Congressional Record a hysterical letter from a constituent accusing the Curtiss-Wright Corporation of various misdeeds going back to the activities of the Curtiss Aeroplane and Motor Corporation in World War I. The letter also practically accused the company of treason for allegedly giving the so-called "secret" of dive-bombing to the Nazis in the thirties.[56] Furthermore, it accused both the company and the government of willful negligence for failing to correct product deficiencies in World War II.

The most extravagant charge was the claim of a "diabolical conspiracy" between Curtiss-Wright and the government to ensure the company an unending supply of war contracts. According to this scenario, Curtiss-Wright was pulling strings to give it control of the post-war aircraft industry.[57] This collusion was supposedly made possible because Curtiss-Wright had certain highly placed government officials acting at its behest, such as Theodore P. Wright, a former Curtiss-Wright executive who was now chief of the Aircraft Resources Control Office of the War Department and also head of the Aircraft Production Board.

Conspiracy theories of this sort have their obvious appeal, but intrigue is normally the staple fare of fiction rather than the real world, and the post–World War II history of Curtiss-Wright clearly demonstrates the complete absurdity of these accusations. Nevertheless, to someone with William Langer's outlook, they made sense, and he continued his drumfire of accusations throughout the spring and summer of 1945.[58]

The Mead Committee, as the former Truman committee was now known, was forced to act and resumed its investigation of the company's wartime performance, this time concentrating on the Buffalo factories. Curtiss-Wright itself reportedly requested the action in order to have a showdown with Langer. Hearings were held in Buffalo and Washington throughout the spring and summer of 1945.[59]

The Mead Committee's final report, published in July 1945, contained no surprises. Attributing Curtiss-Wright's problems to the pressures of an accelerated production schedule, the report faulted the company for making "every effort to obtain quantity rather than quality" manufacturing in the Buffalo airplane plants, hardly a startling revelation. In the words of the report, "production dominated inspection." The committee also criticized the army's inspection operations.

The Mead Committee noted that large-scale aircraft production "presented many difficulties for the manufacturers" and observed that the principal problems faced by Curtiss-Wright were experienced by all of the major manufacturers. Repeating an all too familiar refrain, the report noted the "thin spreading of top management and engineering skill" at Curtiss-Wright. It also listed the lack of experienced workers, shortages of parts and materials, and "constant changes in specifications" by the military services as other major problems for the manufacturers.[60]

Hence Senator Langer was partially vindicated, as the charges of production and testing irregularities were essentially substantiated by the Mead Committee. However, the source of the trouble was neither a conspiracy nor willful wrongdoing. Rather, the culprit was the war emergency, which brought unprecedented expansion of the aviation industry for which companies such as Curtiss-Wright were ill prepared.

The Search for a New Fighter

By 1943 the fortunes of war were slowly shifting to favor the Allies as the flood of weapons from the "Arsenal of Democracy" began to overwhelm the Axis powers. America's aircraft manufacturers that year produced a total of 57,544 combat aircraft, up from 25,582 the previous year. Curtiss-Wright's contribution to the 1943 total consisted of 1,227 SB2Cs, 4,258 P-40s, and 353 C-46s.[61]

Yet all was not well at the Airplane Division. Although the foregoing figures show that the great aviation manufacturing conglomerate continued to make a significant contribution to America's war production, there were disturbing signs that the company was falling behind the competition in the race for new and better airplanes. One of the most important indicators was the company's failed attempt to develop an advanced fighter. Although examples of the latest improvements in fighter design were now rolling off the assembly lines of Lockheed, North American, Grumman, and Republic, Curtiss-Wright was still heavily committed to the P-40 and had no new fighters ready for production.

Nevertheless, the Airplane Division's engineering department was not idle. The company continued to devote much of its energies to correcting the deficiencies of the C-46 and SB2C. At the same time, work proceeded on several advanced fighter projects. Initially, considerable effort had been concentrated on the XP-46, a disappointing design whose performance gave no significant advantage over the P-40. This project had been abandoned by early 1942. Curtiss engineers then turned their attention to several new fighter projects that had been either on the drawing board or under development for some time. Several of these reached prototype status and were flight-tested during the midwar years. As early as the summer of 1941, in fact, both the army and navy had ordered experimental fighters from the Airplane Division. The navy fighter was designated XF14C, and the army model was the XP-62. Unfortunately, both were like so many other Curtiss designs of this period; they fell just slightly short of the mark. The first flight of the XP-62 did not take place until 21 July 1943, and by then it was no longer needed. Its performance, though good, could not match that of the late-model P-47s then on the assembly lines. In other words, an airplane at the peak of its service life was superior to a design just at the beginning of its development cycle. The XF14C, which flew two months later, was a disappointment as well. It also fell short of expectations, received a low priority, and was not delivered to the navy until July 1944. By then, the Grumman F6F and Vought F4U had established themselves as the standard navy fighters, and the Curtiss project was canceled. These Curtiss designs were simply the wrong airplanes at the wrong time, regardless of the merits of the individual designs.

The XP-60 was yet another fighter program that went nowhere. The initial project started life as a modified P-40 but was subsequently canceled when the army decided that Curtiss-Wright should concentrate on P-40 production and license-manufacture of the Republic P-47. The project was kept alive, however, and the XP-60 went through several mutations and finally emerged in early 1944 as the YP-60E, only one airframe of which was completed. It flew for the first time on 15 July 1944 and was declared surplus in December of the same year. Curtiss-Wright had spent four precious years on a project that went absolutely nowhere. The great aircraft manufacturer seemed to have lost its way.

Ironically, in each of these failed fighter projects, Curtiss engineers were merely trying to produce what the military services wanted from them. The P-60 program offers a prime example of an airplane that was beset with constantly changing requirements and priorities. In the incessant push for that qualitative edge, technical improvements were attempted before earlier ones had been completely tested. No other U.S. military airplane with a single model designation ever experienced the number of design and equipment changes that did the P-60 series. In the words of aviation historian Peter Bowers, the P-60 program "is a prime example of a program that [went] nowhere."[62] Echos of the Curtiss Company's tribulations in World War I could be heard in this episode.

Inexorably, events were passing Curtiss-Wright by as the list of failed projects continued to grow. There was ample evidence that the company was in disarray as the words "too little and too late" came to characterize the Airplane Division and its products. Within two years of America's entry into World War II, a company that had been a leader in the industry was well on its way to becoming an also-ran.

Most of the new Curtiss designs in World War II were fatally flawed in one way or another. Curtiss, according to some observers, was a "consolidator" rather than an "innovator" in aircraft development.[63] Many of its aircraft throughout the twenties and thirties, such as the Hawk biplane fighters and their variants, were derivative designs. On the other hand, the C-46, the P-36, and the experimental Y1A-18 were certainly innovative.

Design conservatism was not an exclusive Curtiss-Wright trait. Aircraft design tends to be evolutionary in nature, since engineering experience acquired from a good basic design can be applied to improving and refining it in subsequent models. Moreover, this practice enables a company financing its own development costs to maximize profits by keeping those costs down.

Beyond a certain point, however, conservatism becomes a dangerous policy. Although such an approach may be satisfactory at a time when the pace of technological change is relatively slow, a period of rapid development can quickly make an aircraft design obsolete. The pace of aircraft design was continuing to accelerate under the stimulus of war, and Curtiss-Wright was caught short in the fighter competition. With better luck, greater inspiration, better timing, or a combination of all three, a new fighter based on the P-40 might conceivably have made the grade later in the war. But it never happened. Instead, the P-40, which was a modification of a 1935 design (the Model 75), was continually revamped as production continued at a high level. In the end, the company failed to compete successfully for future fighter business. Its new designs were simply outclassed. In the "uncompromising climate" of World War II aerial combat, "only the best would do and Curtiss . . . was not producing that."[64]

Yet even if Curtiss had successfully developed a superior piston-engine fighter on time, a government production contract may not necessarily have been forthcoming, since the needs of the military services for such an aircraft were being met by other manufacturers. By 1943 the correct balance between quality and quantity necessary for winning the war had been achieved. There was simply no need for another fighter in the inventory unless its potential was so great that it couldn't be dismissed. Such an airplane was America's first operational jet fighter, the P-80, which first flew in early 1944.

None of these problems were unique to Curtiss-Wright. Other manufacturers experienced similar difficulties in their efforts to produce new aircraft for World War II. Consolidated (later Convair), for example, worked for almost five years to produce the B-32 heavy bomber to complement the Boeing B-29. After many delays, the B-32 finally became operational at the very end of the war, only to be scrapped shortly after V-J Day.[65] Nevertheless, Consolidated surmounted these problems and survived and prospered after World War II. This suggests that the design problem by itself fails to fully explain Curtiss-Wright's postwar decline. Questions remain: Why were so many of the later Curtiss designs second-rate, and why did they all have such an excessively long development period? Why was the company consistently six months to a year behind the competition? Definitive answers may never be found. A closer examination of the corporation's management, organization, and structure during the critical years of World War II can nevertheless yield some clues.

Managerial and Engineering Problems

By 1943, the corporation was facing severe managerial problems, symptomatic of which was the turmoil within the Airplane Division, especially at Buffalo. This was reflected in personnel changes that were made in 1943 and 1944, when several hirings, firings, and transfers took place in an attempt to improve efficiency. In 1943 both Frank H. Harrison, manager of manufacturing for the International Harvester Company, and E. J. Harrington, coordinator of planning, production, and material problems for Lockheed, became vice presidents at Curtiss-Wright. That same year, Guy Vaughan announced the appointment of George Montague Williams to the position of company vice president to serve as an assistant to the president "in an executive capacity." Williams, who had been closely associated with the aviation and automobile industries for many years, came to Curtiss-Wright from the Consolidated Vultee Aircraft Corporation (Convair). An important transfer occurred in 1944 when Charles W. France, who had been manager at the Saint Louis factory, was brought to Buffalo on 28 February, where he became plants manager.[66]

The Columbus factory also had its share of managerial problems. An attempt to overcome labor shortages by subcontracting was frustrated by a lack of extra management personnel required to inspect and coordinate the work, although extensive subcontracting eventually took place. In another case, a navy inspection team sent to Columbus in the spring of 1942 to investigate the SB2C-1 program reported that among the many problems at the factory was the failure of Buffalo to provide adequate support at the managerial level.[67] Curtiss-Wright eventually sent additional senior management to Columbus, but these problems were to become chronic throughout the entire organization as the war emergency continued. Management just couldn't keep up.

Many of the corporate giant's troubles lay with the way in which it was organized. The Curtiss-Wright scheme concentrated production under experienced management, creating a very personalized managerial style. The advantage of this style was a high degree of design coordination and quality control. The disadvantage was the dilution of that management as expansion took place. This unwillingness to delegate authority meant that "production could not be expanded indefinitely . . . since management resources would be spread dangerously thin."[68]

The approach favored by companies such as United Aircraft, the parent company of Pratt and Whitney, was to license other manufacturers and thus enlist additional managerial talent, although this approach sometimes created difficulties with technical supervision. The Curtiss-Wright Airplane Division granted licenses to the Canadian Car and Foundry Company (CCF) and to the Canadian branch of the Fairchild Aircraft Corporation to build the SB2C, the only Curtiss airframe license-manufactured in quantity during World War II. The arrangement proved very troublesome for Curtiss-Wright. For example, there were reports that some of the CCF-built Helldivers were inferior to the airframes built by Curtiss and Fairchild. The Aircraft Division of Higgins Boat Industries of New Orleans, Louisiana, contracted to manufacture 500 C-46s but produced only two by the end of the European war. In these instances at least, Curtiss-Wright's fears of license manufacturing were well founded.[69]

Wright Aeronautical resorted to license manufacturing in three instances, when Continental Motors, the Dodge Division of the Chrysler Corporation, and the Studebaker Corporation were granted licenses to build Wright engines.[70] These licenses were given reluctantly and only under pressure from the government. As early as 1940, Wright Aeronautical's management had indicated its desire to retain control over the final assembly of its engines, although it was willing to increase subcontracting for subassemblies. To that end, five major "cooperating companies" became subcontractors. They were the Ohio Crankshaft Company (crankshafts), Otis Elevator Company (crankcases), Hudson Motor Car Company (pistons and rocker arms), Eaton Manufacturing Company (propeller shafts), and Graham-Paige Motors Corporation (master and articulated connecting rods).

An indication of Wright Aeronautical's resistance to the license construction of its engines came as early as November 1940, when the issue of expanded production of the R-2600 came to a head. The engine manufacturer wanted to keep all R-2600 production in one factory and argued for a greater expansion of its plant then under construction at Lockland, Ohio. The government, however, had other plans. William S. Knudsen, former General Motors executive and head of the Production Division of the National Defense Advisory Commission, wanted the R-2600s license-built. Consequently, the Studebaker Corporation was brought into the program over the objections of Wright Aeronautical. The assignment was changed in June 1941, and Studebaker ended up building the R-1820 instead of the R-2600 because the former engine was needed for B-17 production.[71]

Of the two aircraft engine manufacturing giants of World War II, Pratt and Whitney and its licensees produced a total of 355,985 engines, whereas Wright Aeronautical and its licensees manufactured 223,036. A comparison of production in horsepower by type of plant from 1940 to 1943 is also instructive:

	Pratt and Whitney		Wright	
Prewar Plants	162,163	35%	108,278	32%
Branch Plants	7,083	1%	133,972	39%
Licensee Plants	298,976	64%	96,998	29%
	468,222	100%	339,248	100%

These figures suggest that Pratt and Whitney's approach to the problem of expanding aircraft engine production was superior to that of Wright Aeronautical, whose administrative burdens were much greater than its competitor's. Undoubtedly, Wright Aeronautical's lower production figures were due in no small measure to the dilution of its managerial resources. Yet the limited supply of competent licensees, which was a problem for the Airplane Division in airframe production, was a source of aggravation to Pratt and Whitney in the manufacture of engines as well.[72] Hence there were no perfect answers to the question of how best to increase production.

By the midwar years, Wright Aeronautical was hard-pressed to keep up with commitments and had to make some adjustments. For example, the Wright Cyclone R-2600 was originally intended to power the C-46 but was soon displaced by the Pratt and Whitney R-2800. Some sources state that one reason for this switch was the desire to relieve pressure on Wright Aeronautical. Others have claimed that the Curtiss transport would have been underpowered with the Wright engine. Certainly, the R-2800 was in short supply as well. The many delays associated with the development of the trouble-plagued R-3350 have also been attributed to the management at Wright Aeronautical, which was forced to focus its attention on current production problems instead of working with the R-3350.[73]

The Propeller Division did no licensing but added to its plant capacity and opted for subcontracting. On the other hand, Hamilton Standard followed the same policy as its partner in United Aircraft, Pratt and Whitney, and resorted to large-scale licensing. A comparison of the final production figures for propellers suggests once again that licensing yielded better results than subcontracting. The total figure for all Curtiss electric propellers produced from July 1940 to August 1945 was 144,863 units, whereas Hamilton Standard alone manufactured 233,021. Nash-Kelvinator, a major Hamilton Standard licensee, built 158,134 units. In all, 542,632 Hamilton Standard propellers were produced during this period.[74]

Certainly the managerial troubles faced by the Curtiss-Wright Corporation were shared in varying degrees by other companies as well. All of them had to deal with the consequences of a war-induced expansion of the industry; all of them faced a dilution in the numbers of qualified and experienced managerial personnel as branch plants were established; and all of them were inexperienced with large-scale production operations. These burdens became even more onerous as the types of aircraft and engine models increased in variety. A report of the Harvard Business School shortly after the war, commenting on the problem, noted: "Obviously a company producing seven models could not give the same attention to any one model that it could when producing only two or three models."[75] Even the models manufactured in small numbers required extensive preliminary work in engineering development, tooling up, and ordering of materials. In short, the larger the company was and the more diverse its products were, the greater the possibility of production problems. Yet the temptation to overexpand was very real, especially as the demands of the military services appeared limitless.

As a result of these pressures, several companies became very large and very diverse during World War II. For example, Consolidated had seven major plants plus several smaller ones, and Douglas had six.[76] Some manufacturers had as many as six or seven different aircraft models in simultaneous production. None was larger or more diverse than Curtiss-Wright. Although several Curtiss aircraft had very small production runs, the company built as great a variety of airframes as any manufacturer and greater than most. As early as 1941, more than a half-dozen military aircraft types, from trainers to transports, were either under development or in production in Curtiss plants. Nevertheless, only three—the P-40, the C-46, and SB2C—were truly mass-produced. No other Curtiss design was manufactured in quantities greater than 1,000 during these years. The Airplane Division ultimately produced 26,637 airframes between 1 July 1940 and 31 August 1945—19,703 for the USAAF and 6,934 for the U.S. Navy—making the company the fourth largest American airframe producer of World War II, behind North American (41,839), Douglas (30,980), and Consolidated (30,930).[77] In fairness, the size and complexity of the airframes produced must be taken into account in evaluating these figures; otherwise, they are somewhat misleading. For example, much of North American's production was committed to the AT-6 trainer, which was a simpler airplane than the Consolidated B-24 bomber.

As Curtiss-Wright was to learn, the price for excessive product diversity could be very high. The ill-fated C-76 Caravan project remains an unfortunate example of what can happen when a company attempts too much. An all-wood cargo transport, the Caravan was an ill-conceived, dead-end project that squandered time, talent, money, and lives. It offered further proof that Curtiss-Wright was falling victim to poor planning and unwise managerial decisions. The company should never have accepted the project. Just as importantly, the government should never have given it to them. The government could and should have limited the proliferation of different aircraft types produced by any one company, but it did little to correct the problem, as the Truman Committee report observed.

Anyone assessing the managerial complexities of the Curtiss-Wright Corporation must consider that it manufactured several different types of airframes, three distinct engine models, and propellers as well. With the exception of United Aircraft, Curtiss-Wright manufactured a greater variety of aviation products than any other company in the industry. Five aircraft assembly plants, three major and three smaller engine plants, a foundry, and five propeller plants produced Curtiss-Wright aviation products during World War II. Given the immensity of this organization, the swiftness with which it grew, and the war-induced burdens it carried, the wonder is not that it had so many troubles but that it did not have more.

Another factor that undoubtedly contributed to Curtiss-Wright's managerial difficulties was the geographical dispersal of the corporation's many factories. Top management was physically far removed from the day-to-day operations of the Airplane Division. Corporate headquarters was located at 30 Rockefeller Plaza in the center of New York City, whereas headquarters of the Airplane Division was in Buffalo, at the other end of the state. The Columbus and Saint Louis plants were even farther away, not a good geographical arrangement for a company wishing to maintain a highly personalized style of management. The Ohio engine plant was also a considerable distance from Wright Aeronautical's Paterson headquarters, and the Propeller Division had branch plants in western Pennsylvania and Indianapolis. On the other hand, the main plants of Wright Aeronautical were located in Paterson and Wood-Ridge, and the headquarters of the Propeller Division was in Caldwell, all of them just across the Hudson River in New Jersey.

The problem of plant dispersal was not unique to Curtiss-Wright. Other companies also had factories spread throughout the country, some more widely separated than Curtiss-Wright's facilities. All the companies granted their plants varying degrees of autonomy, especially in day-to-day operations. Nevertheless, there are hints that in the case of Curtiss-Wright, the location of corporate headquarters in New York City created a degree of isolation from the company's manufacturing centers. From the perspective of a former Buffalo employee, this isolation left a "big chasm" between 30 Rockefeller Plaza and the western end of the state. There was, he said, simply no New York City presence in Buffalo. Another former employee noted: "The firms competing with C-W [Curtiss-Wright] usually had their leaders right on the sport where design and manufacturing were happening."[78]

Other managerial problems surfaced. Fairly or unfairly, Curtiss-Wright executives developed a reputation for uncooperative and obstinate behavior and for being very difficult to do business with during World War II. This was especially the case when questions arose regarding aircraft design modifications. A persistent refusal to accept design changes allegedly characterized the attitude of management. Former Curtiss-Wright employees, from the engineering staff to the field personnel, have stated that they were discouraged from making any kind of modifications that might impede the flow of airframes moving down the assembly lines. Nothing should be done to impede production, especially of the P-40.[79]

The experience of a Curtiss-Wright technical representative sent to North Africa in 1941 to assist the RAF in training mechanics and assembling P-40s is a case in point. These aircraft, provided through Lend-Lease, were not designed for desert operations and did not have the specialized equipment necessary for proper performance. For example, the engines lacked the dust filters required for desert operations. The filters subsequently shipped for retrofitting tended to clog up almost immediately and became completely useless. Recommendations for changes that were sent from the field back to Buffalo were invariably rejected as too costly and time-consuming. Other quite simple suggestions—such as installing piano hinges on the forward fuselage cowling to permit easy and quick access to the engine—were also rejected for the same reason. The home factory even failed to rectify a flaw in the canopy design that had caused several fatal accidents. From the perspective of this technical representative, everything was geared to increasing production, lowering costs, and maximizing profits.[80]

Although managerial attitudes may have been a factor, the reluctance to make modifications undoubtedly stemmed in large part from extreme pressures to maintain production schedules in the face of sharply increasing demands for qualitative improvements in the P-40 airframe. In late 1943, the fear of enemy superiority in aircraft performance prompted some USAAF unit commanders to send "frantic messages" back to headquarters requesting an immediate upgrade of P-40 models then in production to make them more suitable for combat operations. Yet when the necessary slowdown of production lines occurred to make the requested modifications, unit commanders complained of aircraft shortages. The "logistical difficulties imposed by [the] changes nullified the gains anticipated."[81]

Nevertheless, modifications to the P-40 were made throughout its production life. Neither alleged or real managerial obstinancy nor resistance by field commanders prevented necessary design changes from being made to the airframe. Instead, it was continually upgraded in an attempt to maintain its viability as a combat aircraft. Furthermore, the P-40 was still valuable as a trainer even after it had become obsolete. That 13,738 examples were built during a production run that lasted from 1940 until the end of 1944 testifies to the airplane's versatility and adaptability. As always, the underlying P-40 production problem was the impossibility of reconciling the mutually exclusive goals of large quantity production with ever higher performance levels.

Just as World War II brought overexpansion to Curtiss-Wright's management, so too the engineering staff found itself stretched much too thinly for efficient performance. The transferal of personnel to new plants as they opened aggravated the problem and further weakened existing engineering staffs. The pool of available talent was simply not large enough to accommodate the expansion. This problem was especially acute at Columbus, which was struggling with the SB2C. Conscription threatened to deplete the ranks of capable personnel, and the Ohio Selective Service Board was petitioned to grant deferments to plant workers eligible for the draft.

The SB2C program was affected by the personnel shortage in yet another way. Although the primary airframe was designed and the preliminary drawings were made at Buffalo, the production drawings were the responsibility of the Columbus plant. The completion date for these drawings had to be constantly rescheduled because of the scarcity of engineers.[82]

The proliferation of engineering projects also contributed to the problem, as personnel was forced to shift from one task to another. This meant that talent was either drained away from more promising projects to less viable ones or was divided between two promising ones, thereby diluting work on both. As problems with the SB2C-1 mounted, engineers were shifted to that project from the SO3C, doubtlessly weakening the latter program.[83] Some projects, such as the C-76, never should have been started. Moreover, some experimental projects also suffered from the same malady. Both the XP-60 and XP-62 projects were undertaken almost simultaneously. The company would have been better off concentrating on the former design first and then applying the lessons learned from that project to the latter program. The Airplane Division simply attempted too much at once with a design staff that was being weakened by expansion.[84]

An indication of the troubles besetting the engineering department at the Columbus factory can be found in a memo sent by chief engineer Raymond Blaylock in December 1943 to his department's employees. With extraordinary candor, Blaylock admitted that all was not well and that significant changes were necessary to improve efficiency and productivity. Personnel changes would be forthcoming in the "not too distant future," he said, including a "weeding out" of the "dead wood." Blaylock also admitted that "experience and ability" were "of necessity spread too thin," and that almost without exception, the department was "working on assignments above [its] experience level." Furthermore, he acknowledged that engineering management was "lacking sufficient experienced supervision."[85]

A former Curtiss-Wright engineer, looking back at his company's wartime troubles, claimed that personnel resources were unnecessarily dispersed throughout the various factories of the Airplane Division. On too many occasions, he said, key personnel were taken from a well-functioning design team to staff another division within the organization. The proliferation of design projects diluted personnel resources and weakened the entire organization. "The idea," he said, "is to be the *best* with a limited type of aircraft."[86]

Several individual design projects, such as the XP-62 and XF14C, were victims of bad timing, regardless of their quality. Additionally, the inordinately long development period of these airplanes only compounded Curtiss-Wright's problems. It fell ever farther behind the competition, which was building better airplanes in shorter time. Inevitably, these companies secured the government production contracts. This was especially evident in the advanced fighter project. Although the complexities of this program were much greater than any brief summary can hope to recount, the fact remains that the Airplane Division was about six months to a year behind the rest of the industry in the race to produce a new fighter.[87]

Another victim of bad timing was a navy torpedo bomber, the XBT2C, that came out at the end of the war when military orders were being slashed. This was one design that the Airplane Division seemed to "get right." Curtiss test pilot William Webster called the XBT2C a "great airplane" and criticized the Airplane Division's sales department for failing to promote it properly.[88] More likely, the project was killed by a combination of factors that included not only timing but growing company indecision about its future direction in the industry and government uncertainties about its onetime prime contractor.

As with all of Curtiss-Wright's World War II production difficulties, the timing problem was certainly not insurmountable. Yet solutions were extremely difficult to achieve because the company was so seriously overextended and its resources were strained to the maximum. A more limited commitment and a better allocation of company resources would have enabled Curtiss-Wright to surmount its many wartime problems with less difficulty.

The World War II experience of the Chance Vought Division of United Aircraft provides an interesting counterpoint to the example of Curtiss-Wright. Vought had its hands full with the early F4U Corsair navy fighter. A contemporary of the SB2C, the F4U had its share of defects that required correction before the airplane could become fully operational. Fortunately, Vought's wartime production was limited to two types, the F4U and a navy scout-observation airplane that was used extensively for air-sea rescue work. Hence Vought's resources, relatively speaking, were not stretched as thin as those of the Curtiss-Wright Airplane Division. Vought was able to rectify the Corsair's problems more easily. Moreover, like the other divisions of United Aircraft, Vought resorted to license manufacturing of the F4U to companies such as Goodyear, thereby relieving Vought of additional production burdens.

The War's Legacy

In 1943 the Curtiss-Wright Corporation was at the zenith of its power and prestige. Within two years, however, it had lost its preeminent position. The company had attempted too much in too short a time with resources that were too limited for the demands placed on them. Unfortunately, the government's ravenous hunger for war goods only made an already bad situation worse. Aircraft and engine production had been raised to unprecedented levels, in some instances much too quickly. Such was the case of three Curtiss-Wright products, the SB2C dive-bomber, the C-46 transport, and the R-3350 engine. All three had shown considerable promise, but time was required to fulfill that promise. The search for an edge in performance and numbers had forced each design into production prematurely, with regrettable consequences for Curtiss-Wright and the military services that desperately needed these products. Although the two aircraft and the engine were in operational use by the end of the war and were performing well, the difficulties encountered in developing them had been severe. In the process, confidence in the great company had been severely shaken.

The Airplane Division of Curtiss-Wright was especially weakened by the war experience. Although production of the illustrious P-40 continued unabated until within the last 12 months before V-J Day, Curtiss was particularly hard-pressed to deliver sufficient numbers of more advanced aircraft on time. Worse yet, its newer design projects had been persistently behind the development curve. The World War II experience humbled the once mighty company, which no longer enjoyed the privileged position it once had with its best customer, the military services. The Airplane Division's days of greatness were over.

By the war's end, disappointment and disillusionment had set in. A major question for Curtiss-Wright in 1945 was whether it could regain its equilibrium in the postwar world. It had entered the war enjoying first-mover advantages, but they had been dissipated by the overexpansion of a managerial and engineering base that was too limited for the demands that World War II placed on it. The history of the Curtiss-Wright Corporation at this point suggests that first-mover advantages accomplish little without adequate organization, planning, and subsequent follow-through.

Chapter 7

Demobilization, 1945–1948

The end of World War II brought the Curtiss-Wright Corporation to a crossroads. Questions abounded. What direction should the company take? Should it retain its traditional position as a manufacturer of airframes, engines, and propellers, or should it strike out in a new direction in an attempt to redefine itself and establish a new identity? The stakes were very high, for not only the company's identity but perhaps its very survival hinged on these decisions.

Following the traditional and familiar path would require a revival of the Airplane Division's flagging fortunes. Among the elements essential for such a revitalization was the necessity for new designs, and several were under various stages of development at the war's end. A key element in aircraft design at this time was a new technology that promised to completely transform both civil and military aviation in ways that were only dimly perceived in 1945. It was the gas turbine, or jet engine.

Largely because of wartime constraints, American engine manufacturers in 1945 were well behind both the British and the Germans in jet engine technology. Curtiss-Wright president Guy Vaughan had every intention of catching up as quickly as possible, however. By combining the license manufacturing of British turbojets with a program of research and development financed by wartime profits, Vaughan hoped to give Wright Aeronautical a commanding lead among American aircraft engine manufacturers in jet engine technology.

Evidence strongly suggests that Vaughan's intention was to take Curtiss-Wright down the alternate path toward a new identity as an aircraft engine builder exclusively and away from airframe manufacturing. This would allow the company to direct its energies in a more concentrated manner and perhaps enable it to recapture at least a portion of the renown that it had lost during the war years. More importantly, this strategy would, in Vaughan's eyes at least, help to guarantee his company's survival and prosperity in the difficult years of postwar readjustment. Wright Aeronautical, for many years the dominant partner in the Curtiss-Wright organization, would in effect supplant the other manufacturing divisions entirely.

Jet engine technology would require a large investment in research and development, however. Although Curtiss-Wright's financial resources were more than adequate for this venture, others associated with the company—namely, a group of dissident stockholders— had other ideas. Smoldering in the background was a dispute between management and these stockholders over the disposition of corporate wartime profits and whether they should be used for jet engine research or distributed as a dividend. The larger issue was the control of the great corporation. Who would guide its fortunes in the years to come? In the end, Vaughan and his associates lost the battle, setting into motion a chain of events that ultimately transformed the company and altered its identity in ways never imagined in 1945.

Planning for the Postwar World

The American aviation industry reached its highest rate of production in 1944. Of the 324,750 airframes produced by American aircraft manufacturers between 1939 and 1945, 96,318 were turned out in the 12-month period between January and December 1944. Engine and propeller production followed the same pattern: 1944 was the peak production year, in which 256,911 reciprocating engines out of a total of 812,615 units produced between 1940 and 1945 came off American assembly lines. The total production figure for propellers for the same period was 713,717, of which 243,741 were manufactured in 1944.[1]

America was clearly outproducing both its allies and its adversaries. Together with the quality and numbers of military personnel, this flood of war goods made the difference between victory and defeat in World War II. The Axis powers were simply being overwhelmed by superior quantities of matériel, much of it coming from American factories. As early as 7 December 1941, in fact, the rate of American aircraft production had overtaken the rest of the world, and from that year on, the United States surpassed both Germany and Japan in total airframe production. Together, the two Axis powers manufactured fewer than 180,000 airframes between 1939 and 1944, whereas American aircraft builders alone produced almost 275,000 for the same period. In March 1944, 9,113 airplanes rolled off American assembly lines, a figure that almost equaled the combined production totals of the other four major belligerents (Great Britain, the Soviet Union, Germany, and Japan) for the same time period.[2]

The Curtiss-Wright Corporation's share in this marvel of production was substantial. Despite many production problems, Curtiss-Wright continued to compile a credible record as a supplier of airframes, engines, and propellers to the military services. Like the rest of the industry, the corporation's production soared in 1944. That year, a total of 90 million

Table 1. Aircraft production: World War II

YEAR	JAPAN	GERMANY	GREAT BRITAIN	USA*
1939	4,467	8,295	7,940	5,856
1940	4,768	10,247	15,049	12,804
1941	5,088	11,776	20,094	26,277
1942	8,861	15,409	23,672	47,836
1943	16,693	24,807	26,263	85,898
1944	28,180	39,807	26,461	96,318
1945	11,066**	7,540***	12,070**	49,761

*Includes shipments to U.S. military services and others.

**January–August.

***January–April

Source: Holley, *Buying Aircraft*, 548; Overy, *The Air War, 1939–1945*, 192.

Craven and Cate, *Men and Planes*, 350, lists the combined production for Japan and Germany from 1939 to 1945 at 188,107 units.

horsepower was produced in the factories of Wright Aeronautical, 20 million more than in 1943. In late 1944, the Airplane Division's 15,000th fighter, a P-40N, rolled out the doors of the airport plant in Buffalo. Shortly thereafter, P-40 production came to an end, and the company turned its attention to accelerating the production schedules of the C-46, which by that time had become a reliable transport aircraft. Improved models of the SB2C were also going into service in increasing numbers. On 19 November, the Columbus facility received the Army-Navy "E" for excellence award for production efficiency, in recognition of being ahead of schedule for 12 consecutive months on Helldiver production. To that date, more than 4,000 combat aircraft had been produced at Columbus, most of them Helldivers. Columbus received a second Army-Navy "E" award in 1945. The output of the whole Airplane Division for the month of November 1944, measured in pounds of airframe, was 8.5 times greater than for the entire year 1938. Production of P-40s, C-46s, and SB2Cs in 1944 represented an increase of 65 percent over the previous year and 17 times the 1940 airframe production. Several Propeller Division plants received the "E" award as well. By the company's own accounting, the total dollar value of all Curtiss-Wright shipments from 1940 through 1945 was $5,492,275,000, of which $1,197,705,000 occurred in 1945 alone.[3]

In the meantime, the industry was anticipating the postwar era with a mixture of apprehension and optimism. Everyone knew that the end of the war would bring a time of difficult readjustment. Cancellation of war contracts meant significant cutbacks. Memories of the post–World War I aviation collapse haunted many.

Yet there were significant differences between the two eras. For one thing, military aviation was expected to continue its vital role in the postwar world. More importantly, a dramatic growth in all phases of commercial aviation was anticipated. Observers noted the emergence of an increasingly air-minded society as a result of the wartime experience. Prophecies of a new air age dawning with the end of hostilities were being made. The war had introduced millions of people to the airplane, and air travel was now routine. A worldwide international air transport system was emerging in 1945, as suggested by the creation of the International Civil Aviation Organization (ICAO) and the International Air Transport Association (IATA).[4]

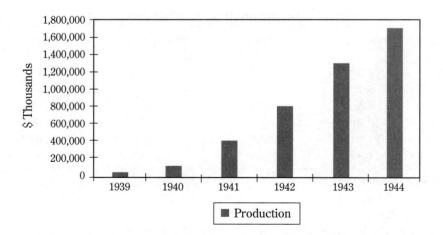

Fig. 9.   Curtiss-Wright production: 1939–1944

In addition to the expected growth of commercial aviation, a similar boom in private or general aviation was also anticipated. Many believed that personal flying would become commonplace in postwar America. Former military pilots would want to continue flying with their own personal airplane; former servicemen without pilot training would be able to afford flight school with the aid of the GI Bill of Rights. Even the most conservative projections of industry and government analysts foresaw a significant expansion of light-aircraft sales and a dramatic growth in private flying. As early as 1943, the Department of Commerce anticipated the postwar demand for light planes at 200,000 units per year.[5] The picture was very rosy; it also was very unrealistic.

Like other companies, Curtiss-Wright took initiatives in 1944 and 1945 to meet the challenges of the new era. The first step came with the creation of a Curtiss-Wright Post-war Planning Committee with subcommittees to consider the issues of postwar aviation. Product development was high on the list.[6] Moreover, a fourth division of the Curtiss-Wright Corporation, the Curtiss-Wright Development Division, located at Bloomfield, New Jersey, was established in April 1943. Although initially concentrating on war production research, the division was already anticipating work on new product and market possibilities for the postwar period.[7]

Fortunately for the industry, the great wartime advances in military aviation had obvious civilian applications. In early 1945, Curtiss-Wright announced several new engineering and technological developments. The Propeller Division, for example, was working on several new products, such as a reversible-thrust propeller that could act as a brake, throwing the air forward and reducing an airplane's landing run and tire wear. Still another product was a new type of so-called "paddle-blade" propeller, then in quantity production, which was claimed to be more efficient than conventional propellers, giving fighter aircraft a 30 percent faster rate of climb. New propeller test facilities were constructed at Caldwell, New Jersey, capable of testing propellers up to 30 feet in diameter. Additionally, the Wood-Ridge, New Jersey, plant built 16 new engine test cells, stressed to handle reciprocating engines capable of 4,000 horsepower.

The Airplane Division was also actively planning for the postwar world. The division's leaders were actively considering several nonaviation as well as aviation products. A light-weight railway passenger car was considered as a possible peacetime Curtiss-Wright product once the reconversion process had taken place.[8]

Aviation products remained a prime consideration, however. The focus of the Airplane Division's activities at this time was the C-46. Work began as early as February 1943 on reconfiguring the military transport as a 44-passenger civilian airliner, the Model CW-20E. The Buffalo plant, where the plane was to be manufactured, undertook the design work.[9]

High hopes rested on this airplane. Its sales would help to cushion the postwar shock of evaporating military contracts. Moreover, the development costs would be minimal, since the basic design was unchanged from the original Model 20. Throughout 1944, Curtiss-Wright officials and representatives of several major airlines, including TWA, American, and Eastern, held discussions about the CW-20E. They culminated in an announcement on 4 October 1944 that Eastern Airlines planned to purchase a fleet of 10 CW-20Es by the fall of 1945.[10]

Central to the postwar plans for the Airplane Division was a completely autonomous research laboratory, conceived by Airplane Division chief Burdette Wright and formally dedicated on 11 February 1943. Contained within its walls were a 750-mile-per-hour wind tunnel and a high-altitude chamber able to simulate altitudes of 60,000 feet at temperatures of minus 85 degrees Fahrenheit. The research laboratory represented a completely new concept. Equal in status within the corporation to engineering, sales, and finance, it was the only aeronautical research laboratory of its kind wholly owned by a private corporation. It represented an investment of approximately $4.5 million.[11]

Of all the possible postwar projects studied by Curtiss-Wright, the one with the greatest potential was revealed when the Wright Aeronautical Corporation announced in early 1945 that work had already begun on the development of gas turbine (jet) engines for aircraft use. In fact, Wright Aeronautical's first direct involvement with turbines had come as early as 1934, when it initiated work on its own version of a device known as a supercharger, a compressor used to increase the density of air supplied to a conventional reciprocating engine. There are two types of superchargers. The first is driven by a step-up gearing from the crankshaft. The second is driven by an exhaust turbine and is called a turbosupercharger.[12]

Further interest in gas turbines had been stimulated around 1940, when industry began hearing rumors of experiments with jet engines then taking place in Great Britain and Germany. Sir Frank Whittle, then an engineer and officer in the Royal Air Force, had conceived the idea of gas turbine propulsion for aircraft use in the late twenties. He continued his work throughout the thirties, and by the spring of 1941, one of his gas turbine engines was installed in an airframe that flew successfully for the first time in May.

Meanwhile, General H. H. Arnold, chief of the U.S. Army Air Corps, learned of these experiments. Not fully understanding the precise nature of this research, he went to England in April 1941 to see for himself just what was going on. What he saw astounded him. Immediately recognizing the military potential of this invention, Arnold made a formal request to the British government for access to the new technology. The British complied, and the two governments negotiated an agreement that gave the U.S. Army the sole authority to develop and build the Whittle engine in the United States. The army contracted the work to General Electric because of that company's long experience with conventional turbines. Both major engine manufacturers, Pratt and Whitney and Wright Aeronautical, were bypassed. At the request of General Arnold, they—together with the other domestic engine manufacturers—were also excluded from membership on the Special Committee on Jet Propulsion that was established by the National Advisory Committee for Aeronautics (NACA) to examine the new technology.

The reasons for Arnold's request remain unclear. The most plausible explanation is that Arnold was extremely anxious to have American engine manufacturers concentrate on piston engine production for the war effort. Jet engine technology was for the future. His immediate concern was the war, and he wanted no resources diverted from the production of existing weapons needed by America's military forces to any project that had little chance of affecting the outcome of the conflict. Reportedly, the army and navy both "absolutely forbade the engine companies to divert any of their resources to the new field until very late in the war" and withheld official information about developments with gas turbines from American engine manufacturers until 1945.[13]

Nevertheless, interest in jet engines remained high throughout the war, and with the end in sight, there was a resurgence of activity in turbine engine research. The implications of this new technology were profound and far-reaching. It promised to revolutionize civil and military aviation. With the conventional reciprocating engine approaching the end of its development cycle, the gas turbine had the potential of improving aircraft performance significantly. Most particularly, much higher speeds would be possible. Hence an engine manufacturer able to exploit this new technology would be well positioned to prosper in the period of contraction following the cancellation of war contracts. This undoubtedly was the thinking of Guy Vaughan as he pondered the Curtiss-Wright Corporation's place in the post–World War II American aviation industry. Vaughan clearly recognized the gas turbine's potential, and as early as January 1945, he directed Wright Aeronautical to push ahead to the "full limit" of the company's abilities with a turbine project already under development, arguing that it had the "best present and long-term prospects" of any project then under consideration.[14]

Demobilization began immediately with the end of hostilities in August 1945. Contracts were canceled almost literally overnight. Of 66 airframe plants that had been in operation in 1944, only 16 were still open a year later. Within six months of V-J Day, more than $21 billion in contracts had been canceled. Total industry sales dropped more than 90 percent between 1944 and 1947, and earnings and employment plummeted.[15]

These conditions were mirrored at Curtiss-Wright. The company experienced an 84 percent reduction in government contracts after V-J Day. This decrease represented the elimination of 1,450 airframes.[16] The consequences of the earlier decision to enlarge production facilities rather than grant licenses to other manufacturers were now being felt. The cancellations left Curtiss-Wright with the burden of excess plant capacity. In fact, retrenchment began even before the Pacific war was over. Operations in Saint Louis came to an end in July 1945. It was a major step in the move to consolidate all Airplane Division activities in Columbus. The Saint Louis factory was turned over to the Defense Plant Corporation amid many recriminations. The Curtiss presence in that city dated from the founding of the Curtiss-Robertson Airplane Manufacturing Company in 1928. Many were now remembering the fears expressed in 1940 that the end of the war would bring an abandonment of the huge manufacturing complex. Those fears had now become reality. The blow was softened, however, when the McDonnell Aircraft Corporation took over the facilities, and many former Curtiss-Wright employees found work with the new company.

All operations in Buffalo ceased in August 1945. The end of the Curtiss era was an especially bitter blow to that city. Curtiss factories had been producing airplanes and engines on the Niagara Frontier since 1915. Old-timers remembered when Jennies had moved down the assembly lines of the Elmwood Avenue plant. Yet mere sentiment was not enough to keep a Curtiss presence in Buffalo. Harsh economic reality dictated otherwise. In announcing the decision to move, company spokesman Robert L. Earle cited a better physical plant setup in Columbus as a major reason for the decision to close the Buffalo facilities; greater production efficiencies could be realized at the Ohio plant. Milder weather in Columbus was also cited as a factor in the decision to move.[17] The loss of the Airplane Division was a blow to Buffalo's pride as well as its economy.

The reductions in plants and equipment were accompanied by several personnel changes. Burdette S. Wright, the longtime vice president and general manager of the Airplane Division, left Buffalo for corporate headquarters in New York City, ostensibly to "assist in reconversion." Robert L. Earle, vice president and general manager of the Propeller Division, was placed in complete charge of the Airplane Division as well, thus effectively combining the two divisions. All of these moves were but a prelude to even greater changes that were to come a few years hence.

The recently created research laboratory was eliminated as well. With production activities about 5 percent of the wartime peak, the corporation asserted that it could not financially justify the continued underwriting of the laboratory's activities. This may or may not have been a correct assessment because claims have been made that the business base for the continued operation of the research laboratory and its wind tunnel actually was quite good. Nevertheless, Curtiss-Wright negotiated a deal with Cornell University whereby the entire facility, including the laboratory building, surrounding property, technical equipment, and material on hand, was donated to Cornell. The total value was estimated at some $4 million.

In making this gift, Curtiss-Wright was able to take a significant tax write-off for 1945, which, thanks to war contracts, was a high-profit year. Consolidated net income for the 12-month period ending 31 December 1945 amounted to $24,430,217.[18] The Airplane Division personnel, sensing the beginning of the end for the Airplane Division, were bitterly disappointed by the loss of the research laboratory.

Despite these cutbacks, the Curtiss-Wright Corporation was in good financial condition. Its reserves were listed at $178 million, making it the financial giant of the industry. Nevertheless, the giant was in trouble. Those reserves proved to be a source of contention between management and stockholders and led to a bitter quarrel over control of the great company. In an ironic twist, Curtiss-Wright's wartime financial success contributed directly to its postwar undoing. It had become too big and too rich. In later years, an executive summarized his company's problems with the sardonic comment: "The Curtiss-Wright Corporation did $5 billion worth of business during World War II and never recovered."[19]

There were other clouds on the horizon. Curtiss-Wright's checkered performance during World War II was a cause for concern over its future. The company's reputation had been damaged, and much goodwill, important for future contracts, had been lost. Product reliability and performance had declined, and in a postwar environment with uncertain markets and increased competition, this could pose problems for the company's ability to secure much-needed government and civil contracts.

The Finletter Commission

The bright promise of world peace in August 1945 proved to be illusory. By 1947 the United States and the Soviet Union had become adversaries in the 40-year global confrontation that came to be known as the Cold War, with the Iron Curtain splitting the European continent between East and West. These events had a profound impact on America. Obsessively concerned with "national security," the nation responded with a militarized foreign policy unprecedented in its history.

Additionally, American public opinion was in the process of being reshaped by books, articles, speeches, and debates emanating from individuals and organizations, both public and private, all stressing the primacy of America's defensive needs in the uncertain world ahead.[20] One of the more significant of these committees was the Air Policy Commission, created by President Truman on 18 July 1947. Chaired by Thomas Finletter, a well-known attorney with State Department connections, the commission submitted its final report in December 1947. The report's title, *Survival in the Air Age,* was a summation of its thesis, which declared that the first line of defense for the United States was air power. Since other nations (i.e., the Soviet Union) were likely to develop nuclear weapons, the only effective way to deter aggression was to concentrate on research and development in the aeronautical sciences and to strengthen both civil and military aviation. The report called for an air force consisting of 70 groups, 15 more than were currently in existence.

The Finletter Commission, as it was popularly known, also analyzed several problems specifically afflicting the aviation industry and observed that its products were both weapons of war and instruments of commerce; its major customer was the government, "which normally took 80 to 90 percent of the [industry's] total output." Furthermore, changing government requirements caused demand to fluctuate, which in turn made it very difficult for the industry to maintain a skilled workforce and keep production costs down. The problem was aggravated by an exceptionally long design and manufacturing cycle. These problems were compounded by the type of product being manufactured, which tended to evolve at a swift pace. This led to "a high rate of design obsolescence and abnormally high engineering costs."[21] In short, the aviation industry was afflicted by fluctuating markets, overcapacity, and a rapidly changing technology.

This was nothing new. These problems had plagued the industry since its birth. Moreover, the solution proposed by the Finletter Commission, which called for an activist and interventionist government policy to stabilize the industry, was reminiscent of similar recommendations made by the Morrow Board in 1925.[22] The difference was the heightened sense of vulnerability to attack that had not existed 22 years earlier. Now, the justification for such a policy was national security:

In a freely competitive economy the number of companies manufacturing a particular product levels off at a point determined by the ordinary laws of economics. In the case of the aircraft industry, however, it would be dangerous to rely on the operation of these laws. The demand factor fluctuates too violently from peace to war. If a reasonable degree of expansibility is to be maintained for periods of emergency, it is necessary to exercise some industry-wide controls in the interests of national security. It may even be desirable to keep a few marginal manufacturers in business who might be forced out if the normal laws of supply and demand were allowed to operate.[23]

The last sentence was to have particular relevance for Curtiss-Wright and its last airplane, the XP-87.

The implications of the Finletter Commission report for the American aviation industry were obvious and profound. The industry was still reconverting to a peacetime economy in 1947, and it was proving to be an extremely painful process. The 1946 domestic production of 35,000 nonmilitary airplanes, including transports and light aircraft, dwindled to 3,545 in 1949. The light plane market was beginning to contract as early as 1947; Piper, the best-known manufacturer of small low-powered personal aircraft, almost went broke.[24]

The giants had their share of problems as well. Convair had a contract to develop the B-36, a massive 6-engine bomber (subsequently 10 engines) that became the mainstay of the Strategic Air Command of the newly created United States Air Force (USAF) during the first decade of the Cold War. Nevertheless, the company lost $36 million in 1947, although that figure was reduced to $16.7 million as a result of tax recovery. Development and production costs on its Model 240 series airliner were greater than anticipated, and an attempt at diversification proved to be "overambitious and poorly thought out." In an effort to preserve its resources and keep its workforce intact, Convair had tried to develop several unorthodox products, such as the prototype of a plastic-and-aluminum packaged home and a hybrid automobile-airplane combination. Convair also became involved in the production of household appliances. None of these projects was successful. Failing to heed Convair's experience with diversification, however, Curtiss-Wright would make a similar move some years later, with similar results.[25]

By 1947 every aircraft manufacturer was experiencing difficulties in varying degrees. The position of the Glenn L. Martin Company continued to deteriorate despite its Model 202 and the later 404 airliners and several military contracts. In the late fifties, Martin abandoned airframe manufacturing altogether and eventually entered the fields of electronics, missiles, and nuclear energy. Even Douglas and Boeing, among the healthiest of the airframe manufacturers, experienced their share of pain in the reconversion process.[26]

Despite the optimism of the air age enthusiasts, the mid-forties was a difficult time for the American aviation industry, and government contracts continued to provide a measure of financial stability. For some, military orders were a matter of survival. Hence the publication of the Finletter Commission report was welcome news. Even though its recommendations were not fully implemented, it provided a broad policy outline for the future development of American aviation.

Promise and Disillusionment

The changes that transformed the Curtiss-Wright Corporation after World War II were played out within the context of these events. By 1947 the once vast manufacturing empire was the proverbial shadow of its former self. Sixteen of 19 plants had shut down. The only ones left were the engine factory and laboratory at Wood-Ridge, New Jersey, the propeller plant at Caldwell, New Jersey, and the aircraft facility at Columbus, Ohio, which was surviving by doing overhaul work and subcontracting. Wright Aeronautical consolidated all of its manufacturing and office facilities in the Wood-Ridge factory, which had been purchased from the government in 1946. The Paterson factories were sold off.[27]

A dramatic decline in personnel accompanied the reduction of the physical plant. The exodus from Curtiss-Wright included thousands of skilled and semiskilled factory workers as well as many from the engineering departments. What had begun as a trickle while the war was still in progress became a flood after 1945 as many of the company's best engineers left. Several stayed on for a while, but by the late forties, the Airplane Division had lost its vitality. Those engineers who remained found themselves competing with one another for the very few aircraft design projects that were still available. Other "old-timers" who had strong ties to the aviation industry such as test pilots and front office personnel also left. With these resignations and with the cutbacks that took place in the years following V-J Day, the Airplane Division experienced a loss of personnel that with only slight exaggeration can be described as a hemorrhage.

The company's downward spiral accelerated to the end of the decade as net profits declined more than $2.5 million, from more than $5.3 million in 1948 to just over $2.75 million in 1949, even though total sales increased by almost $17 million as a result of increased Cold War military spending.[28] To give some perspective on these changes, Curtiss-Wright's share of total sales in the U.S. aviation industry had dropped to 10 percent in 1947, down from nearly 50 percent more than 10 years earlier.[29] Clearly, Curtiss-Wright had slipped badly.

Nevertheless, much potential remained. In addition to the company's substantial cash reserves, several new products were either planned or under development. The Propeller Division continued its work with the reversible-pitch propeller. It also pursued additional propeller research, which included flight testing conducted at the Caldwell facility from 1947 into the early fifties.[30] Additionally, the division received a significant share of commercial aviation's propeller business. Curtiss propellers were found on several major airliners. The division also received the contract to develop the propellers for the mighty Convair B-36. By 1948 the Propeller Division was also beginning to investigate the application of propellers to the new turboprop engines (i.e., gas turbines turning a propeller) being developed by several manufacturers.[31]

Wright Aeronautical was another bright spot. The R-3350 engine, which had been the source of so many headaches during the war, was now evolving into an efficient power plant as it underwent continued refinement and development under the leadership of chief engineer Wilton G. Lundquist. With the carburetion problems largely solved by a fuel injection system, the engine found wide use in a variety of military and civilian aircraft. The engine's efficiency was demonstrated in September 1946, when a Lockheed P2V-1 Neptune named the *Truculent Turtle* established a world record when it flew 11,236 miles without refueling.[32]

The R-3350 also became the basis for a new design, the turbo-compound engine. Arguably the ultimate example of aircraft piston engine development, the turbo-compound was a conventional reciprocating engine that had three small turbines that captured some of the energy in the exhaust gas and fed it directly to the crankshaft, thereby increasing output by some 20 percent. Fuel efficiency was improved dramatically as the original 3,125-horsepower rating was raised to 3,750 horsepower.[33]

The turbo-compound's economy of operation made it a logical choice as the power plant for the new long-range passenger transports that were acquired by the airlines throughout the world in the early fifties. With the surge in postwar commercial aviation, this engine had a substantial market that was growing, at least for the short run. Moreover, its selling price, in the $85,000 range, made it one of the lowest-priced engines per horsepower—less than $23 per horsepower—of any then available. Some claimed that even a Briggs and Stratton lawnmower engine could not match that figure. The turbo-compound became the power plant for such airliners as the Super Constellation and DC-7, which ensured Wright Aeronautical of business with most of the larger airlines worldwide. In addition, the R-3350 was installed in several different military aircraft, such as the P2V.[34] Unfortunately, the turbo-compound was an extremely complex piece of machinery, and it experienced continued operational problems, making it an unpopular engine with flight crews.

Sales from both the Propeller Division and Wright Aeronautical remained strong and were the main source of income for Curtiss-Wright. In 1947, for example, despite overall losses of more than $1 million for the entire corporation, Wright Aeronautical sold $51,260,548 worth of products, on which it realized a net profit of $512,600. At the end of the year, the Propeller Division had unfilled orders of $118,500,000, 80 percent of which were for the military. This was an increase of $3.5 million over the previous year.[35] As late as 1950, the propeller plant at Caldwell was still profitable; as of September that year, it represented 30 percent of all Curtiss-Wright sales and produced half of all propellers manufactured in the United States for the year. The Wood-Ridge plant of Wright Aeronautical generated 65 percent of all Curtiss-Wright sales.[36]

Of the three manufacturing divisions that made up the corporation in 1945, the Airplane Division was the weakest. Vaughan's report to the stockholders at the September 1945 annual meeting noted that aside from experimental work, the only business the Airplane Division had left on its books following V-J Day was the Eastern Airlines order for 10 CW-20E transports. It was also the last production scheduled for Buffalo. On the completion of this order, those factory doors were to close permanently.[37]

As World War II came to an end, the pace of work on the CW-20E picked up significantly. One former Curtiss-Wright engineer who was part of the project said that Buffalo "went full steam ahead with development" of the CW-20E. Moreover, the company initiated a public relations campaign to promote the new transport, which included pictures of the airplane in the livery of several major airlines.

It was all for naught, however, as Eastern canceled its contract with the Airplane Division in the fall of 1945. War surplus airplanes, including the C-46, were now available on favorable terms, allowing the airlines to acquire them as a stopgap measure, "pending production of more advanced models in the future."[38] Great strides had been made in aircraft design during the war years, and the Model 20 was a prewar airplane already seven years old in 1944 and approaching obsolescence. The cancellation of the Eastern Airlines contract hastened the closing of the Buffalo airport plant.

The CW-20E was not the end of the civil transport story, however, as Curtiss-Wright came out with a completely new transport design in the fall of 1945; but it never got beyond the drawing board.[39] An even more ambitious project was the CW-32, a four-engine civil and military cargo transport. A full-scale mock-up was built before the project was abandoned, allegedly for lack of government contracts.[40]

A third project was the XP-87 Blackhawk, a jet-powered all-weather interceptor designed for the air force. Although the airplane showed some promise, the $80 million contract was canceled in 1948.[41] After 40 years, Curtiss-Wright was out of the airplane business. The failure of these designs to reach fulfillment was due to many factors. Company policy was most certainly one of them.

Guy Vaughan's Vision: A Transformed Company

A concerted effort to pursue airframe design and development was required if the Airplane Division was to survive and prosper. Curtiss-Wright needed a program similar to the one undertaken by Boeing several years later when the expertise gained from the development of the B-47 and B-52 programs, together with the profits acquired from military contracts stemming from the Cold War and the Korean conflict, allowed the Seattle-based company to secure a dominant position in the airline market with its highly successful 707 jet transport.[42]

The failure of Curtiss-Wright to pursue the development of its postwar designs and thus anticipate the future Boeing example may well have been due to a conscious decision by management to forsake aircraft production altogether. As early as 1943, in fact, some in the airline industry expressed the feeling that Curtiss-Wright was not really interested in entering the civil transport field. Moreover, rumors were circulating within the company by early 1945 that corporate headquarters in New York City, following a "production, profit and close down" strategy, had planned even before the Cheektowaga plant was built in 1941 to eliminate the Airplane Division once the war was over.[43]

The key figure in these developments was Guy Vaughan, president of Curtiss-Wright from 1935 to 1949. Vaughan presided over the wartime expansion of Curtiss-Wright, and at war's end, he attempted to reshape the corporation to conform to a peacetime economy. Unwittingly he helped to set into motion a chain of events that transformed the Curtiss-Wright Corporation from a major manufacturing enterprise to a second-level subcontractor and investment company. His ultimate failure to achieve his postwar goals was due as much to circumstances beyond his control as to mistakes of leadership.

Guy Vaughan's vision for his company's postwar future was shaped by his own past. One word succinctly summarizes his career: *engines.* He was an engine man and remained one throughout his life. His commitment to the development and production of the internal combustion engine initially led him to the automobile industry and then to aviation, where his journey took him first to Wright-Martin, then to Wright Aeronautical, and finally to the presidency of the Curtiss-Wright Corporation. Although lacking formal training as an engineer, he had an immense fund of practical knowledge of engine development and production. He also had observed the volatile nature of the industry and recognized the differences between airframe and engine manufacturing. His own experience as head of Wright Aeronautical had shown him that of the two types of manufacturing, engine building offered greater stability and more consistent profits. Before leaving Wright-Martin at the end of World War I, he had helped to persuade the company to forsake airframe production and concentrate on engine development.[44] As noted in chapter 4, Vaughan became intimately involved with the development of the Whirlwind and Cyclone engines after his return to Wright Aeronautical and was the leader of the team that negotiated the contract with Douglas that matched the Cyclone R-1820 with the DC-1.[45]

Vaughan opposed the 1929 merger that brought the Curtiss and Wright companies together, believing that it might lead Wright Aeronautical in a sense to compete against itself. On the one hand, he saw the possibility of Wright Aeronautical no longer selling engines to all airframe manufacturers; instead, it would be part of a conglomerate selling "packages," or airframe and engine combinations. On the other hand, Wright Aeronautical might be forced to compete with other engine manufacturers to provide engines for Curtiss aircraft. He also foresaw difficulties in selling engines to other airframe manufacturers, who would be competing with Curtiss in airplane sales. This was not an idle concern, and it may well have contributed to the cancellation of the CW-20E project. According to one source, when Donald Douglas learned that Curtiss-Wright was planning to produce a postwar airliner, he called Vaughan and told him: "I hear you're going into the airframe business. Too bad we're going to have to go to Pratt and Whitney for our new engines—it's been nice doing business with you."[46]

Vaughan's dilemma was not unique. General Motors faced a similar problem after World War II. The automotive conglomerate had first developed a significant presence in the aviation industry in World War I when it produced both engines and airframes for the U.S. government. GM continued to play an active role in the aviation industry after the war by investing in several companies that had an aviation orientation, such as the Allison Engineering Company, which produced the V-1710 engine during World War II. GM had also acquired an interest in North American Aviation, the holding company created by Clement M. Keys in 1928, and continued to play an active role in North American even after the latter company evolved into a major airframe manufacturer in the thirties. GM was North American's largest single shareholder and gave substantial administrative and managerial guidance to the aircraft builder. Additionally, GM's Eastern Aircraft Division manufactured significant numbers of airframes under license from Grumman during World War II, and its Fisher Body Division was the major subcontractor for the North American B-25 bomber.[47]

By the end of the war, therefore, GM was poised to enter the aviation industry as a major builder of airframes and engines while still maintaining its automobile manufacturing business. Its position at this point was roughly analogous to that of Curtiss-Wright. Both companies were large and diverse conglomerates—although GM, with its automotive interests, was more diverse than Curtiss-Wright—and both had a decision to make, namely, whether it was in their respective interests to further develop their airframe and aircraft engine manufacturing capability. In his memoirs, former executive Alfred P. Sloan described GM's position:

Early in [World War II] it became apparent that our involvement in aviation was so large as to raise a question about our permanent place in the industry. Accordingly, we made an effort to redefine our thinking about aviation and the part we should play in it. The principal statement on this important matter is a report which I made in 1942 to the Postwar Planning Group in General Motors. The recommendations in this report were eventually adopted by the corporation's Policy Committee, and they became the basis for our postwar aviation program.[48]

The Postwar Planning Group determined that none of the three major markets in the postwar aviation industry—military, commercial, and private—was large enough to warrant the substantial investment required for aircraft design and development. Excess capacity in the industry, coupled with low-volume production, would probably result in a very low profit margin. On the other hand, the potential for high-volume production—and subsequent profits—was far greater with aircraft engines and accessories.

Moreover, Sloan, echoing Vaughan's concerns, feared that GM's entry into the airframe manufacturing business "might jeopardize the other aviation business of the corporation." The Allison Division was expected to be a "major producer of airplane engines and certain aircraft accessories." These products had considerable sales potential, but to realize it, close engineering cooperation and confidence with the airframe manufacturers was absolutely necessary. Sloan doubted that such a working relationship could be established if GM were in the aircraft manufacturing business as well. GM would be in a position to use the engineering information thus acquired to build its own airframes as a competitor. Therefore the thought that GM could sell engines and accessories to companies with whom they would be competing in airfame manufacturing and sales was to him "incomprehensible." The committee therefore recommended that GM should not get into the business of manufacturing airframes but that it should "develop as complete a position in the manufacture of accessories as its capacity and circumstances make possible."[49]

Hence "General Motors stood to lose rather than gain by attempting to compete with its own customers."[50] Consequently, the automobile giant divested itself of its aviation holdings in June 1948. Significantly, it retained the Allison Division, which became a manufacturer of aircraft turbine engines after World War II. Sloan's reasoning doubtless paralleled Guy Vaughan's thoughts as Vaughan contemplated his own company's future in the years after 1945.

Vaughan had professed a reluctance to assume the presidency of the merged corporation in 1935 and expressed a desire to remain with engine development and sales. Whatever his personal wishes may have been, however, World War II intervened, helping to shape corporate policy, and Curtiss-Wright continued to produce both engines and airframes for the war effort.

As World War II wound down, Vaughan could not quite shake the memory of his experiences at Wright-Martin in 1919, when the aviation industry had suffered an almost total collapse. He also recalled the desperate depression years when, under the leadership of Thomas Morgan, Curtiss-Wright experienced a drastic reduction in the scope of its operations. Consequently, he decided to pursue a very conservative policy, preserving Curtiss-Wright's substantial cash reserves that had accumulated from the huge war contracts. Moreover, he instigated the massive retrenchment program that has already been discussed, and he initiated a policy of diversification into nonaviation products that began when he acquired LGS Spring Clutches, Inc. in 1944.

Vaughan continued to pursue his "cash up front" policy into the postwar years and refused to risk squandering Curtiss-Wright's cash reserves in research projects that in his view showed little promise. Therefore he declined any research not contracted for by the military. In the words of one observer, "he opposed any experimentation or deviation from tried and true paths. . . . He was bearish for the future."[51]

Vaughan's fears were shared by many others in government and the industry who believed there were too many aircraft companies for the available volume of business. One writer claimed that the post–World War II defense program "had barely prevented some financial calamities to happen [sic] to the industry."[52]

Mergers provided a way out of this plight, and several merger rumors involving Curtiss-Wright circulated for some years after World War II. However, Vaughan gave little if any support to these merger ideas while he was president.[53] He apparently believed that Curtiss-Wright's best chance for survival in the long run was to concentrate on engine development. Meanwhile he would carefully husband those enormous cash reserves acquired from war contracts, pending an upturn in the industry.

Curtiss-Wright's failure to develop its postwar aircraft designs can be explained at least partially by Vaughan's policy. Several former employees have claimed that both the XP-87 and CW-32 projects were scuttled by company management, although the official history of the XP-87 compiled by the Air Technical Service Command Historical Office at Wright Field in January 1950 attributes the demise of the Curtiss fighter to design and performance deficiencies. According to this account, flight tests at the USAF test facility at Muroc, California, revealed shortcomings in the original airframe, although the Air Materiel Command expressed confidence that a redesigned and enlarged wing would eliminate them.[54] Nevertheless, the XP-87 program was canceled by USAF Headquarters on 14 October 1948 as a result of a series of comparative flight tests carried out at Muroc on 6 to 7 October with three airplanes, the Curtiss XP-87, the Douglas XF3D, and the Northrop XP-89. The XP-89 emerged as the clear winner. Shortly thereafter, U.S. Air Force Secretary W. Stuart Symington informed Defense Secretary James V. Forrestal that the XP-87 contract had been canceled and the monies saved would be used for developing the Northrop airplane and for procuring an interim all-weather fighter.[55]

Official histories are often as interesting for what they don't reveal as for what they do say. In this instance, nothing is written about a meeting that took place shortly before the cancellation order was given. The meeting was held in the office of Undersecretary of the U.S. Air Force A. S. Barrows between Barrows and Guy Vaughan. According to a rumor that circulated among company personnel, the meeting was extremely acrimonious.[56] Curtiss-Wright had already agreed in the summer of 1948 to absorb more of the cost of redesigning and fabricating a new wing for the XP-87. This action reduced the price of the wing modification from $846,936 to $648,356.[57] Evidently the USAF wanted Curtiss-Wright to absorb still more of the modification costs. Vaughan adamantly refused to go along with the demand, and the USAF responded by canceling the project.

This brief account undoubtedly covers only a small portion of the full XP-87 story, which remains to be written, but nothing in the official history actually contradicts it. The USAF could possibly have accepted the XP-87 had they been able to reach an agreement with the airframe manufacturer on price. As noted, international events were forcing the pace of USAF expansion in 1948. Although the Korean War was still two years away, the Cold War was heating up. A communist coup in Prague the preceding February had swept Czechoslovakia into the Soviet orbit, and the Berlin blockade had begun in June. The USAF was desperate to secure a defensive fighter capable of operating at any time of day in any kind of weather. Some USAF officers, knowing that the Northrop design might be a better aircraft, were nonetheless willing to gamble on the XP-87, knowing that "all available capacity would have to be employed to meet increased Air Force requirements."[58] One is also reminded of the Finletter Commission's recommendations for keeping marginal companies afloat during slack times so that a broad manufacturing base would be available for a national emergency.

Moreover, the XP-89 proved to be a less than perfect choice for an all-weather interceptor. Although it eventually became fully operational, it took longer to develop than expected and had its full share of problems, including structural defects that forced a temporary grounding of the airplane after it had entered squadron service.[59] Therefore, a contract for a production P-87, even with its many problems, might conceivably have been forthcoming had relations between the USAF and the Airplane Division of the Curtiss-Wright Corporation been better. The memories of the Airplane Division's many production difficulties during World War II and its failure to produce a replacement for the P-40 may well have been a factor in the government's decision to refuse to absorb additional development costs on the XP-87; or perhaps Vaughan had resolved to abandon airframe production completely and was unwilling to invest any more money in a project that he felt had little chance of success. In any case, the Airplane Division's reputation had finally caught up with it.

The troubles experienced by the XP-87 program were essentially repeated with the CW-32, an ambitious project undertaken in response to the changing national and international environment. The Finletter Commission report had emphasized the need for "a pool of cargo planes" to respond to a national emergency and asserted that such an airplane not only should have military capability but also should be designed for economical commercial operations as well.[60] Moreover, a congressional report entitled "National Air Policy" stated that the government "should sponsor the design and development of prototype transport and cargo aircraft intended primarily for commercial use, but suitable for certain military purposes."[61] As a result of these proposals, legislation was introduced into Congress to provide for the design, development, and production of such an aircraft.

The CW-32 was Curtiss-Wright's response to these incentives. Although it was under development as a civilian cargo transport even before the Finletter Commission began its deliberations, the military potential of the design was readily apparent. Soon after the publication of the commission's report, Curtiss-Wright was touting the military uses of the airplane. Advertisements showing a heavy field gun being loaded into the Sky Truck, as the CW-32 was known, promoted it as "America's only airplane designed for immediate adaptability to cargo and materiel transport."[62]

Work on the Sky Truck continued at Columbus throughout 1947 and into 1948. Photographs of the full-scale mock-up were published in the aviation press. However, the project was stillborn. Curtiss-Wright never built a prototype or signed a production contract. According to some accounts, another impasse was created when the USAF claimed it was unable to pay for the development costs. Estimating that the price tag for design development would be $15 million, the company board of directors decided to drop the project.[63]

The Changing of the Guard

The collapse of these negotiations can be attributed not only to the reluctance of company management to risk its cash reserves in airframe development but also to a growing managerial crisis within Curtiss-Wright. Reports of the board's dissatisfaction with Vaughan's leadership had surfaced as early as 1946,[64] and by 1948 this crisis was threatening to paralyze the company's decision-making process. Thus, even assuming that Curtiss-Wright wanted to remain in the airframe business, the timing of the XP-87 and CW-32 projects doomed them almost from the start.

While the Airplane Division was going ahead with developmental work on the two designs, Vaughan was moving to implement his postwar plan for Curtiss-Wright. It consisted of two parts. For the short term, he would protect Curtiss-Wright's financial resources through a program of diversification. He initiated the first phase as early as 1944 with the purchase of the assets of LGS Spring Clutches, Inc., of Indianapolis. The company, renamed LGS Spring Clutches Corporation, became a wholly owned Curtiss-Wright subsidiary. Its products had a wide variety of applications in industry and household products. This action was followed by the purchase of the Marquette Metal Products Company and the Victor Animatograph Corporation. These companies produced a variety of nonaviation products such as film projectors and cameras, textile spindles, diesel governors, air compressors, and spring clutches. These acquisitions anticipated a policy that ultimately led to a complete transformation of the aviation giant from a manufacturing company to a diversified investment holding company.

For the long term, Vaughan wanted to concentrate his company's energies and resources on developing turbine engine technology, thereby giving Wright Aeronautical first-mover advantages with these revolutionary engines. The steps contemplated by Vaughan would have placed Wright Aeronautical in good position to take advantage of this technological breakthrough. The cash reserves that were acquired from wartime profits would be used to finance a program of research and development into the new technology. In this way, the company could avoid borrowing in the outside money markets and would be free from any obligations to financial institutions.[65]

The conclusion of hostilities in 1945 gave Vaughan the opportunity to put his plan into effect. Wartime restrictions were lifted, and both Pratt and Whitney and Wright Aeronautical were now free to pursue jet engine development. The two companies had their work cut out for them; both the British and the Germans were well ahead of the United States in turbine technology. Vaughan's scheme, however, would enable Curtiss-Wright to catch up.

He began with a trip to Europe. In early 1946 he took several engineers from Wright Aeronautical with him to Great Britain to survey the aircraft engine scene. What they saw impressed them. Jet fighters were already operational in the RAF, and several manufacturers were working with gas turbines.[66] Vaughan became convinced that the only practical way for Wright Aeronautical to develop and produce jet engines was to secure outside assistance in the form of licenses from one of the British manufacturers. He was especially interested in the Rolls-Royce Avon engine.[67] He also initiated discussions with Sir Roy Fedden of Bristol Aero-Engines for a joint venture into a program of jet engine development. This project died, however, as Vaughan became enmeshed in his own private war for control of Curtiss-Wright. As a result of the ensuing turmoil, Fedden and his associates bowed out of the venture.[68]

The storm broke in early 1948 when a group of stockholders led by New York attorney T. Roland (Ted) Berner launched a vicious proxy fight that challenged Vaughan and his supporters for control of the company. The issue was Vaughan's refusal to pay dividends out of wartime profits. The Berner group, however, wanted dividends. It argued that some $12 per share had been earned on common stock for the seven-year period ending 31 December 1947, but only $4.50 was paid in dividends. Hence they wanted control of the company in order to make a $7 per share cash distribution on the common stock. As an alternative, they proposed the retirement of one-half of the outstanding common stock at $14 per share. Claiming discrimination against the common stock shareholders, the dissidents noted that the Vaughan group owned more than five times as much class A stock as common stock, and that the class A stock was entitled to a noncumulative annual dividend of $2 per share. This group also cited Vaughan's statement that Curtiss-Wright had an excess of $60 million in working capital. Additionally, it observed that the company's position within the industry was declining and declared that such a large amount of cash was therefore unnecessary for the existing scale of operations. The dissidents claimed that Vaughan's conservatism had made the company "sluggish," and that they would revitalize it by bringing in new managerial and technical talent to restore Curtiss-Wright to a competitive position within the industry.

Vaughan responded with the assertion that the $7 per share dividend demanded by the dissidents amounted to more than $52 million and would necessitate a "partial liquidation" of the Curtiss-Wright Corporation. Defending his record, Vaughan stated that the net worth of Curtiss-Wright had increased from $26 million to more than $122 million over the preceeding 14-year period, and that over the same period, some $62 million had been paid in dividends, of which $39 million had gone to common stock shareholders and $23 million had gone to class A shareholders. As for the $60 million of excess working capital, Vaughan declared that he proposed to hold on to it until the future of the industry and the company was clearer. He also reported on several projects then under development, which included the XP-87, a gas turbine engine, and a $17.5 million contract with the navy for the R-3350 turbo-compound engine.[69]

The annual stockholders' meeting in 1948 was particularly acrimonious and was conducted in an atmosphere reminiscent of a comic opera. The meeting convened at the company's office in Wilmington, Delaware, in the third week in April. Berner and his supporters, together with a number of Curtiss-Wright officials, arrived at the appointed time; but Vaughan and his group, who were coming from New York, were delayed because their train broke down. In Vaughan's absence, Berner and another Curtiss-Wright official were elected cochairmen. They then convened the meeting, which was under way when the Vaughan group arrived. At that point, the Curtiss-Wright official who was cochairman invited Vaughan to take charge of the meeting, but Berner refused to recognize Vaughan and continued to preside.

Nevertheless, Vaughan took over the chairman's table, and Berner was moved to the side. A bizarre spectacle unfolded. Two simultaneous meetings were conducted by two separate chairmen, each working at cross-purposes with the other. The result was chaos as the session degenerated into a shouting match. Vaughan ignored Berner and proceeded with the election of 11 directors, after which he answered a few perfunctory questions and, declaring the business of the annual stockholders' meeting thus completed, adjourned the session.

Berner, however, maintained that Vaughan had not been properly recognized and that his actions were therefore unauthorized and illegal. He adjourned his meeting to be reconvened the following month. However, the Vaughan group subsequently obtained a court order enjoining the Berner forces from reconvening the annual meeting.[70]

Berner and his supporters suffered a tactical defeat in this attempt to take control of the company. But the damage was done. That tumultuous stockholders' meeting set into motion a chain of events that soon led to a complete change of corporate leadership. The position of Vaughan and his associates was fatally weakened, and within a year they were out of the picture completely. That mountain of money had become a magnet, drawing Wall Street interests into the scene. Despite declining sales—the company would lose the $80 million contract for a production version of the XP-87 in October 1948—Curtiss-Wright was a wealthy company in good financial health. Its reserves stood at $103 million, of which $75 million was in cash and short-term government securities. As noted, this was some $60 million more than normal surplus requirements.[71] With these kinds of financial reserves, the stockholders' call for a dividend is understandable. It was also myopic. Short-term interests were taking precedence over long-term considerations. The episode demonstrated that stockholders' demands do not always coincide with the needs of long-term corporate growth.

In an attempt to deal with the mounting crisis, Vaughan asked Paul V. Shields, a personal friend and head of the Wall Street firm of Shields and Company, for help and advice. Shields became chairman of the executive committee and took charge of stockholder relations. Vaughan resigned as president and became chairman of the board in December 1948. His handpicked successor for the presidency was William Jordan, a Curtiss-Wright associate who had been with both the Columbus Division and Wright Aeronautical.[72]

It was the beginning of the end of the Vaughan era. By 31 January 1949, Shields was in effective control as he brought in four new directors, including T. Roland Berner. Moreover, two longtime associates of Vaughan were retired. They were William D. Kennedy, general manager of Wright Aeronautical, and Burdette S. Wright. The substance of Shields's power was confirmed the following May when he was named chairman of the board and chief executive officer and Vaughan and Jordan both announced their retirement. Vaughan had hoped to remain with the company in an advisory capacity, but that wish was never granted.

Berner's victory in the dividend war had come as early as the summer of 1948, when the board of directors declared a dividend of $2.00 per share on the class A stock, amounting to $1,907,336. A $1.00 per share dividend on common stock was declared on 26 August and again on 3 December, amounting to $14,860,666. The following February, the directors declared a second $2.00 per share dividend on the class A stock and a regular quarterly dividend of 25¢ per share on the common stock.[73]

Vaughan's decision to step down was motivated in part by his physical condition. No longer a young man—he was in his mid-sixties—his hearing had begun to fail, an affliction that was a source of mounting frustration to him. Moreover, he was becoming increasingly weary of the corporate battles that he was being forced to fight. Aviation had become a "troublesome business" to him.[74]

The presidency of Guy W. Vaughan spanned one of the most turbulent periods in American aviation history. In 1935, the year of his appointment, the industry was struggling to survive the effects of the Great Depression. Thirteen years later, it not only had made a critical contribution to victory in a war of unprecedented fury and scope but was now a major feature of the American industrial landscape. Under Vaughan's leadership, Curtiss-Wright had been an important part of aviation's contribution to that victory, and the company was still a major force in the industry, its many problems notwithstanding. Despite his critics' assertions to the contrary, Vaughan still had the vision and energy in 1945 to move his company in new directions.

Nevertheless, he was unable to achieve his goals. In retrospect, he failed to move with sufficient boldness and determination to implement the changes he envisioned. For a while, he seemed to be hedging his bets. In early 1944, for example, he voiced impatience with the failure of the Airplane Division to do more with jet airframe development.[75] Moreover, several projects, some of which have already been discussed, were going ahead at the Airplane Division in 1944 and 1945, presumably with his approval. This suggested that he envisioned an active postwar role for the Airplane Division. Additionally, Vaughan had given at least tacit support to the 1943 decision to build the research laboratory and wind tunnel in Buffalo. Hence a degree of uncertainty regarding the future of the Airplane Division may have weakened his resolve.

Undoubtedly, the main reason for Vaughan's inaction, however, was the developing boardroom battle for control of the company. His energies were being consumed in this power struggle. If his plan was to make Curtiss-Wright an engine manufacturer exclusively, he failed to consider what effect the postwar $178 million surplus would have on the stockholders. He simply underestimated the significance of greed in human affairs. The incident foreshadowed the type of shareholder-driven activity that would preoccupy corporations in the seventies and eighties.

Curtiss-Wright's post–World War II troubles can be traced directly to that pile of cash accumulated during the war. The unrest within the company's leadership at this point had very little to do with aviation but almost everything to do with money as stockholders scrambled to get their hands on it. This creeping managerial crisis further weakened the company's ability to develop new aircraft designs, meet production deadlines, and maintain a competitive edge in an increasingly tight market. Hence, even if Vaughan was not consciously working to take Curtiss-Wright out of the business of building airframes, managerial problems were.

Consequently, the three manufacturing divisions, with little direction or support from corporate headquarters, were essentially on their own. This was an especially difficult problem for the weakest of the three, the Airplane Division. Wright Aeronautical and the Propeller Division were better able to weather the storm because they had products that had been developed earlier and were moving down the assembly lines before the leadership crisis erupted. The Airplane Division, however, was caught in the whiplash of this crisis and, lacking a viable product, did not survive. More importantly, the crisis itself was not resolved but continued to fester for the next decade and more, further sapping the company's energies and resources.

A Clouded Future

The half decade after World War II was a critical time for the entire aviation industry. The prosperous days of seemingly limitless expansion were over. As government contracts were slashed, each company struggled to carve out a niche for itself in a new and uncertain world of rapid change. As always, government contracts remained the industry's lifeblood, but now they were few and far between. Many feared a replay of the retrenchment that had followed World War I a generation earlier. The differences between the two eras were profound, however. New products and new markets, brought about by dramatic changes in world politics, were soon accompanied by a resumption of government contracts. Although the level of activity was smaller than it had been before 1945, the Cold War helped to bring about a recovery of the industry's fortunes.

How well the Curtiss-Wright Corporation would respond to these new challenges depended on its top leadership. The events of the five years following World War II gave little cause for optimism. By 1949 chaos reigned in the front office. The vicious proxy fight of the previous months had left the company weakened and ill-prepared to chart a clear course for the future. A changing of the guard had taken place, but strong leadership with a clear vision of the future had not emerged. Instead, the focus was shifting to profit taking at the expense of investment. A serious conflict was developing between the short-term interests of the stockholders and the long-term needs of the corporation. This did not bode well for its future health. Serious issues had yet to be addressed. What should Curtiss-Wright's place be in the new postwar order? How should the company direct its energies? What kind of product development should it pursue? What sort of identity should it assume in the decades to come? These and other questions remained unanswered as the company entered the decade of the fifties. A vigorous and well-planned course of action was desperately needed. This, in turn, required a high degree of managerial skill and perhaps a bit of luck. Curtiss-Wright, it seemed, lacked both.

Chapter 8

A New Identity, 1949–1990

Nineteen forty-nine was a watershed year for the Curtiss-Wright Corporation. Guy Vaughan and the men who worked with him were true aviation pioneers. Some had been fliers. Many were engineers. All had been closely and directly connected with aviation in its formative years. They knew the industry and its people intimately. The leadership that took over in 1949, however, represented a "new breed" of manager. Virtually without exception, they came from the world of corporate finance and investment banking and had almost no direct connection with, or understanding of, the aviation industry.

The following years became a "time of troubles" as the company struggled to survive in a new and increasingly uncertain world. Managerial unrest continued to take its toll. Meanwhile, a preoccupation with profit taking contributed to a steadily deteriorating manufacturing base as the company became cash rich and product poor. By the mid-fifties, management had clearly lost its way. Curtiss-Wright no longer had a distinct identity; the company had no viable product to develop and sell, and overdiversification was dissipating its resources.

Ultimately, the Curtiss-Wright Corporation was transformed from one of the top-tier manufacturers of aviation products into an investment company that became a second-level supplier of subcomponents to the industry. It was an extremely painful process, and Curtiss-Wright paid heavily for the ignorance of its new management.

The Paul Shields Era

In January 1950, Paul Shields addressed a meeting of the New York Society of Security Analysts. His remarks gave a clear indication of the new path that the Curtiss-Wright Corporation would be taking under his leadership as chairman of the board. Claiming that the company had become "tired out" after World War II, he said that Curtiss-Wright executives "had pretty well run their string out. There wasn't the drive: there wasn't the initiative necessary for the times." He declared that Curtiss-Wright was "completely off base on its development program" and indicated that he intended to move the company away from its traditional manufacturing base of airframes, engines, and propellers into such fields as electronics, guided missiles, rockets, and atomic power, where the profit margin was greater. This was not an unreasonable proposal because, along with turbojets, guided missiles and their related technologies were about to become a major component of growth within the industry. The problem lay with his motivation. He wanted a quick profit, not long-term investment. Shields had already conveyed his intentions several months earlier when he scuttled a proposal by William Jordan to build a turboprop engine with company funds.

Although he declared his faith in aviation's future, Shields was less sanguine about the industry's profitability. "I have never been very bullish on aviation as an investment vehicle," he said. "It has been a more or less chaotic industry, not particularly well managed, and entirely too dependent upon government subsidy, lacking in the tough, hard-headed business view." Hereafter corporate activities at Curtiss-Wright would be confined "to things of purely commercial value, the results of which will show up in the profit and loss statement."

He claimed that engineering expenses had been far too high, and he proudly announced that he had already cut them by more than half, partly by significantly reducing the size of the engineering staff. Company manufacturing, he said, had been carried on by men who were engineers and who, by the nature of their training, were not businessmen; "they are not profit-and-loss conscious." In this new era, the Curtiss-Wright Corporation would be guided by an industrial management team concentrating on "things of purely commercial value." Profit taking became more important than engineering research and product development. Fred Rentschler had left Wright Aeronautical because it had displayed this same attitude in 1924. The actions taken by Paul Shields in 1950 would have a profound effect on the long-term future of the company.[1]

In 1948 the J. B. Field Company, an investment analysis firm, published a report on Curtiss-Wright. It stated that Wright Aeronautical was the "backbone" of the corporation and that it was then attempting to establish a foothold in the jet engine field. Moreover, Curtiss-Wright had come through the post–World War II reconversion process "in excellent financial condition. No other aircraft company can approach Curtiss-Wright from the standpoint of liquidity. However, this gives Curtiss-Wright more of the attributes of an investment company than an aircraft manufacturing enterprise."

The report also noted the company's deteriorating position within the industry, citing the continued decline of the Airplane Division plus the fact that Pratt and Whitney's engine shipments in 1946 were more than three times those of Wright Aeronautical. Focusing on Curtiss-Wright's fundamental problem, the Field report observed that the scale of operations was much too small to support existing capitalization. This meant that Curtiss-Wright's "exceptionally strong cash position is . . . both a strength and a weakness. For one thing, the management becomes a target of pleas for a special distribution of funds to stockholders, and subject to pressure for the purchase of other enterprises."[2]

The Field report summarized the company's problems and predicted its future behavior quite accurately. Diversification became the hallmark of Curtiss-Wright policy after 1950 and, together with profit taking, persisted with a vengeance for the next 20 years. Furthermore, the problem of overcapitalization, which had been so bothersome to Clement Keys after World War I and to Thomas Morgan in the depths of the Great Depression, remained a perennial problem after World War II.

In the meantime, world events continued to affect the American aviation industry as relations between the United States and the Soviet Union deteriorated rapidly after 1947. The changes in the international order reflected by the Finletter Commission report helped to shape a new foreign policy that called for the containment of what appeared to be the Soviet Union's expansionist tendencies. Destined to remain the foundation of American foreign policy for the next 40 years, containment policy was becoming increasingly militarized by the end of the decade. Events seemed to justify this reaction. By 1950 Soviet forces were firmly ensconced in Eastern Europe, the Iron Curtain was a stark reality, NATO had come into existence, and the Cold War suddenly heated up with the invasion of South Korea by the North Korean Army on 24 June. The implications of these developments for the aviation industry were obvious.

As America began to rebuild its military forces, the basic assumptions underlying the Finletter Commission report were expanded and reinforced in a document produced by the Truman administration in April 1950. Apocalyptic in tone, National Security Council Report no.68 (NSC-68) stated that the issues facing America were "momentous, involving the fulfillment or destruction not only of this Republic but of civilization itself." Consequently, the report called for a "rapid, massive military build-up" to resist what was now popularly known as "Soviet aggression."[3] The heart of the program was to be a weapon not yet developed, a thermonuclear, or hydrogen, bomb. Significant expenditures would also go for conventional weapons. Administration officials anticipated a four-fold increase in military spending, from $13 billion to $50 billion.[4] The outbreak of the Korean War two months later seemed to confirm the validity of NSC-68.

These developments contributed substantially to the restored health of the American aviation industry. Within two weeks of the North Korean attack, Cessna had a $5 million army contract for 400 liaison airplanes, and four weeks after the Cessna contract was signed, Lockheed had doubled its backlog of orders, from $200 million to $400 million.[5] Thus the nation began to gird for its long twilight struggle with the Soviet Union, and the aviation industry once again became the beneficiary of government largesse in the growing international competition for military supremacy.

Yet there was no return to the heady days of World War II; that level of prosperity was not repeated during the Korean War or afterward. The scope of this new conflict was much more limited, and mobilization took place at a far lower level. The following quote, though somewhat imprecise because of qualitative differences (e.g., greater complexity of the newer aircraft), nevertheless gives a rough comparison: "The production of military aircraft in 1952, the last full year of the Korean War, was just over 7,000 compared with the 96,000 of 1944."[6]

In addition, the industry itself was undergoing profound change. By 1955, aviation's pioneering era was over. Many of the giant aircraft and engine companies of World War II had been founded by businessmen and managers who also were gifted engineers, some of them completely self-taught. Men such as Donald Douglas and Jack Northrop, who led the companies that bore their names, along with James "Dutch" Kindelberger at North American, Guy Vaughan at Curtiss-Wright, Fred Rentschler at United Aircraft, and Hall Hibbard at Lockheed, all had a wealth of practical experience with the development of their products. Moreover, their civilian customers had come out of the same mold. Individualistic, innovative, and willing to take great risks, they almost literally had grown up with aviation. Eddie Rickenbacker, the World War I flying ace who was head of Eastern Airlines, and Jack Frye, a former airmail pilot who had become president of Transcontinental and Western Airlines (later Trans-World Airlines), typified the men who were the airline executives in 1945.

As with the first generation of aviation pioneers, however, time was passing these men by. Although several continued to play a significant role for some years to come, their influence as a group was beginning to wane. In the words of one writer, the older type of leader was being replaced by managers who were "more corporate, and less aviation oriented." This change signaled "the end of a great era."[7] In short, the changes that transformed Curtiss-Wright after World War II were reflected throughout the entire industry.

Much of this change was driven by technology and the products themselves. More sophisticated, more complex, and more expensive than those of an earlier era, they required greater financial resources than ever before and demanded a higher degree of formal bureaucratic organization to develop and market.

Foremost among these new products was the jet engine, which was already altering the aeronautical landscape by the early fifties. Developments in rocketry and space research promised to transform the industry completely. A new term, "aerospace," soon supplanted "aviation" as the descriptive word for the industry. Traditional aeronautical engineering was moving into new regimes dominated by electronics and similar kinds of high technology. Missiles, rockets, jet engines, and even earth satellites were the wave of the future.[8]

Commercial aircraft production grew modestly as jet transports entered the scene and private or general aviation activity expanded moderately; however, purchases of military aircraft actually declined somewhat in the sixties as guided missile technology became a significant component of military aviation. Moreover, the size and complexity of new aircraft made them increasingly expensive, further limiting the numbers purchased.

As a consequence of these post–World War II changes, many older companies were forced to reorganize and redirect their investment strategies during the fifties and sixties. The industry was undergoing additional consolidation and diversification. Martin became part of a conglomerate that had interests in cement, lime and rock products, and chemicals. Its new name was the Martin-Marietta Corporation. North American Aviation became North American Rockwell, later Rockwell International. Bell Aircraft changed its name to Bell Aerospace Corporation before becoming part of Textron, Inc., which was a holding company in the textile industry. Douglas encountered serious financial and managerial problems and was eventually forced to merge with McDonnell Aircraft in 1967, creating the McDonnell Douglas Corporation. In 1954, United Aircraft, while keeping its Sikorsky division (which was now concentrating on helicopters), sold off its Chance Vought airframe division, concluding—as had Guy Vaughan almost a decade earlier—that manufacturing both engines and conventional airframes was a losing proposition. Vought became part of a conglomerate, Ling-Temco-Vought, in 1961.[9]

These years were no kinder to Curtiss-Wright, whose problems continued to multiply as its fortunes declined. Paul Shields realized the importance of the new technologies that were reshaping the industry. Moreover, Wright Aeronautical had the financial means and engineering talent in 1950 to become a major force in the new world of turbojets, rockets, and missiles. Shields was nevertheless unwilling to commit those resources to the research and development indispensable to a successful venture into these new fields, preferring profit taking instead.

As outlined in his speech to the New York Society of Security Analysts, he attributed his company's continuing decline in profits to large expenditures for engineering research and development by Wright Aeronautical, and he moved to reduce these costs. Consequently, ongoing research, especially in turbine engines, was either curtailed or killed. Total engineering development expenses were cut from $1.1 million to $500,000 monthly, and some 500 engineers from Wright Aeronautical were let go as the name of the game now became quick profits, even at the risk of future profitability. Some people to this day feel that Wright Aeronautical never recovered from this body blow.[10]

Despite these setbacks, Wright Aeronautical, together with the Propeller Division, remained the profitable mainstay of Curtiss-Wright throughout the fifties as it had been since the 1929 merger. Wright's most important product was still the R-3350 and its derivative, the R-3350 turbo-compound. They both continued to find wide use in a variety of military and civilian aircraft.

These engines were big money makers. Sixty-five percent of Curtiss-Wright's sales in 1950 came from the engine factory at Wood-Ridge, New Jersey, and 30 percent of its sales were generated by the propeller plant at Caldwell. Moreover, the Caldwell plant was producing half of all the propellers manufactured in the United States. At the time of his retirement in 1951, Shields claimed that the company held contracts for the production of more than $1 billion worth of engines and propellers.[11]

The piston engine era was coming to an end, however. Although reciprocating engines would continue to occupy a niche in the market, turbine engine technology represented the future in aircraft engine development. Many within Wright Aeronautical, including William Jordan, Vaughan's successor, knew it. Jordan also knew that Wright Aeronautical could move into the jet era only by manufacturing a foreign design under license, by using the company's own money for research and development, or by a combination of both. Public research and development money was scarce in 1948 and 1949, and federal officials, well aware of Curtiss-Wright's cash reserves, wanted the company to put up its own money.

The work on turbine engines already done at Wright Aeronautical had yielded several very promising projects, including two with particular potential, the TJ6 and TJ7. Some have claimed that both were far superior to the engine then being developed by Pratt and Whitney that eventually became the J57, one of the most successful jet engines of that era. In 1949 Jordan approached air force officials, secured a government contract for only one dollar for each of the two engines, and got the go-ahead to proceed with the project with the understanding that Wright Aeronautical would assume the development costs. A meeting was then set up between the board of directors and Jordan and one of his associates to secure the board's approval for the contracts.

The mission was doomed. As the two men entered the boardroom, Jordan's associate said: "My heart sank. I recognized that there was not one aviation man on the board. They were people either out of banks or Wall Street." The board was adamant. No Curtiss-Wright money would be spent on jet engine research and development. Shields in particular was very critical of the research monies already spent, a paltry $7 million. After some discussion, the board went into a brief executive session. Not surprisingly, their decision was final. No Curtiss-Wright monies would be spent on developing the TJ6 and TJ7. At that point, Jordan stood up, put on his hat, said, "Gentlemen, I'm through," and left the room. He had resigned on the spot.[12] Shields was now in total control.

Paul Shields remained board chairman until his retirement in October 1951, when he claimed that his "objectives had been achieved." He was replaced by Roy T. Hurley, who had been director of manufacturing engineering at the Ford Motor Company before coming to Curtiss-Wright in 1949.

Roy Hurley as President

Hurley was a throwback to the nineteenth-century entrepeneurs. Born the son of a plumber in the Harlem district of Manhattan in 1896, he received only a New York City grammar school education. Nevertheless, he had a drive and ambition that carried him to the top of the corporate ladder. He was proud of his humble origins. Described by others as an "up through the ranks production man," Hurley referred to himself as a "pick-and-shovel operating man." Along the way, he acquired a widespread knowledge of engineering and industrial management techniques. In later life, he said: "I took all the correspondence courses and read all the textbooks."[13]

Roy T. Hurley.
Curtiss-Wright Corporation.

Hurley began his career in 1916 as an aircraft engine mechanic with the B. F. Sturtevant Company, of Hyde Park, Massachusetts. During World War I, he was an inspector of airplanes and engines for the U.S. Army at the Wright-Martin Aircraft Corporation in New Brunswick, New Jersey, the ancestor company of Wright Aeronautical. In 1921, at the age of 25, he became chief engineer of the B.G. Aircraft Spark Plug Company of New York City, leaving in 1927 to become vice president and general manager of the Moto-Meter Gauge and Equipment Company of Long Island.

Hurley left Moto-Meter in 1931 to form the Hurley-Townsend Company of New York to manufacture a spark plug of his own design. He joined the Bendix Corporation in 1935 as a staff executive on production matters when Bendix acquired Hurley-Townsend. During World War II, he became deputy chief of ordnance and a civilian production adviser to the Ordnance Division of the U.S. Army. Returning to Bendix, he was named vice president of manufacturing on 14 September 1944. He joined the Ford Motor Company in 1948.

Hurley became president of the Curtiss-Wright Corporation in September 1949, replacing the recently resigned William Jordan. Unfortunately for Curtiss-Wright, Hurley's production experience was mostly in the automobile business rather than aviation, and he failed to realize the differences between the two industries. He was not the first man to make this mistake. The experience of John North Willys in World War I should have been a warning to Hurley. Several years after he became president, a dissatisfied Curtiss-Wright customer was quoted as saying of the company, "We aren't getting aircraft responsibility; we're getting automobile responsibility."[14] Further compounding these problems was Hurley's obsession with profits, which proved to be his undoing and further weakened the manufacturing base of the company.

Hurley took control of a wealthy but seriously troubled company. The departure of Curtiss-Wright from Columbus in November 1950 had brought an end to the Airplane Division. Wright Aeronautical and the Propeller Division still had plenty of business, but turbine engine technology was moving ahead rapidly, and thanks to Paul Shields, Wright Aeronautical had been left at the starting gate.

Hurley tried to improve Curtiss-Wright's fortunes in several ways. First he reversed his predecessor's policy and resumed work on gas turbines. Second, he initiated an aggressive sales program for the various models of the R-3350 engine. The outbreak of the Korean War practically guaranteed the success of this effort. Finally, as piston engine sales began to decline in the mid-fifties, Hurley pushed diversification to unprecedented levels.

A necessary step in the long journey back to turbine engines was the restoration of a skilled workforce, and Hurley initiated an extensive recruiting program to attract engineering talent back to Wright Aeronautical. It met with modest success.[15] Then, taking a page out of Guy Vaughan's book, Hurley looked across the Atlantic to Great Britain, where some of the first jet engines had been produced and where turbine engine technology was moving ahead rapidly. Wright Aeronautical's main U.S. competitor, Pratt and Whitney, was already building Rolls-Royce jets under license.

Hurley took several trips to England in 1950 and visited Bristol Aero-Engines and Armstrong Siddeley. Each company was working on an advanced jet engine. Bristol was developing the Olympus, and Armstrong Siddeley was working on the Sapphire. Hurley secured licenses for both engines and planned a two-stage scheme for bringing Wright Aeronautical into the gas turbine age. First, he wanted to mass-produce an American version of the Sapphire. Then he planned to use the Olympus, which was just in its developmental stage, as the basis for a new, more powerful engine.[16]

The Sapphire was manufactured by Wright Aeronautical as the J65, although once the substantial redesign problems associated with creating an American version were overcome, it was essentially a different engine. Production began in 1952, and by 1958 more than 10,000 units had been built.[17] Although it experienced many developmental problems and was perhaps not the best choice for a production engine, the J65 was a financial success. For many years, it was the power plant for a variety of military aircraft in the United States and throughout the world. It also helped to keep Wright Aeronautical going.

The Olympus was another story. Overweight and underpowered, it was completely uncompetitive with the contemporary Pratt and Whitney engines. Part of the problem lay with USAF requirements, which demanded 13,500 pounds of thrust for the new generation of jets. Bristol engineers believed this stipulation to be beyond the capability of the original Olympus, and this prompted the engineers at Wright Aeronautical to redesign the unit. This effort failed. According to Sir Stanley Hooker, chief engineer at Bristol, this decision "was the final nail in their coffin," and Wright Aeronautical never again produced a competitive gas turbine engine. The decimation of the engineering department by Paul Shields undoubtedly contributed to this debacle. Although the two companies continued their collaboration into the late fifties, they failed to develop a production engine.[18]

In the meantime, sales of the R-3350 remained good, and the Propeller Division continued to do well. Military purchases increased significantly, thanks in large part to the Korean War, and sales to the airlines remained strong. The end result was a dramatic improvement in Curtiss-Wright's financial health over the short term. Total income in 1951 was almost $15 million as compared with $13.6 million in 1950, although net income was down by $370,348 from the 1950 total of $7,278,564. This decline was the result of a tax increase of $1.7 million in 1951, plus substantial expenditures for capital expansion. For example, the jet engine plants at Wood-Ridge, Caldwell, and Garfield, New Jersey, were enlarged, and three new corporate manufacturing divisions were established. The first was an Electronics Division, located in Carlstadt, New Jersey, which produced flight simulators. Second, Curtiss-Wright reestablished its presence in Buffalo with the creation of the Metals Processing Division. Together with work in metallurgical research, the new division produced castings, forgings, and extrusions. A third division was the Columbia Protektosite Company, also of Carlstadt, New Jersey, which manufactured plastic products.[19] The total cost of this capital investment was just over $19 million, which was partially offset by a backlog of orders totaling more than $1 billion.[20] Hurley also created a Specialities Division "specifically to institute a program of diversification," and within two years, three additional divisions, the Research Division, Curtiss-Wright of Canada, Ltd., and the Industrial and Scientific Products Division, had been created.[21]

In 1953 total sales for the corporation reached $438.7 million, an increase of 34 percent over the previous 12 months. The profit margin reached 8.1 percent, a 1.7 percent improvement over the 1952 figure. Substantial capital expenditures for enlarged and improved plants and equipment continued into 1953. An independent estimate revealed that Curtiss-Wright had increased its gross plant account during the eight-year period since 1945, most of it occurring during the Korean War buildup. Moreover, the company's financial position remained strong. Working capital at the end of 1953 was listed at $91.3 million. The comparable figure for United Aircraft, Curtiss-Wright's major domestic competitor, was $79.9 million. Total dividend payout averaged 53 percent of available earnings. Surprisingly, research and development expenditures in 1953 remained high, almost $47 million, which was roughly $11.3 million higher than for 1952.[22]

Unfortunately, this prosperity was as deceptive as it was short-lived. The armistice bringing the Korean War to an end was signed in 1953. In the following year, the maiden flight of the prototype Boeing 707 took place. These two events had far-reaching implications for Wright Aeronautical. With the cessation of hostilities, demand for the R-3350 by the military services began to decline rapidly, whereas the flight of the 707 ushered in a new era in airline travel, which had been pioneered by the ill-fated de Havilland Comet. The age of commercial jet transports had arrived.

At this point, Roy Hurley stumbled badly. As late as 1958, he was still committed to further refining and producing the big piston engines, mistakenly believing that they could be made economically competitive with the large jets. He also assumed that a significant airline and military market for conventional reciprocating engines would continue indefinitely.[23] He was wrong, and Curtiss-Wright ultimately paid a very high price for his stubborn shortsightedness. Furthermore, this myopia was combined with an insatiable quest for profits that further eroded Curtiss-Wright's position within the industry.

An episode that occurred at a corporate management meeting about this time is illustrative. The meeting was attended by about 300 department heads and managers from 17 divisions. Roy Hurley presided. He asked them all to look under their chairs. There they each found a silver dollar with a 15 percent section removed and replaced with gold. They were all told to make the coin a pocket piece and look at it every day as a reminder that their goal each day should be a 15 percent net profit. Good products and satisfied customers were no longer important. Profit taking was all that mattered. He even took the corporate engineering fund, which had been used for engineering research, and converted it to profit.[24]

Additionally, Hurley tried to squeeze every last cent of profit from the R-3350. This engine had been developed largely on U.S. Navy contracts, and many within the Pentagon were very unhappy with Curtiss-Wright for not investing its own funds more heavily in research and development. By the mid-fifties, the company was paying out more than half of its earnings in dividends rather than investing in research and development, which had now become a low-priority item. Consequently, government contracts began to dry up, and within four years, from 1954 to 1958, Curtiss-Wright plunged from 8th to 53d among suppliers of defense equipment nationwide.[25]

Curiously, this state of affairs seemed to suit Hurley just fine. Even though 65 percent of the company's personnel and facilities in 1958 were at work on government contracts,[26] he made it clear in a variety of ways that he had no interest in government contract money. For example, he testified before the House Armed Services Committee that Curtiss-Wright did not want any of the government's rocket business.[27] He was shrewd enough to hedge his bets, however, and accepted some government money such as a research and development project to produce new fuels. Curtiss-Wright also became a prime contractor to develop the Dart, an antitank missile that went into limited production in a plant at South Bend, Indiana, which had been leased from the Studebaker-Packard Corporation. Nevertheless, Hurley was convinced that his company's future lay with commercial ventures, and he remained generally opposed to government contracts. The government was happy to oblige him.

Why would the head of a company that was part of an industry so highly dependent on government contracts consciously reject government business? The answer is simple. His single-minded concentration on short-term profits had taken command of his thinking. He was convinced that the profit return from government contracts was too low. Moreover, the profits he did get from those contracts were constantly being dissipated by renegotiation. Hurley took great pride in "working to make a dollar," and in his view, the best way to achieve that goal was to concentrate on commercial business. In other words, working for the government was a "crummy" way to make money, as he once told an associate.

Hurley noted with great satisfaction that Curtiss-Wright's after-tax earnings in 1956 had surpassed those of United Aircraft by a significant margin, even though United had generated a much greater total sales volume. That year, United earned $37 million on $953 million in sales, whereas Curtiss-Wright earned $43 million on sales of just $571 million. Hurley was quoted as saying: "That is what we are after in manufacturing—dollars to put in shareholders' pockets, not ribbons to pin on their coats." For him, the only kind of leadership that mattered was profit leadership.[28] The Shields legacy continued.

Hurley compounded Curtiss-Wright's problems with a display of arrogance toward his customers that bordered on irresponsibility. It was rooted in his conviction that the R-3350 had a permanent niche in the aircraft engine market and was indispensable to his customers, turbine engines notwithstanding. According to his reasoning, his engine's overall performance, especially fuel economy, ensured its continued viability in the jet age. Consequently his customers needed him more than he needed them. It was, in short, a seller's market, or so he believed. He therefore dismissed customers' complaints with a cavalier take-it-or-leave-it attitude.

He developed a reputation for price gouging, such as charging the airlines excessive prices for parts to overhaul the R-3350 at 200 hours, which was an exceptionally short overhaul period. He also pulled similar kinds of stunts on the government. On at least one occasion, he tried to charge the navy a profit on an engineering change that didn't work. Some of these policies were later corrected, but Curtiss-Wright's reputation was severely damaged by his shenanigans.[29]

Hurley also unnecessarily angered many within the airline industry with what some observers described as his "merchandising" strategy for the Zephyr jet engine then being developed cooperatively by Wright Aeronautical and Bristol. He took out full-page advertisements in magazines and newspapers describing the Zephyr as a "quiet" engine, claiming that it performed at a full "30 decibels quieter than present commercial jet engines." The sales campaign also asserted that the Zephyr was much "cooler," operating at a significantly lower temperature than competing engines. Cooler operation meant less engine fatigue, which translated into fewer repairs and longer engine life. Since the only comparable commercial engine then in airline service was a civilian derivation of the Pratt and Whitney J57 that powered most of the high-performance military aircraft then operational with the U.S. armed forces, Hurley's promotional campaign was a direct slam at the Pratt and Whitney engine and its customers.

The airlines were furious. They interpreted the Zephyr advertisement as a direct attack against them. C. R. Smith of American Airlines sent a scathing letter to Hurley, denouncing his "holier than thou" attitude and suggesting that the whole advertising campaign would cause him and his company serious damage. Said another executive:

First he tells the public our new aircraft will be a nuisance, which is not true; now he's about to tell our shareholders that we are squandering their money on high-cost engines with a short life, which is also not true. This airline will never buy another Curtiss-Wright engine!

Hurley's response was vintage Hurley:

I'm selling C-W's jets, not jets for competitors. Furthermore, the resentment of the airlines is in large part explained by our monopoly position in the big reciprocating-engine field, an impossible position for a supplier. The airlines have every reason to dislike us. . . . We are convinced our facts are right and that the airlines will have to come to us eventually.[30]

Unfortunately for Hurley and for his company, the airlines did *not* have to come to Curtiss-Wright eventually. Inevitably, fuel economy for the big turbojets improved, and the commercial market for the R-3350 evaporated. Moreover, the Zephyr was never able to break in to the market now dominated by the J57. By this time, Wright Aeronautical was several years behind Pratt and Whitney in turbine engine technology, and General Electric was moving rapidly to fill the void caused by Wright Aeronautical's decline. Hurley's behavior had succeeded only in further alienating the very people that Curtiss-Wright needed the most, its customers.

Curtiss-Wright needed a leadership devoted to improving its customer relations rather than one fixated on profit taking. It also needed more generous support for research and development. The R-3350 had become Wright Aeronautical's cash cow, which provided the income and cash flow that should have been used for intensive development of new products, especially new turbine engines. The company's big piston engine had reached the effective end of its development cycle, and the Zephyr was going nowhere. Hurley failed to heed lessons found in his own company's history. The revival of the Curtiss Aeroplane and Motor Company's fortunes in the twenties had been due largely to the commitment made by Clement Keys to intensive research and development.

Diversification: The Search for a Product

By 1958 Wright Aeronautical was without a viable product. Pratt and Whitney had become the acknowledged leader in jet engine production, holding 70 percent of all government prime contracts and 100 percent of all commercial contracts for the big transports. By one account, Pratt and Whitney owed its dominant position "in large part to the fact that it [had] poured money into research with a lavish hand." Wright Aeronautical, by contrast, had been "niggardly" with its investment in turbine engine research and development. Consequently, it was about to become an also-ran in an industry in which it had held a commanding position scarcely more than a decade earlier.[31]

As the era of the reciprocating engine came to a close and sales of the R-3350 plummeted, profits and income declined precipitously. Net income in 1956 was over $43 million; by 1965 it was less than $8 million.[32] In response, Hurley began pushing the Curtiss-Wright Corporation in all directions in the search for new products, particularly those that might yield an immediate return. The diversification policy foreshadowed by Vaughan would soon be pursued with a vengance. Wright Aeronautical continued its work with turbine engines but began investigating ramjets, liquid-fueled rocket technology, and the Wankel rotary-piston engine, sometimes called a rotary-combustion engine. Curtiss-Wright acquired rights to the Wankel under a 1958 licensing agreement with the German firm of NSU Werke and was given world aviation rights plus Western Hemisphere land and water rights. Research with this unusual engine continued for the next 20 years as a variety of applications were studied, including automobiles, boats, motorcycles, and even lawnmowers, pumps, and snowplows.[33] None of these projects succeeded financially, however.

The X-19 Project

In 1958 Curtiss-Wright began experimental work on a radically new type of aircraft, a vertical takeoff and landing (VTOL) airplane. Early that year, Henry Borst, the chief aerodynamicist at the Propeller Division, approached Joseph M. Mergen, the division's director of engineering, with an idea for an airplane able to take off and land vertically like a helicopter but capable of conventional flight. The concept was based on propeller research that had been carried out by the government. Further inquiry was warranted. Consequently, a $10,000 design study was initiated, and within a month, the engineering team had produced on paper an airplane with a normal fuselage and tail but a rather stubby set of wings with large propellers at the tips. These propellers could rotate 90 degrees to provide both horizontal and vertical thrust.

At that point, the Propeller Division contacted the military services, and the response was very positive. Armed with this support, Mergen and his group approached Roy Hurley, who had just returned from a trip to Europe. Although enthusiastic about the concept, he was less than happy with the prospect of the government getting into the picture. "Who was the idiot who sent you to the military with this?" he said. "This is too good for the military. . . . This will be a company project and we will share it with no one."[34] The conversation continued and eventually turned to the question of development costs. Mergen told Hurley that $2 million would be needed to build and fly a proof-of-concept model. Hurley responded that he would need board approval for that kind of money and instructed Mergen and his staff to prepare a presentation for the board.

Several days later, Mergen entered the company boardroom armed with the appropriate documentation. He also had a small box that contained a simple 25¢ "ceiling walker" toy to prove the validity of the idea. Given to him by Henry Borst, the toy consisted of a balsa wood stick with propellers on each end that were powered by a rubber band. A piece of chewing gum on the front end caused the toy to transition to horizontal flight after being launched vertically.

Although the board members were favorably impressed with the concept, they balked at the price. Ted Berner spoke up: "Two million is a lot of money. Can't we make a model for a couple thousand and see if it works?" Mergen said he could do it for 25¢, whereupon he produced the ceiling walker. He wound up its rubber band and launched it. The tiny craft gave a flawless performance. Suitably impressed, the board voted the $2 million, and the VTOL project was off and running.[35]

Hurley was behind the project 100 percent. "This would be a fulfillment of his dream. His chance to offer to the commercial market a vehicle that was better than anything else, yet built totally by his own company."[36] Hurley was described as an "absolute genius at putting ideas and programs together,"[37] and his organizational and administrative talents were never more apparent than with the VTOL program. Nevertheless, his stubborn determination to keep the project exclusively in company hands proved costly and eventually contributed to his undoing.

The debate over the choice of an engine, one of the first and most important decisions that had to be made, is a case in point. In the earlier negotiations, the army had indicated its willingness to supply two Lycoming T53 gas turbine engines for the VTOL project. Although Mergen and his group had been forced to terminate those discussions under Hurley's orders, they approached the army again. Much to their surprise and delight, the army agreed to supply the Lycoming turbines because they wanted to have them tested. The only cost to Curtiss-Wright would have been a report on the engine's performance. Once more, Hurley rejected the offer: "You are giving the airplane away. Taking those engines is like being a little pregnant. Little by little they will get it all."[38] Consequently, instead of securing engines from the army at virtually no cost, the project team had to spend close to half a million dollars to acquire an appropriate power plant.

A proof-of-concept airplane, the X-100, was built and successfully tested. Moreover, the program was completed on time and within the $2 million budget. In the meantime, Hurley was pushing for the development of a commercial VTOL transport. He was persuaded by the design team to accept something a bit less ambitious and finally settled on an executive transport, which was given the designation X-200. Once more, however, the engine issue threatened to unravel the whole project. Hurley insisted that the prototype executive transport have as many Curtiss-Wright-designed and -manufactured components as possible, including Wright engines. However, the VTOL concept required turboprop engines because conventional reciprocating engines did not have a sufficient power-to-weight ratio, and Wright Aeronautical had no appropriate turboprops. Hurley said, "No Curtiss-Wright engine, no airplane!"

The issue was temporarily resolved when everyone agreed to use the new Wankel engine for which Curtiss-Wright had just acquired the world aviation rights. Unfortunately, it was still very much in the experimental stage, which meant that the project team now had to develop both an unconventional power plant and an unconventional airframe. From an engineering perspective, this was a bad idea.

As work on the X-200 proceeded, an ambitious public relations campaign was launched to promote Curtiss-Wright products, especially the Wankel engine, the VTOL airplane, and a new product called an "air-car," which was designed to float on a cushion of air. One of their most elaborate exhibits was unveiled at New York City's Rockefeller Plaza in the spring of 1960. It consisted of two floors of exhibits that included full-scale mock-ups and models as well as movies and the usual assortment of charts, graphs, and drawings.

Curtiss-Wright launched this campaign with good reason. It was running out of products and the lead time to develop them. Although there was plenty of money in the company coffers, its reputation had deteriorated badly in the late fifties. Price gouging, high-handed sales tactics, poor service, and inattention to product quality all had undermined the company's reputation. It was losing customers, and something was needed to turn things around quickly. Time was running out on a company whose cash flow problems were mounting rapidly.

Consequently, Hurley was forced to divide his company's energies between longer-term projects such as the X-200 and those that had a shorter lead time, like the various applications of the Wankel engine. Wright Aeronautical's engineers were thus ordered to work on short-term Wankel projects that were easy to produce, such as small stationary engines and lawnmower engines, for which there was a large potential market. This meant, however, that work on larger long-term projects, such as the power plant for the X-200, was languishing. As in World War II, Wright Aeronautical's engineering staff had become overextended. It was an impossible situation for the engineers on the VTOL project. Forbidden to abandon it, they were not allowed to use another engine even though the Wankel was not being developed.

At this point, the board of directors stepped in. Ted Berner, evidently well aware of the situation, approached Mergen at the Rockefeller Plaza show and asked him how the VTOL project was coming along, whereupon Mergen told Berner about the engine problems. Some weeks later, Hurley resigned. Several factors contributed to his dismissal; the VTOL project was certainly one of them.

Hurley's departure paved the way for a contract with the air force. Berner, the new company president, addressed himself to the X-200 project immediately after assuming his duties and asked Mergen what should be done with it. Mergen replied, "Redesign it for turbine engines and sell it to the military."[39] Although not overly fond of research and development expenditures, Berner accepted the recommendation and gave Mergen $2.5 million and 18 months to redesign and sell the airplane. Additionally, a VTOL Systems Division of the Curtiss-Wright Corporation was created to oversee the project, and Mergen was made division president and general manager. In the meantime, other companies such as Bell, Hiller, Vought, and Ryan were working on their own versions of a VTOL aircraft for the military services.

The VTOL Systems Division became a small, completely integrated airplane company within the Curtiss-Wright Corporation. It had its own sales and marketing organization, plus accounting, engineering, advanced design, planning, tool design, and manufacturing departments. As the redesign work on the X-200 got under way, plans were made to sell the concept to the military services. A multipurpose mission was developed for the aircraft, which included combat surveillance, counterinsurgency, transport, and air-sea rescue. The Curtiss-Wright VTOL project was picked up by the USAF as part of the Tri-Service Program, a cooperative venture of the three military services to explore and develop vertical and short takeoff technologies. Management for the project was assigned to Wright-Patterson Air Force Base, Dayton, Ohio, and the aircraft was given a new designation, X-19.

The first of the two projected X-19 aircraft was rolled out at the Curtiss-Wright test facility at Caldwell, New Jersey, on 23 July 1963. Although it appeared rather conventional when viewed from the side, the top view showed a radically different kind of airplane. Two short wings were mounted in tandem at the top of the fuselage. The larger rear wing was mounted where the horizontal tailplane was normally located, and the smaller front wing was placed just behind the cockpit. Propellers attached to each wingtip could rotate from the horizontal to the vertical plane as with the original X-100 test vehicle.

Testing at Caldwell began immediately and continued until the following summer, when the test site was moved to the FAA's National Aviation Facility Experimental Center west of Atlantic City, New Jersey. A less congested area, it would permit more extensive flight testing. As could be expected with such a radically new type of aircraft, it immediately encoun-

Curtiss X-19.

Courtesy of Harold Andrews.

tered many pitfalls, causing delays. Ironically, the source of some of the problems lay with the layout of the airframe, which lacked proper space for good flight control design. Curtiss-Wright had abandoned airframe construction long ago and no longer had expertise in designing aircraft.

Testing on the X-19 continued at Atlantic City until 25 August 1965, when the first prototype crashed as a result of a fatigue failure of the magnesium nacelle housing to which one of the propellers was attached. Although Curtiss-Wright resumed work on a second X-19 prototype, the project was doomed. By December 1965, the government decided to abandon the X-19. Curtiss-Wright had made its last venture into airframe development.[40]

Still More Diversification

In the meantime, another issue had arisen while Hurley was still president. Cash flow was becoming a source of increasing concern by the mid-fifties. As the X-19 project got under way toward the end of the decade, profits were deteriorating, and the company needed a product that would generate sales for the short term. Hurley's search for that product was beginning to move Curtiss-Wright far beyond the limits of the aerospace industry. He carried his diversification policy to incredible extremes. Beginning as early as 1955, he unveiled a grandiose scheme for a large, completely self-contained research center in a remote area of west-central Pennsylvania near Clearfield called Quehanna. Too diverse and too ambitious, the Quehanna project never lived up to expectations. While it existed, however, it investigated a host of products that ranged from foam materials to atomic energy.

By 1958 Hurley was frantically scrambling for any product that would give a quick return. He moved Curtiss-Wright into almost every field imaginable, from construction and earth-moving equipment to oceanography, to ultrasonics, to solar energy, and even to the manufacture of sunglasses. One company executive said that Hurley "would try anything on the theory that the law of averages would be for him 50 percent of the time." Berner explained Hurley's policy as follows: "When you don't know where you're going, you go every place at once."[41]

Hurley also pushed Curtiss-Wright into consumer product development, from household furnishings to automobiles. One such product was a plastic material developed at Quehanna and manufactured under the Curtiss-Wright brand name of "Curon." It had a variety of household applications such as sponges and rug undercushions. This venture reflected Hurley's antigovernment bias; he intended "to increase and maintain a healthy portion of Curtiss-Wright's business in non-aircraft and non-defense business." His critics pointed out, however, that the company was not, and had never been, a consumer-oriented enterprise; hence it lacked the requisite managerial skills and organizational structure to pursue this line of business.[42] Inevitably, the Curon plastics project was a failure. Like the earlier ill-starred "air-car" and an offshoot, the "air-boat," Curon was eventually consigned to oblivion.

Another example of Hurley's diversification policy was a poorly conceived venture into the automobile manufacturing business. In July 1956 Curtiss-Wright and the Studebaker-Packard Corporation announced conclusion of a contract bringing the two companies together in a three-year "joint program" in which Curtiss-Wright agreed to take over the management of the ailing automobile manufacturer. Included in the deal was a $35 million stock option that gave Curtiss-Wright a 52 percent control of Studebaker-Packard. This agreement was viewed as a preliminary step toward a formal merger at an unspecified time in the future. In addition, Curtiss-Wright agreed to purchase Studebaker-Packard's defense inventories, consisting largely of jet engine parts, and to take a 12-year lease on two of the company's plants in Utica, Michigan, and South Bend, Indiana. The agreement further stipulated that all automobile manufacturing would be consolidated at the South Bend plant, and that Curtiss-Wright would get the defense business. Studebaker-Packard was a major defense subcontractor for jet engines, and this agreement promised to give Curtiss-Wright some $500 million in defense contracts, an arrangement that would obviously help to alleviate the corporation's cash flow crisis. As with the Dart missile contract, Hurley once more managed to overcome his aversion to government business.

More significant, however, Hurley viewed this merger as a means of further diversifying into a civilian market. Speaking of the Curtiss-Wright/Studebaker-Packard connection in August 1956, he praised the benefits of commercial work over defense contracts and said: "The day has come to an end when you can save a company by defense business." His commitment to diversification was reflected in Curtiss-Wright's six-month financial report in August 1956, which revealed that 50 percent of the company's $20.4 million net earnings came from commercial business.[43]

The Studebaker-Packard deal also included a tie-in with the German auto manufacturer Daimler-Benz, which agreed to give the American auto company the distribution rights in the U.S. for their Mercedes line of luxury and sports cars and promised to give Curtiss-Wright access to what was described in the press as "unspecified German developments in diesel and gasoline engine fields." This included fuel injection technology, which had been pioneered by Daimler-Benz.[44]

The Studebaker-Packard Corporation had been created out of a 1954 merger between two declining old-line auto manufacturers. The Packard Motor Car Company produced its first automobile in 1900 at Warren, Ohio, and quickly developed a reputation for building high-quality luxury cars. The Studebaker Corporation of South Bend, Indiana, traced its origins to the Studebaker Brothers Manufacturing Company, which was formed in 1852 to make carriages and wagons. By the time it turned to manufacturing automobiles in 1904, it was the world's largest builder of horse-drawn vehicles.[45] Although both companies flourished independently for many years, their fortunes began to wane after World War II, and the 1954 merger only postponed their ultimate demise.

Hurley obviously believed that a bright future awaited Curtiss-Wright in the automobile business. There was logic in his position. The market was growing in the mid-fifties—an estimated 10 million units per year was predicted for the immediate future—and Curtiss-Wright could supply the venture capital that would give Studebaker-Packard an opportunity to capture a small segment of that expanding market with an "economy car." Although the obstacles were formidable, the potential returns were great.[46] Moreover, Hurley was returning to a business he knew well. Unfortunately, the same could not be said for the company that he headed. The Curtiss-Wright Corporation knew nothing about the automobile industry, and the ill-considered union of two struggling companies failed to produce any positive results for either. "It was a case of a company with problems taking on a company with problems, and the result was inevitable: disaster."[47]

Once again, Hurley had miscalculated badly. He failed to account for Curtiss-Wright's slender managerial resources, which were inadequate to deal with the responsibilities of directing Studebaker-Packard. A lack of sufficient managerial talent, which had been the Achilles heel of the Curtiss-Wright Corporation throughout its often stormy history, had reappeared.

In retrospect, the idea was absurd, and the outcome should have been foreseen. The big three auto manufacturers, Ford, General Motors, and Chrysler, had a stranglehold on the American automobile industry, and the combined resources of Curtiss-Wright and Studebaker-Packard were insufficient either to break it or to loosen it just enough to create a profitable niche for themselves. The experience of Kaiser-Frazer, which had entered the industry at the end of World War II but had left by 1955, should have been a warning to Hurley. In 1967 Ted Berner recalled those events:

We had fifteen divisions. We didn't have enough management talent for them. The only big money-maker was the big-engine division. Our top corporate staff spent most of their time in South Bend.

What right did we have to take on General Motors and Ford when we had plenty of problems at home? Our customers grew more unhappy than ever, and rightly so. Hurley had come from the auto industry. He wanted to show General Motors, Chrysler and Ford what he could do.[48]

One wonders why the board of directors—of which Berner was a member—took no action to restrain Hurley. They obviously could have blocked this agreement had they been of a mind to do so; but unlike the days when Paul Shields was in control, the board had become too compliant.

Paradoxically, Curtiss-Wright continued to enjoy reasonably good financial health even as this series of dead-end projects came and went. The company's cash position remained strong despite the damage wrought by Hurley's imprudent diversification maneuvers. Even though corporate sales plummeted from $598.6 million to $144.1 million and earnings dropped from $40 million to $8.7 million between 1957 and 1967, its cash position more than doubled for the same period, from $43 million to $96 million. The company's cash reserves in early 1966 were listed at $90 million, a figure representing almost 50 percent of its common equity.[49]

Roy T. Hurley resigned as board chairman and president of the Curtiss-Wright Corporation in May 1960, ending months of bickering with disgruntled stockholders and the board of directors. He came to a board meeting on 25 May with a request that was tantamount to an ultimatum: he wanted greater authority and a freer hand in the operations of the company; otherwise, he would resign from his positions as president, board chairman, and director. He was quoted as saying: "I'm not mad at anyone. If you fellows don't want it that way [i.e., giving him greater authority and a freer hand] I'll be glad to do what you want." After requesting that Hurley leave the room, the board considered his proposal and voted unanimously to accept his resignation.[50]

The annual stockholders' meeting in April had been a prelude to the May action. At that April meeting, Hurley was forced to face the wrath of stockholders who were extremely dissatisfied with the precipitous decline in company profits. After the arduous grilling was over, Hurley was reported to have exclaimed: "I'm called a bum and I'm called a genius, but I think I'm somewhere in between."[51]

He undoubtedly was correct. There were, after all, some successes. He had been instrumental in improving engine production efficiency by introducing changes on the shop floor, including an automated assembly line that was considered by some to be the most advanced in the aircraft engine industry. Hurley claimed that these changes had doubled the rate of engine production at two-thirds the cost.[52] Together with the increased sales of engines and propellers that accompanied the Korean War, his innovations had contributed significantly to the company's improved profitability. He also brought Wright Aeronautical into the jet age with the J65.

Nevertheless, he stayed with reciprocating engines too long. Sales melted away as turbojets and turboprops came to dominate the aircraft engine market, and Curtiss-Wright soon found itself without a product. Logic suggests that Hurley should have reinvested the earnings from the sales of the R-3350 engine and its derivative, the turbo-compound, into aircraft engine development instead of taking those profits as dividends. He should have applied his company's energies to aircraft engine development, something it knew well. Instead, he chose diversification in the search for a salable product. He succeeded only in dissipating corporate resources. Research and development activities languished, and work on servicing and improving existing products was neglected. Inevitably, customer relations deteriorated. All of this suggests that diversification is successful only with proper organization and sufficient managerial resources. Curtiss-Wright lacked both.

Hurley's talents lay in dealing with practical engineering and production problems. He was, in the words of one observer, a "shop superintendent type,"[53] a description with which Hurley himself doubtless would have agreed. So long as the product was up-to-date and sales remained good, those talents could be put to good use. By the mid-fifties, however, technological change had made the company's main product, the R-3350, obsolete, and different talents were required to respond to new circumstances. Curtiss-Wright needed someone with a broad perspective who could give the company both direction and a sense of identity. Regrettably, Hurley was not up to that task. His abilities were insufficient to cope with the problems that eventually overwhelmed him.

From Contractor to Subcontractor: Ted Berner Takes Command

The new board chairman was the same Ted Berner who had led the original stockholders' revolt in 1948.[54] He evidently accepted his new position somewhat reluctantly. However, as in 1948, he had been an outspoken critic of the company's leadership, and this time he was in effect told by the board to "put up or shut up." According to his account, the directors said, "All right, you know so much about what's wrong with this company, you take over."[55]

One of his first responsibilities was to find a new president. It proved to be an impossible task. According to Berner:

Nobody would accept the job. It was considered the worst job in American industry. One of the men I asked said: "You haven't a customer in the world who isn't dissatisfied with your engines." Finally the board told me: "You become President."[56]

T. Roland Berner.
Curtiss-Wright Corporation.

Hence, after six months as board chairman of the Curtiss-Wright Corporation, Ted Berner now found himself president as well. He had never before held an executive position. He was a corporate lawyer by training and had spent his entire career in the legal profession. Berner graduated from Harvard University in 1931, received a degree from Columbia Law School in 1935, and shortly thereafter joined a Manhattan law firm. He served with the navy in World War II. After his discharge in 1945, he set up his own law practice, specializing in minority stockholder disputes with management.[57] He was a Curtiss-Wright stockholder himself with some 1,200 shares, and his wife's family had also held shares in the company since the twenties.[58] Although young and unknown in 1948, he was outspoken and combative and did not hesitate to question Guy Vaughan's leadership. Berner believed that the corporation had outgrown the abilities of its management, and he wanted more than a dividend for the stockholders. He also demanded greater stockholder representation on the board and asked for what was described at the time as a "revitalization" of the management.[59] When Vaughan completely ignored Berner, the battle was joined. Although Berner lost the first round, he eventually won the war. And now, 12 years later, he had just won a similar war with another Curtiss-Wright president. Along the way, he had acquired a reputation as a gadfly.

Nevertheless, Berner could not be held completely blameless for Curtiss-Wright's troubles in 1960. He had been a member of a passive board of directors that had given Hurley a virtual free hand to reorient the company. The abortive Studebaker-Packard deal in 1956 exemplified the board's acquiescence to Hurley's freewheeling actions. Hurley had presented the idea to them as a "heads we win, tails Studebaker loses" proposition, and they meekly went along. Ultimately, it became, in Berner's words, "tails on both sides." Yet no one on the board, not even Berner, had spoken up against the deal. Berner justified his actions by arguing that a president should be backed by his directors "as long as possible." "Maybe," he added, "we went beyond that."[60]

Now he was in the driver's seat and was expected to deliver. A top-priority issue was the declining quality of Curtiss-Wright products and the consequent deterioration of customer relations. In response to this problem, he initiated an immediate program to improve the performance and reliability of Wright engines, a move that he hoped would restore his company's credibility with its customers, including the government. It was a tough sell. The preceding five years or more had been disastrous for customer relations. Moreover, confidence in Wright aircraft engines, especially the R-3350, was almost nil. The situation was so bad that on one occasion, an airline president was so angry with Curtiss-Wright that he refused even to see Berner.[61] Ironically, the improvement of engine quality actually reduced the company's revenues because it significantly lowered spare parts sales, which had been a very lucrative source of income. Nevertheless, Berner was willing to lose this money in order to regain customer confidence and rebuild his company's reputation. It was a wise move.

Other changes following Hurley's departure came quickly. In June, the company announced that it would place greater emphasis on "company-originated product development and less development acquired through licensing of foreign projects."[62] Although this statement implied a renewed emphasis on research and development, the promise was not fulfilled. Other changes included a reversal of Hurley's policy of reducing government contracts in favor of commercial business. At this time, the ratio of defense to commercial business stood at about 50-50, with military and defense contracts in decline. The rejuvenated X-19 project was part of this reorientation.

Berner also indicated that he intended to bring an end to the excessive product diversification that had become the hallmark of Curtiss-Wright. He rightfully pointed out that under Hurley, Curtiss-Wright's product line had become "too broad and too thin." Too many products were chasing too few sales. Berner's problem was to sort out and reorganize what was referred to by outside observers as the company's "jumbleshop."[63] This action was expected to produce an even lower sales volume, although higher profit margins were anticipated. Hence certain product lines were doomed. At the top of this list was the Curon Division. Berner was never happy with Curtiss-Wright's foray into consumer products, and this was his opportunity to unload a costly operation. It was sold to Reeves Brothers, a textile company.[64]

Once the decision was made to eliminate specific products, the opposite side of the coin had to be considered, namely, the development of a viable product. Unfortunately, Curtiss-Wright was facing an identity crisis, and Berner, like his predecessor, apparently had no clear idea of what to do with his company.[65] He was accused of indecisiveness. Said one critic, a former Curtiss-Wright executive: "Berner seems unsure of himself—afraid to really commit himself to anything that has risk."[66] Other observers claimed that Berner and his board lacked a viable corporate strategy. They simply didn't know where they wanted to go. Berner struggled with this problem for the better part of the following decade. Ultimately, the Defense Department helped him to decide, albeit in a very painful way.

Shortly after becoming president in 1960, Berner received two staggering blows from the government. In his words, "The ceiling fell in." The first came from Rear Adm. William Rayborn, head of the Polaris missile program, who informed Berner that the government was canceling its contracts with Curtiss-Wright, which was manufacturing components for the rocket engines that powered the missile. Rayborn told Berner, "Your company has been heading our delinquency list for six months. You're holding up the whole program. You're ruining us."

It would get worse. Shortly after Berner's conversation with Admiral Rayborn, he received a call from Washington and was informed that the Department of Defense had decided to expand the missile program. This meant that aircraft procurement would be reduced significantly, which in turn implied a curtailment of aircraft engine procurement. At the time, five companies were manufacturing engines for military aircraft. Berner quoted the government official as saying: "We can't support five companies. We can only support two, and you're not one of them. We're giving all our orders to General Electric and Pratt and Whitney."[67] This decision signaled the end of J65 production, which in any case had been surpassed by new technologies. This action effectively eliminated Wright Aeronautical from the jet engine market. General Electric had finally displaced Wright Aeronautical as one of the "big two" aircraft engine manufacturers in the United States, although other manufacturers such as Allison with its turboprops remained in the field.

Nevertheless, Berner hung on. He persuaded Admiral Rayborn to give Curtiss-Wright several weeks to improve its performance on the Polaris project and suggested to the unnamed government official that Wright Aeronautical could develop a new jet engine that would be competitive in performance and cost with the General Electric and Pratt and Whitney engines.

I said: "Suppose we develop a jet engine twice as good at half the cost. What then?" He said: "You don't have an engine like that." I said, "No, but we can develop one." He said: "If you do, we'll buy it." I was stupid. I believed him. I was really stupid. I didn't understand how a bureaucracy works.[68]

About this same time, interest in the new supersonic transport (SST) project was running high, and the government announced a competition for an engine to power the airplane. The two front-runners were General Electric and Pratt and Whitney, both of whom had received research and development money from the government. Berner, in a last desperate bid to keep Wright Aeronautical in the jet engine business, and remembering his conversation with the government official, decided to enter the competition using the company's own money. He claimed that costs to develop a production engine would amount to $50 million per year for five years.

Although Wright engineers built a prototype engine, the company failed to get a government contract to develop it, and the project was dropped. The government, remembering Curtiss-Wright's sorry record in the recent past, may have doubted the manufacturer's ability to meet its contractual obligations and decided to eliminate it from the competition.[69] Berner explained the cancellation differently. He claimed that Wright Aeronautical's entry was superior to the competition, and he expressed frustration at his failure to sell it:

We had the talent, we had the technique, and we didn't make it. Our engineers discovered the secret: high-inlet temperature. We designed an engine that would carry four times the payload at half the price of the Pratt and Whitney engine. Boeing was amazed. I don't know why the hell I wasn't able to sell this engine. I guess I wasn't smart enough. I did try.

He also charged that the government purposely changed the rules midway through the competition in order to eliminate Curtiss-Wright. Since both General Electric and Pratt and Whitney had government research and development money, they were able to adapt. Curtiss-Wright, working with its own money, could not afford the changes and was forced to drop out. Berner claimed the government would have had difficulty accepting a Curtiss-

Wright engine that had been developed with private funds after millions in public money had been given to General Electric and Pratt and Whitney. He explained:

> The government changed the rules. For General Electric and Pratt and Whitney, that was no problem. They had all this government R&D money. We couldn't afford it. What's more, once GE and Pratt and Whitney saw our engine, it was no trick for them to develop one just as good.
>
> I should have realized the government would change the rules. If you're a bureaucrat and you give two companies millions for R&D and then you go and buy your engine elsewhere, how do you look? How do you justify yourself?[70]

Although the Berner rendition of these events has a certain plausibility, it also is more than a little self-serving. For example, his claim that Wright Aeronautical had an engine capable of carrying four times the payload at half the price of the comparable Pratt and Whitney engines is highly unlikely. Hence the former version of the SST engine story is undoubtedly much closer to the truth. Whatever the reason for Wright Aeronautical's failure to secure that contract, this venture cost the company close to $15 million.[71]

It was now the mid-sixties. Curtiss-Wright had $96 million and didn't know what to do with it. The company was facing an all too familiar problem: too much cash and no product.[72] The old questions remained: What direction should Curtiss-Wright take? What kind of a company should it become? What sort of identity did it want? Six years after acquiring control of the Curtiss-Wright Corporation, Ted Berner still seemed to have no clear answer to these questions. Writers in 1960 speculated that he would be "looking for acquisitions and mergers rather than trying to rebuild C-W from the inside."[73] That option still seemed to be viable in 1966. One observer, noting the company's low earnings and substantial holdings of cash and securities, wondered aloud if it would become a prime candidate for a takeover or, more likely, if it "would turn itself into a holding company,"[74] which it technically had been ever since its creation in 1929. Those statements proved to be prophetic. As in the past, Curtiss-Wright's large cash reserves determined its future policy as a series of proxy fights and takeover bids again dominated the activities of company management.

By 1963 Curtiss-Wright had reportedly made several merger approaches to various companies without success. One of the more highly publicized of these was an attempt late that summer to secure a controlling interest in the Garrett Corporation, a company in the aerospace industry. Curtiss-Wright offered to buy 700,000 shares of stock, a purchase that would have given it 46.5 percent of Garrett's outstanding common stock. An earlier merger proposal by Curtiss-Wright had been turned down by Garrett, and this latest takeover bid— Curtiss-Wright management called it "an investment"—was rejected as well. Garrett initially sought protection from the federal courts, claiming that a Curtiss-Wright/Garrett merger would be a violation of the Clayton Anti-trust Act. The battle continued until November 1963, when Curtiss-Wright, after extending its offer deadline twice and raising its offer from $50 to $57 per share, finally gave up. At that point, Garrett withdrew its federal court suit.[75]

Curtiss-Wright's most spectacular takeover bid took place some 15 years later when Ted Berner took on the Kennecott Copper Corporation, the nation's largest copper producer. Berner's actions were somewhat akin to that of a mouse attempting to swallow an elephant because Kennecott was at least three times the size of Curtiss-Wright (some said it was five times larger; others claimed it was as much as seven times larger).[76] The proceedings also were reminiscent of his 1948 proxy fight with Guy Vaughan and his spectacular theatrics at the Curtiss-Wright stockholders' meeting that year. He gave a repeat performance at the May 1978 Kennecott stockholders' meeting.

Somewhat earlier, Curtiss-Wright had spent $77 million, of which $45 million was borrowed money, to purchase 10 percent of Kennecott's stock. Berner then precipitated a proxy war for control of Kennecott. He proposed to sell off the Carborundum Company, a recent Kennecott acquisition, for $567 million and pay out $663 million to the shareholders either in a stock buyback or in dividends, a formula that was almost identical to the one he had used against Guy Vaughan 30 years earlier.[77] Berner claimed that the Carborundum acquisition was a bad deal and that the money would have been better spent either in modernizing Kennecott's facilities or in paying a dividend to stockholders.[78] Kennecott's management retaliated by securing a federal court injunction declaring that Curtiss-Wright was in violation of securities and antitrust law and enjoining Curtiss-Wright from voting the shares it owned and the proxies it had secured. This decision was reversed on appeal just 12 minutes before the Kennecott stockholders' meeting was scheduled to begin. Curtiss-Wright was allowed to vote its shares.

Armed with this latest court order, Berner made what his contemporaries described as a "theatrical, fist-waving entrance" into the grand ballroom of the Plaza Hotel in Manhattan, where the meeting was to be held. He dashed up to the stage shouting, "A stay has been granted! I'm Ted Berner and I'm here!" Frank R. Milliken, the Kennecott board chairman, was caught totally by surprise. The meeting was called to order after a 15-minute delay that gave the adversaries an opportunity to establish mutually agreeable procedures. Each side was given 40 minutes—which both ignored—to present its case. What followed was a display of verbal pyrotechnics that bore at least a superficial resemblance to that long-ago Curtiss-Wright stockholders' meeting. Noted one observer: "Cutting verbal swordplay by both sides" was punctuated by a "fusilade at both from the overflow crowd of 1,200."[79]

In the end, the Curtiss-Wright challenge was beaten back, and some analysts claimed that Kennecott emerged from the battle stronger than when it began. Berner's proposal was dismissed by the financial community as "imprudent."[80] Berner came out of this episode with a rather badly tarnished image. One reporter said that he "came across as just another carping publicity seeker."[81] As for Curtiss-Wright, it gained little from the battle except adverse publicity. In the meantime, its performance throughout the sixties and seventies continued to be lackluster, with profits for the 20-year period averaging $11.4 million per year. Sales for the same period ranged from a low of $144.1 million in 1966 to a high of $336.7 million in 1976.[82]

The Kennecott proxy battle proved to be but a preliminary skirmish in a war between the copper-producing giant and the onetime colossus of the aviation industry. In the end, the conflict worked against Curtiss-Wright's best interests because it set into motion a chain of events that threatened the company's survival as an independent corporation and gained nothing. If the 1978 stockholders' fight was the first shoe to fall, the second was dropped in 1980 when, in an ironic reversal of positions, Kennecott made a bid to take over Curtiss-Wright.

Although frustrated in his first attempt to take control of Kennecott, Berner had persisted, and by the fall of 1980, he owned 14.3 percent of Kennecott's stock. This made Curtiss-Wright the copper producer's largest single stockholder.[83] Obviously positioning his company for another takeover bid, Berner announced his intention to acquire a 25 percent holding. Thomas Barrow, Kennecott's new board chairman, was determined to thwart Berner and counterattacked with what has been described as a "pre-emptive strike."[84] Barrow decided to take over Curtiss-Wright. As one onlooker commented: "The apple had bitten the worm."[85] Kennecott made a purchase offer to Curtiss-Wright stockholders of $40 dollars a share, which was almost twice the market price. Berner retaliated with a buyback offer of $46 per share.

And so it went for the next several weeks. The struggle escalated as each offer produced a counteroffer. By January 1981, Kennecott had acquired 32 percent of Curtiss-Wright stock, making it Curtiss-Wright's largest shareholder. Kennecott tried to further increase its holdings when it made a tender offer to purchase 49.6 percent of Curtiss-Wright stock and offered to buy back the 14.3 percent of its own stock currently held by Curtiss-Wright.

This proxy war soon degenerated into a personal vendetta between Berner and Barrow. Neither company was being well served by its leaders. The energy and money wasted would have been better spent in rebuilding and modernizing the manufacturing facilities of each and in developing new products.

By February, the struggle had become a standoff. Neither side was able to defeat the other, and a truce was declared as each company recovered its own stock with the mutual promise of a 10-year truce in the proxy battle. As might be expected, each side declared itself the winner. Objective assessments gave the victor's wreath to Kennecott, however, because Curtiss-Wright lost its Dorr-Oliver Division in the settlement. Dorr-Oliver Incorporated was a manufacturer of process equipment that transported solids suspended in liquids or gasses. This equipment had a wide variety of applications in various industries. Curtiss-Wright had purchased a controlling interest in Dorr-Oliver in 1968 and secured 100 percent control in 1979. That year, the division accounted for almost half of total Curtiss-Wright sales and revenues and close to 40 percent of its near $34 million earnings.[86]

But that division was now going to Kennecott Copper. Berner tried to put the best face on the exchange by noting that Curtiss-Wright had paid some $70 million for Dorr-Oliver but in exchange was receiving its own stock back from Kennecott at an inflated price of $112 million—some said the figure was $122 million—which was more than 70 percent above book value. Moreover, the stock that Kennecott was buying back for $168 million had cost Curtiss-Wright only $110 million. By the time the dust settled, Kennecott had paid out some $290 million to bring the proxy fight to an end, and Curtiss-Wright had pocketed $34.1 million from the sale, allowing it to post net earnings of $85.3 million for 1981, its most profitable year in the 35-year period from 1960 to 1995.[87]

Once again, Curtiss-Wright found itself cash rich but product poor, and one writer noted that the corporation had emerged from the settlement "as a shrunken hodgepodge" with a variety of products ranging from nuclear control valves to spare engine parts.[88] It also no longer had its most profitable division, and what remained were units showing varying degrees of profitability. The industrial and process equipment sectors were healthy, but the nuclear division was producing for a declining industry in 1980, and the engine division was manufacturing only spare aircraft engine parts, most of which were going to the J65, which was being phased out.[89]

In the end, the proxy war had accomplished little. Vital resources had been wasted in a battle of egos, and neither company had much to show for it. Nevertheless, Ted Berner reprised his earlier role in the Kennecott imbroglio when shortly thereafter he made a similar bid to take over Western Union. This battle ended in 1983 with an agreement by Curtiss-Wright not to increase its Western Union holdings beyond 25 percent. In 1985 the company posted a $42 million deficit as a result of the disposition of the Western Union investment. This action more than wiped out the profit accrued from the sale of Dorr-Oliver four years earlier.[90]

While all of the boardroom proxy battles were going on throughout the sixties and seventies, Curtiss-Wright was struggling to reposition itself within the aerospace industry. After the collapse of the 1960 negotiations for an engine to power the projected SST, Berner decided that General Electric and Pratt and Whitney would continue to dominate the big aircraft engine market for the foreseeable future. Consequently, he elected to turn his company into a major "first-tier supplier" to its erstwhile competitors in the airframe and engine business. And that is where Curtiss-Wright eventually found its niche in the aerospace industry: as a subcontractor.

Despite promises to the contrary, the company continued to diversify, although not as extensively as in the Hurley years. In 1976 the U.S. Department of Energy awarded Curtiss-Wright a multiyear contract to develop a process for generating electricity by means of a turbine engine fired by gasses produced from high-sulphur coal. Although a pilot plant was constructed, the company abandoned the project at the end of 1983.

A development of the late sixties was the creation of the Wood-Ridge Nuclear Facility, which manufactured a variety of products for the nuclear industry. These included nuclear valves, control and instrumentation devices, and stainless steel components for nuclear reactors. By the late seventies, severe problems within the nuclear industry had forced a sharp decline in sales of these products, and the Wood-Ridge facility was closed at the end of 1980. Nevertheless, the company has continued to manufacture components for the industry and government.

Wright Aeronautical, which had become a division within the parent corporation in October 1951, survived throughout the sixties and seventies by providing overhaul services for jet engines. It also pursued development work on the Wankel engine. Time was running out, however. With no marketable products on the horizon, the 40-year-old Wood-Ridge plant was closed on 30 November 1983. Two months later, on 30 January 1984, Curtiss-Wright sold its entire Wankel engine business to the John Deere Company. Thirty-three years after leaving the airplane business, Curtiss-Wright was out of the aircraft engine business as well. What was left of the once great Wright Aeronautical Corporation had passed into history.[91]

By the early eighties, the various divisions and subsidiaries of the Curtiss-Wright Corporation, which for the most part had been acquired through direct purchase, were producing a wide range of products for several segments of American industry. They included precision spring clutches, manual impact wrenches, air compressors, aircraft windshield wiper systems, seamless alloy pipe, relief valves of various types, and aircraft control systems.[92] In addition, the Metal Improvement Company, a wholly owned Curtiss-Wright subsidiary, used a process for cold-shaping metal products known as shot peening. In this process, the part to be molded is bombarded with small spherical media known as "shot," which act as tiny peening hammers shaping the metal. The process improves resistance to fatique and stress failure and increases the hardness and wear resistance of the part. The process has a wide variety of industrial applications, including the forming of metal components used in aircraft structures and engines.[93]

As Curtiss-Wright entered its second half century, it had evolved from an airframe, aircraft engine, and propeller manufacturer to an investment company. Its 1979 annual report summarized the metamorphosis succinctly: "In the course of half a century, Curtiss-Wright Corporation has successively, and successfully, transformed itself from an airplane company to an airplane engine company to a diversified, multi-industry, multi-national concern."[94] The report also might have added that its management had acquired a reputation as a corporate raider.

Its managerial structure had been completely changed as well. Shortly after the cancellation of the X-19 project in 1965, Berner decided to make some sweeping managerial changes. He eliminated all the individual divisions that had previously maintained almost complete autonomy in such matters as sales and engineering and replaced them with "work centers" or "market centers" for specific products and services. These centers were created to encourage "aggressive marketing campaigns." Works managers replaced former presidents and general managers. The general office took over all sales, profit and loss, and engineering responsibility. These changes were the last straw for those few old-timers who were still around. From their perspective, this reorganization spelled the end of what was left of a once great company. Within a year, most of them had departed.[95] The transformation that had begun in 1948 was now complete.

T. Roland Berner's death in March 1990 ended a 30-year era in the history of the Curtiss-Wright Corporation. His achievements were considerable. The most significant was the reversal of his company's decline and its restoration to a position of respectability and reliability among its customers. He had preserved its independence and had secured a place for the onetime industrial giant as a subcontractor in a volatile and fickle industry.

His failures are evident as well. In some ways, Berner attempted too much, and eventually he fell into the same trap as his predecessor. There was too little research and development, too much diversification, and, for a time at least, no viable product. Moreover, company assets had been squandered in several ill-considered attempts by Ted Berner to play the role of a corporate raider. Berner's failures are easy to see with hindsight. Yet it was evident to contemporary observers that those proxy fights that vitiated his company's resources were totally unnecessary.

As the Curtiss-Wright Corporation approaches the twenty-first century, it is still very much a part of the industry that it helped to create. Much has changed, however. No longer a manufacturer of airplanes, engines, and propellers, it has become, in its own words, a "diversified multi-national manufacturing concern." Its headquarters in Lyndhurst, New Jersey, oversees an organization that employs approximately 1,500 people and maintains overseas as well as domestic operations. Total sales in 1995 amounted to $154.4 million, and net earnings were $18.2 million.

Three main business units are at the heart of the corporation. The first is the Flight Systems Group, which is devoted to the design, development, and manufacture of flight control and actuation systems for military and commercial aircraft. This division also maintains a commercial aircraft overhaul business. The second division, the Metal Improvement Company (MIC), was established in 1946 and was acquired by Curtiss-Wright in 1968. In 1994, it had 31 facilities throughout North America and Europe. MIC is best known for its special metalworking technologies, such as shot peening, and services the metalworking industry worldwide. It is the oldest and largest technical shot-peening company in the industry. The Target Rock Corporation, the third of the company's main divisions, is also a wholly owned subsidiary acquired in 1961. It produces electronic control valves for a variety of military and industrial uses. The primary technological thread tying these units together is the precision working of metal and metal alloys.[96] These three divisions constitute the central core of the company's operations and have been essential to its continued viability within the aerospace industry. Thus the long search for a new identity and a new product that began after World War II has been brought to a successful conclusion.

The Curtiss-Wright Corporation: A Survivor

The Curtiss-Wright Corporation has a rich heritage. It traces its lineage to the beginning of the air age. The very name evokes images of three great pioneers of aviation history. Once at the center, the company is now a junior partner in the aerospace industry. The onetime industrial giant has adapted and survived in an unstable industry that has had recurring periods of rapid expansion and disastrous contraction. Prosperity and poverty have been twin companions of the many companies that have entered these treacherous waters. Few remain. One of those survivors is the Curtiss-Wright Corporation, which has retained its identity as a distinct organization at a time when other companies have either merged or been completely subsumed into a larger corporate structure, or have closed their doors completely. Curtiss-Wright's history has mirrored the tides of fortune and misfortune that have gripped the industry from the beginning.

The two founding companies were leaders in the initial expansion that followed the birth of the air age. They enjoyed the surge of business that came with World War I and endured the hardships that followed the armistice. The Lindbergh boom of the late twenties helped to bring the two companies together as one giant corporation in 1929. It soon faced the disastrous downturn that accompanied the Great Depression. The corporation responded by liquidating many of its assets and greatly reducing the scope of its activities. A third expansion came with World War II, but it was soon followed by yet another period of severe contraction after the end of hostilities. Although the onset of the Cold War helped to restore profitability to the industry, managerial instability at Curtiss-Wright contributed to a "time of troubles" for the company that lasted for many years. Conflicts between stockholders and management over the disposition of its assets accompanied a growing uncertainty about the company's direction and identity. Inevitably, Curtiss-Wright entered a period of decline as its formerly dominant position within the industry continued to erode. After years of mismanagement, the company arrested its slide and stabilized itself within a rapidly changing industry by becoming a diversified investment company.

We can only speculate about what the Curtiss-Wright Corporation would have looked like 50 years after World War II had the energies expended in preserving its cash resources and acquiring subsidiaries in the perennial quest for immediate profits been directed instead toward long-term research and development in aircraft or engines, or both. A company whose aircraft and engines once equipped the airlines and air forces of the world is now associated with subcomponents such as leading-edge flap actuators, solenoid valves, windshield wiper systems, and seamless alloy pipe. As important as these products are, they seem to be a far cry from the Whirlwind and Cyclone engines and the Hawk, Condor, and even the Jenny airplanes of so long ago. In the hard-nosed business world, such nostalgia is usually dismissed as romantic nonsense. Yet one cannot help but wonder if it is not just a bit more than that.

Appendix A:
Curtiss-Wright
Corporate Genealogy
and Organizational Charts

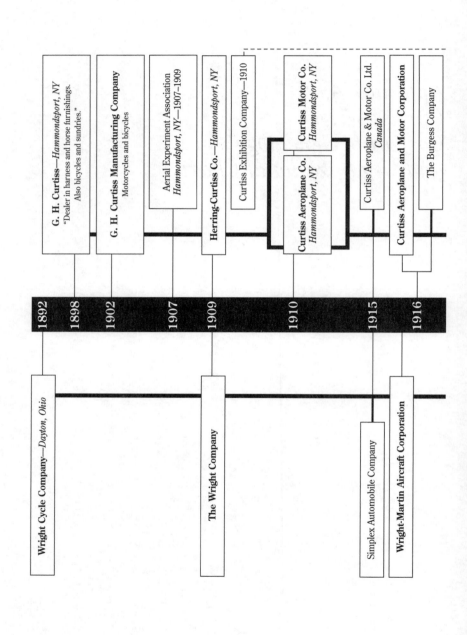

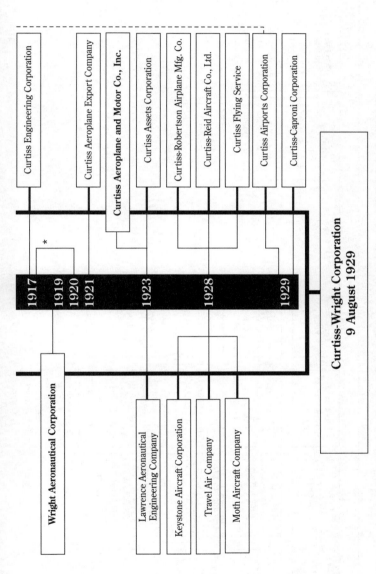

Curtiss Engineering Corporation

Curtiss Aeroplane Export Company

Curtiss Aeroplane and Motor Co., Inc.

Curtiss Assets Corporation

Curtiss-Robertson Airplane Mfg. Co.

Curtiss-Reid Aircraft Co., Ltd.

Curtiss Flying Service

Curtiss Airports Corporation

Curtiss-Caproni Corporation

1917
*
1919
1920
1921

1923

1928

1929

Wright Aeronautical Corporation

Lawrence Aeronautical Engineering Company

Keystone Aircraft Corporation

Travel Air Company

Moth Aircraft Company

**Curtiss-Wright Corporation
9 August 1929**

* The Willys Overland Company had a controlling interest in the Curtiss Aeroplane and Motor Corporation (1917–1920)

Curtiss-Wright Corporation genealogy, 1892 to 1929.
Courtesy of James Miceli Design.

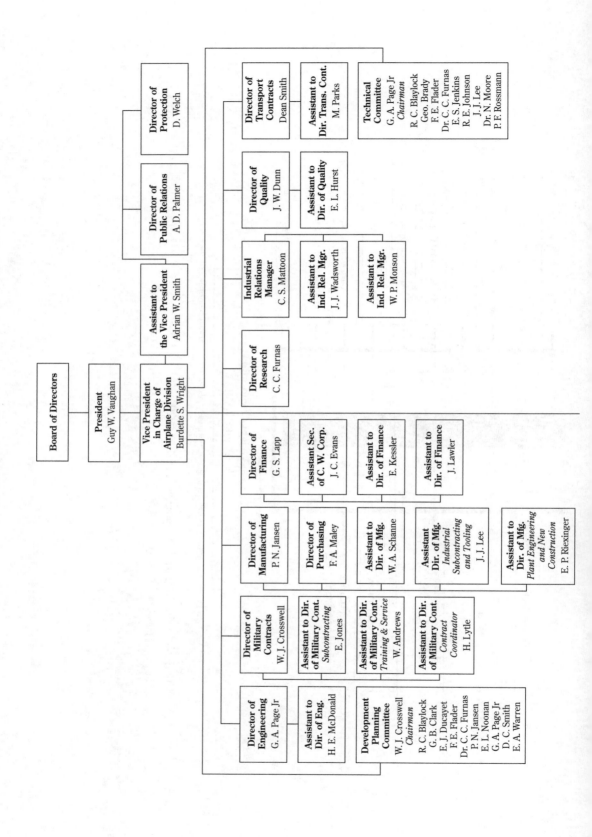

Board of Directors

President
Guy W. Vaughan

Vice President in Charge of Airplane Division
Burdette S. Wright

Assistant to the Vice President
Adrian W. Smith

Director of Public Relations
A. D. Palmer

Director of Protection
D. Welch

Director of Research
C. C. Furnas

Industrial Relations Manager
C. S. Mattoon

Assistant to Ind. Rel. Mgr.
J. J. Wadsworth

Assistant to Ind. Rel. Mgr.
W. P. Monson

Director of Quality
J. W. Dunn

Assistant to Dir. of Quality
E. L. Hurst

Director of Transport Contracts
Dean Smith

Assistant to Dir. Trans. Cont.
M. Parks

Technical Committee
G. A. Page Jr
Chairman
R. C. Blaylock
Geo. Brady
F. E. Flader
Dr. C. C. Furnas
E. S. Jenkins
R. E. Johnson
J. J. Lee
Dr. N. Moore
P. F. Rossmann

Director of Finance
G. S. Lapp

Assistant Sec. of C. W. Corp.
J. C. Evans

Assistant to Dir. of Finance
E. Kessler

Assistant to Dir. of Finance
J. Lawler

Director of Manufacturing
P. N. Jansen

Director of Purchasing
F. A. Maley

Assistant to Dir. of Mfg.
W. A. Schanne

Assistant Dir. of Mfg.
Industrial Subcontracting and Tooling
J. J. Lee

Assistant to Dir. of Mfg.
Plant Engineering and New Construction
E. P. Riexinger

Director of Military Contracts
W. J. Crosswell

Assistant to Dir. of Military Cont.
Subcontracting
E. Jones

Assistant to Dir. of Military Cont.
Training & Service
W. Andrews

Assistant to Dir. of Military Cont.
Contract Coordinator
H. Lytle

Director of Engineering
G. A. Page Jr

Assistant to Dir. of Eng.
H. E. McDonald

Development Planning Committee
W. J. Crosswell
Chairman
R. C. Blaylock
G. B. Clark
E. J. Ducayet
F. E. Flader
Dr. C. C. Furnas
P. N. Jansen
E. L. Noonan
G. A. Page Jr
D. C. Smith
E. A. Warren

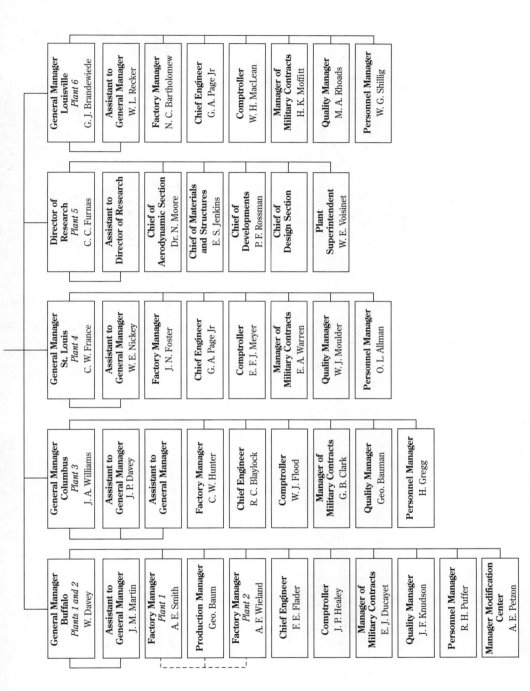

Curtiss-Wright Corporation—Airplane Division organizational chart, 1942.
Courtesy of the National Archives and Records Service, record group 18, central decimal files 004.03, Curtiss Airplane Division organization and salaries, box 32.

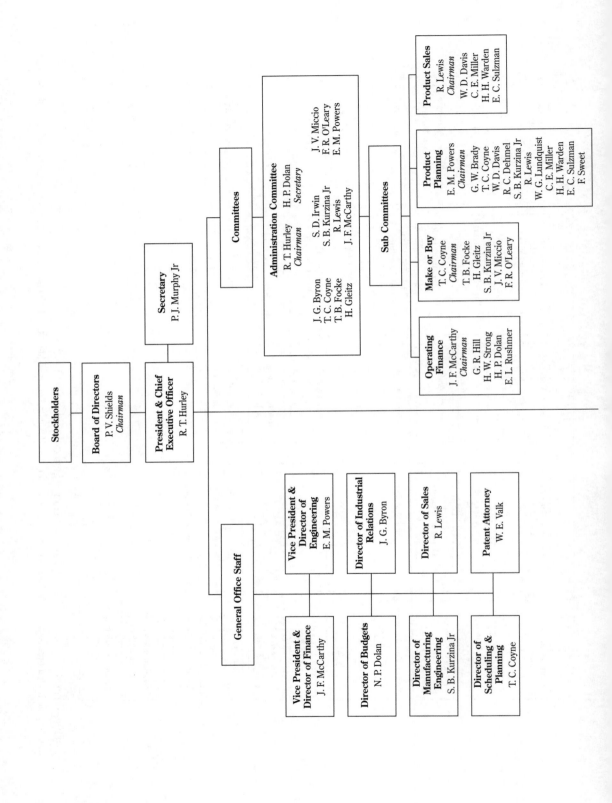

Stockholders

Board of Directors
P. V. Shields
Chairman

President & Chief Executive Officer
R. T. Hurley

Secretary
P. J. Murphy Jr

Committees

Administration Committee
R. T. Hurley   H. P. Dolan
Chairman   *Secretary*

S. D. Irwin   J. V. Miccio
S. B. Kurzina Jr F. R. O'Leary
R. Lewis   E. M. Powers
J. F. McCarthy

J. G. Byron
T. C. Coyne
T. B. Focke
H. Gleitz

Sub Committees

Operating Finance
J. F. McCarthy
Chairman
G. R. Hill
H. W. Strong
H. P. Dolan
E. L. Rushmer

Make or Buy
T. C. Coyne
Chairman
T. B. Focke
H. Gleitz
S. B. Kurzina Jr
J. V. Miccio
F. R. O'Leary

Product Planning
E. M. Powers
Chairman
G. W. Brady
T. C. Coyne
W. D. Davis
R. C. Dehmel
S. B. Kurzina Jr
R. Lewis
W. G. Lundquist
C. E. Miller
H. H. Warden
E. C. Sulzman
F. Sweet

Product Sales
R. Lewis
Chairman
W. D. Davis
C. E. Miller
H. H. Warden
E. C. Sulzman

General Office Staff

Vice President & Director of Engineering
E. M. Powers

Director of Industrial Relations
J. G. Byron

Director of Sales
R. Lewis

Patent Attorney
W. E. Valk

Vice President & Director of Finance
J. F. McCarthy

Director of Budgets
N. P. Dolan

Director of Manufacturing Engineering
S. B. Kurzina Jr

Director of Scheduling & Planning
T. C. Coyne

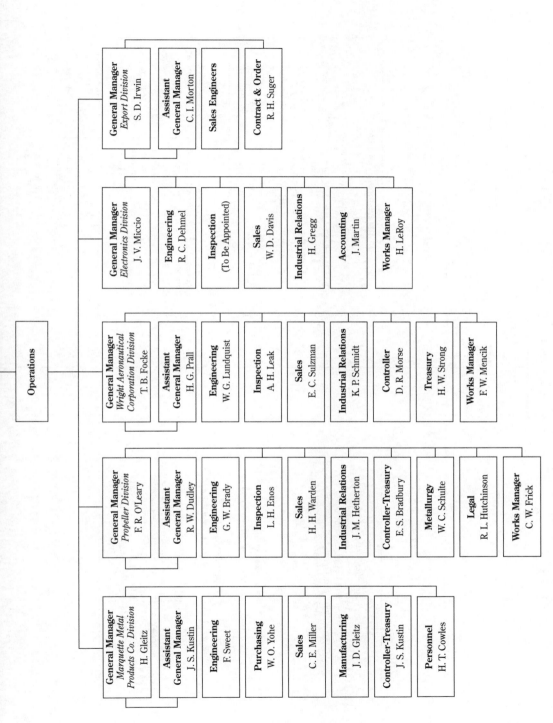

Curtiss-Wright Corporation organizational chart, January 1951.   Courtesy of the late Robert E. Johnson.

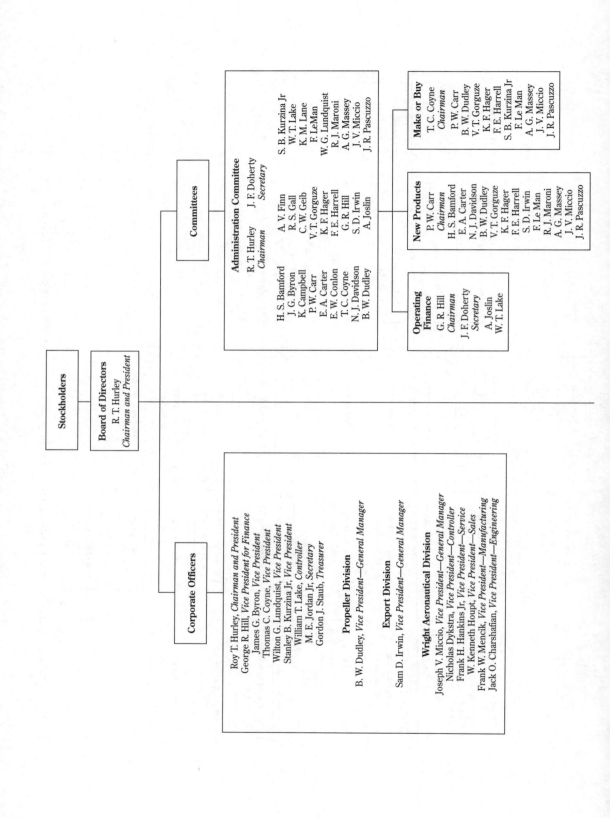

Stockholders

Board of Directors
R. T. Hurley
Chairman and President

Committees

Corporate Officers

Roy T. Hurley, *Chairman and President*
George R. Hill, *Vice President for Finance*
James G. Byron, *Vice President*
Thomas C. Coyne, *Vice President*
Wilton G. Lundquist, *Vice President*
Stanley B. Kurzina Jr, *Vice President*
William T. Lake, *Controller*
M. E. Jordan Jr, *Secretary*
Gordon J. Staub, *Treasurer*

Propeller Division
B. W. Dudley, *Vice President—General Manager*

Export Division
Sam D. Irwin, *Vice President—General Manager*

Wright Aeronautical Division
Joseph V. Miccio, *Vice President—General Manager*
Nicholas Dykstra, *Vice President—Controller*
Frank H. Hankins Jr, *Vice President—Service*
W. Kenneth Houpt, *Vice President—Sales*
Frank W. Mencik, *Vice President—Manufacturing*
Jack O. Charshafian, *Vice President—Engineering*

Administration Committee
R. T. Hurley   J. F. Doherty
Chairman   *Secretary*

H. S. Bamford	A. V. Finn	S. B. Kurzina Jr
J. G. Byron	R. S. Gall	W. T. Lake
K. Campbell	C. W. Geib	K. M. Lane
P. W. Carr	V. T. Gorguze	F. LeMan
E. A. Carter	K. F. Hager	W. G. Lundquist
E. W. Conlon	F. E. Harrell	R. J. Maroni
T. C. Coyne	G. R. Hill	A. G. Massey
N. J. Davidson	S. D. Irwin	J. V. Miccio
B. W. Dudley	A. Joslin	J. R. Pascuzzo

Operating Finance
G. R. Hill
Chairman
J. F. Doherty
Secretary
A. Joslin
W. T. Lake

New Products
P. W. Carr
Chairman
H. S. Bamford
E. A. Carter
N. J. Davidson
B. W. Dudley
V. T. Gorguze
K. F. Hager
F. E. Harrell
S. D. Irwin
F. Le Man
R. J. Maroni
A. G. Massey
J. V. Miccio
J. R. Pascuzzo

Make or Buy
T. C. Coyne
Chairman
P. W. Carr
B. W. Dudley
V. T. Gorguze
K. F. Hager
F. E. Harrell
S. B. Kurzina Jr
F. Le Man
A. G. Massey
J. V. Miccio
J. R. Pascuzzo

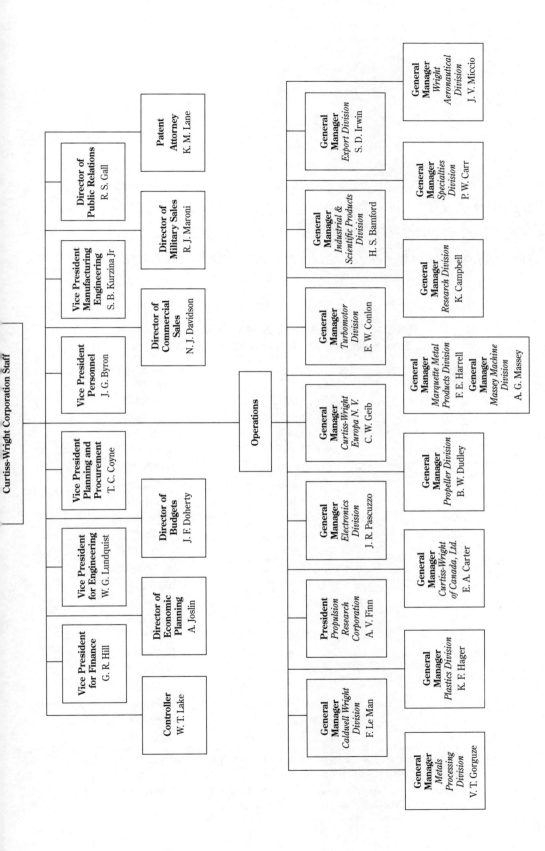

Curtiss-Wright Corporation Staff

Controller
W. T. Lake

Vice President for Finance
G. R. Hill

Director of Economic Planning
A. Joslin

Vice President for Engineering
W. G. Lundquist

Director of Budgets
J. F. Doherty

Vice President Planning and Procurement
T. C. Coyne

Vice President Personnel
J. G. Byron

Director of Commercial Sales
N. J. Davidson

Vice President Manufacturing Engineering
S. B. Kurzina Jr

Director of Military Sales
R. J. Maroni

Director of Public Relations
R. S. Gall

Patent Attorney
K. M. Lane

Operations

General Manager
Metals Processing Division
V. T. Gorguze

General Manager
Caldwell Wright Division
F. Le Man

General Manager
Plastics Division
K. F. Hager

President
Propulsion Research Corporation
A. V. Finn

General Manager
Curtiss-Wright of Canada, Ltd.
E. A. Carter

General Manager
Electronics Division
J. R. Pascuzzo

General Manager
Propeller Division
B. W. Dudley

General Manager
Curtiss-Wright Europa N.V.
C. W. Geib

General Manager
Marquette Metal Products Division
F. E. Harrell

General Manager
Massey Machine Division
A. G. Massey

General Manager
Turbomotor Division
E. W. Conlon

General Manager
Research Division
K. Campbell

General Manager
Industrial & Scientific Products Division
H. S. Bamford

General Manager
Specialties Division
P. W. Carr

General Manager
Export Division
S. D. Irwin

General Manager
Wright Aeronautical Division
J. V. Miccio

Curtiss-Wright Corporation organizational chart, 1955.   Courtesy of the late Gerard Abbamont.

Appendix B:
Wright Aeronautical and
Curtiss-Wright Total Sales and Net Income

**Table 1   Wright Aeronautical Corporation:
Total Sales and Net Income, 1929–1950**

YEAR	TOTAL SALES	NET INCOME
1929	$10,379,245	$900,837
1930	5,477,560	−2,198,429
1931	9,557,825	196,619
1932	6,510,547	250,853
1933	5,053,680	364,606
1934	9,339,851	966,153
1935	7,757,461	423,295
1936	11,377,466	1,057,098
1937	16,654,393	2,090,192
1938	21,862,295	3,288,772
1939	28,881,058	3,740,626
1940	67,537,213	6,656,284
1941	208,345,060	10,255,874
1942	449,545,679	8,904,711
1943	579,228,172	3,599,866
1944	778,229,095	9,673,145
1945	536,878,082	13,260,868
1946	40,065,459	4,178,442
1947	51,260,548	512,600
1948	49,798,799	1,517,020
1949	74,910,259	1,296,835
1950	77,537,239	3,988,040

Wright Aeronautical merged with Curtiss-Wright on 31 October 1951 as a division of the parent corporation.

Source: Curtiss-Wright Annual Reports; Moody's Manual of Investments: American and Foreign Industrial Securities.

**Table 2   Curtiss-Wright Corporation:
Total Sales and Net Income, 1929–1995**

YEAR	TOTAL SALES	NET INCOME
1929	$26,047,904	–$668,532
1930	19,325,197	–9,012,919
1931	21,651,585	–4,126,060
1932	12,406,720	–606,182
1933	10,450,728	136,785
1934	14,009,533	359,736
1935	11,119,581	2,886
1936	18,929,364	1,643,976
1937	24,116,084	1,983,609
1938	33,102,962	3,598,739
1939	48,654,143	5,218,259
1940	138,720,151	15,746,874
1941	373,083,364	25,717,512
1942	770,594,882	13,143,515
1943	1,295,236,317	12,883,347
1944	1,716,935,177	14,331,062
1945	1,197,705,084	24,430,217
1946	71,984,015	2,472,091
1947	83,161,988	–1,365,258
1948	111,747,027	5,313,298
1949	128,578,227	2,750,361
1950	135,662,864	7,278,564
1951	176,625,380	6,908,216
1952	326,183,643	9,047,514
1953	438,728,482	11,402,791
1954	475,084,435	19,377,279
1955	508,703,445	35,081,045
1956	571,064,793	43,153,518
1957	598,621,622	40,075,582
1958	388,841,934	25,053,382
1959	329,188,469	14,302,858
1960	270,591,689	10,031,167
1961	203,487,992	5,970,561
1962	228,726,236	9,880,848
1963	226,682,779	10,063,238
1964	157,334,756	8,913,988
1965	148,328,561	7,992,080
1966	144,114,000	8,684,030
1967	173,709,719	11,530,965

(continued)

Appendix B

YEAR	TOTAL SALES	NET INCOME
1968	170,580,471	13,043,281
1969	261,874,412	12,243,000
1970	264,523,978	3,382,227
1971	248,671,291	703,000
1972	235,561,000	5,533,000
1973	253,078,000	8,883,000
1974	273,275,000	10,354,000
1975	326,358,000	14,341,000
1976	336,679,000	19,078,000
1977	309,904,000	16,299,000
1978	318,357,000	17,547,000
1979	170,362,000	33,771,000
1980	185,539,000	39,746,000
1981	194,929,000	85,308,000
1982	185,582,000	20,805,000
1983	180,417,582	18,503,000
1984	144,369,000	1,886,000
1985	159,942,000	−42,361,000*
1986	166,444,000	22,747,000
1987	165,064,000	31,612,000
1988	170,999,000	27,995,000
1989	187,083,000	30,413,000
1990	198,884,000	6,884,000
1991	191,250,000	21,253,000
1992	179,737,000	21,687,000
1993	158,864,000	−5,623,000
1994	156,001,000	19,303,000
1995	154,446,000	18,169,000

*Disposition of Western Union investment.

Source: Curtiss-Wright Annual Reports; Moody's Manual of Investments: American and Foreign Industrial Securities.

Notes and References

1. Introduction

1. Michael E. Porter, *Competitive Advantage: Creating and Sustaining Superior Performance* (New York: Free Press, 1985), 1–5.
2. Alfred D. Chandler Jr., *Scale and Scope: The Dynamics of Industrial Capitalism* (Cambridge, Mass.: Harvard University Press, 1990), 231, 594.
3. Ibid., 598–601.
4. Ibid., 28–36.

2. Origins to the End of World War I, 1909–1918

1. Thomas P. Hughes, *American Genius: A Century of Invention and Technological Enthusiasm, 1870–1970*. (New York: Viking, 1989), 13–16.
2. Ibid., 20–24.
3. C. R. Roseberry, *Glenn Curtiss: Pioneer of Flight* (New York: Doubleday, 1972), 5–6.
4. Ibid., 10.
5. Ibid., 12–13.
6. Ibid., 16–17.
7. Ibid., 2–3, 18–20.
8. Ibid., 22.
9. Tom D. Crouch, *The Bishop's Boys: A Life of Wilbur and Orville Wright* (New York: W. W. Norton, 1989), 313–14.
10. Ibid., 313–14.
11. Julliette A. Hennessy, *The United States Army Air Arm, April 1861 to April 1917* (Washington, D.C.: Office of Air Force History, 1985), 15–16.
12. Roseberry, 48–49, 56, 67.
13. Ibid., 71–72.
14. Crouch, 352–53.
15. Ibid., 362–64.
16. Roseberry, 150.
17. Ibid., 151–52.
18. Ibid., 115–16, 153–54.
19. Crouch, 400–401.

20. Roseberry, 152–53, 156–60, 164–65.

21. Peter M. Bowers, *Curtiss Aircraft, 1907–1947* (London: Putnam, 1979), 37; Crouch, 401–2.

22. Crouch, 402–3; Roseberry, 61–63, 190–91.

23. Roseberry, 237–44; Crouch, 412.

24. Crouch, 413.

25. Crouch, 414; Roseberry, 252–57.

26. Roseberry, 231–36, 262–78, 285–86.

27. Ibid., 257.

28. Ibid., 309.

29. Ibid., 311–12.

30. Crouch, 457.

31. Bowers, 28, 44; Roseberry, 279.

32. George Van Deurs, *Wings for the Fleet: A Narrative of Naval Aviation's Early Development, 1910–1916* (Annapolis: United States Naval Institute Press, 1966), 16.

33. Ibid., 19–21, 23–29.

34. Bowers, 45–47.

35. Bowers, 40–42; *Aero* 3, no. 8 (25 November 1911): 157; Eiichiro Sekigawa, *Pictorial History of Japanese Military Aviation* (London: Ian Allen, 1974), 11.

36. Bowers, 49–51.

37. John H. Morrow Jr., *The Great War in the Air: Military Aviation from 1909 to 1921* (Washington, D.C.: Smithsonian Institution Press, 1993), 46–48.

38. Clark G. Reynolds, *Admiral John H. Towers: The Struggle for Naval Air Supremacy* (Annapolis: Naval Institute Press, 1991), 34.

39. Crouch, 460–63.

40. Hennessy, 103, 105.

41. Bowers, 34–35, 61–65.

42. Herschel Smith, *Aircraft Piston Engines: From the Manly Balzer to the Continental Tiara* (New York: McGraw-Hill, 1981), 15–16; Roseberry, 319.

43. Bowers, 57–60; Roseberry, chap. 20.

44. Morrow, 29–57, 59–87.

45. Ibid., 78–79, 85–89, 129–30.

46. Owen Thetford, *British Naval Aircraft since 1912,* 6th rev. ed. (London: Putnam, 1991), 85, 417; Bowers, 150–51.

47. Bowers, 69; Roseberry, 394–97.

48. Thetford, 416–18; Bowers, 120–21, 136–37, 151; *Aerial Age Weekly* 2, no. 16 (3 January 1916): 374.

49. Roseberry, 401.

50. *Aerial Age Weekly* 2, no. 17 (10 January 1916): 399; vol. 2, no. 19 (24 January 1916): 447–48; vol. 2, no. 22 (14 February 1916): 519.

51. Edward M. Young, "Clement M. Keys," in *Encyclopedia of American Business History and Biography: The Airline Industry,* ed. William M. Leary (New York: Bruccoli Clark Layman, 1992), 258–66.

52. *Aerial Age Weekly* 3, no. 14 (24 July 1916): 562–68.

53. Thetford, 87, 417; Bowers, 92, 152–53.

54. Hennessy, 128, 135.

55. Hennessy, 154–55; Bowers, 92, 112, 122–23, 150–53; *Aerial Age Weekly* 4, no. 8 (6 November 1916): 195.

56. Hennessy, 196–97.

57. Bowers, 71.

58. Morrow, 266; Michael S. Sherry, *The Rise of American Air Power: The Creation of Armageddon* (New Haven, Conn.: Yale University Press, 1987), 17–18.

59. Morrow, 266; Jacob Vander Meulen, *The Politics of Aircraft: Building an American Military Industry* (Lawrence: University Press of Kansas, 1991), 12–22.

60. Vander Meulen, 25–26.

61. Morrow, 268–69.

62. Welman A. Shrader, *Fifty Years of Flight: A Chronicle of the Aviation Industry in America, 1903–1953* (Cleveland: Eaton Manufacturing Company, 1953), 19.

63. Bowers, 144–45; Vander Meulen, 33.

64. Vander Meulen, 32; *Curtiss Flyleaf* 1, no. 2 (August 1917); *Aerial Age Weekly* 5, no. 7 (9 July 1917): 562.

65. *Aerial Age Weekly* 5, no. 16 (2 July 1917): 522.

66. U.S. Congress, Senate, Subcommittee of the Senate Committee on Military Affairs, *Hearings on Aircraft Production,* 65th Cong., 2d sess., 1918, 120–22.

67. Vander Meulen, 33; *Hearings on Aircraft Production,* 70–71, 110–15.

68. *Hearings on Aircraft Production,* 88–90.

69. Ibid., 128.

70. Ibid., 86–87.

71. Ibid., 87, 93.

72. Morrow, 342.

73. *Hearings on Aircraft Production,* 97–98, 128–31; Morrow, 342.

74. Bowers, 144.

75. *Hearings on Aircraft Production,* 96.

76. Bowers, 82–83, 90–96, 112–13, 126–29; Peter M. Bowers and Gordon Swanborough, *United States Navy Aircraft since 1911,* 2d ed. (London: Putnam, 1990), 111–12, 122–24, 125–27, 130–32; Theodore Roscoe, *On the Seas and in the Skies: A History of the U.S. Navy's Air Power* (New York: Hawthorn Books, 1970), 95–97, 126.

77. Roscoe, 125.

78. Roseberry, 406.

79. Smith, 69–70.

80. Bowers, 138–43.

81. John B. Rae, *Climb to Greatness: The American Aircraft Industry, 1920–1960* (Cambridge: MIT Press, 1968), 221–23.

3. Decline and Expansion, 1919–1929

1. Maurer Maurer, *Aviation in the U.S. Army, 1919–1939* (Washington, D.C.: Office of Air Force History, 1987), 11.

2. C. R. Roseberry, *Glenn Curtiss: Pioneer of Flight* (New York: Doubleday, 1972), 426.

3. *Aircraft Yearbook for 1920* (New York: Manufacturers Aircraft Association, 1920), 171, 175.

4. Ibid., 173, 177–79.

5. Peter M. Bowers, *Curtiss Aircraft, 1907–1947* (London: Putnam, 1979), 174–80.

6. Ibid., 178–81.

7. Maurer, 12; Bowers, 168–69.

8. *Aircraft Yearbook for 1926* (New York: Manufacturers Aircraft Association, 1926), 301.

9. Jacob Vander Meulen, *The Politics of Aircraft: Building an American Military Industry* (Lawrence: University Press of Kansas, 1991), 42.

10. Ibid., 41–44.

11. Wesley Phillips Newton, *The Perilous Sky: U.S. Aviation Diplomacy and Latin America, 1919–1931* (Coral Gables, Fla.: University of Miami Press, 1978), 21–24, 31–33.

12. *Aircraft Yearbook for 1921* (New York: Manufacturers Aircraft Association, 1921), 187.

13. John Moody, *Moody's Analysis of Investments 1921* (New York: Moody's Investors Service, 1922), 1183.

14. Bowers, 169.

15. *Air Transportation,* 27 July 1929, 51.

16. U.S. Congress, House, Select Committee of Inquiry into Operations of the United States Air Service, *Hearings (Lampert Hearings),* 68th Cong., 1st sess., 1924, pt. 2, p. 1131. Hereafter cited as *Lampert Hearings.*

17. Ibid., 1130.

18. Ibid., 1132.

19. Moody, *Moody's Analysis of Investments 1921,* 1182; *Lampert Hearings,* 1130; C. M. Keys, "The Curtiss Aeroplane and Motor Corporation after the War," *Aerial Age Weekly* 13, no. 13 (6 June 1921): 295–96.

20. Keys, "The Curtiss Aeroplane and Motor Corporation after the War."

21. "The Curtiss-Wright Corporation," *Aero Digest* 24, no. 4 (April 1934): 31–32.

22. Bruce Robertson, ed., *United States Army and Air Force Fighters, 1916–1961* (Fallbrook, Calif.: Aero Publishers, 1961), 25.

23. Bowers, 184–88.

24. *Lampert Hearings,* 1144, 1404–5; Ray Wagner, *American Combat Planes,* 3d enlarged ed. (New York: Doubleday, 1982), 111; Bowers, 189–91.

25. *Lampert Hearings,* 1144, 1404.

26. Wagner, 111.

27. Bowers, 191.

28. Maurer, 165.

29. Thomas G. Foxworth, *The Speed Seekers* (New York: Doubleday, 1975), 3–5.

30. Foxworth, 62–64; Herschel Smith, *Aircraft Piston Engines: From the Manly Balzer to the Continental Tiara* (New York: McGraw-Hill, 1981), 69–70.

31. Bowers, 228–29.

32. Bowers, 230–32; Foxworth, 65.

33. Bowers, 230–35; Foxworth, 52–53.

34. "Reorganization of the Curtiss Corporation," *Aviation* 14, no. 14 (26 March 1923): 342–43.

35. "Reorganization of the Curtiss Corporation"; Moody, *Moody's Analysis of Investments 1924,* 537.

36. Moody, *Moody's Analysis of Investments 1924,* 537; *Curtiss Aeroplane and Motor Company, Inc., Annual Report for 1924.*

37. Wagner, 53–55.

38. Wagner, 53–55; Bowers, 241–45, 267.

39. Bowers, 240.

40. Ibid., 285–87.

41. *Curtiss Aeroplane and Motor Company, Inc., Annual Report for 1925.*

42.   I. B. Holley Jr., *Buying Aircraft: Materiel Procurement for the Army Air Forces: The United States Army in World War II,* Special Studies 7 (Washington, D.C.: Office of the Chief of Military History, 1964), 45.

43.   Lloyd Morris and Kendall Smith, *Ceiling Unlimited: The Story of American Aviation from Kitty Hawk to Supersonics* (New York: Macmillan, 1953), 208–11.

44.   Holley, 46–47; *Aircraft Yearbook for 1926,* 5–17.

45.   *Aircraft Yearbook for 1926,* 111.

46.   *Aircraft Yearbook for 1927,* 5.

47.   *Aircraft Yearbook for 1927,* 5; Nick A. Komons, *Bonfires to Beacons: Federal Civil Aviation Policy under the Air Commerce Act, 1926–1938* (Washington, D.C.: Smithsonian Institution Press, 1989), 80–88.

48.   Maurer, 191–97, 199; *Aircraft Yearbook for 1927,* 347–53.

49.   Holley, 113–18.

50.   *Curtiss Aeroplane and Motor Company, Inc., Annual Report for 1926.*

51.   Morris and Smith, 258–73, 281.

52.   *Curtiss Aeroplane and Motor Company, Inc., Annual Reports,* 1926–1929.

53.   Elspeth Freudenthal, *The Aviation Business: From Kitty Hawk to Wall Street* (New York: Vanguard Press, 1940), 128.

54.   Wagner, 31–34; Bowers, 240, 245–52, 264, 286–301.

55.   Smith, 74–75; Bowers, 253–60.

56.   Charles M. Melhorn, *Two-Block Fox: The Rise of the Aircraft Carrier, 1911–1929* (Annapolis: Naval Institute Press, 1974), 98–99; Smith, 106.

57.   Peter M. Bowers, *Boeing Aircraft since 1916,* 2d ed. (London: Putnam Aeronautical Books, 1989), 162–63.

58.   Bowers, *Curtiss Aircraft, 1907–1947,* 377–78.

59.   Pynchon and Company, *The Aviation Industry* (New York: Pynchon and Company, 1929), 34.

60.   *Curtiss Aeroplane and Motor Company, Inc., Annual Reports,* 1926–1929.

61.   Earl Reeves, *Aviation's Place in Tomorrow's Business* (New York: B. C. Forbes, 1930), 94.

62.   Reeves, 95; "C. M. Keys Is Dead; Financed Aviation," *New York Times,* 13 January 1952.

63.   Clement M. Keys, "Aviation and Its Future," *U.S. Air Services,* March 1929, 43–48.

64.   Keys, "Aviation and Its Future"; Reeves, 94–97; Alfred D. Chandler, *Scale and Scope: The Dynamics of Industrial Capitalism* (Cambridge, Mass.: Harvard University Press, 1990), 17–18, 21–23, 37–38.

65.   Chandler, 28–31.

66.   Reeves, 95–97.

67.   Reeves, 82–83, 85, 92; Moody, *Moody's Manual of Investments 1929,* 1753–55; *Moody's Manual of Investments 1930,* 886–91.

68.   *Curtiss Aeroplane and Motor Company, Inc., Annual Report for 1927; Curtiss Aeroplane and Motor Company, Inc., Annual Report for 1928; Curtiss Aeroplane and Motor Company, Inc., Annual Report for 1929;* Moody, *Moody's Manual of Investments 1929,* 1753–55; Bowers, 314–15.

69.   "North American Aviation, Inc.," *Aero Digest* 24, no. 2 (February 1934): 22–29; Reeves, 96.

70.   *Curtiss Aeroplane and Motor Company, Inc., Annual Report for 1928; Curtiss Aeroplane and Motor Company, Inc., Annual Report for 1929;* Moody, *Moody's Manual of Investments 1930,* 889.

71.   *Financial Handbook of the American Aviation Industry* (New York: The Commercial National Bank and Trust Company of New York, 1929), 61–67.

72.   Charles W. Foss, "Merger Groupings in Aviation," *Airways Age* 10, no. 4 (April 1929): 426.

73.   Ibid., 426–27.

74.   *Aircraft Yearbook for 1929,* 25, 61.

75.   Pynchon and Company, 9.

76.   Ibid., 10.

77.   Freudenthal, 92.

78.   Thomas C. Cochran, *200 Years of American Business* (New York: Dell, 1977), 155.

79.   John B. Rae, *Climb to Greatness: The American Aviation Industry, 1920–1960* (Cambridge, Mass.: MIT Press, 1968), 39–40.

80.   Ibid., 40–41.

81.   Foss, "Merger Groupings in Aviation"; *Aircraft Yearbook for 1929,* 18–19, 34.

82.   Foss, 427.

83.   Rae, 24–25; Ronald Miller and David Sawers, *The Technical Development of Modern Aviation* (New York: Praeger, 1970), 18, 50–51, 53–67.

84.   *New York Times,* 30 June 1929.

85.   Chandler, 32–33, 42–45.

86.   Crouch, 405, 409–10.

87.   Ibid., 455–64.

88.   Ibid., 465.

89.   "The Wright-Martin Corporation and the Hispano Suiza Motor," *Aerial Age Weekly* 3, no. 23 (21 August 1916): 685–86; *Hearings on Aircraft Production, 1918,* 316.

90.   "Wright Company, New York, and Glenn L. Martin Company, Los Angeles, Merge," *Aerial Age Weekly* 3, no. 22 (14 August 1916): 653–54; "The Wright-Martin Merger," *Aviation* 2, no. 2 (15 August 1916): 25.

91.   *Hearings on Aircraft Production, 1918,* 316–21; *Aircraft Yearbook for 1919,* 275.

92.   *Hearings on Aircraft Production, 1918,* 319–21; Glenn L. Martin Company, *Box Kites to Bombers: The Story of the Glenn L. Martin Company* (Baltimore: Glenn L. Martin Company, n.d.) 17–18.

93.   *National Encyclopedia of American Biography,* 160.

94.   Guy W. Vaughan, CO 700100 National Air and Space Museum; "Guy Warner Vaughan," *Curtiss Wright Review* 1, no. 4 (July 1930): 4; "Turning the Spotlight on Mr. Vaughan," *Wright Engine Builder* 1, no. 1 (July 1921): 8.

95.   *Hearings on Aircraft Production, 1918,* 318–19; *Aircraft Yearbook for 1919,* 278–79.

96.   Rae, 223.

97.   *The Pratt and Whitney Aircraft Story (United Aircraft Corporation, 1950),* 20; *Aircraft Yearbook for 1920,* 241–47.

98.   Wagner, 44–48, 132.

99.   Moody, *Moody's Analysis of Investments 1924,* 2562.

100. Foxworth, 60–62, chap. 17.

101. Rae, 27–28; Smith, 104; Eugene E. Wilson, *Slipstream: The Autobiography of an Aircraftsman* (New York: McGraw-Hill, 1950), 17.

102. Rae, 27–28; Wilson, 17.

103. Smith, 104–5; Wilson, 49–50.

104. Wilson, 50–51; *Pratt and Whitney Aircraft Story,* 29.

105. Wilson, 51–52; Rae, 28–29; *Pratt and Whitney Aircraft Story,* 32–45.

106. *Wright Aeronautical Corporation Annual Report for 1927.*

107. *Wright Aeronautical Corporation Annual Report for 1927;* Smith, 107.

108. *Wright Aeronautical Corporation Annual Report for 1928.*

109. Wilson, 51.

110. *New York Times,* 27 June 1929.

111. *Financial Chronicle,* April–June 1929, 4328.

112. Moody, *Moody's Manual of Investments 1930,* 886.

113. Howard Mingos, "The Harriman of Aviation," *New York Herald Tribune,* 2 June 1929.

114. Sherman Gwinn, "Aviation Is About to Become of Age," *American Magazine* 108 (September 1929): 51–53.

115. *New York Times,* 9 September 1929.

4. Decline and Resurgence, 1930–1937

1. *Aircraft Yearbook for 1937,* 442.

2. John B. Rae, *Climb to Greatness: The American Aircraft Industry, 1920–1960* (Cambridge, Mass.: MIT Press, 1968), 84.

3. Rae, 58; Ronald Miller and David Sawers, *The Technical Development of Modern Aviation* (New York: Praeger, 1970), 47–48; Laurence K. Loftin Jr., *Quest for Performance: The Evolution of Modern Aircraft* (Washington, D.C.: National Aeronautics and Space Administration, 1985), 88–91.

4. Loftin, 53–69.

5. Broadus Mitchell, *Depression Decade: From the New Era through New Deal, 1929–1941,* vol. 9 of *The Economic History of the United States* (New York: Holt, Rinehart and Winston, 1947), 27–28.

6. R. R. Doane, "Aeronautical Finance in 1930," *Aviation,* January 1931, 45.

7. Moody, *Moody's Manual of Investments 1931,* 2744.

8. R. Sidney Bowen Jr., "The Aeronautic Industry during 1929," *Aviation,* 15 February 1930, 306–10; Charles R. Lawrance, "Where the Industry Stands," *Aviation,* December 1931, 678–81.

9. C. M. Keys, "Caution and Courage," 291, and Frederick B. Rentschler, "Military Aviation—Air Mail—A Needed Readjustment in Progress," 292–93, in "What Are the Prospects for 1930?" *Aviation* 28, no. 7 (15 February 1930).

10. *Curtiss-Wright Corporation Annual Report for 1929.*

11. *Aviation* 28, no. 2 (11 January 1930): 75; *New York Times,* 6 September 1930.

12. *Curtiss-Wright Corporation Annual Report for 1929.*

13. Clement M. Keys, "The Business of Aviation, 1929–1930," *Airway Age* 11, no. 1 (January 1930): 40–42.

14. Mitchell, 30.

15. Jeremy Atack and Peter Passell, *A New Economic View of American History from Colonial Times to 1940,* 2d ed. (New York: W. W. Norton, 1994), 588.

16. Ibid., 597–98, 584.

17. R. Sydney Bower Jr., "Trends of the Industry during 1930," *Aviation* 30, no. 1 (January 1931): 15–17.

18. *New York Times,* 6 September 1930.

19. Moody, *Moody's Manual of Investments 1931,* 2744–45; *Curtiss-Wright Annual Report for 1930.*

20. Moody, *Moody's Manual of Investments 1931,* 2744–45; *Curtiss-Wright Annual Report for 1930;* Peter M. Bowers, *Curtiss Aircraft, 1907–1947* (London: Putnam, 1979), 386–87.

21. Jacob Vander Meulen, *The Politics of Aircraft: Building an American Military Industry* (Lawrence: University Press of Kansas, 1991), 114–15.

22. *Wright Aeronautical Corporation Annual Report for 1930.*

23. Moody, *Moody's Manual of Investments 1931,* 2747–48; Keys, "Caution and Courage," 291.

24. *Curtiss-Wright Annual Report for 1930; Moody's Manual of Investments 1931,* 2747–48.

25. C. R. Roseberry, *Glenn Curtiss: Pioneer of Flight* (New York: Doubleday, 1971), 450–56.

26. *Curtiss-Wright Annual Report for 1931.*

27. *New York Times,* 9 August 1931.

28. *New York Times,* 25 June 1931.

29. Ibid.

30. *Aircraft Yearbook for 1934,* 421.

31. Thomas A. Morgan, "Memorandum to the Chairman of the Board, Curtiss-Wright Corporation," 19 October 1932, in QMC 28, Records of the Bureau of Aeronautics, General Correspondence, Record Group 72, National Archives, Washington, D.C. Hereafter cited as Morgan Memorandum.

32. Ibid.

33. Morgan Memorandum; *Curtiss-Wright Annual Report for 1931;* Vander Meulen, 114–15; *Wright Aeronautical Corporation Annual Report for 1931.*

34. *Curtiss-Wright Annual Report for 1931.*

35. *New York Journal,* 7 January 1932.

36. E. C. Sauer and S. C. Simon, "North American Aviation, Inc.," 24 April 1934, Washington, D.C. Report prepared for the Senate Special Committee to Investigate Foreign and Domestic Ocean and Air Mail Contracts, North American, Box 17, Entry 145, Record Group 46, United States Senate, National Archives, Washington, D.C.

37. Ibid., 8–9.

38. Morgan Memorandum.

39. Morgan Memorandum; *Curtiss-Wright Annual Report for 1932; Wright Aeronautical Corporation Annual Report for 1932.*

40. Morgan Memorandum; *Curtiss-Wright Annual Report for 1932;* Moody, *Moody's Manual of Investments 1933,* 1580.

41. *Aircraft Yearbook for 1933,* 62.

42. Benjamin S. Kelsey, *The Dragon's Teeth? The Creation of United States Air Power for World War II* (Washington, D.C.: Smithsonian Institution Press, 1982), 51.

43. Ibid., 78–79.

44. Ray Wagner, *American Combat Planes,* 3d enlarged ed. (New York: Doubleday, 1982), 161.

45. Ibid., 328–30.

46. Ibid., 163–65.

47. Ibid., 193–97.

48. Peter M. Bowers, *Boeing Aircraft since 1916,* 2d ed. (London: Putnam Aeronautical Books, 1989), 214–15, 220–21; Bowers, *Curtiss Aircraft,* 333–35.

49. Edwin H. Rutkowski, *The Politics of Military Aircraft Procurement, 1926–1934: A Study in the Political Assertion of Consensual Values* (Ohio State University Press, 1966), 141.

50. House Committee on Military Affairs, "Transcript of the Testimony in the War Department Investigation, April 5, 1934–April 15, 1936," 73d Cong., 2d sess., to 74th Cong., 2d sess., 1934–1936. Record Group 233, House of Representatives, National Archives, Washington, D.C., 5 April 1934, 36.

51. "Transcript of the Testimony in the War Department Investigation, April 5, 1934–April 15, 1936."

52. Bowers, *Curtiss Aircraft,* 274.

53. Ibid., 275–77.

54. Bruce Robertson, ed., *United States Navy and Marine Corps Fighters, 1918–1962* (Fallbrook, Calif.: Aero Publishers, 1962), 68–69.

55. Wagner, 334–36.

56. Louis Eltscher, "A Tale of Two Condors," *Skyways: The Journal of the Airplane, 1920–1940,* no. 14 (April 1990): 13.

57. Ibid., 13.

58. Bowers, *Curtiss Aircraft,* 391; Miller and Sawers, 98–103.

59. I. B. Holley Jr., *Buying Aircraft: Materiel Procurement for the Army Air Forces: The United States Army in World War II,* Special Studies 7 (Washington, D.C.: Office of the Chief of Military History, 1964), 26–29.

60. Ibid., 17–20.

61. Bowers, *Curtiss Aircraft,* 278; James H. Doolittle with Carroll V. Glines, *I Could Never Be So Lucky Again* (New York: Bantam, 1991), 105–9; Dan Hagedorn, "Curtiss Types in Latin America," *Air Enthusiast* 45 (March–May 1991): 69, 71.

62. Bowers, *Curtiss Aircraft,* 202, 281, 311–12, 404.

63. Hagedorn; Bowers, *Curtiss Aircraft,* 281; Moody, *Moody's Manual of Investments 1935,* 2357.

64. Bowers, *Curtiss Aircraft,* 281–84, 330.

65. Wm. Barclay Harding, *The Aviation Industry* (New York: Charles D. Barney, 1937), 27–28.

66. Ibid., 27.

67. Vander Meulen, 114–16.

68. Miller and Sawers, 86–87.

69. *Aircraft Yearbook for 1934,* 419.

70. Holley, 14–15.

71. Guy Vaughan, "Comments by Industry Leaders," *Aero Digest* 20, no. 3 (April 1932): 55.

72. Ibid.

73. Miller and Sawers, 86.

74. Ibid., 48–49.

75. Herschel Smith, *Aircraft Piston Engines: From the Manly Balzer to the Continental Tiara* (New York: McGraw-Hill, 1981), 107; *Aircraft Yearbook for 1931,* 293–94, 548.

76. Bill Gunston, *The Development of Piston Aero Engines* (Sparkford, England: Patrick Stephens, 1993), 18, 51, 67–68.

77.   Arthur Pearcy, *Douglas Propliners, DC-1–DC-7* (Shrewsbury, England: Airlife Publishing, 1995), 25–26.

78.   Wagner, 164, 196–98, 370–73.

79.   Gunston, 131; Smith, 118–19, 125.

80.   *Wright Aeronautical Corporation Annual Reports;* Moody, *Moody's Manual of Investments for 1931–1935.*

81.   Pearcy, 59.

82.   Gunston, 131.

83.   *New York Times,* 8 March 1935.

84.   Maurer Maurer, *Aviation in the U.S. Army, 1919–1939* (Washington, D.C.: Office of Air Force History, 1987), 299–303, 315–17, 352.

85.   *Aircraft Yearbook for 1937,* 460–61.

86.   *Aircraft Yearbook for 1935,* 15, 83; *Aircraft Yearbook for 1937,* 460.

87.   J. M. Roberts, *Europe, 1880–1945* (New York: Longman, 1989), 504–11; *Aircraft Yearbook for 1936,* chap. 3.

88.   R. A. Buchanan, *The Power of the Machine: The Impact of Technology from 1700 to the Present* (London: Viking Press, 1992), 231–32.

89.   Holley, 22.

90.   Wagner, 166, 171–72.

91.   Page Shamberger and Joe Christy, *The Curtiss Hawks* (Kalamazoo: Wolverine Press, 1972), 90–91.

92.   Wagner, 238–39, 241–42.

93.   Ibid., 242–43.

94.   Ibid., 242.

95.   Ibid., 336, 350.

96.   *Aircraft Yearbook for 1937,* 374.

97.   Wagner, 202–3.

98.   *Aircraft Yearbook for 1937,* 284; *Aviation's Directory of Planes and Engines* (New York: Aviation, 1937), 113.

99.   Bill Gunston, *World Encyclopedia of Aero Engines,* 3d ed. (Sparkford, England: Patrick Stephens, 1995), 175–76; Smith, 125.

100.   *New York Times,* 5 September 1936; *Curtiss-Wright Corporation Annual Report for 1936;* Moody, *Moody's Manual of Investments 1939,* 1578; letter from Guy W. Vaughan Jr., June 1995.

101.   *Curtiss-Wright Corporation Annual Report for 1936; Curtiss-Wright Corporation Annual Report for 1937;* Moody, *Moody's Manual of Investments 1939,* 1578–79.

102.   Wagner, 244–46.

103.   Ibid., 242.

5. Rearmament, 1938–1941

1.   R. J. Overy, *The Air War, 1939–1945* (New York: Stein and Day, 1980), 26.

2.   Gerry Beauchamp, "Falcons of France," *Wings* 26, no. 3 (June 1996): 8–24, 33–37, 47–55.

3.   Derek Wood and Derek Dempster, *The Narrow Margin: The Battle of Britain and the Rise of Air Power, 1930–1940* (London: Arrow Books, 1967), 82; Overy, 26.

4.   Overy, 213.

5.   Ibid., 28.

6. Wesley Frank Craven and James Lea Cate, *The Army Air Forces in World War II,* vol. 6, *Men and Planes* (Chicago: University of Chicago Press, 1955), 191; I. B. Holley, *Buying Aircraft: Materiel Procurement for the Army Air Forces, the United States Army in World War II,* Special Studies 7 (Washington, D.C.: Office of the Chief of Military History, 1964), 200. Much of the material in this section is based on these two published sources, especially Craven and Cate, chapter 5, and Holley, chapter 7.

7. Craven and Cate, 301–2; Holley, 198–200.

8. "Curtiss Expands Plant Facilities," *Curtiss Flyleaf* 22, no. 1 (April 1938): 9, 16; "Building Expansion Program Completed," *Curtiss Flyleaf* 23, no. 3 (Winter 1940): 9, 18. "The Curtiss-Wright Corporation," *Aero Digest* 24, no. 4 (April 1934): 28; *Curtiss and Associated Companies* (New York: James C. Willson, 1929), 20.

9. Gerry Beauchamp, "Hawks for Hire," *Wings* 8, no. 2 (April 1978): 26; See also John McVickar Haight Jr., "France's Search for American Military Aircraft before the Munich Crisis," *Aerospace Historian* 25, no. 3 (Fall 1978): 141–52.

10. Enzo Angelucci and Peter Bowers, *The American Fighter* (New York: Orion Books, 1985), 161–62.

11. Beauchamp, "Hawks for Hire," 59.

12. John B. Rae, *Climb to Greatness: The American Aircraft Industry, 1920–1960* (Cambridge, Mass.: MIT Press, 1968), 112; Angelucci and Bowers, 162.

13. Craven and Cate, 173.

14. Ibid., 183.

15. Ibid., 172–73, 183–84.

16. Holley, 180.

17. Tom Lilley et al., *Problems of Accelerating Aircraft Production in World War II* (Boston, Mass.: Division of Research, Graduate School of Business Administration, Harvard University, 1947), 40.

18. Craven and Cate, 190; Rae, 130–31.

19. Holley, 37.

20. Wm. Barclay Harding, *The Aviation Industry* (New York: Charles D. Barney, 1937), viii.

21. "C-W New Deal May Head Shake-Up in Plane Industry," *American Aviation* 12, no. 18 (15 February 1949): 10.

22. Holley, 38–39.

23. Lilley, 40–41.

24. Holley, 180–86; Craven and Cate, 305–10; Rae, 122.

25. Peter Mansoor, "The Impact of World War II on the Economy of Columbus, Ohio" (unpublished essay, Ohio State University), 7, courtesy of Peter Mansoor; Craven and Cate, 309.

26. Richard A. Morley, "The Ohio-Curtiss Airplane Connection (Curtiss-Wright Airplane Division in Columbus, 1940–1950)," *Journal of the American Aviation Historical Society* 36, no. 3 (Fall 1991): 186; Craven and Cate, 309; Mansoor, 8.

27. Albert Kahn, "Design of Plan for Mass Production," *Aero Digest,* October 1941, 157, 159; "Interesting Facts about the Buffalo Airport Plant," National Air and Space Museum, "General I" loose-leaf notebook.

28. Frederick W. Roos, "Curtiss-Wright St. Louis," *Journal of the American Aviation Historical Society* 35, no. 4 (Winter 1990): 301; Kahn, 159.

29. Morley, 186–88; Kahn, 159.

30. "Civic Ceremonies Mark Ground Breaking at Buffalo, St. Louis, Columbus," *Curtiss Flyleaf* 24, no. 1 (January–February 1941): 6; "Production Engines Invoiced," Wright Aeronautical Corporation, courtesy of the late Gerard Abbamont; Mansoor, 9, 11, 18.

31. "Plans Completed for Management of Expanded Curtiss Facilities," *Curtiss Flyleaf* 24, no. 1 (January–February 1941): 8–9; Burdette S. Wright diaries, vol. 13, June 1940.

32. Guy W. Vaughan, "Curtiss-Wright Expands," *Aero Digest,* June 1938, 41. Beauchamp, "Hawks for Hire," 38; Holley, 201.

33. "Fifteen Curtiss-Wright Factories Speed Defense Output," *Aero Digest,* October 1941, 164, 166; Lilley, 33; Rae, 130–31; "Chronological History of Curtiss-Wright," *Aero Digest,* October 1941, 152–55.

34. *Curtiss-Wright Corporation Annual Report, 1939; Curtiss-Wright Corporation Annual Report, 1940;* telephone conversation, 27 February 1987, with the late Arnold Kossar, vice president for Engineering, the Curtiss-Wright Corporation; "Fifteen Curtiss-Wright Factories," 166, 169; "Curtiss Propeller Division of Curtiss-Wright Corporation Organized," *Curtiss Flyleaf* 22, no. 1 (April 1938): 12; Robert Earle, "Propeller Division Moves into New Home," *Curtiss Flyleaf* 22, no. 2 (Summer 1938): 13; Holley, 562–63; Craven and Cate, 355–56.

35. "Curtiss-Wright: Biggest Aviation Company Expands Its Empire," *Life* 11, no. 11 (15 September 1941): 50; "Fifteen Curtiss-Wright Factories," 160.

36. "Biggest Aviation Company Expands Its Empire," 50; "Production for Victory: Curtiss-Wright Corporation Consolidated Shipments for Years 1938–1941," *Curtiss-Wright Annual Report for 1941;* Rae, 142; Craven and Cate, 350, 352; Holley, 548; Overy, 192. For a discussion of Curtiss-Wright's propensity for accepting all contracts, see Joseph V. Mizrahi, "Climax for Curtiss-Wright," *Wings* 25, no. 5 (October 1995): 26–43.

37. Peter M. Bowers, *Curtiss Aircraft, 1907–1947* (London: Putnam, 1979), 423, 451; George F. P. Kernaham, "The Trials of the Helldiver," *Journal of the American Aviation Historical Society* 36, no. 4 (Winter 1991): 244.

38. "Chronological History of Curtiss-Wright," 153–54; "Wright Engines," *Aero Digest,* October 1941, 232–35; "History of the Wright Aeronautical Corporation," University of Texas Collection; Holley, 580; Lilley, 10–12.

39. Robert E. Johnson, "Why the Boeing B-29 Bomber, and Why the Wright R-3350 Engine?" *Journal of the American Aviation Historical Society* 33, no. 3 (Fall 1988): 177; Lindsay Peacock, "Boeing B-29 . . . First of the Superbombers," *Air International,* August 1989, 70.

40. Bowers, *Curtiss Aircraft,* 433.

6. War Production, 1942–1945

1. I. B. Holley, *Buying Aircraft: Materiel Procurement for the Army Air Forces, the United States Army in World War II,* Special Studies 7 (Washington, D.C.: Office of the Chief of Military History, 1964), 320–21; Wesley Frank Craven and James Lea Cate, *The Army Air Forces in World War II,* vol. 6, *Men and Planes* (Chicago: University of Chicago Press, 1955), 314.

2. Holley, 321.

3. John B. Rae, *Climb to Greatness: The American Aircraft Industry, 1920–1960* (Cambridge, Mass.: MIT Press, 1968), 143.

4. Craven and Cate, *Men and Planes,* 319.

5. The 1942 production figures for other American fighters were as follows: 1,973 P-39s, 634 North American P-51s, and 532 Republic P-47s (Holley, 550).

6. Memorandum from Frederic Flader to Curtiss-Wright employees, 28 October 1943, entitled "A Letter from the Chief Engineer"; Craven and Cate, *Men and Planes*, 212.

7. Holley, 550.

8. Wesley Frank Craven and James Lea Cate, *The Army Air Forces in World War II*, vol. 7, *Services around the World* (Chicago: University of Chicago Press, 1958), 5.

9. Craven and Cate, *Services around the World*, 24; National Archives, Record Group 18, E-22, Case History of C-46 Airplane Project.

10. National Archives, Record Group 18, file 452.1-E, Transports, Entry 294, Box 747.

11. Craven and Cate, *Services around the World*, 25.

12. Peter M. Bowers, *Curtiss Aircraft, 1907–1947* (London: Putnam, 1979), 423.

13. Richard A. Morley, "The Ohio-Curtiss Airplane Connection (Curtiss-Wright Airplane Division in Columbus, 1940–1950)," *Journal of the American Aviation Historical Society* 36, no. 3 (Fall 1991): 184.

14. Harold Andrews, "The Curtiss SB2C Helldiver," in *Aircraft in Profile*, vol. 6 (Garden City, N.Y.: Doubleday, 1970), 60–61. George F. P. Kernahan, "The Trials of the Helldiver," *Journal of the American Aviation Historical Society* 36, no. 4 (Winter 1991): 243–45; Bowers, *Curtiss Aircraft*, 423.

15. Interview with the late Ira Ross, former director of the Cornell Aeronautical Laboratory, 9 January 1985.

16. Kernahan, 250; Ross interview.

17. Kernahan, 246; Andrews, 61; Bowers, *Curtiss Aircraft*, 423.

18. Kernahan, 245.

19. Richard A. Morley, "The Ohio Curtiss Airplane Connection (An Addendum)," *Journal of the American Aviation Historical Society* 3, no. 2 (Summer 1992): 104–6; Andrews, 61.

20. Andrews, 62; Kernahan, 246.

21. Andrews, 62; Bowers, *Curtiss Aircraft*, 430.

22. Morley, "The Ohio-Curtiss Airplane Connection (Curtiss-Wright Airplane Division in Columbus, 1940–1950)," 189; Andrews, 62–63, 67; Kernahan, 245; Peter Smith, "Curtiss Helldiver," *Flypast*, no. 41 (December 1984): 34–35; *Engineering History, SB2C Airplane*, courtesy of Robert C. Mikesh.

23. Kernahan, 249.

24. Morley, "The Ohio-Curtiss Airplane Connection (Curtiss-Wright Airplane Division in Columbus, 1940–1950)," 190.

25. Kernahan, 249.

26. Ibid., 249–50.

27. Kernahan, 250; Andrews, 63; George W. Gray, *Frontiers of Flight: The Story of NACA Research* (New York: Alfred A. Knopf, 1948), 162–64.

28. Kernahan, 246, 248–49; Peter Mansoor, "The Impact of World War II on the Economy of Columbus, Ohio" (unpublished essay, Ohio State University), 10, courtesy of Peter Mansoor; Morley, "The Ohio-Curtiss Airplane Connection (Curtiss-Wright Airplane Division in Columbus, 1940–1950)," 189.

29. Kernahan, 256.

30. Robert E. Johnson, "Why the Boeing B-29 Bomber, and Why the Wright R-3350 Engine?" *Journal of the American Aviation Historical Society* 33, no. 3 (Fall 1988): 177.

31. Ibid., 177, 178.

32. Lindsay Peacock, "Boeing B-29 ... First of the Superbombers," *Air International*, August 1989, 70.

33. Johnson, 177, 181–82.

34. Ibid., 179.

35. Peacock, 71; Johnson, 179.

36. Johnson, 179–80.

37. Johnson, 180, 181; Robert Schlaifer and S. D. Heron, *Development of Aircraft Engines—Development of Aviation Fuels* (New York: Pergamon Press, 1950), 525–26, 539–40, 542.

38. Wright Aeronautical Corporation, "Report of Pacific Trip," by John T. Wentzel, 28 July 1945. Courtesy of the late Gerard Abbamont.

39. Johnson, 181.

40. Harry S. Truman, *Memoirs: Year of Decisions,* vol. 1. (Garden City, N.Y. Doubleday, 1955), 167.

41. Truman, 167, 168.

42. *Additional Report of the Special Committee Investigating the National Defense Program,* 78th Cong., 1st sess., report 10, pt. 10, vol. 10758, 10 July 1943, 12.

43. *Additional Report,* 25.

44. Ibid., 13.

45. Peter M. Bowers, "The Heritage of the Hawk," *Airpower* 13, no. 3 (May 1983): 14, 15.

46. Ibid., 15.

47. *Additional Report,* 14–15.

48. Ibid., 15.

49. Merle Miller, *Plain Speaking: An Oral Biography of Harry S. Truman* (New York: Berkley Publishing, 1973), 168.

50. Truman, 184; *Additional Report,* 18, 25; "Truman on Aircraft," *Newsweek,* 19 July 1943, 62.

51. "Truman on Aircraft"; "Langer Revives Truman Charges in Curtiss Case," *Buffalo Evening News,* 25 April 1945.

52. "Guy Vaughan Speaks for Curtiss-Wright on Truman Report," *U.S. Air Services,* August 1943, 26.

53. "Calling the Tally on the Truman Report," *Aviation* 42, no. 8 (August 1943): 111.

54. *Additional Report,* 12.

55. Ibid., 26.

56. *Congressional Record—Senate,* 11 January 1945, 200.

57. Ibid., 201.

58. "Senator Charges Curtiss Sold Defective Planes to Services," *Buffalo Evening News,* 20 April 1945.

59. "Mead Decides on Immediate Curtiss Probe," *Buffalo Evening News,* 24 April 1945; "Langer Revives Truman Charges."

60. "Emphasis on Quantity Rather than Quality, Senate Group Asserts," *Buffalo Evening News,* 26 July 1945; "Report on Curtiss Mingles Criticism with Compliments," *Buffalo Evening News,* 27 July 1945.

61. Tom Lilley et al., *Problems of Accelerating Aircraft Production during World War II* (Boston: Division of Research, Harvard University Graduate School of Business Administration, 1947), 93.

62. Peter M. Bowers, "Last Flight at Curtiss-Wright," pt. 1, *Airpower* 15, no. 3 (May 1985): 44.

63. Peter M. Bowers, "Demons by the Dozens," *Wings* 11, no. 5 (October 1991): 50.

64. Bowers, "Last Flight," 47.

65. Steven S. Harding, "Flying Terminated Inventory," *Wings* 23, no. 2 (April 1993): 39–48.

66. *Air Transportation,* November 1943, 45; *The Curtiss Wrighter,* 9 July 1943, 2; Burdette S. Wright Diaries, vol. 24, 26 February 1944.

67. Kernahan, 246.

68. Holley, 562.

69. Kernahan, 257; John M. Davis, Harold G. Martin, and John A. Whittle, *The Curtiss Commando* (Tonbridge, Kent, England: Air Britain, 1978), 5.

70. An undated postwar memorandum of the Wright Aeronautical Corporation entitled "Production Engines Invoiced" also lists Chevrolet, Kaiser, and Caterpillar as licensed builders of Wright engines. Courtesy of the late Gerard Abbamont.

71. Lilley, 33.

72. Holley, 580; Lilley, 34.

73. Lilley, 34; Conversation with Harold Andrews.

74. Holley, 563; For a discussion of the problems of centralization, decentralization, and coordination in wartime production, see Sir Alec Cairncross, *Planning in Wartime* (New York: St. Martin's Press, 1991).

75. Lilley, 66.

76. Ibid., 65–66.

77. Holley, 561.

78. Robert W. Fausel, *Whatever Happened to Curtiss-Wright?* (Manhattan, Kans.: Sunflower University Press, 1990), 16; interview with Alvin C. Green, 9 May 1995.

79. Walter Tydon, *Saga of the P-40* (unpublished manuscript).

80. Green interview.

81. Holley, 517–18.

82. Kernahan, 246.

83. Ibid.

84. Bowers, "Last Flight," 47; others have questioned the viability of both designs.

85. "Engineering Questionnaire—Report On." Memo from R. C. Blaylock to all employees of the engineering department, Curtiss-Wright Corporation, Airplane Division—Columbus Plant, Columbus, Ohio, 30 December 1943. Courtesy of Marion T. Hockman.

86. Fausel, 30–31. Boeing's success with its large multiengine transport aircraft illustrates the validity of this argument. Yet Curtiss's experience in the twenties suggests that there have been times when the ability to market a breadth of model types has also been advisable.

87. "Editor's Note," in Bowers, "Last Flight," 10.

88. Richard A. Morley and Gerry Beauchamp, "The Last Aircraft from Curtiss," *Le Fana de l'Aviation* (Clichy, France): part 1, November 1993; part 2, December 1993; part 3, January 1994.

7. Demobilization, 1945–1948

1. I. B. Holley, *Buying Aircraft: Materiel Procurement for the Army Air Forces, the United States Army in World War II,* Special Studies 7 (Washington, D.C.: Office of the Chief of Military History, 1964), 548–49; Wesley Frank Craven and James Lea Cate, *The Army Air Forces in World War II,* vol. 6, *Men and Planes* (Chicago: University of Chicago Press, 1955), 350.

2. Craven and Cate, 350; Holley, 548, 553; R. J. Overy, *The Air War, 1939–1945* (New York: Stein and Day, 1980), 192.

3. "Record Output of Warplanes, Engines, and Propellers in 1944 Reported by Curtiss-Wright; New Marks Ahead," news release, 1 January 1945. AO107700 Curtiss C-46 "Commando," Documentation no. 1, National Air and Space Museum (Hereafter cited as NASM); "Production Soars in '44," *Curtiss Flyleaf* 27, no. 1 (January–February 1945): 7; "Production Engines Invoiced—Wright Aeronautical Corporation." Prepared by Engine Section, Order and Contract Division, General Sales and Service Department. Courtesy of the late Gerard Abbamont; Correspondence with George F. P. Kernahan, 29 November 1994.

4. Roger E. Bilstein, *Flight in America, 1900–1983* (Baltimore and London: Johns Hopkins University Press, 1984), 167–70, chap. 5; Joseph J. Corn, *The Winged Gospel* (New York: Oxford University Press, 1983) chaps. 5–6.

5. Bilstein, 195; also see Corn, 91.

6. Burdette S. Wright Diaries, vol. 25, 6 June 1944.

7. "Production Soars in '44," 9; "Record Output,"; *Air Transportation,* April 1943, 44; "Curtiss-Wright Head Announces Formation of New Division to Assist War Efforts and Develop Post-War Products," news release, 8 April 1943, Guy W. Vaughan, CO 700100 NASM.

8. Burdette S. Wright Diaries, vol. 25, 31 May 1944.

9. "Operating Cost, 44-passenger Version of Model CW-20E," Aircraft AO110800, NASM; Curtiss CW-20, AO115600, NASM.

10. Burdette S. Wright Diaries, vols. 23, 24, 25, many references; "Eastern Announces $25 Million Expansion of Its Great Silver Fleet," 4 October 1944, Guy W. Vaughan, CO700100, NASM.

11. "Experiment in Research." Address by Clifford C. Furnas, delivered at the "1950 Niagara Dinner" of the Newcommen Society of England, held at the Buffalo Club, Buffalo, N.Y., 4 May 1950. Courtesy of Howard Wolko; "Cornell Aeronautical Laboratory," *Aero Digest,* March 1947, 59.

12. Robert Schlaifer and S. D. Heron, *Development of Aircraft Engines—Development of Aviation Fuels* (New York: Pergamon Press, 1950), 502; "Wright Aeronautical Corporation Current Postwar Plans and Policies," 14 April 1944, NASM.

13. Schlaifer and Heron, 458–59, 490.

14. "Proposed Engineering Approval of Mr. G. W. Vaughan," Wright Aeronautical Corporation, 1 January 1945. Courtesy of the late Robert E. Johnson.

15. John B. Rae, *Climb to Greatness: The American Aircraft Industry, 1920–1960* (Cambridge, Mass.: MIT Press, 1968), 173.

16. "Cutback Closes Curtiss Plants Temporarily," *Buffalo Evening News,* 16 August 1945, 1.

17. "Wright Goes to New York. R. L. Earle Will Head Curtiss Division Here," *Buffalo Evening News,* 18 September 1945.

18. "Curtiss Profit Put at $24,430,217," *Buffalo Evening News,* 16 July 1945; "Experiment in Research," 11–12; "Cornell Aeronautical Laboratory," 59.

19. Conversation with the late Arnold Kossar, vice president, Engineering, the Curtiss-Wright Corporation; Hilton Hornaday, "Curtiss Decision to Move Is Taken with a Grain of Salt," *Buffalo Evening News,* 24 September 1945.

20. Bilstein, 185.

21. Rae, 193–94.

22. Ibid., 194–95.

23. Ibid., 194.

24. Rae, 189; Devon Francis, *Mr. Piper and His Cubs* (Ames, Iowa: Iowa State University Press, 1973), 134.

25. Rae, 177–78, 181–82, 199.

26. Ibid., 175–76.

27. "Curtiss Eyes Commercial Field, Will Build New Air Freighter," *Buffalo Evening News,* 10 January 1947; "C-W Drops Plane Making," *Business Week,* 6 November 1948, 40; *Aviation,* May 1946, 123, and June 1946, 119.

28. Selig Altschul, "How Martin, C-W, Have Improved," *Aviation Week,* 27 March 1950, 39.

29. Selig Altschul, "Curtiss-Wright Business Analyzed," *Aviation Week,* 2 August 1948, 32; "C-W Drops Plane Making."

30. Several interviews with the late Herbert O. Fisher, chief production test pilot for the Curtiss-Wright Corporation. Fisher conducted most of the postwar flight tests for the Propeller Division at Caldwell, N.J.

31. Joseph M. Mergen, *Always There: Reflections of One Engineer* (Mishawaka, Ind.: n.p., 1992), 68–69, 83; the late Joseph Mergen was chief engineer with the Propeller Division. Interview, 21 November 1992.

32. Bill Gunston, *World Encyclopedia of Aero Engines* (Wellingborough, England: Patrick Stephens, 1986), 178–79; Herschel Smith, *A History of Aircraft Piston Engines: From the Manly Balzer to the Continental Tiara* (Manhattan, Kans.: Sunflower University Press, 1986), 128–29.

33. Mergen, 95.

34. Ibid., 95, 96.

35. "C-W Reported Set for Business Boost," *Aviation Week,* 12 April 1948, 24.

36. "No More Planes," *Business Week,* 9 September 1950, 106–7.

37. "Curtiss Has Few Orders Left on Books, Vaughan Says," *Buffalo Evening News,* 26 September 1945.

38. "500 Employees Being Laid Off by Curtiss Here," *Buffalo Evening News,* 31 October 1945; *Aviation,* December 1945, 227.

39. Burdette S. Wright Diaries, vol. 33, several references; "Curtiss-Wright Model CW-28," press release of Curtiss-Wright Corporation, 24 September 1945.

40. "C-W Reported Set for Business Boost"; interview with Marion C. Hockman, 7 January 1987.

41. Peter M. Bowers, *Curtiss Aircraft, 1907–1947* (London: Putnam, 1979), 508–10; "Case History of the XF-87 All-Weather Fighter," compiled by the Air Technical Service Command Historical Office, Wright Field, January 1950, and published in the *American Aviation Historical Society Journal* 38, no. 1 (Spring 1993): 20–31.

42. Bilstein, 228–29.

43. Burdette S. Wright Diaries, vol. 23, 27 October 1943; Alvin E. Green letter, 3 December 1994.

44. "Chronological History of Curtiss-Wright," *Aero Digest,* October 1941, 152.

45. Robert S. Johnson, "Who Really Gave Us the DC-3?" *American Aviation Historical Society Journal* 29, no. 3 (Fall 1984): 206.

46. Interview with Guy W. Vaughan Jr., 13, 14, and 15 July 1987; Douglas, quoted in Robert W. Fausel, *Whatever Happened to Curtiss-Wright?* (Manhattan, Kans.: Sunflower University Press, 1990), 64.

47. Jack Dean, "North American's Flying Gun," *Wings* 23, no. 4 (August 1993).

48. Alfred P. Sloan Jr., *My Years with General Motors* (Garden City, N.Y.: Doubleday, 1964), 371–72.

49. Ibid., 373.

50. Rae, 180.

51. "C-W New Deal May Head Shake-Up in Plane Industry," *American Aviation* 12, no. 18 (15 February 1949), 10; "The Curtiss-Wright Fight," *Newsweek*, 26 April 1948, 66–68.

52. "C-W New Deal."

53. A prewar merger between Curtiss-Wright and the Atlas Corporation was discussed but never finalized. Burdette S. Wright Diaries, vol. 12; "Curtiss, Lockheed Discussing Merger," *Buffalo Evening News*, 19 October 1945; "Curtiss Decision to Move Is Taken with a Grain of Salt," *Buffalo Evening News*, 24 September 1945; "Curtiss Has Few Orders Left on Books, Vaughan Says," *Buffalo Evening News*, 26 September 1945; "Aircraft Manufacturer Mergers?" *Buffalo Evening News*, 19 October 1945.

54. "Case History of the XF-87 All Weather Fighter," 30.

55. Ibid., 31.

56. Walter Tydon letter, 28 June 1993.

57. "Case History of XF-87 All Weather Fighter," 29; AO135900 Curtiss XP-87 Blackhawk Doc., NASM.

58. "Case History of XF-87 All-Weather Fighter," 30.

59. "Northrop F-89: Scorpion with a Nuclear Sting," *Air International*, July 1988, 44–50, and August 1988, 86–92.

60. Quoted in "The CW-32 Cargo Transport," Report no. 32-F10, Curtiss-Wright Corporation. AO111300, Curtiss CW-32 1947 Cargo Transport, NASM.

61. "The CW-32 Cargo Transport."

62. News release, AO111300 Curtiss CW-32, NASM; "Stenographic Report of Proceedings." President's Air Policy Commission, 29 September 1947. "The Outlook for Cargo Planes." Statement of Admiral L. B. Richardson, USN (Ret.), vice president, Curtiss-Wright Corp. Q0001720 President's Air Policy Commission, NASM; *Aero Digest*, August 1948, 52.

63. Hockman interview.

64. Remarks of E. C. Sulzman at reunion of Wright Aeronautical employees, Cocoa, Florida, 11 May 1989. Videotape courtesy of the late Robert E. Johnson.

65. Vaughan interview.

66. Sulzman remarks.

67. Memo, Guy W. Vaughan to Paul V. Shields, 26 March 1949. Courtesy of the late Robert E. Johnson.

68. Vaughan interview.

69. "C-W Proxy Fight," *Aviation Week*, 26 April 1948, 18; "The Curtiss-Wright Fight."

70. "Court May Settle C-W Control Fight," *Aviation Week*, 3 May 1948, 13; "C-W Control," *Aviation Week*, 17 May 1948, 16.

71. "C-W Reported Set for Business Boost."

72. "C-W New Deal"; "After the Rainy Day," *Time*, 14 February 1949, 81–82.

73. "C-W New Deal"; "Curtiss-Wright Shake-Up," *Newsweek*, 19 May 1949, 73; "Curtiss-Wright Changes Continue," *Aviation Week*, 7 February 1949, 13; *Curtiss-Wright Annual Report for 1948*, 3.

74. Rae, 90; Vaughan interview.

75. Burdette S. Wright Diaries, vol. 25, 29 May 1944.

8. A New Identity, 1949–1990

1.   Transcript of luncheon meeting, New York Society of Security Analysts, 6 January 1950.

2.   Selig Altschul, "Curtiss-Wright Business Analyzed," *Aviation Week,* 2 August 1948, 32.

3.   Walter LaFeber, *The American Age: American Foreign Policy at Home and Abroad since 1750* (New York: W. W. Norton, 1989), 481; "NSC-68. A Report to the National Security Council," *Naval War College Review,* May–June 1975, 53.

4.   LaFeber, 481.

5.   John B. Rae, *Climb to Greatness: The American Aircraft Industry, 1920–1960* (Cambridge, Mass.: MIT Press, 1968), 197.

6.   Ibid.

7.   Mike Machat, "Dark Days at Douglas," *Airpower* 23, no. 6 (November 1993): 39.

8.   See Stuart W. Leslie, *The Cold War and American Science* (New York: Columbia University Press, 1993) for a discussion of the impact of these new technologies on the aviation industry, esp. 110–13; also see G. R. Simonson, "Missiles and Creative Destruction in the American Aircraft Industry, 1956–1961," *Business History Review* 38, no. 3 (Autumn 1964): 302–14.

9.   Rae, 189, 213; Roger E. Bilstein, *Flight in America, 1900–1983* (Baltimore: Johns Hopkins University Press, 1984), 264 n.

10.   Joseph M. Mergen, *Always There: Reflections of One Engineer* (Mishawaka, Ind.: n.p., 1992), 87–88; "C-W Policy Changes Outlined," *Aviation Week,* 6 February 1950, 32.

11.   "Curtiss-Wright Shift," *Newsweek,* 15 October 1951, 70; "No More Planes," *Business Week,* 9 September 1950, 106–7.

12.   Remarks of E. C. Sulzman at a reunion of Wright Aeronautical employees, Cocoa, Florida, 11 May 1989. Videotape courtesy of the late Robert E. Johnson.

13.   "The Has-Been," *Forbes,* 1 October 1966, 31; "Rescue by Curtiss-Wright?" *Time,* 21 May 1956, 96; "Roy T. Hurley, 75, Aviation Leader," *New York Times,* 6 November 1971.

14.   "The Well-Deserved Decline of Curtiss-Wright," *Forbes,* 15 November 1967, 25.

15.   Mergen, 96.

16.   Sir Stanley Hooker, *Not Much of an Engineer* (Shrewsbury, U.K.: Airlife, 1984), 141–42.

17.   "Interesting Facts about the J-65 Turbojet Engine," February 1958, Wright Aeronautical Division, Curtiss-Wright Corporation, B1040300 Propulsion Brochures, Wright Aero General Jet Engines, National Air and Space Museum.

18.   Hooker, 143.

19.   "Production Engines Invoiced—Wright Aeronautical Corporation." Prepared by Engine Section, Order and Contract Division, General Sales and Service Department. Courtesy of the late Gerard Abbamont.

20.   Wm. Kroger, "Curtiss-Wright Faces a Busy Year," *Aviation Week,* 24 March 1952, 16; *Curtiss-Wright Annual Report for 1952.*

21.   *Curtiss-Wright Annual Report for 1954,* 4, 5.

22.   Selig Altschul, "UAC, C-W Report Postwar Peaks," *Aviation Week,* 26 April 1954, 79.

23.   Hooker, 142–43; Wm. B. Harris, "Curtiss-Wright Throws Away the Book," *Fortune,* January 1958, 112–17.

24.   Mergen, 100, 102.

25.   "The Has-Been," 31.

26.   Harris, 112.

27.   Mergen, 101–2.

28. Harris, 113.
29. Mergen, 101–2.
30. Harris, 117; Copy of Smith letter courtesy of the late Robert E. Johnson.
31. Harris, 113.
32. "The Has-Been."
33. Mergen, 127.
34. Ibid., 117–18.
35. Ibid., 119.
36. Richard C. Koehnen, "Never Say Die," *Wings* 13, no. 1 (June 1983): 37.
37. Mergen, 119.
38. Ibid., 120.
39. Ibid., 130.
40. Mergen, 130–41; Jay Miller, *The X-Planes* (Arlington, Tex.: Aerofax, for Orion Books, 1988), 143–45; Koehnen, 44–48.
41. "Facing Reality," *Forbes,* 15 November 1967, 25; "The Has-Been"; "The Well-Deserved Decline of Curtiss-Wright," 24; Harris, 112–13; "Clash That Upset Curtiss-Wright," 24; *Business Week,* 11 June 1960, 32–34.
42. "Curtiss-Wright Adds $50 Million to Original Quehanna Investment"; "New Curtiss-Wright Management Prepares to Reorient Company," *Aviation Week,* 13 June 1960, 30.
43. "Curtiss-Wright Aids Ailing Carmaker," *Aviation Week,* 13 August 1956, 26.
44. Ibid.
45. John B. Rae, *The American Automobile Industry* (Boston: Twayne Publishers, 1984), 25, 27.
46. "Builder of Bargains," *U.S. News and World Report,* 26 April 1957, 18; "Two Famous Cars—Can they Come Back?" *U.S. News and World Report,* 17 August 1956, 59–61.
47. "The Well-Deserved Decline of Curtiss-Wright," 25.
48. "The Well-Deserved Decline of Curtiss-Wright," 25; see also Rae, *The American Automobile Industry,* 99.
49. "The Has-Been"; Harris, 112; "Facing Reality," 24–25.
50. "New Curtiss-Wright Management Prepares to Reorient Company," 31.
51. "Exit Hurley," *Time,* 6 June 1960, 94.
52. "Curtiss-Wright's Comeback," *Time,* 23 November 1953, 108.
53. "Clash That Upset Curtiss-Wright," 33.
54. Ibid., 32.
55. "The Well-Deserved Decline of Curtiss-Wright," 26.
56. Ibid.
57. "Exit Hurley."
58. "Clash That Upset Curtiss-Wright," 33–34.
59. "Curtiss-Wright Shake-Up," *Newsweek,* 9 June 1949, 73.
60. "Clash That Upset Curtiss-Wright," 33.
61. "The Well-Deserved Decline of Curtiss-Wright," 26.
62. "New Curtiss-Wright Management Prepares to Reorient Company," *Aviation Week,* 13 June 1960, 30.
63. "Clash That Upset Curtiss-Wright," 34.
64. "Curtiss-Wright Begins Product Orientation," *Aviation Week,* 5 September 1960, 65.
65. "Clash That Upset Curtiss-Wright," 34.
66. "The Has-Been."
67. "The Well-Deserved Decline of Curtiss-Wright," 26; *Curtiss-Wright Annual Report for 1960,* 4.

68. "The Well-Deserved Decline of Curtiss-Wright," 26.
69. "The Has-Been," 31.
70. "The Well-Deserved Decline of Curtiss-Wright," 26.
71. "Facing Reality," 24.
72. Ibid., 24, 25.
73. "Clash That Upset Curtiss-Wright," 34.
74. "The Has-Been."
75. "Garrett Opposes Curtiss Offer," *Aviation Week and Space Technology,* 16 September 1963, 39; "Garrett Asks Court to Prevent Curtiss-Wright Purchase of Stock," *Aviation Week and Space Technology,* 30 September 1963, 33; "C-W Extends Garrett Stock Plan," *Aviation Week and Space Technology,* 21 October 1963, 30; "Garrett, Signal Propose to Merge after Curtiss-Wright Raises Offer," *Aviation Week and Space Technology,* 28 October 1963, 33; Garrett, Signal Oil Continue Merger Plan, *"Aviation Week and Space Technology,"* 11 November 1963, 32.
76. "A Good Old Proxy Fight," *Newsweek,* 15 May 1978, 109; A. F. Ehrbar, "Kennecott after the Battle," *Fortune,* 5 June 1978, 126; "Battle in the Boardrooms," *Time,* 9 February 1981, 72.
77. Ehrbar, 128.
78. "Battle in the Boardrooms."
79. "A Good Old Proxy Fight."
80. Ehrbar, 124–25.
81. Ibid., 130.
82. "Proxy Raid by an Old Brigade," *Time,* 10 April 1978, 83; "A Good Old Proxy Fight"; *Moody's Manual of Investments: American and Foreign Industrial Securities,* and *Moody's Industrial Manual,* for years 1960–1995.
83. "Behind Kennecott's Bid for Curtiss-Wright," *Business Week,* 15 December 1980, 30.
84. "Battle in the Boardrooms."
85. Ibid.
86. *Curtiss-Wright Corporation Annual Report for 1979,* 2, 10.
87. "Winner in a Close Decision," *Fortune,* 23 February 1981, 15; "Out of a Failed Merger, 'Victory' for Both Sides," *Business Week,* 9 February 1981, 25; *Moody's Industrial Manual, 1982.*
88. "Winner in a Close Decision."
89. "Winner in a Close Decision"; "Behind Kennecott's Bid for Curtiss-Wright," 31.
90. *Curtiss-Wright Corporation Annual Report for 1983,* 3; *Curtiss-Wright Corporation Annual Report for 1986,* 2.
91. *Curtiss-Wright Annual Report for 1972,* 8–12; *Curtiss-Wright Annual Report for 1979,* 3; *Curtiss-Wright Annual Report for 1981,* 14; *Curtiss-Wright Corporation Annual Report for 1983,* 2–3; *Moody's Manual of Investments: American and Foreign Industrial Securities, 1952.*
92. *Curtiss-Wright Annual Report for 1983,* 4.
93. *A Special Report to Stockholders: A Primer on Shot Peening.*
94. *Curtiss-Wright Corporation Annual Report for 1979,* 10.
95. Mergen, 143; *Curtiss-Wright Annual Report for 1968,* 8.
96. *Curtiss-Wright Annual Report for 1972,* 13; *Curtiss-Wright Corporation Annual Report for 1979,* 9–10; *Curtiss-Wright Corporation Annual Report for 1991,* 5–10; *Curtiss-Wright Corporation Annual Report for 1994,* 6; *Curtiss-Wright Corporation Annual Report for 1995,* introduction, 3–4.

Bibliographical Essay

The literature devoted to the Curtiss-Wright Corporation is extremely limited, although several reference books on Curtiss aircraft have been published over the years. The best of these is Peter M. Bowers, *Curtiss Aircraft, 1907–1947* (Putnam, 1979). However, almost nothing has been written about the corporation itself. The only exception is Robert W. Fausel, *Whatever Happened to Curtiss-Wright?* (Sunflower University Press, 1990), which is essentially a compilation of responses to a series of questions posed by the author, who was a company test pilot for many years, to former Curtiss-Wright employees about their experiences at the company. Hence, the book is not history per se, although it does give some valuable insights into company operations during and after World War II.

Of the several biographies of the Wright brothers that have been published, the most recent is Tom Crouch, *The Bishop's Boys* (W. W. Norton, 1989). The most comprehensive biography of Glenn Curtiss is C. R. Roseberry, *Glenn Curtiss: Pioneer of Flight* (Doubleday, 1972).

I. B. Holly, *Buying Aircraft: Materiel Procurement for the Army Air Forces* (Office of the Chief of Military History, 1964), is part of the Special Studies on the U.S. Army's participation in World War II. This book is an important source for information on the aviation industry's contribution to World War II. Another important series is Wesley Frank Craven and James Lea Cate, *The Army Air Forces in World War II* (University of Chicago Press, 1958), especially volume 6, *Men and Planes,* and volume 7, *Services around the World.* A third important series is Maurer Maurer, *Aviation in the U.S. Army, 1919–1939* (Office of Air Force History, 1987).

The history of the American aviation industry has been the subject of several recent books, including Jacob Vander Meulen's *The Politics of Aircraft: Building an American Military Industry* (University Press of Kansas, 1991), Roger E. Bilstein's *Flight in America, 1900–1983: From the Wrights to the Astronauts* (Johns Hopkins University Press, 1984), and Bilstein's *The American Aerospace Industry* (Twayne, 1996). An important older work is John B. Rae, *Climb to Greatness: The American Aircraft Industry, 1920–1960* (MIT Press, 1968).

Much has been written about the Curtiss-Wright Corporation and its predecessor companies in publications such as *Aerial Age Weekly, Airways Age, Aviation,* the *Aircraft Yearbook,* and *Aero Digest.* Some company publications, such as *The Curtiss Flyleaf, The Curtiss-Wrighter,* the *Wright Engine Builder,* and *Trade Winds,* have survived in specialized collections. These kinds of materials can be found in aviation libraries and archives such as the National Air and Space Museum of the Smithsonian Institution in Washington, D.C., the Pima Air Museum in Tucson, Arizona, the Ohio History of Flight Museum in Columbus,

Ohio, and the Aviation Hall of Fame of New Jersey in Teterboro, New Jersey. Otherwise, very few corporate records, aside from various annual reports, have been preserved. Of those that remain, most are held in the private collections of former Curtiss-Wright employees. The personal papers of Clement Melville Keys are housed in the National Air and Space Museum.

Records of the federal government found in the National Archives, such as the various congressional investigations and files of the U.S. Army and Navy, are a rich source of primary material on the aviation industry, including Curtiss-Wright.

Another important source of information for the more recent past has been many interviews with former employees of the Curtiss-Wright Corporation. Their experiences and insights have given a personal dimension to the company's history.

The following is a select bibliography.

Books relating to Curtiss Aircraft or to the Curtiss-Wright Corporation

Bowers, Peter M. *Curtiss Aircraft, 1907–1947.* London: Putnam, 1979.
Christy, Joe, and Jeff Ethell. *P-40 Hawks at War.* New York: Charles Scribner's Sons, 1980.
Fausel, Robert W. *Whatever Happened to Curtiss-Wright?* Manhattan, Kans.: Sunflower University Press, 1990.
Rubenstein, Murray, and Richard M. Goldman. *To Join with the Eagles: Curtiss-Wright Aircraft, 1903–1965.* Garden City, N.Y.: Doubleday, 1979.
Shamburger, Page, and Joe Christy. *The Curtiss Hawks.* Kalamazoo, Mich.: Wolverine Press, 1972.

Books relating to Glenn Curtiss and the Wright Brothers

Crouch, Tom. *The Bishop's Boys: A Life of Wilbur and Orville Wright.* New York: W. W. Norton, 1989.
Howard, Fred. *Wilbur and Orville: A Biography of the Wright Brothers.* New York: Alfred A. Knopf, 1987.
Roseberry, C. R. *Glenn Curtiss: Pioneer of Flight.* Garden City, N.Y.: Doubleday, 1972.
Scharff, Robert, and Walter S. Taylor. *Over Land and Sea: A Biography of Glenn Hammond Curtiss.* New York: David McKay, 1968.

Books relating to the Aviation Industry

Bilstein, Roger E. *Flight in America, 1900–1983: From the Wrights to the Astronauts.* Baltimore, Md.: Johns Hopkins University Press, 1984.
Rae, John B. *Climb to Greatness: The American Aircraft Industry, 1920–1960.* Cambridge, Mass.: MIT Press, 1968.
Vander Meulen, Jacob. *The Politics of Aircraft: Building an American Military Industry.* Lawrence, Kans.: University Press of Kansas, 1991.

Index

Acts of Congress. *See* U.S. Congress
Aerial Age Weekly, 22
Aerial Experimental Association, 9–10, 11, 17
Aero Club of America, 9–10
Aeronautical Society of New York, 11
aerospace industry, 144, 154, 161, 164, 165
aircraft carriers. See *Enterprise; Lexington; Saratoga; Yorktown*
aircraft demand, 2–4
Aircraft Disposal Company, 28
Aircraft Production Board, 20–22, 24
airlines. *See specific airlines*
airmail, 39, 40, 71, 75
Air Materiel Command, 135
Airplane Division. *See* Curtiss-Wright Airplane Division
airplanes: Bell, P-39, 96, 97; Bristol fighters, 21–22; Caproni Bombers, 21; de Havilland Comet, 148; DH-4, 34; Reid Rambler, 39; Republic P-47, 97, 108, 113; Spad 13, 21; Thomas Morse MB, 30; as weapons of war, 16, 19, 26

BOEING
Boeing 707, 132, 148
Boeing B-17, 76–78, 116
Boeing B-29, 4, 93, 105, 111, 114
Boeing B-47, 132
Boeing B-52, 132
Boeing Model 80, 42
Boeing Model 83/F4B/P-12, 38, 54, 65, 70
Boeing Model 247, 66
Boeing Model 299, 76, 78
Boeing Model 299/Y1B-17, 78
Boeing P-26, 64, 77
Boeing P-26A, 64
Boeing PW-9, 33
Boeing XB-9, 64
Boeing XB-29, 106
Boeing XP-936/XP-26, 64–65

CHANCE VOUGHT
Vought F4U Corsair, 100, 113, 120
Vought UO-1, 49

CONSOLIDATED
Consolidated B-24, 117
Consolidated (Convair) B-32, 93

CONVAIR
Convair B-36, 129, 130
Convair Model 240, 129

CURTISS
A-1, 12
A-2, 12
A-12 Shrike, 64, 69, 77
A-25, 101, 102
B-2, 37–38
B-F2C-1, 65
C-76, 117, 119
Condor, 38, 58, 66
CR-2, 32
CS-1, 31–33
CS-2, 31
CW-14/14B Osprey, 68–69
CW-32, 132, 135–36
Eagle, 27
F6C-1, 33
Fledgling, 67
Flying Boat #2, 13
H-4, 17
H-12, 18–19
H75, 96
H75A, 84
Hawk II, 68–69
Hawk III, 69, 79–80
Hawk 75, 79–80
HS1L, 22
JN, 15, 22
JN-2, 19
JN-3, 17–19
JN-4, 18–20, 27–28, 45
JN-4A, 19
JN-4D, 20–21
Kingbird, 57
Model 18, 23–24
Model 18-T, 23

Index

Model 20, 80, 93, 97–98, 125
Model 75, 77–78, 79, 83, 84
Model 76/Y1A-18/A-18, 77, 114
Model 81, 83
Model CW-20E, 125, 131
Model D, 12–14
Model E, 12–14
Model F, 13–15, 19
Model G, 14–15
Model J, 15–17
Model MF Seagull, 27
Model N, 15–17
Model T, 17
N-9, 19
NBS-1, 31
O-1, 34
O-52, 94
Oriole, 27, 29
P-1, 33, 37
P-6, 37, 66–67
P-6A, 37
P-6E, 65
P-36, 80, 85, 95, 114
P-60, 113
PW/PW-9, 33
R-4, 19
R-6, 32
Robin, 38–39, 56
SB2C-1, 102, 103, 115, 119
SBC-3, 78
SC, 103
SO3C, 103, 119
SOC, 78
SOC-1, 66–67
T-2, 49
T-3, 49
T-32/AT-32 Condor II, 66, 69
TS-1, 30, 49
XB2C-1, 100–101
XBT2C, 120
XF11C-1, 65
XF11C-2/F11C-2, 65
XF14C, 113, 119
XP-40, 85
XP-46, 113
XP-60, 109, 113, 119
XP-62, 113, 119
XP-87, 129, 132, 135, 138
XP-934, 64
XSBC-2, 78
XSBC-3, 78
Y1A-8, 64
Y1P-36, 78, 79, 80
YP60E, 113
See also *America*; *Canada*; C-46; Falcon; *Golden Flyer*;
   Hawk; *Hudson Flyer*, *June Bug*; P-40; *Red Wing*;
   SB2C; *Silver Dart*; *White Wing*

CURTISS-WRIGHT
X-19, 152
X-100, 152, 153
X-200, 152, 153

DOUGLAS
Douglas B-18, 78
Douglas C-47, 97
Douglas DC-1, 66, 73
Douglas DC-2, 66, 73, 78, 104
Douglas DC-3, 66, 73, 74, 78, 97, 104
Douglas DC-7, 131
Douglas DST, 78
Douglas SBD, 104
Douglas XF3D, 135

FOKKER
Fokker attack plane, 64
Fokker F-10, 42
Fokker F.VIIa, 49

FORD
Ford 4-AT Trimotor, 49
Ford 5-AT Trimotor, 42

GRUMMAN
Grumman F3F, 65
Grumman F6F, 113
Grumman TBF Avenger, 102
Grumman XF2F/F2F, 65

KEYSTONE
Keystone Bombers, 64
Keystone LB-6, 37, 42

LOCKHEED
Lockheed Orion, 54
Lockheed P2V, 131
Lockheed P2V-1, 130
Lockheed P-38, 97
Lockheed P-80, 114
Lockheed Super Constellation, 131

MARTIN
Martin B-10A, 73
Martin B-26, 102
Martin M-130, 76
Martin Model 139W, 73
Martin Model 202, 129
Martin Model 404, 129
Martin XB-907/B-10, 64, 73

NORTH AMERICAN
North American AT-6, 117
North American B-25, 133
North American P-51, 97, 108

NORTHROP
Northrop 2E, 73
Northrop A-17/A-17A, 64–65, 77
Northrop XP-89, 135

SEVERSKY
Seversky P-35, 78, 80
Seversky SEV 1XP, 77–78

Air Policy Commission. *See* Finletter Commission
Airports Division. *See* Curtiss-Wright Airports Division
Air Technical Service Command Historical Office, 135
Allies, World War II, 88, 95, 96, 97, 98; strategy of, 105
Allison Engineering Company. *See* General Motors, and Allison Engineering Company
America, 15–16
American Airlines, 78, 125
American Airways, 66
Andrews, Major General Frank M., 86
Argentina, 67, 80
Argentine navy, 28
Armee de l'Air, 82, 90, 94
Armstrong Siddeley company, 147
Arnold, General H. H., 105, 126
"Arsenal of Democracy," 86, 95, 112
Asia, 2, 67; Southeast Asia, 98
Austria-Hungary, 14
automobile industry, 19–20, 45, 47
Aviation, 56, 110
Aviation Corporation (AVCO), 41–42
Aviation Credit Corporation, 42
Avro Company, 15
Axis, 82, 95, 97, 112; and World War II production, 123

Baker, Newton, 30, 75
Baldwin, Frederick W. "Casey", 9
Baldwin, Thomas Scott, 9
Barrow, Thomas, 162–63
Barrows, A. S., 135
Beaver, Pennsylvania, 91
Beech, Walter, 51
Bell, Alexander Graham, 7, 9–10
Bell Aerospace Corporation, 144, 153
Bell Aircraft Corporation, 54, 96
Bendix Corporation, 146
Berlin, Donovan, 77
Berlin blockade, 135
Berliner-Joyce Aircraft Company, 60
Berner, T. Roland (Ted), 137, 154; criticism of Hurley, 156; Curtiss-Wright Corporation, revitalization of, 159–61; death of, 165; president and board chairman of Curtiss-Wright, 157–58; proxy fight with Guy Vaughan, 137–39, 158; successes and failures of, 165; takeover bids, 161–63; X-19 project, 151, 153

B. F. Sturtevant Company, 146
B.G. Aircraft Sparkplug Company, 146
Birmingham. See Ely, Eugene T.
Bishop, Cortland Field, 10
Blaylock, Raymond, 119
Bloomfield, New Jersey, 125
Boeing, William, 42
Boeing Aircraft and Transportation Company, 41
Boeing Aircraft Company, 41
Boeing Airplane Company, 30, 33, 37–38, 53, 64; capital expansion of, 1940, 89; innovative aircraft, 66; post-World War II reconversion, 129
Boeing Air Transport, 41
Bolivia, 68
Borst, Henry, 151
Bowers, Peter, 113
Brazil, 67
Brazilian navy, 28
Briggs and Stratton, 131
Bristol Aero-Engines company, 137, 147
Britain. *See* England
British Admiralty, 19
British Royal Naval Air Service (RNAS), 16–18
British Royal Navy, 101
Buffalo, New York, 7, 11, 12, 18; Churchill Street plant, 17, 28; closing of all plants in, 127, 131; Curtiss-Wright presence reestablished in, 148; Elmwood Avenue plant, 21; Genesee Street plant, 89–90, 98, 125; Kenmore plant, 60–61, 108; manufacture of military and large aircraft, 39; production reorganization, 1930, 58–59; reduction of Curtiss facilities, 1920, 28; transfer of staff from, 71. *See also* Berlin, Donovan; Damon, Ralph
Bureau of Aeronautics, 31, 37
Burgess, W. Starling, 18
Burma, 98

C-46, 93, 95, 97–98, 114; and China airlift, 99; corrections of deficiencies in, 113; and mass production of, 117; and Pratt and Whitney R-2800, 116; production, premature, 120; production problems, 102
Caldwell, New Jersey plant, 91, 125, 130, 131, 145; expansion of, 148
Canada, 17
Canadian Car and Foundry Company, (CCF), 101–2, 115
capital/capitalization, 3, 17, 20, 21, 27; and assets write-off, 1931, 60; capital expansion, 1933–39, 81, 88; and commercial aviation, 35; decline of, 57; and engine manufacturing, 70; and Field report, 142; and Keys' vision, 39–41; lack of, in industry, 30, 36, 87; overcapitalization, 32–33, 87, 142, 161, 163. *See also individual companies*
Caproni, Gianni, 40
Carborundum Company, 162
Carlstadt, New Jersey plant, 148

Cessna Aircraft Company, 143
Chaco War, 68
Chambers, Washington Irving, 12
Chance Vought Corporation, 37, 42, 51, 53, 66; development of F4U fighter, 120; separation from United Aircraft, 144; VTOL aircraft, 153
Chance Vought Division of United Aircraft. *See* Chance Vought Corporation
Chandler, Alfred, 5
Cheektowaga, New York, 132. *See also* Buffalo, New York, Genesee Street plant
Chilean air force, 67
Child, Lloyd, 100
China, 52, 68, 69, 73, 80; and American Volunteer Group (AVG) 97, 98
Chrysler Corporation, 156
Clifton, New Jersey, 91
C. M. Keys and Company, 29, 61
Cold War, 128, 129, 132, 135, 140; and Iron Curtain, 128, 142
Colombia, 68
Columbia Law School, 158
Columbia Protektosite Company, 148
Columbus, Ohio, plant, 89–90, 101, 115, 130; closing of, 147; and consolidation of Airplane Division in, 127; problems with unskilled work force, 102–3; and SB2C production, 104
Commando. *See* C-46
commercial aviation, 27–29, 40–41
competitive bidding, 2, 27–28, 30–31, 33–36
Consolidated Aircraft Corporation, 89, 114, 117
Consolidated Vultee Aircraft Corporation, 115
containment policy, 142–43
Continental Motors, 115
Convair, 129
Coolidge, President Calvin, 35
Cornell University, 127
Curon, 155
Curtiss, Glenn Hammond, 1–2, 7, 9–10, 11–14, 16–18; confidence in aviation's future, 26–27; and Curtiss Engineering Corporation, 23; and Curtiss-Wright Corporation, 51; and Curtiss-Wright merger, 43; death of, 58; design of tractor airplanes, 44; and flying boats, 24; and Willys, John North, 20–21
Curtiss Aeroplane and Motor Company, Inc., 33, 40, 43, 51–52, 56–57; annual report for 1926, 36; dividends and profits between 1924–1928, 34, 38; export sales of, 68–69; fighter contract, 77; financial losses of, 74; first-mover advantages, 36; merger with Wright Aeronautical Corporation, 51–52; new projects between 1930–1935, 76–77; reorganization in 1930–1931, 60–61; reorganization in 1936, 79; sale of new designs to Air Corps and Navy, 64–67; and technological change, 76; Wright Aeronautical, comparison with, 63
Curtiss Aeroplane and Motor Company, Ltd., of Canada, 17

Curtiss Aeroplane and Motor Corporation, 2–3, 17–18, 20–21, 22–25; aircraft engine production, 47, 48, 50; contraction, post-World War I, 26, 28–30; and criticism by William Langer, 111; reorganization of, 27; World War I production, 20, 24, 26
Curtiss Aeroplane Company, 2, 12–14, 16–17
Curtiss Aeroplane Division, Buffalo, 79, 81, 83
Curtiss Aeroplane Export Corporation, 30, 40, 67
Curtiss Airports Corporation, 40
Curtiss Assets Corporation, 33
Curtiss-Caproni Corporation, 40, 79
Curtiss Engineering Corporation, 23–24
Curtiss Exhibition Company, 12, 17, 40
Curtiss Flying Service, 40, 74
Curtiss Motor Company, 12, 14–15; earnings, 17
Curtiss Propeller Division, 79, 84, 116; consolidation with Airplane Division, 127; expansion between 1939–1941, 91; new products, post-World War II, 125; profitability between 1947–1950, 131, 144, 147; X-19 project, 151–54. *See also* engines, turboprop
Curtiss-Reid Aircraft Co., Ltd., 39
Curtiss-Robertson Airplane Manufacturing Co., 39, 56, 59, 127
Curtiss-Wright Airplane Company of Delaware, 79
Curtiss-Wright Airplane Company of Missouri, 59–61, 66, 68–69, 76, 79
Curtiss-Wright Airplane Division, 90, 94, 95, 97, 108; C-46 production, 99; closing of, 147; consolidation in Columbus, 127; CW-32, 136; decline of, 120–21, 142; new products, post-World War II, 125; personnel loss, post-World War II, 130; problems of, 112–13; and proxy fight, 1948, 137–39; revitalization, need for, 122; status in Curtiss-Wright Corporation, 1945, 131; termination of, 140, 147; and USAF, 135; World War II production, 117, 124; XP-87, 136
Curtiss-Wright Airports Corporation, 57–58, 60, 62, 74, 79
Curtiss-Wright Airports Division, 79
Curtiss-Wright Corporation, 3–6, 51–52, 53, 56–57; and acclaim of public, 1943, 97; Airplane Division, plans to eliminate, 132; automobile business, 156; capital expansion, from 1950–1953, 147, 148; capital expansion, three-stage program, 84, 89–93, 96; cash reserves of, 128, 134, 137, 156, 161; combat aircraft, 1943 production of, 112; contraction of, post-World War II, 130; contributions to war effort, 111; corporate headquarters of, 117–18, 127, 132; creation of, 51–52, 58; criticisms of, 98, 99, 106–12; at crossroads in 1945, 122; dependence on Wright Aeronautical, 70, 73–74; diversification, non-aviation, 136, 142, 151, 154–57, 164; diversification, in World War II, 117; export sales in early 1930s, 67–69; facilities, geographical dispersal of, 117–18; financial recovery of, 76, 80–81; first-mover advantages of, 5, 83, 95, 96, 121, 137;

income and financial condition in 1945, 128; income in 1950–1951, 147; lawsuits, defendant in, 110; leadership, 1935 change of, 75; licenses and licensees, 91, 95, 101, 113, 115–16, 122, 127, 137, 145, 147; losses between 1929–1933, 59–63; losses between 1945–1950, 130; management crisis in 1949, 139–40, 141, 147; military sales, importance of, 63; money capital, need for, 87; and neutrality legislation, 90; overexpansion of, 94, 95; performance in World War II, 128; Postwar Planning Committee, 125; problems during World War II, managerial and engineering, 114–20; profits of, 87, 130, 149, 155, 162, 163; reorganization in 1936, 79; reorganization of, 1940, 90; retrenchment after 1929, 55–63; sales, 124, 145, 156, 162; sales decline, between 1954–1958, 148; and Shields presidency, 141–42; as subcontractor, 164; and takeover bids, 161–63; and world rearmament, 75, 83, 84; World War II fighter program, 112–14; X-19 project, 151–54; XP-87 project, 132, 135, 138. *See also specific company plants*
Curtiss-Wright Curon Division, 159
Curtiss-Wright Development Division, 125
Curtiss-Wright Dorr-Oliver Division, 163
Curtiss-Wright Electronics Division, 148
Curtiss-Wright Export Corporation, 60, 67, 69, 79
Curtiss-Wright Export Sales Division, 79
Curtiss-Wright Flying Service, 52–60, 62
Curtiss-Wright Industrial and Scientific Products Division, 148
Curtiss-Wright Metals Processing Division, 148
Curtiss-Wright of Canada, Ltd., 148
Curtiss-Wright Research Division, 148
Curtiss-Wright Research Laboratory, 103, 125–26, 127
Curtiss-Wright Specialties Division, 148
Curtiss-Wright VTOL Systems Division, 153

Daily Mail, 15
Daimler-Benz, 155
Damon, Ralph, 60–61, 66, 76
Dart antitank missile, 149, 155
Dayton, Ohio, 45, 49, 153
Defense Plant Corporation, 89, 127
Desberon Motor Co., 45
Dodge Division of Chrysler Corporation, 115
Dorr-Oliver, Incorporated, 163
Douglas, Donald, 73, 133, 143
Douglas Aircraft Company, 34, 37, 42, 53, 64; aircraft assembly plants of, 1942, 96; capital expansion of, 1940, 89; and engine choice for transports, 73; innovative aircraft, 66; reconversion process, post-World War II, 129; and world rearmament, 84; World War II production, 117
Dutch East Indies, 45

Earle, Robert L., 127

Eastern Aircraft Division. *See* General Motors, Eastern Aircraft Division
Eastern Airlines, 78, 125, 131
Eastern Air Transport, 57, 66
Eaton Manufacturing Company, 115
Edison, Thomas, 7
Ely, Eugene, 12, 13
employment, 4, 14, 16, 19
engines: air-cooled, 38, 43, 47–50, 51, 65, 71; Allison V-1710, 84–85; Armstrong Siddeley Sapphire, 147; Bristol Olympus, 147; Hispano-Suiza ("Hisso"), 44, 46–47; jet, 122, 126, 137; Liberty, 21, 47; liquid-cooled, 38, 47–50, 58, 65; Lycoming T-53, 152; turboprop, 130, 142, 152, 157, 160

CURTISS
C-12, 32
Conqueror, 37, 64–65, 68–69, 71
D-12, 2, 31, 33–34, 36, 38, 49, 52, 71
K-12, 23, 31
Model O, 15
Model OX, 15–16
Model OX-5, 27
Model OXX, 15
V-X, 17

PRATT AND WHITNEY
Pratt and Whitney Hornet, 50, 72, 73, 74, 78
Pratt and Whitney J57, 145, 150
Pratt and Whitney R-1535 Twin Wasp Junior, 73
Pratt and Whitney R-1830 Twin Wasp, 73, 78, 80
Pratt and Whitney R-2800, 116
See also Pratt and Whitney Aircraft Company, Wasp engines

ROLLS-ROYCE
Rolls-Royce Avon, 137
Rolls-Royce Falcon, 22

WRIGHT
Cyclone, 42, 50, 65, 71–73, 78–79, 95
G series Cyclone/G-100, 78
J-1, 48
J-4, 48
J-5 Whirlwind, 49–50
J-6, 50
J65, 147, 160, 163
Model E, 48
P-2, 50
R-1510 Whirlwind, 73
R-1670, 73
R-1820 Cyclone, 74, 76–77, 93, 95, 104, 116
R-1820 Cyclone E, 72
R-1820 Cyclone F, 73
R-1820 Cyclone F-50, 73
R-1820 Cyclone G, 73
R-2600 Cyclone, 79, 93, 95, 104, 109, 115–16

TJ6, 145
TJ7, 145
Wankel, 151, 152, 153
Zephyr, 149–50
See also R-3350 (Cyclone); Wright Aeronautical Corporation

England, 2, 16–17, 18–19, 21, 24, 28; aircraft, World War II production of, 82–83, 123; Curtiss flying boats, purchase of, 23; estimation of German strength, 83; financing of American industrial expansion, 88, 90; jet engine technology, 122, 126, 137; military establishment, need for expansion of, 82; purchasing mission of, 84, 85, 90; rearmament program, 75
Enterprise, 78
E. R. Thomas Co., 7
Export Sales Division. *See* Curtiss-Wright Export Sales Division

Fabre, Henri, 12
Fairchild Aircraft Corporation, 102, 115
Fair Lawn, New Jersey, 91
Falcon, 34, 37, 64, 67–68, 73; development life, end of, 76
Fedden, Sir Roy, 137
Finletter, Thomas, 128
Finletter Commission, 128–30, 135, 136, 142–43
Fisher Body Division. *See* General Motors, Fisher Body Division
Flight Systems Group, 165
Flying Tigers. *See* China, and American Volunteer Group (AVG)
Ford, Henry, 14
Ford Motor Company, 145, 146, 156
Forrestal, James G., 135
Fort William, Ontario, 101
France, 2, 4, 11, 19, 21; aviation industry, 81, 82, 84; estimation of German strength, 83; military establishment of, 82; purchasing missions, 84, 85, 90; rearmament acceleration, 75; and Simplex Automobile Company, 44
France, Charles W., 115
French Air Ministry, 90
Frye, Jack, 143

Garden City, Long Island, 23, 28, 39, 59
Garfield, New Jersey plant, 148
Garrett Corporation, 161
gas-turbine. *See* engines: jet; turboprop
General Electric Company, 126, 150, 156, 160–61, 163
General Motors, 84, 96, 108, 133–34; and Allison Engineering Company, 84, 133, 134; Eastern Aircraft Division, 133; Fisher Body Division, 96, 133
Geneva Disarmament Conference, 75
Germany, 13, 16, 19, 82, 83; aircraft, new, World War I, 21; invasion of Poland, 86; jet engines, 122, 126,

137; Hitler's rise, 75; U Boats, 23, 105; World War II aircraft, production of, 82, 123
G. H. Curtiss Manufacturing Company, 8–10
GI Bill of Rights, 125
Glenn L. Martin Co., 31, 45, 64, 66
Glover, Byron A., 103
Golden Flyer, 11
Goodyear company, 120
Gordon Bennett Trophy, 11
Göring, Hermann, 75
Graham-Paige Motors Corporation, 115
Great Britain. *See* England
Great Depression, 52, 53, 83. *See also* stock market crash
Grumman Engineering Aircraft Corporation, 54, 65, 102, 113, 133

Hamilton Standard. *See* United Aircraft
Hammondsport, New York, 7–9, 13, 17, 28, 58
"Happy Hooligan," 7
Harriman, Edward, 51
Harrington, E. J., 114
Harrison, Frank H., 114
Harvard Business School, 117
Harvard University, 45, 158
Hawk, 33–34, 37, 52, 65–69, 73; design, as derivative, 114; development life, end of, 76
Hayden, Stone and Company, 41, 44–45, 47
Helldiver. *See* SB2C
Hercules: bicycle, 7; motorcycle, 8
Heron, Samuel, 49–50
Herring, Augustus, 10–12
Herring-Curtiss Company, 10, 11–12, 45
Hibbard, Hall, 143
Higgins Boat Industries, 115
Hiller Aircraft Company, 153
Himalaya Mountains. *See* "Hump"
Hitler, Adolf, 75
Hollywood films, 97
Hooker, Sir Stanley, 147
Hoover administration, 63
House Armed Services Committee, 149
Houston, George, 47
Hoyt, Richard F., 3, 41–43, 45, 47, 49; and Curtiss-Wright merger, 51; death of, 75; and retrenchment after 1929, 57–60, 62
Hudson Flyer, 12, 58
Hudson Motor Car Company, 115
Hulse, Barton T. "Red," 101
"Hump," 98, 99
Hurley, Roy T., 145–47, 149, 154–57; chairman of the board at Curtiss-Wright, 145; and customer relations, 149–50; and jet engine development, 147; president of Curtiss-Wright in 1949, 146; and profit taking, 148, 149, 150; resignation, 1960, 156–57; successes and failures of, 157; and X-19 project, 151–52

Hurley-Townsend Company, 146
Hydroaeroplane, 12, 13

Imperial Russian Navy, 14–17
India, 98–99; Assam Valley of, 98, 99
International Air Transport Association (IATA), 124
International Civil Aviation Organization, (ICAO), 124
International Harvester Company, 114
International Motor Truck Corporation, 47
Italy, 28, 82

Japan, 13, 75, 82, 96, 98; aircraft production, 123; bombing of, 105, 106
J. B. Field Company report, 142
John Deere Company, 164
Johnson, Robert E., 106, 107
Joint Army and Navy Technical Board, 220
Jordan, William, 138, 142, 145; resignation of, 145, 146
June Bug, 9–11

Kaiser-Frazer Corporation, 156
Kartveli, Alexander, 77
Kennedy, William D., 138
Kennicott Copper Corporation, 161–63
Kepperly, James E., 21
Keys, Clement M., 2–3, 18, 29–32, 34–36, 38–41; and Curtiss-Wright merger, 43, 51–52, 55; and export markets, 67; grand vision, 38–43, 74, 80; and Great Depression, 56–60, 62; management and marketing strategy of, 30, 39; North American Aviation, Inc., creation of, 40–41; and overcapitalization problem, 142; purchase of Curtiss company, 29; resignation from Curtiss-Wright, 62
Keystone Aircraft Corporation, 42, 51, 57, 60–61
Kindelberger, James "Dutch," 143
Kirkham, Charles, 23, 31
Kleckler, Henry, 15
KLM, 78
Knight automobile engines, 46
Knudsen, William S., 115–16
Korean War, 132, 135, 143, 147, 148; and sales of engines and propellers, 157

labor unrest. *See* Paterson, New Jersey, strike at; Wright Aeronautical Corporation, strike at
Langer, William, 111–12
Latin America, 4, 52, 67
Lawrance, Charles R., 3, 48–50
Lawrance Aero-Engine Company, 3, 48
Lawsuits. *See* Curtiss-Wright Corporation, lawsuits, defendant in; Wright patent suit
League of Nations, 75
Lehman Brothers, 41–42
Leticia affair, 68
Lexington, 38
LGS Spring Clutches Corporation, 136
LGS Spring Clutches, Inc., 134, 136

licenses and licensees, 2, 22–23, 44, 47, 84; and F4U production, 120; and GM manufacture of Grumman aircraft, 133; and World War II production, 88. *See also* Curtiss-Wright Corporation, licenses and licensees; Pratt and Whitney Aircraft Company, licenses
Lindbergh, Charles, 3, 36, 49
Lindbergh boom, 87
Ling-Temco-Vought, 144
Lockheed Aircraft Corporation, 84, 85, 113; capital expansion of, 1940, 89; and Korean War, 143
Lockheed Martin, 1
Lockland, Ohio, plant, 89, 91, 93, 96, 105; Truman Committee criticism of, 109–10
Long Island City, 46
Loos, Charles W., 60
Los Angeles, 11, 39, 40, 45
Los Angeles International Air Meet, 11
Louisville, Kentucky, plant, 90, 96
Luftwaffe, 75, 83, 86
Lundquist, Wilton, G., 130
Lyndhurst, New Jersey, 165

Madagascar, 105
management, 4, 6, 17; changes of, 1965, 164; and Curtiss-Wright merger, 51, 58; staff, lack of, during World War I, 20, 24–25; and stockholder interests, conflict with, 87. *See also* Curtiss-Wright Corporation: management crisis in 1949; problems during World War II; Keys, Clement M.: management and marketing strategy of; North American Aviation, Inc., creation of; *specific companies*
Manchuria, 75
Manufacturers Aircraft Association, 20
manufacturing. *See* production
Marblehead, Mass., 18
markets/marketing, 1–5, 8–9, 10, 11, 12; air-cooled engine, development of, 49; aviation industry, 26; dealerships, 27; military purchases, importance of, 26, 63, 65; purchasing missions of France and England, 84, 85, 89; and spare engine parts sales, importance of, 71. *See also* Curtiss-Wright Corporation, sales; Keys, Clement M., management and marketing strategy of; sales; *specific companies; specific countries*
Marquette Metal Products Company, 136
Martin, Glenn L., 44–45
Martin Company, 73, 76, 84, 89
Martin-Marietta Corporation, 144
McCook Field, 45, 49
McCurdy, J. A. D., 9–10, 17
McDonnell Aircraft Corporation, 127
McDonnell Douglas Corporation, 144
Mead, George, 48–50
Mead, Senator James, 107
Mead Committee, 112

Mergen, Joseph M., 151–52, 153
Metal Improvement Company, 164, 165
Miami, 40
Miller, Merle, 109
Milliken, Frank R., 162
Mingos, Howard, 51
Mitchell, Brigadier General William, 35
mobilization day (M-day), 86
Montreal, 39
Moody's Investors Service, 47
Morgan, Thomas, 3, 60–62, 70, 74, 134; board chair-
    man of Curtiss-Wright Corporation, 75; and over-
    capitalization, problem of, 142; testimony before
    House subcommittee, 65
Morgan, William A., 21
Morrow, Dwight, 35
Morrow Board, 35, 129
Moto-Meter Gauge and Equipment Company, 146
Munich agreement, 82, 83
Muroc, California, 135

Nash-Kelvinator, 116
National Advisory Committee for Aeronautics
    (NACA), 42, 103, 126
"National Air Policy," 136
National Air Transport, 39, 51–52
National Aviation Corporation, 42
National Aviation Facility Experimental Center, 153
National City Bank of New York, 41
National Defense Advisory Committee, 116
National Security Council Report no. 68 (NSC-68),
    143
NATO, 142
Netherlands, 45
New Brunswick, New Jersey plant, 44, 46–47
New York Automobile Show, 9
New York City, 18, 39, 40, 41, 43–44. *See also* Curtiss-
    Wright Corporation, corporate headquarters;
    Lindbergh, Charles
New York Herald Tribune, 51
New York Society of Security Analysts, 141, 144
New York Times, 51
Niles-Bement-Pond Co., 49
North American Aviation, Inc., 40–42, 53, 60–61, 84,
    113; capital expansion of, 1940, 89; and General
    Motors, 133; new assembly plants, 1941, 96;
    World War II production, 117
North American Rockwell, 144
Northcliffe, Lord, 15
Northrop, John K. (Jack), 143
Northrop Corporation, 64–66, 77
Northrop Grumman, 1
NSU Werke, 151
Nutt, Arthur, 32, 71

Ohio Crankshaft Company, 115
Ohio Selective Service Board, 119

Olds Motor Works, 46
Otis Elevator Company, 115

P-40, 83, 84, 85, 94; combat, 1942, 96; criticisms of,
    108; desert operations, 118; first-mover advan-
    tages, conferred by, 95; production of, 85, 96–97,
    117, 118–19
Pacific Air Transport, 41
Packard Motor Car Company, 34, 47, 50, 155
Pan-American Airways, 76
Paris, 36
patent dispute, 10, 12, 14, 16, 20
Paterson, New Jersey, plant, 47, 50, 57–58, 60;
    enlargement of, 90, 91; R-3350 project, review of,
    105; strike at, 71; sale of, 130; transfer of person-
    nel to, 71–72
Pennsylvania. See Ely, Eugene
Pensacola, Florida, 19
Perrin, Brigadier General Edwin S., 99
Peru, 28, 68
Peruvian navy, 28
Pitcairn Aviation, Inc., 40
Pittsburgh Screw and Bolt Corporation, 91
Plaza Hotel, 162
Polaris missile project, 159, 160
Porter, Michael, 5
Postwar Planning Group. *See* General Motors
Prague, Czechoslovakia, 135
Pratt and Whitney Aircraft Company, 38, 41–42,
    49–51, 53, 150; airlines' influence on, 71; competi-
    tion with Wright Aeronautical, 76–77; dominance
    in jet engine manufacturing, 160–61, 163; engine
    shipments in 1946, 142; jet engines, 126, 137;
    licenses, 116, 147; market dominance in 1958,
    150; markets and profits, 70–71; neutrality legisla-
    tion, 90; Wasp engines, 38, 42, 49–50, 70, 73–74;
    and world rearmament, 84
Prince, J. F., 51
production, 14, 17, 21–22, 24, 26; American aviation
    industry during World War II, 123; capacity,
    improvement of, 88; of combat aircraft in 1943,
    112, 113; of engines, 47, 49–50, 90; expansion of,
    88, 96, 104; and fear of over-expansion, 87; of
    fighters in 1941–1942, 96–97; government appeal
    for increase in 1941, 96; and Great Depression,
    53, 55–57; growth between 1925–1928, 38; and
    job shop process, 86; "line production," 88; mass
    production, 19–20, 22, 83; mobilization, Air Corps
    objectives of, 86; over-extension, 94, 95; and post-
    World War II demobilization, 127; and produc-
    tion processes unwritten, 20; of propellers, 116;
    quantity vs. quality, 81, 86, 93–94, 96, 108; and
    stability of engine designs, 70–71; in United
    States, 36; and U.S. Army Air Corps mobilization
    objectives, 86; and World War II total aircraft,
    117, 123–24; and Wright-Martin, 46. *See also* air-
    planes, Curtiss, T-32/AT-32 Condor II; P-40, pro-

duction of; SB2C, production of; *individual companies*
Profits. *See individual companies*
Pulitzer Trophy Races, 32
Pynchon and Co., 41

Quehanna research center, Clearfield, Pennsylvania, 154–55

R-3350 (Cyclone), 93, 95, 104, 116, 147; and crash of XB-29, 105; design problems of, 106–7; flight testing of, 105; production of, premature, 120; production problems, 105–6; sales, decline of, 148, 150; and Truman Committee, 109–11; turbo-compound modification of, 130, 131, 138, 144, 157
Rayborn, Rear Admiral William, 159–60
Reconstruction Finance Corporation, 89
records, speed, 3, 11, 23, 32
Red Wing, 9
Reeves Brothers company, 159
Reid Aircraft Co., 39
Reims Air Meet, 11
Rentschler, Frederick, 42–43, 47, 49–51, 56, 142; pioneer of aviation, 143
Republic Aviation Corporation, 96, 113
research and development, 18, 20, 21, 29–31, 33; contracts, need for, 66; decline of, 142, 144, 148–51, 155, 156, 157, 159; and engine performance and airlines, 72; of jet engines, 122–23, 137; Keys' commitment to, 29, 31–32, 51, 150; Propeller Division, 130; of propellers, constant-speed, 79; Quehanna research center, 154–55; radial engines, 49; refusal of management to authorize, 145; and stability of engine designs, 70–71; supersonic transport, engine for, 160; X-19 project, 151–54. *See also* technological revolution, early 1930s
Rickenbacker, Edward (Eddie), 143
Robertson, Missouri, 60
Robertson, Major William, 39
Robertson Aircraft Corporation, 39
Rochester, New York, 7
Rockefeller Plaza, 152, 153
Rockwell International, 144
Roosevelt, President Franklin D., 75, 86, 88, 92
Roosevelt administration, 63
Royal Air Force (RAF), 83, 85
Royal Flying Corps, 19
Royal Siamese Air Force, 80
Russell, F. H., 51
Russia, 13, 128, 142–43
Ryan Aeronautical Company, 153

Saint Louis, Missouri, plant, 39, 56, 59, 61, 66; closing of, 1945, 127; new facilities, 1940, 89–91, 98. *See also* airplanes, Curtiss, Model 20
Saint Louis Airplane Division, 79, 90

Saint Louis Exhibition, 8
sales: of engines, between 1925–1928, 38, 50; exports, 13, 27, 67–69, 80, 81, 83; Model D to U.S. Army, 13; Model E seaplanes, foreign sale of, 13; 1930 decline in, 56; 1954–1958 decline in, 148; return on, between 1930–1936, 71; scarcity of, 25; to South America, 28. *See also* markets/marketing
San Diego, California, 12–13
Saratoga, 38
SB2C, 93, 95, 97, 101–2; correction of deficiencies in, 113; criticisms of, 108, 109; design problems of, 99–100, 102–3; performance in military service, 104; and personnel shortage problems, 119; production of, 101–3, 117, 120
Schneider Trophy Races, 32
schools, flying, 12, 13, 14, 28, 40. *See also* Wright Company
Scientific American Trophy, 9–11
seaplanes, 2, 12
Selfridge, Thomas, 9
Seversky, Alexander P. de, 77
Seversky Aircraft Company, 54, 77, 79–80
Shanghai incident, 68
Shields, Paul V., 138–39, 144, 147; commitment to profit taking, 144; and new directions for Curtiss-Wright, 1950, 141–42; retirement of, 145
Shields and Company, 138
shot peening, 164
Siam, 69
Sikorsky division. *See* United Aircraft corporation, Sikorsky division of
Silver Dart, 11
Simplex Automobile Company, 44–45, 47
Sino-Japanese War, 80
Sky Truck. *See* airplanes, Curtiss, CW-32
Sloan, Alfred P., 133–34
Smith, C. R., 150
Smith, J. A. B., 51, 60–61
Sopwith Company, 15
Soviet Union. *See* Russia
Spanish navy, 17
Special Committee on Jet Propulsion, 126
Special Wright Engine Committee, 106
Sperry Gyroscope Co., 40, 60
Spirit of St. Louis, 49
Standard Automobile Co., 46
stock market crash, 3, 52, 55, 61
Strategic Air Command, 129
strategic bombing, 76, 93, 106
Studebaker Brothers Manufacturing Company, 155
Studebaker Corporation, 115, 116, 155
Studebaker-Packard Corporation, 149, 155, 156; South Bend, Indiana, plant, 149, 155; Utica, Michigan, plant, 155
"superbomber," 93
supercharger/turbosupercharger, 126
supersonic transport (SST), 160, 163

Survival in the Air Age, 128
Symington, W. Stuart, 135

Target Rock Corporation, 165
Taylor, Philip, 72
technological revolution, early 1930s, 54–55, 63–64, 66, 76, 87
Textron, Inc., 144
Thomas, B. Douglas, 15
Toronto, 17–18
Towers, John, 14
Transcontinental Air Transport, 39, 42, 51
Transcontinental and Western Airlines. *See* TWA
Trans-World Airlines. *See* TWA
Travel Air Co., 42, 51, 59
Tri-Service Program, 153
Truculent Turtle. See airplanes, Lockheed, Lockheed P2V-1
Truman, Harry S., 107, 128
Truman Committee, 107–12, 117
turbo-compound engine. *See* R-3350 (Cyclone), turbo-compound modification of
TWA, 78, 125, 143

United Aircraft and Transportation Corporation, 41–43, 55
United Aircraft Corporation, 3, 42–43, 51, 115, 116; profits between 1935–1938, 87; Sikorsky division of, 144. *See also* Pratt and Whitney Aircraft Company
United Airlines, 78
United Kingdom. *See* England
U.S. Air Force (USAF), 129, 135, 147; and X-19 project, 153
U.S. Army, 2, 9–11, 13–14, 19, 20–22; and Allison V-1710, 84; conflicting instructions to Curtiss, 21; Curtiss airplanes, orders for, 19; GHQ Air Force, 86; Hawk fighters, purchase of, 34; and Hispano-Suiza engine, 46; and Wrights, 43
U.S. Army Air Corps, 4, 35–37, 49, 65, 67; and airmail crisis, 75; cargo airplanes, 97–98; contracts with Aeroplane Division, 80, 81; expansion of, 1941, 86; fighter competitions, 77–80, 83, 85; five-year expansion program, 37, 40, 60, 63; P-12 fighter, 70; P-36, contract for, 80; purchase of Cyclone engine, 50, 73; and radial engine, 42; and technological revolution, early 1930s, 63–64
U.S. Army Air Forces (USAAF), 85, 96, 97, 108
U.S. Army Air Service, 24, 33–35, 47, 49; aircraft on hand, 1925, 34
U.S. Army Ordnance Division, 146
U.S. Army Signal Corps, 12, 13, 14, 19
U.S. Army Signal Corps Equipment Division, 21
U.S. Circuit Court of Appeals, 14
U.S. Congress, 13; Air Commerce Act, 1926, 35; Air Corps Act, 36; appropriations, 13, 19, 20, 27, 28, 63, 75, 80, 86; Army and Navy Five Year Aircraft Program Acts, 35; Clayton Anti-Trust Act, 161;
Fourth Neutrality Act, 85; Kelly Air Mail Act, 71; Lend Lease, 88, 118; McNary-Watres Act, 71; National Defense Act, 19; National Industrial Recovery Act, 65; Vinson-Trammell Naval Bill, 75; and World War I aviation, 27–28
U.S. Department of Commerce, 125
U.S. Department of Defense, 159, 160
U.S. Department of Energy, 164
U.S. Marine Corps, 101
U.S. Navy, 2–3, 12–14, 19–20, 22–24, 31; Aeroplane Division, contracts with, 81; Curtiss aircraft sales to, 65, 67, 78; Cyclone engines for patrol planes, 72–73; and F4B fighter, 70; five-year expansion program, 40, 60, 63; Hawk fighters, purchase of, between 1925–1938, 34; naval aviation, expansion of, between 1935–1936, 75, 78; naval aviation, reductions in, 63; and radial engine, 42, 49–50; Wright engines, purchase of, 47–48, 72–73
U.S. Navy Bureau of Aeronautics, 93, 99, 100, 103
U.S. Navy Department, 36, 108
U.S. Senate, 104; Special Committee to Investigate the National Defense Program, 107. *See also* Mead Committee; Truman Committee
U.S. War Department, 26, 36, 108

Vaughan, Guy W., 4, 45–47, 50, 55, 60; cash reserves, preservation of, 134, 136; and "cash up front policy," 88, 134; chairman of the board in 1948, 138; defense of company's war record, 110; fear of industry instability, 88; and jet engines, 122, 126–27, 137; opposition to merger of Curtiss and Wright companies, 133; pioneer of aviation, 143; president of Curtiss-Wright, 75–76, 78; and proxy fight, 1948, 137–39; and reorganization of Curtiss-Wright in 1936, 79; reluctance to invest in new projects, 134; retirement in 1949, 139; and sales to France, 81; successes and failures of, 139; trip to Great Britain, 137; vision for his company's postwar future, 132–36, 139; and Wright Aeronautical, 62, 71–72, 74. *See also* Curtiss-Wright Corporation; Wright Aeronautical Corporation
Vera Cruz, Mexico, 14
vertical take-off and landing airplane (VTOL), 151–54
Victor Animatograph Corporation, 136

W. A. Harriman company, 42
Wall Street, 17, 42
Wall Street Journal, 17–18
Wanamaker, Rodman, 15
Warren, Ohio, 155
Webster, C. W., 67
Webster, William, 120
Western Air Express, 42
Western Union, 163
White Wing, 9
Whittle, Sir Frank, 126
Wichita, Kansas, 60, 107

William Morris Imbrie and Company, 17
Williams, George Montague, 114–15
Willgoos, Andrew, 48–50
Willys, John North, 20–21, 23, 24, 29, 146
Willys Overland Company, 20–21
Wood-Ridge, New Jersey, plant, 91, 96, 105, 125, 131; closing of, 164; engine sales in 1950, 145; expansion in 1951, 148; Wright Aeronautical, sole remaining facility of, 130
Wood-Ridge Nuclear Facility, 164
World's Work, 18
World War I, 2, 19, 22, 45; airplane as weapon in, 16; Armistice, 24, 26; contraction of industry after, 26; equipment in, quality and quantity of, 83; political order, post-war collapse of, 75
World War II, 3, 4, 6, 83, 95, 97; Burma Road, 98; "Hump," 98, 99, 108; Midway, Battle of, 101; North African campaign, 85, 108; Pacific campaign, 103–4; Pearl Harbor, 93, 96, 101, 105, 108; Polish campaign, 86; Russian Front, 108; V-J Day, 114, 120, 127, 130, 131
Wright, Burdette, 60, 90, 125, 127, 138
Wright, Orville, 1, 7, 43, 58
Wright, T. P., 60–61
Wright, Wilbur, 1, 7, 43
Wright Aeronautical Corporation, 3–4, 37–38, 41–43, 47–51, 55; airlines' influence on, 71; capabilities of, 1950, 144; Curtiss company, comparison with, 63; Curtiss-Wright, importance to, 69–70, 73–74;

decline of, 150, 151; end of engine manufacturing, 160–61; engineering research and development expenditures, cuts in, 144; engineers, overextension of, 153; expansion of, 1940, 90; export sales of Cyclone, 73; financial performance in 1930–1931, 57, 60; foreign contracts, 1939, 84; J65, importance to, 147; jet engines, 126, 137, 145; markets and profits, 71; merger with Curtiss Aeroplane and Motor Company, 51–52; operations at peak capacity, 1939, 91; Paterson factory, 58; profitability, post-World War II continuation of, 130, 131, 144; R-1820 engine choice for Douglas airliners, 73; R-1820 sales, 73, 74, 104; R-3350 engine problems, 104; R-3350 sales, 147, 148, 150–51; radial engine, importance of, 70–74, 76, 78; readjustment, post-war, 122; sales in 1940, 83; sales in 1950, 145; strain on facilities, 105; strike at, 57, 58, 60, 71; termination of, 164; Vaughan as head of, 62; Wankel engine, 153, 164; World War II production, 124. *See also* R-3350 (Cyclone)
Wright Brothers, 9–12, 43, 58
Wright Company, 2, 43–45
Wright-Martin Aircraft Corporation, 2–3, 20, 45–47; and Roy T. Hurley, 146
Wright patent suit, 11, 14, 16, 20, 43
Wright-Patterson Air Force base, 153

Yorktown, 78

The Authors

Louis Eltscher taught history and politics in the College of Liberal Arts at the Rochester Institute of Technology until his retirement in 1994, when he was named professor emeritus. He has written several articles on aviation history and was the Alfred V. Verville Fellow at the National Air and Space Museum, 1986–1987.

Edward Young is a managing director at Moody's Investors Services. The author of several articles on aviation history, he has also written *Aerial Nationalism: A History of Aviation in Thailand* (Smithsonian Institution Press, 1994).

The Editor

Dr. Kenneth J. Lipartito is associate professor of history at the University of Houston, Houston, Texas. He holds a Ph.D. in history from the Johns Hopkins University and has published extensively in the field of economic and business history. He is the author of *The Bell System and Regional Business: The Telephone in the South* and *Baker and Botts in the Development of Modern Houston.* His work has appeared in the leading journals, including the *American Historical Review,* the *Journal of Economic History,* the *Business History Review,* and *Industrial and Corporate Change.* In 1989–1990, Dr. Lipartito was appointed Newcomen Fellow at the Harvard Business School, and in 1995 he was awarded the IEEE Life Members Award for the best article in the history of electrical technology, as well as the Newcomen Society Award for Excellence in Business History Research and Writing by the Business History Conference.